W9-AFI-057

SANCTUARIES OF SEGREGATION

SANCTUARIES
of
SEGREGATION

The Story of the Jackson Church Visit Campaign

CARTER DALTON LYON

University Press of Mississippi / Jackson

www.upress.state.ms.us

Designed by Peter D. Halverson

The University Press of Mississippi is a member of the
Association of American University Presses.

"Easter in Jackson, MS, 1964" previously appeared in *Methodist History* (Volume
XLIX, Number 2, January 2011, pp. 99-115)

First printing 2017

∞

Library of Congress Cataloging-in-Publication Data

Names: Lyon, Carter Dalton, author.
Title: Sanctuaries of segregation: the story of the Jackson church visit
campaign / Carter Dalton Lyon.
Other titles: Story of the Jackson church visit campaign
Description: Jackson, MS : University Press of Mississippi, [2017] | Includes
bibliographical references and index.
Identifiers: LCCN 2016034776 (print) | LCCN 2017003610 (ebook) | ISBN
9781496810748 (cloth : alk. paper) | ISBN 9781496810755 (epub single) |
ISBN 9781496810762 (epub institutional) | ISBN 9781496810779 (pdf single)
| ISBN 9781496810786 (pdf institutional)
Subjects: LCSH: Civil rights movements—Mississippi—Jackson—History—20th
century. | African Americans—Civil
rights—Mississippi—Jackson—History—20th century. | Civil
rights—Mississippi—Religious aspects—Christianity. | Civil rights
workers—Religious life—Mississippi—History—20th century. |
Segregation—Religious aspects—Christianity—History—20th century. |
Jackson (Miss.)—Church history—20th century. | Jackson (Miss.)—Race
relations.
Classification: LCC F349.J13 L95 2017 (print) | LCC F349.J13 (ebook) | DDC
323.1196/073076251—dc23
LC record available at https://lccn.loc.gov/2016034776

British Library Cataloging-in-Publication Data available

To my parents,
Richard and Kathryn Lyon;
and to my wife, Sally,
and our two daughters, Lucy and Ann Carter

Contents

SANCTUARIES OF SEGREGATION

Introduction

Even after a devastating week, Anne Moody and her classmates were still optimistic that this Sabbath would be different. The Sunday before, they had fanned out across the city to attend worship services at a variety of white Protestant churches for the first time, but because they were black, no churches admitted them. Just days later, Medgar Evers, their leader and one of the adults who had driven them to the churches that Sunday, was murdered in his driveway. Now, a day after his funeral and another confrontation with city police, the students once again presented themselves at the doors of many of the city's white churches. They remained confident that engagement with white Christians could help bridge the divide in the city, especially given the tumult of the preceding days. On this Sunday, most of the churches continued to reject them, but one let them inside. Ushers at St. Andrew's Episcopal—a church just steps away from the governor's mansion, occupied by Ross Barnett—admitted and seated Moody and three others. The young women were uncomfortable and nervous, and a journalist reported a few curious glances in their direction from the congregation, but the group did not encounter any obvious animosity. Exiting the church, they were greeted by its rector, Rev. Christoph Keller, who was pleased to see them and invited them to visit again. Moody later wrote that his words seemed genuine. In a moment captured by a photographer and printed in newspapers around the nation the next day, she descended the stairs with the three others. For the first time in a long while, she "began to have a little hope."[1]

In 1963 and 1964, the steps of churches in Jackson, Mississippi, were among the front lines in the national struggle over civil rights. For ten months, integrated groups attempted to attend Sunday worship at twenty-two all-white Protestant and Catholic churches. While civil rights activists utilized church visits or "kneel-ins" as a tactic of nonviolent direct action in various parts of the South, Jackson was the only city where groups mounted a sustained campaign to protest segregation by attempting to worship in white churches that spanned the denominational spectrum. Faculty and students at Tougaloo College, under the direction of their chaplain, Rev. Edwin King, initiated the Jackson church visit campaign in June 1963, after years of controversy within Mississippi churches over the issue of segregation, and in the wake of a boycott and sit-in campaign against Jackson businesses and public accommodations. Rev. King and the other activists aimed to stir the consciences of white Christians, hoping to motivate silent white moderates who could help steer the state toward a peaceful resolution to the burgeoning crisis. Christian principles of love for one's neighbor, brotherhood, and equality dominated the strategy of the activists and the out-of-state ministers who sometimes accompanied them. They felt that if change were going to come, breaking down barriers of segregation in the Christian church would be a logical place to begin. The Tougaloo groups intended to engage white church people in dialogue and publicly testify to the oneness of mankind, but they also hoped to tug at the hearts of local white ministers, particularly those who had not used their pulpit to denounce racial injustice.

During the course of the campaign, the church visits sparked internal debates within congregations over segregation in their churches. Most of the churches maintained closed-door policies and consistently turned away black visitors. In a few of the churches that refused to admit African Americans, ministers recognized that closed church doors conflicted with their Christian consciences, and they took a stand for open doors. Their convictions cost all of them their jobs; ultimately they either resigned or church members forced them out. Then, starting October 1963, just after the Jackson Citizens' Council announced a campaign to "save these churches from integration," police began arresting visitors who were denied entrance. This tactic remained in effect for the next six months. In all, police made forty arrests, mostly of out-of-state ministers who came to Jackson out of solidarity with the Tougaloo activists. Still, not all of the churches in Jackson refused to allow African Americans to join in Sunday worship. A few, such as a Lutheran and two Presbyterian churches, admitted black visitors early in the campaign before segregationists forced the church doors closed. Moreover, the Catholic, Episcopal, and Unitarian churches consistently admitted black visitors. These churches, while in the minority, served as useful counterpoints to a community of otherwise closed churches.

By May 1964, when most of the churches remained closed and it became clear that the Methodist Church would not mandate open doors in all of its churches, Rev. King and the Tougaloo activists halted the campaign and turned their attention to the Mississippi Summer Project. For them, the church visit campaign exposed the failure of the white church to be a relevant force in helping to address the momentous problem facing Mississippi. Rev. King and the students felt that they had given white church people a chance. Now that these congregations had passed on the opportunity, the activists would pursue a more wide-ranging civil rights program, one that included even more non-Mississippian campaigners.

Surviving records of the weekly showdowns on church steps— found in government documents, newspapers, letters, minutes of church meetings, contemporary manuscripts, and interviews with eyewitnesses—illuminate the motivations of the opposing sides. Significantly, the record reveals a few rare opportunities for dialogue between activists and white lay people. For the Tougaloo students and the out-of-state ministers who sometimes accompanied them, opportunities to convey their thinking to ushers or other white church people were even more important than providing a visible witness to their convictions. On some occasions, the police, in actions constituting unprecedented state intervention in the affairs of a local church, stepped in to prevent more dialogue. When police arrested church visitors for trespassing, breach of peace, or disturbing divine worship, they sometimes did so on their own initiative, without being specifically asked to do so by the minister or a layperson. In those instances when an usher had clearly solicited police intervention, the event demonstrated state collusion with a church member, regardless of the wishes of the minister involved or the policies of the denomination.

Despite receiving substantial local and, at times, national and international news coverage, the story of the Jackson church visit campaign is a largely neglected chapter in the history of the civil rights movement. Works about the movement and religion in Mississippi sometimes discuss the Jackson church visits, sometimes called kneel-ins. The seminal analysis of the movement in the state—John Dittmer's *Local People*—provides a brief summary of the goals and highlights of the campaign. Charles Marsh, in *God's Long Summer*, devotes a chapter to the campaign's leader, Rev. King, and another chapter to the pastor of a Jackson church targeted by students on a few Sundays. Marsh illuminates some of the focal points of the campaign—namely the Sunday of the first arrests and the barring of two Methodist bishops from Galloway Memorial Methodist Church—and provides a thorough analysis of the theological beliefs and motivations of Rev. King. In *Freedom's Coming*, Paul Harvey presents a concise synopsis of the campaign within the context of other efforts by Christians to challenge theological racism. Four historians, Carolyn Dupont in *Mississippi Praying*, Joseph Crespino in *In Search of Another Country*, Randy J. Sparks in *Religion in Mississippi*, and Ellis Ray Branch in *Born of Conviction*, and, most recently, Joseph Reiff's *Born of Conviction: White Methodists and Mississippi's Closed Society*, discuss the campaign within the framework of the controversy over race in the Mississippi Conference of the Methodist Church during the 1950s and 1960s. Stephen Haynes's *The Last Segregated Hour*, which focuses on the impact of a church visitation campaign in Memphis, Tennessee, provides an outline of the Jackson campaign and a comprehensive overview of the tactic of church visits and kneel-ins during the movement. To date, only one published work gives a firsthand account of the events, *Agony at Galloway*, published in 1980. In it, Rev. W. J. Cunningham chronicles his time as senior pastor at Galloway Memorial Methodist Church during the climax of the turmoil.

On one level, an analysis of the Jackson church visits sheds light on the relationship between congregations and their pastors, and between local churches and their regional or national bodies during one of the major crises in American religious history. The argument that most white church people in the South conformed to the culture during this period is a familiar one, grounded in two works from the era, Kenneth K. Bailey's 1964 book, *Southern White Protestantism in the Twentieth Century*, and Samuel S. Hill Jr.'s 1966 analysis, *Southern Churches in Crisis*. Bailey points to the practical and theological concerns that set denominational leaders and pastors apart from rank-and-file church people. Most white pastors, he emphasized, were seminary trained and detached from the cultural milieu of the South. Those ministers who did speak out against segregation received overwhelmingly negative responses. Hill, on the other hand, sees Southern white ministers and laymen as more of a united front, joined by a theological understanding elevating the conversion experience and changing individual behavior over concern for racial equality.

The nature of the Southern white church response to the civil rights movement continues to receive scholarly attention. Some, like Charles Marsh, see a commitment to a certain theology guiding many segregationist church people's reactions in the 1950s and 1960s. In *God's Long Summer*, Charles Marsh finds the evangelical impulse in the thinking of Rev. Douglas Hudgins, pastor of First Baptist Church in Jackson, Mississippi. Marsh argues that because of his particular theology, Rev. Hudgins spoke out against his denomination's endorsement of the *Brown* decision and allowed his ushers to bar African Americans from worshipping in his church in the 1960s. While Rev. Hudgins affirmed the congregationalism inherent in Southern Baptist practice, he believed that political concerns—which for him included the civil rights question—intruded on the purity of the event of salvation. In *Getting Right With God: Southern Baptists and Desegregation, 1945–1995*, Mark Newman also recognizes the role of theology in justifying segregation among many within the Southern Baptist Convention, though he emphasizes that Southern Baptists historically prized other beliefs and institutions—such as law and order, public schools, and global missionary efforts—that conflicted with the argument to maintain segregation after *Brown*. These other commitments ultimately helped to guide Baptists toward accepting the end of legalized segregation and disfranchisement. Yet not all historians emphasize what amounted to collusion between segregationists and Southern white ministers and church people. In *A Stone of Hope: Prophetic Religion and the Death of Jim Crow*, David Chappell sees little religious rationale or biblically based arguments in the discourse of racial conservatives, and remains unconvinced that ministers and church leaders were central or even necessary to the segregationist cause. He argues that after *Brown*, most segregationists saw their own churches and denominations as their enemies. As a result, Chappell finds that white supremacists lost in their effort in part because they did not have the backing and support of the white church. Paul Harvey, in *Freedom's Coming*, demonstrates how this defeat of what he calls theological racism occurred. While those committed to a theology of segregation lost whatever claims to a Bible-based defense once they failed to have the law on their side, Harvey sees a larger process at work, one that helped undermine the Christian segregationist argument. He traces a racial interchange between black and white evangelicals from the cultural exchanges of music and folk traditions to the interracial traditions of holiness and Pentecostal churches, which then gave rise to informal and institutional zones for Christian interracialism. Working together within these spaces, black and white Christians drew inspiration from the evangelical concerns of redemption, salvation, and the omnipotence of God in daily life to foment a social revolution that successfully destabilized theological racism and helped to defeat Jim Crow.

A recent work, Carolyn Dupont's *Mississippi Praying*, provides the most thorough and helpful analysis to date on the role of white evangelicals in the fight to sustain segregation in Mississippi in the decades after World War II. Examining local church communities and church people, she challenges Chappell's findings, seeing white evangelicals as central to the racist cause in the state. Though some white evangelicals labored to ensure fairness and such principles as freedom of the pulpit, most white Baptists, Methodists, and Presbyterians in Mississippi actively defended white supremacy, using their own particular theologies and political philosophies. Churches were not mere captives to a white supremacist culture; churches provided clear institutional support for white supremacy, and church people were as vigorous inside the church doors as they were outside in trying to repel desegregation.

This study enters the discussion on the white church response to the civil rights movement of the early 1960s at an even more acute angle, from the vantage point of a city, the local congregation, and the individual church person. The story of the Jackson church visit campaign reveals a complicated milieu of contested spaces and divergent beliefs. On one side, a fierce localism prevailed among many of the white churches of Jackson—though this localism had to be asserted and won, as its victory was never predetermined. Many churches in Jackson saw themselves as private houses of worship subject to their own racial policies, regardless of whether or not they were connectional bodies affiliated with or chartered by a larger denomination. At a basic level, the fight to open or close the doors of churches was a fight over the meaning of "church" itself and the ideal of connectionalism. When the official boards of local Methodist churches voted to forbid African Americans from attending services, they did so with total disregard for Methodist Church policies and beliefs. Not only did the pastor retain complete authority in admitting or declining to admit individuals to worship, recently adopted statements and creeds from national Methodist Church conferences affirmed the right of all persons to worship, irrespective of color or nationality. Yet on the local level, the people who maintained responsibility for enforcing the policy of the denomination, especially the bishop and the district superintendent, either believed that desegregating the local church would fracture the conference—or worse, they displayed racist behavior. White ministers looking for leadership to help buttress their own efforts in bringing their congregations more in line with Methodist Church values were left unsatisfied in Jackson. As a result, some departed the state, while others struggled to work within the segregationist structure, content to labor on as pastors and shepherds to errant flocks.

This dilemma of the so-called moderate religious leader or pastor, one who opposed racial discrimination but favored a patient, gradualist approach to desegregation, could be seen in communities throughout the South, but was highlighted most distinctly during the Birmingham campaign of 1963. When a number of high-profile white religious leaders in the state denounced the timing and tactics of the movement in the city, Dr. Martin Luther King Jr. replied with his "Letter from a Birmingham Jail," a cogent defense of religious leaders who argued that segregation was immoral and un-Christian and the response must therefore be immediate, direct, and nonviolent. King reserved particular scorn for white moderate pastors, but some were beginning to reassess their predicament. In *Blessed Are the Peacemakers*, S. Jonathan Bass provides a comprehensive analysis of the "letter" and the men to whom it was addressed. Upon uncovering the stories of the eight white religious leaders and the pressures that each faced—particularly from segregationists and other extremists—Bass finds the group to be far more sympathetic than King and others appreciated at the time. If King had bothered to seek out the men—or vice versa—he would have found a range of beliefs about the racial crisis. The over-simplified category of "moderate" was not a particularly accurate label for them.

Some white pastors in Jackson fit the designation as moderates, but my analysis of a specific church community reveals many examples of white ministers and church people from a variety of denominations in Jackson denouncing segregation in moral and overtly religious terms. The leadership of some of the pastors was crucial in guiding churches through the turmoil in part created by the church visit campaign. In some cases, the guidance that ministers provided proved not to be assertive enough; in other instances, pastors who denounced compulsory segregation found themselves removed from their congregations. Most of the white ministers in Jackson who took a stand against segregation during the early to mid-1960s were out of their pulpits within a few years. While it may be true, as some scholars assert, that most white ministers were reluctant to confront the immorality of racial discrimination, one must not lose sight of those who did, particularly those whose stories have not yet been told.

The church visit campaign also reveals many instances of moderate and liberal white lay people proclaiming their convictions. A few directly joined the church visit campaign, bringing black guests with them to white churches where they belonged or regularly attended. Some decided they could not remain at a closed church, and announced their views by simply switching membership to an open church. Others recognized that their churches needed their voices, and they chose to fight from within, determined to help steer their churches toward inclusiveness. While some churches remained closed to blacks, at least for the time being, the campaign demonstrated that these closures were not preordained. The actions of moderates and liberals within churches in Jackson, combined with weekly attempts to break the color barrier, ensured that segregationists had to fight to close the churches to African Americans.[2]

An examination of the Jackson church visit campaign provides a window into understanding the forces advocating and resisting social change on a local and individual church level. While James Silver gave America an inside view on how racial conservatives maintained a monopoly of power in the state in his 1964 book, *Mississippi: The Closed Society*, my analysis demonstrates how that society operated on a more fundamental level, though I suggest that this society was never as closed as Silver found it to be. Both activists and segregationists understood what was at stake. Civil rights volunteers, many of whom joined the movement because of their Christian convictions, recognized the power of their argument that segregation was not only unconstitutional, it was a sin. They intended to remind white Christians throughout their struggle and their weekly visits to churches, feeling that if positive and non-violent change would ever occur in Mississippi, it would happen because white Christians saw their cause as a moral one. Though segregationists rejected the religious argument the Tougaloo activists made—or instead framed it in sociological or political terms—they understood the value of maintaining closed church doors. Ushers at some white churches routinely blocked integrated groups of students, teachers, and ministers from participating in worship because they knew they could not concede the moral grounds for integration if they wanted their side to prevail in other areas.

Additionally, segregationists recognized that their churches constituted one of the last communal spaces they controlled. The church visit campaign began at a time when segregationists were losing their grip on Jackson and on the state. Though city officials and civic leaders quashed civil rights demonstrations in late May and early June 1963, the mayor began to make a series of concessions that had the effect of gradually eroding white control in the capital city. Moreover, the campaign began just as President Kennedy sent Congress a civil rights bill that would eventually force the desegregation of all public facilities in the city. With Jackson schools beginning to phase in integrated classrooms in the fall of 1964, white churches were becoming the last sanctuaries for segregationists. Not surprisingly, then, some white church people called in various agents of city and state government, from the Jackson police to the Mississippi State Sovereignty Commission, to assist in turning African Americans away from white churches. Midway through the campaign, the Jackson Citizens' Council tried to assert its power, announcing a plan to "save the churches from integration." Jackson's two main daily newspapers—the morning *Clarion-Ledger* and the afternoon *Jackson Daily News*—reinforced the narrative segregationists created about the campaign, emphasizing its "outside" origins and the law-breaking tactics of its participants. Segregationists and white church people and church leaders in Jackson were indeed co-conspirators in the fight against civil rights. Segregationists, like the Tougaloo activists, understood that the keys to unlocking segregated Jackson could be found in the city's church doors.

Examining the Jackson church visit campaign provides a window into the decision-making process of national denominations and the changes that some made in their racial policies in 1963 and 1964. Because of the visits in Jackson, for instance, the bishops of the Methodist Church clarified their views on segregation in the church and denounced the arrests in the city, though the subsequent quadrennial General Conference of the Methodist Church declined to mandate immediate desegregation of the denomination. While the closed churches and arrests in Jackson were not the only events in the country that highlighted the controversy over racism in the church, my analysis suggests that Jackson was clearly on the minds of church leaders and conference delegates as they considered changes in the racial policies of the denomination.

Finally, an examination of the Jackson church visits provides a useful context for understanding what happened next, with the Mississippi Summer Project of 1964 and then the initiation of the Delta Ministry, the key civil rights project of the National Council of Churches' (NCC) new Commission on Religion and Race (CRR). As Rev. King reasoned, the activists had given the white church community in Mississippi a chance to accept its moral responsibility. Presented with the opportunity to achieve change internally, Mississippians would now see a flood of outsiders arriving to join in the civil rights cause. Rather than accepting change voluntarily, as the Tougaloo activists hoped, white Mississippians would instead be subject to the weight of federal law and court orders.

[2]

"When Integration Comes to Mississippi, It Will Enter through the Front Doors of Churches"

1954–60

When the Supreme Court handed down the landmark *Brown* decision in 1954, a move applauded by most Christian denominations, many white racial conservatives immediately recognized the range of possibilities coming out of the high court's ruling. The governor of Mississippi, Hugh White, spoke for many when he lamented, "If the Supreme Court decision is observed in my church I will be forced to find some other place to worship."[1] Organized attempts to desegregate white churches in the state did not commence for another nine years, but when they did occur, these efforts represented the culmination of a lengthy struggle over the issue of race in churches and denominations in Mississippi. When Protestant denominations, including those representing the three largest in Mississippi— the Southern Baptists, the Methodist Church, and the Presbyterian Church in the United States (Southern)—announced their approval of the 1954 *Brown* decision, their reaction should have surprised no one, for all three denominations couched their support in explicitly Christian terms and pointed out that they were already becoming more involved in social justice programs. As many historians have noted, however, owing to conflicts over the ideal of racial equality, in the ensuing years cleavages developed between local churches and conferences in the South and their regional or national bodies.

This dichotomy between national church beliefs and individual church practice was especially stark in the capital city of Mississippi. Some congregations in Jackson publicly condemned their denomination's reactions to *Brown*, and church people organized to subvert their denominations' beliefs and policies. When that effort proved insufficient, state legislators tried to tax "non-segregated" churches, as they called it, and then pushed through a measure to set up a process whereby individual congregations could wrest control of their church buildings from the national body. Supporters of the "church property bill" did not hide their motivations, routinely pointing out that the legislation was meant to preempt the integration of churches. As one of the authors of the bill explained, when integration came to Mississippi, "it w[ould] enter through the front door of churches."[2] Racial conservatives recognized that churches were one of the key contested spaces in which they would have to fight to sustain Jim Crow. Civil rights activists throughout the South understood the power of segregation in churches as well, and, beginning in 1960, began a campaign of kneel-ins to testify to the iniquity of racial discrimination. Though no local activists in Mississippi conducted organized attempts to desegregate white churches before 1963, some churches in Jackson prepared for that possibility, realizing that not even their new statutes would prevent or dissuade African Americans from trying to attend their churches.

The General Assembly of the US Presbyterian Church (Southern) convened in a previously scheduled conference just weeks after the Supreme Court announced the *Brown* ruling. It was the first denomination that had an opportunity to react. The Southern Presbyterians, meeting in Montreat, North Carolina, approved a lengthy resolution affirming the court's reasoning over the objection of a sizable minority of delegates, including Governor Hugh White and Chalmer Alexander, one of Jackson's city commissioners. Pointing to various passages throughout the Bible that establish the dignity of man and the oneness of mankind, a majority of Southern Presbyterian lay leaders and ministers agreed with the court that segregation was not just separation, but subordination. While declining to address specific steps to ending discrimination in American society, the General Assembly did make specific recommendations for changing racial practices in the life of the church. They urged the desegregation of all bodies and educational institutions within the denomination's domain, including local churches.[3] A few days later, the elders of First Presbyterian Church in Jackson announced that they would not follow recommendations to lower racial barriers in the church. The elders believed that the resolution approved at the General Assembly "so seriously threaten the peace and purity of the Church that they must not go unanswered." They declared that "segregation of the races is not discrimination," and decided to "maintain [the church's] traditional policy and practice of distinct separation of the races." The *Clarion-Ledger* reported that First Presbyterian was "one of the first" to rebuff the pronouncements of the Southern Presbyterians.[4] While it remained unclear whether or not the elders of First Presbyterian were merely codifying a longstanding practice, as they said themselves, this was the first time they definitively voted to exclude African Americans from the services and activities of the church.

A few days after the Southern Presbyterians met, the Southern Baptist Convention assembled in St. Louis, Missouri. Although they did not ground their rationale in specific passages from scripture, as the Presbyterians had, the Southern Baptists nevertheless affirmed that the court's decision was in harmony "with the Christian principles of equal justice and love for all men." Yet the Southern Baptists' statement declined to address the issue of segregation within church bodies.[5] Despite the restrained language of the resolution, its overall stance in affirming the Supreme Court's ruling was loudly rejected by many white Baptists in Jackson. The pastor of First Baptist, Dr. Douglas Hudgins, opposed the resolution, arguing that the denomination had no reason to enter into the debate in the first place. He believed that the Supreme Court decision was an educational and political question, not a religious one. Curiously, Dr. Hudgins left the convention before the vote on the statement, but in his absence the president of the convention read Hudgins's opposition to the vote aloud. Dr. Hudgins elaborated on his thinking in a sermon at First Baptist soon after the convention, stressing the democratic and autonomous nature of congregations. He underscored the belief that churches are fellowships at a fundamental level adding, "If the fellowship of the church [is] broken, the idealism of the first is very definitely retarded."[6] For Hudgins, issues like desegregation distracted from and ultimately injured the fundamental bond of Christians within a church.

The day after the vote on the resolution, the *Jackson Daily News*, owned by Thomas and Robert Hederman, two lay leaders at First Baptist, carried a front-page story quoting in full reactions from various deacons at First Baptist, followed by an editorial calling the denomination's move "a deplorable action." Overall, the deacons emphasized that the resolution was not binding and that it was unlikely that "Negroes [would] invade the First Baptist Church," as one deacon put it. But a few deacons proffered views grounded in white supremacy. For instance, Alex McKeigney, an assistant to the attorney general, asserted, "The facts of history make it plain that the development of civilization and of Christianity itself has rested in the hands of the white race." He argued that any activity that broke down the safeguards of racial separation would be a "direct contribution to the efforts of those groups advocating intermarriage between the races—a course which if followed to its end will result in driving the white race from the earth forever, never to return." Ross Barnett, a local attorney and a former (and future) candidate for governor, pointed out that the resolution was "very probably brought about by paid lobbyists, members of the NAACP, and people who are not in sympathy with either race, but who are motivated by selfish purposes." He believed that "if this problem was left to the colored people of Mississippi they would vote overwhelmingly for continued segregation." A few pages later, the Hedermans instructed their readers not to worry, that leading laymen and pastors in Southern Baptist churches in Jackson believed "without dissent" that the move would not "change the complexion of Baptist congregations in this city."[7] For now, deacons at First Baptist remained confident in their forecast that, unlike their counterparts at First Presbyterian, no African Americans would attempt to worship at First Baptist.[8]

While the assemblies of Southern Baptists and Presbyterians provided a instant responses to the *Brown* decision, lay leaders and ministers of the Methodist Church were not scheduled to meet in general conference until 1956. In the mean time, the church's Council of Bishops convened in Chicago in November 1954 and issued a resolution endorsing the Supreme Court's ruling, pointing to pronouncements at the previous general conference in 1952 that declared racial discrimination to be un-Christian. They held that "one of the foundation stones of our faith is the belief that all men are brothers, equal in the sight of God." The bishops pledged to offer leadership in support of these principles, though, like the Southern Baptists, they declined to detail specific methods of demonstrating their beliefs.[9]

Complicating the bishops' response was the fact that the Methodist Church itself continued to practice segregation, a legacy of the reunification of Northern and Southern Methodists in 1939. The Plan of Union united the Methodist Episcopal Church (North), the Methodist Episcopal Church, South, and the Methodist Protestant Church. As part of the compromise intended to satisfy many white Methodists in the South, the new Methodist Church maintained five regional jurisdictions and a sixth separate nonregional jurisdiction for African American churches, the Central Jurisdiction. Before unification, the black churches in the Central Jurisdiction were segregated within the Methodist Episcopal Church (North), though most of them were physically located in the South, the products of mission efforts by the Church North following the Civil War. The new structure of the Methodist Church provided some advantages to the black churches of the Central Jurisdiction, namely that as a jurisdiction, they now had over 16 percent of the policy-making power, even though they accounted for only 4 percent of the total membership of the Methodist Church. Yet many black and white Methodists saw the Central Jurisdiction as a symbol of segregation and moved to integrate the jurisdiction into the rest of the denominational structure in succeeding years.[10] Fifteen years later, at the time of the *Brown* decision and the bishops' response to it, the segregated structure of the Methodist Church remained intact. Like other Methodists, the bishops recognized they could no longer proclaim the brotherhood of man as it applied to public schools while failing to apply the principle to their own denomination.

Immediately following the pronouncement from the Methodist Council of Bishops supporting the Supreme Court decision, the Bishop of Mississippi, Marvin Franklin, moved to downplay the bishops' resolution. In an article printed in the *Clarion-Ledger* and reprinted in the *Mississippi Methodist Advocate*—his first published comments on *Brown*—Bishop Franklin explained that he and the eight other bishops in the Southeastern Jurisdiction urged the Council of Bishops against making any statement at all, that it was not the right time for such a move. Bishop Franklin tried to assuage fears that the bishops' resolution would mark the beginning of the end of the segregated structure of the Methodist Church, concluding, "The resolution will have little or no effect on Mississippi Methodists." Pointing to his own place within the perceived regional uniformity apropos of segregation, Bishop Franklin maintained, "No one in the Southeast is crusading for the resolution or what it calls for."[11]

While Southern Baptists and Presbyterians in Jackson denounced their denominations' stands, and at least one church voted to close its doors to black visitors, segregationist laymen of the Mississippi and North Mississippi Conferences of the Methodist Church organized a new group to counter the aims established by a majority of the Council of Bishops. In advance of the 1956 general conference, in order to maintain pressure on the Methodist Church to maintain its segregated structure regardless of Bishop Marvin Franklin's assurances, about two hundred conservative Methodist church people in Mississippi convened at the Robert E. Lee Hotel in Jackson in late March 1955 to form Mississippi Association of Methodist Ministers and Laymen (MAMML).[12] Shoring up the impression of uniformity about the issue, the *Jackson Daily News* announced to its readers on the front page, "Methodists Firmly Favor Segregation." The new group mirrored the recently created Association of Methodist Ministers and Laymen of Alabama, and leaders of the Alabama organization attended the meeting in Jackson. Dr. G. Stanley Frazer of St. James Methodist Church in Montgomery, Alabama, told Mississippi Methodists to stand united behind their bishops, for integrationists were using "the Church to destroy every trace of accepted racial customs."[13]

The founding of MAMML came just days after the formation of the Jackson Citizens' Council, a group headed by Ellis W. Wright, a laymen at Galloway Memorial Methodist Church, C. H. "Dick" King, and William J. Simmons. At their first meeting, Circuit Judge Tom Brady, author of *Black Monday*, reminded Jacksonians of the city's strategic importance, as "it's in the capitals that the opposition wage their wars." Responding to the view affirmed by many national Christian leaders that segregation and racial discrimination were morally wrong, Judge Brady contended, "The laws of nature . . . have decreed segregation," adding, "If segregation is wrong, God Almighty stands condemned."[14] As Will Campbell, a native Mississippian and a staff member with the NCC, observed in the early 1960s, the Citizens' Council and other segregationist groups often characterized their effort as a holy crusade, believing that God was on their side. Segregationist leaders, such as Robert B. Patterson, the executive secretary of the Citizens' Councils of America, who was at the March meeting in Jackson, saw churches as ground. In a meeting in New Orleans, Patterson explained, "By organizing within churches, foes of integration could bring pressure on ministers to support segregation and change the position of state and national church organizations which have endorsed mixing of the races." Patterson reminded his fellow Citizens' Council members, "We love our churches just like we love our schools, and we want to preserve them."[15] Churches were both a sanctuary for segregation and a space to exert influence in the national debate over integration.

Despite attempts to construct an image of uniformity on the issue of the desegregation of the Methodist Church in the state, new examples of nonconformity within the Mississippi Conference emerged just weeks after the formation of MAMML and the Jackson Citizens' Council. Delegates to the annual meeting in Jackson of the Women's Society of Christian Service (WSCS) of the Mississippi Methodist Conference voted two to one to affirm a charter that vowed to desegregate the national woman's division. Though the charter did not alter the structure or policies of the WSCS in Mississippi, it nevertheless constituted a statement of ideals and goals supported by a vast majority of women delegates to the convention. The vote by the women delegates of the Mississippi Methodist Conference was placed in even sharper relief a few weeks later when their counterparts in the WSCS for the North Mississippi Conference refused to affirm the charter in a 181 to 14 vote.[16] The move by a majority of delegates to the Mississippi Methodist Conference, while doing little to change practices in Mississippi, helps explain why MAMML and the Jackson Citizens' Council were so vigorous in organizing resistance to the elimination of racial barriers in churches.

When delegates to the General Conference of the Methodist Church convened in Minneapolis in 1956, they voted to begin the process of desegregating the denomination. But to satisfy white Southern Methodists, particularly the bishops of the Southeastern Jurisdiction, the convention decided that such moves should only happen voluntarily. To accomplish that end, they approved amendment IX, which paved the way for black churches to transfer out of the Central Jurisdiction, specifying that a local church could transfer to the annual conference in its geographical location by a two-thirds vote of the church and the conference. Likewise, annual conferences could transfer to another jurisdiction by a two-thirds vote of the conference and the jurisdiction. The Central Jurisdiction would cease to exist only when all the annual conferences completed the transfers.[17] Bishop Marvin Franklin voiced his approval of the compromise, saying that there was now a possibility of "a period of growing goodwill between the races." The following year, the Mississippi Conference indicated its support for voluntarism in the church, voting 271 to 15 in support of amendment IX, while the North Mississippi Conference voted narrowly, 115 to 107, to reject the amendment. A majority of the annual conferences nationwide voted to approve amendment IX, and it became effective in April 1958.[18]

Though no denomination moved to mandate desegregation in their bodies in the years immediately following the *Brown* decision, the specter of integrated churches compelled some state legislators to take a series of unprecedented measures to protect the racial purity of their churches. In March 1956, just a month prior to the Methodist vote affirming gradualism in desegregating the denomination, legislators in both the state house and senate introduced bills to deny religious organizations property tax exemptions if they practiced racial integration in any of their facilities or programs. With the bills languishing in senate and house committees, Sen. George Yarbrough of Red Banks, in northern Mississippi, introduced a separate amendment to a bill that would require churches and religious groups to pay property taxes if they insisted upon operating on an integrated basis. The measure would also apply to hospitals and any other charitable organization that received tax exemptions. The senate adopted the amendment without any discussion or a roll call vote, though it soon became clear that many senators did not fully comprehend its meaning when they voted, so the senate reconsidered the measure a few days later.[19]

The vote to reconsider the amendment provoked an intense debate on the senate floor. A few opponents to the amendment rose to affirm their support of segregation, but to denounce the measure as a dangerous intervention in the affairs of churches. One senator argued that the measure would "turn brother against brother" and deprive people of their religious freedom.[20] She pointed out that the bill would potentially forbid missionaries to minister to people of other races. Like others, she announced her support for segregation in social affairs, but maintained that religious integration was an entirely different matter. She told her colleagues, "I don't want my children to say their parents helped keep anyone from worshipping God." Yet defenders of the bill maintained that it did not target any particular church or denomination. Sen. George Yarbrough, the amendment's author, claimed, "We are simply telling all organizations that if you integrate you lose your tax exemption." Another supporter, Sen. Robert Everett of Ruleville, added, "If they are going to integrate—they'll have to pay to do it." In the end, the senate voted 25 to 14 to refuse to reconsider the previous vote, meaning that the amendment passed and the measure now moved to the house.[21]

The day after the state senate discharged the bill to the house, Governor J. P. Coleman announced his strong opposition to the bill, effectively rendering the measure dead. In explaining his rationale, Governor Coleman invoked the historic doctrine of separation of church and state, maintaining, "Our forebears tried to resolve that question by declaring that the government had no voice in the church and the church no voice in the government." He reasoned that if people were unhappy with the issues of race in their churches or denominations, then they, not the government, should deal with it.[22] The editors of the *Jackson Daily News* endorsed the governor's stand, calling the bill "a radical measure." Yet the editors pointed out that the passage of the bill in the senate "should awaken church leaders, regardless of creed or denomination, to realization of the grim earnestness of the fight being staged against the Supreme Court decree." Specifically, the bill should remind certain ministers that when they "proclaim that the battle against integration in our schools is 'sinful' and 'against the law of God,' [they] array themselves in opposition to the traditional Southern way of life and must take the consequences when so doing."[23] For the editors of the *Jackson Daily News*, the bill should serve notice to those dissenting from the perceptions of custom and uniformity. When some ministers denounced segregation, even in moral or religious terms, they did so at their own peril.

The second piece of legislation to assist individual congregations in sustaining racial barriers came four years later and met with greater success than the 1956 church tax bill. In February 1960, state senate and house members introduced measures to set up a process whereby a church could withdraw from its parent denomination while maintaining title to church property. State policymakers enacted a statute in 1952 that tried to do this—giving individual congregations legal title to their real property—but this law did not apply to most churches, particularly those chartered under the Methodist Church, which operated as trusts. As originally written, the 1960 bills would give each Protestant congregation the right to retain their church property if 65 percent of its members approved. Consideration of the bills came on the heels of adoption of a similar measure in Alabama in 1959. Authors of the Mississippi proposals made clear that the measures were intended to protect white churches from integration, seeing it as a way for local churches to avoid desegregation if national denominations continued to move in that direction, or if a parent organization appointed a black pastor to a white church. The fear of integrated churches was at the forefront, but at least one of the senate bill's twenty-six authors, Sen. Edgar Lee, saw the measure as a stopgap in the effort to prevent desegregation overall. He warned that when integration comes to Mississippi, "it will enter through the front doors of churches." He advised opponents to the bill that they would be "the first to hear the screams of coffee-colored grandchildren."[24]

While the authors of the bills avoided any discussion pointing to the Methodist Church as the target of the measure, MAMML stepped in to declare that the church property bill was the best way to ensure segregation in the local congregation if Methodist leaders tried integration. Following the introduction of the bill, MAMML informed its members in its monthly information bulletin of a recent "noble experiment" in California, where a church apparently fell apart after church leaders appointed a black pastor to a white congregation. The newsletter included a copy of the Alabama church property bill and urged readers to support the legislation currently being considered in Mississippi. The following month, MAMML catalogued the recent pronouncements of national Methodist Church leaders and bodies, indicating, "Our Southern Bishops and Church leaders have been unable to halt the move in the direction of integration so far." Pointing to what they saw as the inevitability of Methodist Church desegregation, MAMML concluded that the church property bill "will act as an insurance policy," permitting the local congregation to become trustee of church property.[25]

The authors of the senate and house church property bills were caught off guard when the measures engendered nearly universal condemnation from Protestant and Catholic leaders in Mississippi and several pastors in Jackson itself. Sidestepping an attack on the true motivation for the measures—to avoid integration of churches—these ministers and lay leaders focused on the means to that end, emphasizing that the measure constituted an unnecessary and unconstitutional state intrusion in the affairs of religious bodies and individual congregations. Bishop Marvin Franklin, who at the time was president of the Council of Bishops of the Methodist Church, announced that the proposed bills "could be the first steps toward the destruction of the Protestant churches in Mississippi and a serious blow to freedom of speech." Two Methodist ministers in Jackson seconded Bishop Franklin's alarm. Dr. Roy C. Clark of Capitol Street Methodist Church denounced the bill from the pulpit, saying, "There is no problem in any church in America which is so severe that it needs the radical remedy of bringing the power of government into the regulation of church affairs." Dr. W. B. Selah of Galloway Memorial Methodist Church told a Jackson civic group that the bill was "a clear violation of the principle of separation of church and state," adding, "The churches can handle their own affairs." Lay leaders in the Jackson district of the Mississippi Conference, including J. P. Stafford, pointed out that Mississippi political leaders were being hypocritical, decrying unprecedented federal interference in state affairs on one hand, while asking for unprecedented state interference in local affairs on the other hand.[26]

In response to criticism from various church leaders, authors of the church property measures changed some of the language of the bills, no longer specifying that it applied to Protestant groups. Instead, the second set of bills identified beneficiaries, trusts, or educational, charitable, or religious organizations as those the measure affected. Though some congregations were autonomous and maintained direct control over their church property, others, including those in the Methodist Church, operated under organizational and property structures that would be applicable under the new law. The authors, counseled by attorney John Satterfield and others in MAMML, hoped that the alterations would alleviate some of the concerns about the constitutionality of the original bill. As the authors indicated, the bills did not constitute class legislation since legislation applied to all churches, not just Protestant congregations. They reasoned that the bill was

no different from other statutes that regulated churches and religious organizations, so they felt the bill did not constitute a significant violation of the
constitutional mandate of separation of church and state.

The changes made to the second church property bill did little to damp-
en opposition to the measure, but the bill survived and passed both houses.
Governor Ross Barnett, a Sunday school teacher and deacon at First Baptist Church in Jackson, signed the legislation into law on March 31, 1960.
Though discouraged with the outcome, Bishop Franklin acknowledged the
law would have little effect on Methodist churches in the state, since it was
improbable that his denomination would force racial integration on any
churches.[27] Yet at the time, it represented a symbolic victory for segregationist church people in Mississippi. Moreover, as Dr. Clark recalled a few
years later, the bill was the "opening gun" of conservative agitation about
race within the church in Mississippi.[28]

A month after the church property measure became law, Methodists assembled in Denver, the first assembly since the adoption of amendment IX,
which provided for voluntary desegregation of churches and conferences
and gradual abolition of the Central Jurisdiction. Until the May 1960 meeting, only six churches nationwide, representing just a fraction of a percent
of the Central Jurisdiction membership, transferred out of the Central Jurisdiction under the provisions of amendment IX. Because of this dilatory
pace, the bishops of the Central Jurisdiction wanted a more detailed plan
and schedule for transfers, yet the committee called upon to investigate the
desegregation of the church at the 1956 general conference, the Commission
of Seventy, recommended a continuation of the status quo. Delegates to the
general conference overwhelmingly affirmed the commission's suggestion
but created a new group, the Commission on Interjurisdictional Relations,
to promote interracial brotherhood and further study the realization of
amendment IX in advance of the 1964 general conference in Pittsburgh. Curiously, the Council of Bishops named John Satterfield, counsel for MAMML
and presiding president of the American Bar Association, as a member of
the new commission. Recognizing that the conference effectively voted to
maintain the status quo with regard to the segregated system of the Methodist Church, the Central Jurisdiction set up its own group, the Committee
of Five, to work with the Commission on Interjurisdictional Relations and
other groups studying the dissolution of the Central Jurisdiction. As one of
its five members, Dr. William Astor Kirk, later recalled, he and the other four
on the committee immediately focused on how to rid the denomination of
involuntary segregation as a means of ending the Central Jurisdiction.[29]

While voting to extend the policy of gradual segregation, delegates to the 1960 general conference voted to reaffirm the belief that racial segregation was un-Christian. They declared that the "House of God must be open to the whole family of God," and reminded Methodists that membership and participation in Holy Communion in local churches in the denomination were open to all.[30] For national Methodist Church leaders, these principles clearly meant that churches in the denomination must follow open door policies. For instance, two leaders who would figure prominently in the Jackson church visit campaign, Thelma Stevens, chairman of staff of the Christian Social Relations of the Woman's Division, and Dr. A. Dudley Ward, chairman of the Board of Christian Social Concerns of the Methodist Church, coauthored a 1962 pamphlet explaining the actions taken at the 1960 general conference. They stated unequivocally, "*No person may be excluded from the Methodist Christian fellowship by the vote of the congregation, the Quarterly Conference, or the Official Board.*" (emphasis original) They pointed out that the pastor had sole responsibility for admitting persons into the church, and that membership in the church was not subject to any restrictive actions on the part of a local congregation.[31] Though it was apparent to Methodist leaders that segregated churches were inconsistent with church teachings, the reality was that denomination remained segregated, a practice the 1960 general conference did little to alter. Failure to resolve this contradiction gave segregationists in Mississippi the space they needed to assert even more control over the policies and direction of their congregations.

Just as Mississippi adopted the church property bill and the Methodist Church voted to maintain volunteerism in its desegregation plan, a new direct action, youth inspired movement burst upon the scene. Impatient with the slow process of desegregation, college students throughout the South initiated sit-ins at a variety of public facilities beginning in early 1960, and formed the Student Nonviolent Coordinating Committee (SNCC) to the sustain this new phase of the movement. Meeting in Atlanta in August, SNCC leaders announced their intention to challenge the segregation practiced by white churches and recommended that activists begin what they called "kneel-ins." Student leaders felt that "the time has come to awaken the dozing consciences of white Southerners by carrying the problem of segregation to the church," believing that "the white Southerner has failed to realize the moral wrongness of segregation." By attempting to attend church, activists simply wanted to present the problem of segregation to the white Southerner. Though they termed it a kneel-in to correspond with other similarly named nonviolent direct action tactics, like the sit-in or the wade-in, there was no intimation that the tactic would involve anything other than attempting to attend a worship service in a white church. SNCC leaders did not suggest, for instance, that activists should physically kneel at the church in the event that church officials barred their entry, or do anything that might invite police intervention. In fact, SNCC was quick to point out that this was not even a protest in the conventional sense. The statement in their newsletter maintained, "The attitude of the students kneeling in is not one of protest but a feeling that only when all are united under God can there be true brotherhood." The students were appealing not only to the consciences of white Americans—trying to convince them of the immorality of segregation—but they wanted to remind Christians that "the church [was] a house of God, to be attended by all people, regardless of race, who wish to worship there." In their August newsletter, SNCC leaders predicted that "the kneel-ins will be one of the next important phases of the student movement."[32]

Beginning in Atlanta in August 1960 and spreading elsewhere in the state and to other major cities throughout the South over the next several months, student led groups fanned out to seek worship in at least two hundred churches from across the denominational spectrum.[33] Responses from white church people varied, but when churches barred their entry, the activists simply departed, feeling that being turned away meant they had achieved their objective. As one Atlanta student recalled, "The attempt itself was a success, because the minds and hearts of the people who turned us away were undoubtedly stirred."[34] In most cases, the students participated in church visits in concert with other local direct action protests, and the visits were thus just one facet of a larger campaign to desegregate local spaces. Though no organized attempts to try to attend white churches occurred in Jackson or in any other city in the state during this time, the 1960 round of visits served as a precedent and demonstrated the potential of utilizing church visits as a tactic.

One of the leaders of the 1960 kneel-ins who would prove central to the Jackson church visit campaign was Joan Trumpauer, at the time a white student at Duke University. While she was at home in northern Virginia in August, she coordinated a series of church visits in Alexandria. Unlike their counterparts further south, all of the churches from a variety of denominations in Alexandria admitted integrated groups of students. Trumpauer and many of the others who participated in the Alexandria kneel-ins had been active in the movement in their college towns. Frank McCain, for instance, was one of the original four who participated in the Greensboro Woolworth sit-ins in February. Yet, as SNCC leaders envisioned, the opportunity to engage white Christians on Sunday and serve as a public witness to the brotherhood of mankind held special meaning for the church visitors. Though Trumpauer saw different sources for her beliefs and activism—ancestors on her father's side were militant suffragists—she took seriously the lessons she learned at Sunday school at her Presbyterian church and recognized that many Christians were not putting these convictions into practice. In high school, for instance, organized discussion groups at her church helped prepare the way for desegregation at a time when many white residents were clamoring to close the public schools.[35]

The kneel-ins of 1960 coincided with other nonviolent methods of manifesting the injustices inherent in compulsory segregation. Yet for civil rights activists, the kneel-in had an even more perspicuous purpose. Activists utilized tactics such as the boycott, for instance, to impact the wallets of white citizens, while they visited white churches to tug on the heartstrings of white Christians. Students recognized that, at least on one level, they were involved in a battle of ideas. They were trying to convince white Christians that the issue was not just upholding the Constitution; it was also about applying Christian principles. The white church provided a key space to clarify and redefine the nature of the struggle. Like the state senator from Mississippi, many activists believed that when integration arrived, it would go through the front doors of white churches.

[3]

Jackson Ministers Proclaiming Their Convictions
1961–63

As kneel-ins spread to many major cities throughout the South, beginning in August 1960, students and other activists in Mississippi's capital city were just getting organized. A few students in Jackson conducted their own individual protests in the wake of the Greensboro sit-ins, and Medgar Evers, the Mississippi field secretary for the National Association for the Advancement of Colored People (NAACP), coordinated a boycott of businesses for the Easter 1960 shopping season. But the Tougaloo Nine library sit-in in March 1961 marked the real launch of the organized protests and grassroots activities of the Jackson movement. During this sit-in, Jackson police arrested nine Tougaloo students and NAACP youth council volunteers at the city's large whites only library on North State Street. The protest and trial energized Jackson's black youth and inspired more sit-ins and protests in other public spaces, but not at any white churches. While activists in 1961 and 1962 clearly aimed to focus their efforts on economic discrimination, targeting venues and institutions supported with their tax dollars, they also avoided kneel-ins simply because they expected the doors of churches to be closed.

Following the passage of the church property bill, some congregations became even more proactive in their efforts to keep black visitors out. Two months after the Tougaloo Nine sit-in, the arrival and arrests of Freedom Riders focused more attention on the city's segregated spaces and convinced some white church people that they might begin to encounter black activists at their church doors for the first time. Lay leaders in at least two of Jackson's most historic churches prepared for that possibility by voting to close their doors to all African American visitors in 1961. Controversies over race within white churches accelerated during this time and reached a boiling point during the crisis surrounding James Meredith's integration of the University of Mississippi in the fall of 1962. The sharpest public disagreements within churches occurred in the Methodist Church, where a moderate manifesto adopted by a group of pastors provoked a backlash that centered on the racial purity of white churches in Mississippi.

As Freedom Riders started arriving in Jackson in May 1961, city authorities began making preparations for follow-up protests. In early June, Mayor Allen Thompson informed the minister of his church, Dr. W. B. Selah of Galloway Memorial Methodist, that he had received reliable information that the Freedom Riders intended to send a group of black activists to Galloway to attend morning worship on June 4. Mayor Thompson told Dr. Selah that he had ordered police to keep the activists out of the churches. Dr. Selah immediately discussed the mayor's decision with the chair of the church's official board, and both agreed that the city did not have authority to decide who could enter a church. As Dr. Selah reasoned, if the city could "say who enters a church, it can also say who stands in the pulpit." The lay leader and Dr. Selah prevailed upon Mayor Thompson, who promptly rescinded the order for police intervention.[1] Though no activists attempted kneel-ins in the capital during these months, lay leaders at Galloway and another large downtown church, First Christian, prepared for that possibility in the succeeding weeks and voted to forbid African Americans from attending services. The two congregations joined First Presbyterian as the three Jackson churches known to maintain closed-door policies through 1961. Unlike the experience at First Presbyterian, however, laymen at First Christian and Galloway initiated the exclusionary polices over the strong objections of their respective ministers.[2]

The pastor of First Christian Church was Rev. Roy S. Hulan, who arrived at the church just months after the *Brown* decision in 1954. The congregation's pulpit screening committee specifically asked him if he intended to preach on the race issue, a concern made paramount not only by the Supreme Court ruling, but also by admission of a black woman into a Sunday school class and a worship service at the church on a recent Sunday morning. He told the committee that he was from Tennessee and understood the attitudes of Southerners well, but that he intended to preach the gospel as he understood it.

Just as Rev. Hulan assumed the helm of the church, his denomination—the Disciples of Christ—became a trustee of Tougaloo Southern Christian College. In addition to being a respected black college in the region, Tougaloo was one of few places in the Jackson area where interracial gatherings occurred frequently. Consistent with his commitment to outreach, Rev. Hulan visited Tougaloo on a regular basis, serving as a guest preacher at chapel services. In the ensuing years, he encouraged his church members to establish greater ties to the college. The racial attitudes of his congregation ran the gamut, and some openly demanded that the church sever its ties to the school owing to a perception that it was a hotbed of communist and other leftist activity in the state.

Rev. Hulan successfully resisted these calls, but he was unable to prevent the closing of the church doors in 1961. At some point late that spring, his general board voted to authorize church ushers to bar the entry of African Americans to services at First Christian. The general board instructed the ushers to tell any black visitor that the church would provide transportation to a nearby all-black affiliated church. The board's statement rejected the timing and legitimacy of the African Americans' tactic, reasoning that the church was "not ready for an integrated fellowship," and attending the church would not create "the best atmosphere in which to carry on mutually helpful communication." Though the board made the move over Rev. Hulan's protest, no blacks tested First Christian's closed-door policy for another two years.[3]

Like his counterpart at First Christian, Dr. Selah, the long-time senior pastor of Galloway Memorial Methodist Church, one of the largest Methodist churches in the state, presided over a congregation with a range of views on race. On one side, membership included many of the city's political and business leaders. Jackson's segregationist mayor, Allen Thompson, and the past president of the United States Chamber of Commerce, Boyd Campbell, were longtime members. Key leaders of the Jackson Citizens' Council, such as Richard Morphew and Ellis and John Wright, attended Galloway and served on the official board. Yet membership also included a sizable contingent of racial moderates and liberals, many of which taught at the state's white Methodist college, Millsaps. Like many in his flock, Dr. Selah clearly grappled with the issue of race and, in the years just after the *Brown* decision, did little to publicly challenge the status quo. For instance, he gave the invocation at a Jackson Citizens' Council meeting in January 1956, telling members, "Only in an atmosphere of goodwill can black and white people live together, for we do have to live together."[4] In 1958, Dr. Selah tackled the issue of segregation head-on in a sermon titled "The Climate of Freedom," in which he stated unambiguously, "It would be tragic for both races in the deep South to put black and white children in the same school." He believed that "we have to take the ethical teachings of Jesus . . .

and formulate policies to apply these principles to the actualities of life in each locality."⁵ Yet after his official board considered barring African Americans from worship at Galloway, one can detect a departure from this type of language as he began insisting instead on the inevitability of desegregation in Mississippi. He became less equivocal about the immorality of compulsory segregation, especially in churches.

The 1961 debate over Galloway's attendance policy came on the heels of three consecutive official board meetings during which laymen deliberated the church's contributions to the NCC. The ecumenical group, which provided educational resources for churches but also took political stands at odds with conservatives, had long been a target, particularly of MAMML. At the March meeting, just two weeks before the Tougaloo Nine sit-in, one of the laymen declared that the some of the material that the NCC recommended for reading by youth was "communistic, revolutionary, vile and unfit for human consideration." He brought two articles written by Langston Hughes and Buckin Moon, two writers the NCC recommended youths consider reading. Smith asked his fellow laymen to write the NCC and demand that they "stop such unchristian work from being continued."⁶

While issues of race often surfaced within the context of discussions over the liberal leanings of the NCC, the official board of Galloway Memorial Methodist confronted the issue more directly in June 1961 in preparation for potential visits by black activists. As Jackson police began arresting Freedom Riders at the Greyhound terminal nearby, the official board considered a resolution that would instruct ushers to reject anyone, regardless of race, who sought admission "for the purpose of creating an incident."⁷ Dr. Selah later wrote that the laymen who voted for the resolution were "not the kind of men who in normal times would seek to bar colored people from the church service," but that they "sincerely feared that if the Freedom Riders were admitted in this hour of tension there might occur an incident." In his mind, the laymen believed that the Freedom Riders were outside agitators who "were not coming in a sincere spirit of worship but were coming to make trouble."⁸ Dr. Selah was one of the first to speak and reasoned that the church should just let the visitors in, since they likely hoped to be turned away. Dr. Selah told the board that he would have a prepared statement he would read to the congregation if the church admitted African Americans. He would tell them, "It is not sinful for white people to prefer to worship with white people or for colored people to prefer to worship with colored people," but that "the sin comes when a church seeks to put up a color bar before the Cross of Christ." He would add, "To discriminate against a man because of the color of his skin is contrary to the will of God." Yet the minutes indicate only one other member spoke out against the resolution, which passed overwhelmingly, 102 to 31. Interpreting the actions of the board years later, a future senior pastor at Galloway, Rev. W. J. Cunningham, wrote, "Barring Negroes from worship in white congregations was another way of fighting back" against "outside intervention." For the majority on the board, "the churches were the last line of defense."[9]

Though no Freedom Riders or other black activists tried to attend Galloway the summer of 1961, the closed-door policy remained in effect, and Dr. Selah began to preach more forcefully on the immorality of compulsory segregation. He admitted later that he made up his mind shortly after the June vote that he would resign if blacks were ever barred from Galloway.[10] In November 1961, he delivered a sermon entitled "Brotherhood" that expanded upon the beliefs he articulated during the official board meeting in June. He devoted most of his sermon the argument that racial and religious bigotry was weakening the country at the very moment when unity was needed in the fight against communism, though he confronted the recent actions of the official board. He reminded his congregation, "We will be judged not by our theological opinions but by the way we treat men," adding that God is "concerned with the way we treat His other children." The laws of Christian love and brotherhood dictated as follows:

> We must seek for all men, black and white, the same justice, the same rights, and the same opportunities to find the abundant life we seek for ourselves. Nothing less than this is Christian love. To discriminate against a man because of color is contrary to the will of God. Forced segregation is wrong. We should treat men not on the basis of color but on the basis of conduct.

Though Dr. Selah declined to specify the political implications of this principle, it was nevertheless a significant departure from the language and tone from his statements just years before, when he deemed school desegregation "tragic" and stated that segregation was not necessarily un-Christian. He was now calling compulsory segregation un-Christian, indicating a subtle shift in his thinking. But in the context of Jackson in 1961, his language constituted a fundamental rebuttal to the arguments and policies of the city and state governments, the Citizens' Council, and his own official board. While leaving it to the congregation to deduce the political consequences of the principles of brotherhood and love, he did go on to spell out the religious implications, saying that the laws meant Christians must welcome other Christians into the house of God, regardless of race. Though he grounded his reasoning in Christian fundamentals, he also tried to convince his church of the practicality and usefulness of the open-door policy. He pointed out that even if African Americans visited Galloway, it was unlikely a black person would seek to join the church. Moreover, the black pastors in Jackson with whom he talked told him that African Americans in the city were uninterested in intermingling with whites, although they did resent the color bars in white churches. As he related to his congregation, one black minister told him that if the church took "the dare out of it . . . ninety percent of the problem is solved."[11] In Dr. Selah's view, closed church doors created more problems than they solved and, more fundamentally, gainsaid Christian principles of brotherhood and love.

While white Jacksonians were content to dismiss the Freedom Ride campaign as outsider induced troublemaking, they could not ignore local citizens' efforts to challenge the segregationist power structure. The integration of the state's flagship university by a native Mississippian in 1962 had a range of symbolic and tangible effects, convincing many black residents that change was possible, while serving notice to segregationists that nothing—no school, restaurant, or church—was exempt from integration. In the wake of the integration crisis at the University of Mississippi, a group of mostly young white Methodist ministers, all native Mississippians, released a manifesto articulating their convictions about race and freedom of speech. Though not all members of the group of twenty-eight received actual threats in response, they shared a sense that one of the ways to navigate the current crisis was to foster an environment in which white Mississippians truly accepted a free exchange of viewpoints. As Rev. Jerry Furr, one of the chief architects of manifesto and Dr. Selah's associate at Galloway Memorial Methodist, told Professor James Silver of the University of Mississippi, the ultimate object in releasing the statement was "in the direction on convincing Mississippians not only that ministers and educators have a right to speak their minds but to convince Mississippians that they must insist on the free expression and discussion of all ideas."[12] The fact that all of the twenty-eight were native Mississippians was crucial to achieving this objective. Since segregationists could not brand them with the usual pejorative label, "outsiders," the ministers hoped that Mississippians would see the group's members as their own.

On January 2, 1963, the denomination's statewide newspaper, the *Mississippi Methodist Advocate*, published what came to be known as the "born of

conviction" statement. The twenty-eight pastors affirmed four main principles and points: "freedom of the pulpit" where ministers can preach in an
atmosphere of "responsible belief and free expression"; the social creed of
the 1960 Methodist *Discipline*, which stated that "God is Father of all people
and races, that Jesus Christ is His Son, that all men are brothers, and that
man is of infinite worth as a child of God"; commitment to keep public
schools open; and, anticipating the refrain that equated race mixing with
communism, an "unflinching opposition to Communism."[13] The ministers'
statement was decidedly moderate, for it did not explicitly endorse desegregation, but stated that white Christians must accept African Americans
as brothers. The ministers were making the case for a Christian defense
of integration. From the bishop to lay leaders in local churches, most understood the implications of the ministers' statement: Segregation denied
Christian brotherhood.

Although the "born of conviction" statement remained consistent with
the official positions of the national Methodist Church, including pronouncements of the most recent Bishops' council, the response from conference leaders varied. Mississippi's bishop, Marvin Franklin, who wrote
a weekly column in the *Methodist Advocate*, never publicly endorsed the
statement or defended the twenty-eight. For the ministers, this lack of support from leaders of the Mississippi Conference was not really a surprise.
As Dr. Roy C. Clark of Capitol Street Methodist Church in Jackson later explained, during this period in Mississippi, ministers "were not sure whether
or not the ecclesiastical hierarchy would really support them or not." This
climate of uncertainty made the ministry difficult for those who felt "there
was a moral dimension to dealing creatively and relevantly with what was
happening in the life of the culture." Bishop Franklin refrained from commenting on the manifesto in the January 2 issue and in future issues. Yet
he and the district superintendent issued a joint statement in mid-January
emphasizing the autonomy of local churches. They pointed out that according to the constitution of the Methodist Church, the church "places racial
relationships on a voluntary basis," and "integration is not forced upon any
part of our church." The conference lay leader, Dr. J. P. Stafford, the lay counterpart to Bishop Franklin, broke with his bishop's position, affirming the
"born of conviction" statement in the January 9 edition of the *Methodist
Advocate*. In addition, Francis Stevens, the conference associate lay leader
and a member of Broadmeadow Methodist Church in Jackson, announced
his support for the entire statement, predicting that most laymen would

agree with the twenty-eight ministers as well and would support the ministers' right to voice their convictions.[14]

Sensing the inconsistent message among church authorities in Mississippi, MAMML stepped in to steer the public discourse. A week after publication of the "born of conviction" statement, the pro-segregation Methodist group issued a response, asking all congregations to state their position on integration.[15] MAMML now boasted five thousand members statewide, the vast majority of them laymen. A Jackson businessman and member of Capitol Street Methodist Church, Garner M. Lester, headed the group. Though preventing the desegregation of the Methodist Church at all levels became the raison d'être of MAMML, this had not been the most pressing concern among members. Until 1963, the organization met periodically and issued monthly bulletins in which they exposed liberal statements in Sunday school literature, or discussed controversial actions by non-Mississippi Methodist leaders and the NCC. Yet the statement by the twenty-eight ministers exposed a crack in what had been perceived to be a largely pro-segregation wall among Mississippi Methodist ministers. Even though the "born of conviction" statement expressed a moderate deviation from the norm, MAMML leaders sensed that their segregated church was in danger.

MAMML issued their own declaration, authored by Dr. Medford Evans, a Citizens' Council staff member and Methodist layman. Evans addressed the principles espoused by the twenty-eight, while also offering an extensive rebuttal to the larger issue of integration. The statement affirmed a minister's freedom of speech if what he preached truly reflected his conscience, but added that a minister "must be ready to accept the consequences if what he says offends the consciences of those to whom he looks for support."[16] While MAMML did not detail what the consequences would be if the minister challenged the congregations' sense of right and wrong, the statement illustrated the logic embraced by those churches that were in the process of forcing out their ministers. If the conscience of the minister did not align with the conscience of the congregation as expressed by the church's official board, then the board reserved the right to ask the bishop to reassign the congregation's minister. MAMML felt that the "born of conviction" statement exemplified a "spirit of authoritarianism" that went against John Wesley's teachings, specifically his opposition to ecclesiastical positions "when they seemed to him contrary to the will of God."[17]

After calling for limitations on "freedom of the pulpit," MAMML's statement predictably turned to the larger issue of integration. While declaring, "It is unChristian to endanger segregation," the statement proffered a lesson in history. Evans asserted that "the United States has been a segregated country from the start," and that the country "has furnished the world the greatest example in history of two races, radically different in physical and psychological characteristics, living together in peace." If the integrationists attained their goals, the statement warned of a repetition of what occurred in the Congo, "where wholesale rape, murder, and pillage have been the fruits of doctrinaire racial equalitarianism." In addition, MAMML disputed the central contention of the ministers who signed the "born of conviction" statement and the Methodist Church's position that "all men are brothers." Since the Bible, particularly the teachings of St. Paul, prescribed segregation by sex or position, MAMML believed that segregation by race was no different. If Paul's "restrictions on women and on servants (he meant slaves, actually) did not violate the spirit of oneness in Christ, then certainly our Southern system of race relations—with its demonstrated benefits—does not." Addressing the possibility of black church visits, the statement significantly acknowledged that it would be "impossible for man to deny this admittance and it would be sinful to try." Yet no one had tried in Mississippi, since blacks "have churches of their own." The declaration ended with an appeal to all Methodist churches to conduct secret ballots concerning their views and policies on the issue of segregation.[18]

While Francis Stevens's prediction of widespread public support in the state for the twenty-eight never materialized, one crucial Methodist minister, Dr. Selah, did join with the two conferences lay leaders in embracing their convictions. Dr. Selah's associate at Galloway, Rev. Jerry Furr, was the only minister from a Jackson church who at the time signed the "born of conviction" statement. Rev. Furr's stance carried added significance not only because of the church's size and stature within Mississippi Methodism, but because many city leaders were members, including Jackson's pro-segregationist mayor. Dr. Selah openly endorsed his assistant's position and made explicit what the twenty-eight ministers implied: Christian brotherhood required open church doors. In a statement released to the local press and reprinted nationwide, Dr. Selah reiterated what he had been proclaiming recently from the pulpit, "There can be no color bar in a Christian church." While he said, "It is not sinful for white people to prefer to worship with white people," he added, "the sin comes when a church seeks to erect a color bar before the Cross of Christ." To clarify the political implications of his beliefs, he stated, "We should voluntarily desegregate all public facilities."[19] Though the notion of voluntary desegregation fit the language of many racial conservatives, who aimed to thwart federal laws or court orders by insisting upon a local time frame, and echoed the tactic of voluntarism that prevailed at the time in his denomination, Dr. Selah's statements constituted a sharp rebuke to the status quo. The leading segregationists in Jackson were not interested in desegregating any facility, whether it was a church or a school.

Dr. Selah's sermons clearly put him at odds with the majority of those on the official board, and by extension, with the majority in his congregation. Given Rev. Furr's signature on the "born of conviction" statement, Dr. Selah's public support for his assistant and for desegregation in general, and MAMML's instructions of a few days earlier, the official board of Galloway Memorial Methodist decided to clarify its position relative to the church's ministers. One layman presented a motion to censure both ministers and to request the bishop to recall their appointments, but the motion failed.[20] Instead, the board proposed a new resolution on January 14, 1963, which the laymen adopted and released to the press:

> The recently published statements by the pastors of this Church are their personal opinions and are not necessarily the views and opinions of the individual members of Galloway Memorial Methodist Church. It is not un-Christian that we prefer to remain an all-white congregation. The practice of segregation of the races is a time-honored tradition. We earnestly hope that the perpetuation of that tradition will never be impaired.[21]

Unlike the June 1961 resolution initiating the closed-door policy, the January 1963 statement specifically racialized those whom greeters would bar from entering. In addition to protecting something perceived as tradition, the resolution rationalized the exclusion policy by arguing that it was not inconsistent with Christian teachings. The board was clearly borrowing from the reasoning of Dr. Selah, though they overlooked the distinction he tried to make between compulsory and voluntary segregation. During and after the debate over the 1961 policy, Dr. Selah contended that it was not sinful for whites to choose to worship with other whites; the sin occurred when that preference became mandatory. By secret ballot, the board voted 145 to 14 to approve the resolution.[22] Debate over the minister's statements was not limited to official board meetings. John and Margrit Garner, new church members, noted a lengthy debate over their ministers' positions during their adult Sunday school class the day before the vote. Most in their class supported Dr. Selah and Rev. Furr, but other church members were calling one other, "urging them to stop their pledge and take their children out of the Sunday school."[23]

In the weeks following Galloway's official board vote to continue their closed-door policy, the positions of their two ministers remained tenuous. The Sunday after the January 14 vote, Dr. Selah had to cut short his sermon because of pains in his stomach. Diagnosed with a severe bleeding ulcer and requiring several blood transfusions, Dr. Selah remained out of the pulpit for the next month.[24] When the issue of Dr. Selah and Rev. Furr's futures as ministers at Galloway came before the official board in April, the two ministers presented a united front. While it was unlikely that the board would ask the bishop to remove Dr. Selah, given his tenure at the church and stature throughout Methodism, Rev. Furr's status was more uncertain. When the board met, Dr. Selah told them that if the board asked for Rev. Furr's reassignment, he would have to step down. Dr. Selah's reasoned that he "must stand behind the members of [his] staff in their right to express their honest convictions, especially when their convictions, as in Mr. Furr's case, are in line with the position of the Methodist Church and the gospel." For his part, Rev. Furr backed away from Dr. Selah's overall position on race and spoke to the salient practical issues before the church. He told the board that he was "not, and have never been, in favor of the integration of Galloway Church," and that it was not his "intention to work for this objective in the future."[25] In the end, the board voted to return both Dr. Selah and Rev. Furr for another conference year.[26]

While the "born of conviction" statement garnered most of the attention, there were other prominent Methodist pastors in Mississippi who shared the principles of the manifesto but, like Dr. Selah, were not asked to sign the statement. One of these was Dr. Roy C. Clark, the pastor of Capitol Street Methodist Church in Jackson. In the days following the release of the manifesto, he worked to build support among other ministers for a statement supporting the twenty-eight and their freedom of speech. Dr. Clark, a second-generation Methodist minister in the Mississippi Conference, grew up in the state and graduated from Millsaps College and Yale Divinity School. After leading smaller churches throughout Mississippi for nine years, he accepted a call to Capitol Street Methodist in 1953. By that time, he recalled later, he had already engendered the hostility of the power structure in the conference because of his resistance to their conservative initiatives and because of his connection to Yale. He recollected that he "was almost in a different universe" from the conference leadership.[27] Much of his work on racial justice concentrated on maintaining a dialogue with

those representing the full spectrum on civil rights, though he later admitted that he made the mistake of grounding many of these discussions in
sociology rather than Christian theology. During the summer of 1961, he
visited several Freedom Riders in jail after receiving frantic calls from their
parents. He later remembered a discussion with one jailed white activist
who was a fundamentalist, but felt called to the movement because of his
Christian convictions and identification with blacks in his hometown, Chicago. The experience helped demonstrate to Dr. Clark that sincere Christians were part of the struggle, that Freedom Riders and other civil rights
activists were not just a bunch of communists.[28] He tried to keep the lines
of communication open to those in his own church who strongly objected
to his statements on race, an endeavor that became more intractable in the
early 1960s, when his opponents at Capitol Street began circulating yearly
petitions asking the bishop to remove him.

A solid majority on the official board backed Dr. Clark's ministry, but by
late 1962, the board had gone about as far as it could sticking up for him.
A few lay leaders approached him and reiterated their support and respect,
but they announced that they could no longer defend him if he continued
to denounce segregation. He reasoned that these men were under considerable pressure from the Citizens' Council and were fearful of losing their
jobs. After nearly a decade as pastor at Capitol Street, he recognized that
his ministry was at an end and asked Bishop Franklin for a reassignment.
Bishop Franklin, however, encouraged him to stay. The bishop told Dr.
Clark, "You and Bill Selah have your feet on the neck of the Citizens' Council," adding that they were both in full command of the situation. When Dr.
Clark persisted in requesting a transfer, Bishop Franklin finally came up
with a solution. With Dr. Selah nearing retirement, Bishop Franklin offered
Dr. Clark an exchange: He would transfer to the church previously held by
Dr. Selah's successor. Now all he had to do was wait for Dr. Selah to step
down.[29]

On January 13, 1963, Dr. Clark directly addressed the "born of conviction" manifesto in a sermon preached to his congregation at Capitol Street
Methodist. His audience included many Citizens' Council members and local segregationist leaders, such as Garner Lester, the president of MAMML.
For Dr. Clark, the pressing issue facing Methodists in Mississippi at the moment was not segregation or desegregation, since he sensed that most overwhelmingly favored segregation. He estimated that if it were put to a vote
before the conference, the vote would be about 95 percent in favor of maintaining segregated churches.[30] Instead, the crucial question was whether he

and others who "sincerely believe by our light from Christ that justice and love require modification in the segregated way of life, have the same right to believe as we do and to express this belief and to work for it in appropriate ways without prejudice and reprisal against ourselves or our families?"[31] Though Dr. Clark seemed resigned to the fact that most of his flock opposed his views on segregation, he recognized that upholding the freedom of the pulpit was necessary to guiding his church toward moderation.

Whether in response to the "born of conviction" manifesto or the request by MAMML that churches state their positions, Methodist congregations throughout the state discussed freedom of the pulpit and the underlying issue of integration. Based on a reading of Bishop Franklin's correspondence in the months following the ministers' statement, dozens of churches reported discussions at official board meetings. Most expressed opposition to "born of conviction." Consistent with reactions at Galloway and other churches whose ministers signed the statement, these congregations understood the larger issue: whether or not Christian brotherhood necessitated integration. The majority of those church boards that expressed opposition to the ministers' statement also expressed opposition to integration. For instance, the congregations of the Dekalb Circuit, which included Meridian, issued a joint resolution stating they did "not believe in the Integration of our Churches, because no useful purpose could be served."[32] Like MAMML, these churches understood that far more than "freedom of the pulpit" was at stake. Congregations recognized that the ministers' belief in the brotherhood of mankind threatened their system of segregation, both inside and outside their church doors.

If Mississippians failed to appreciate the implications of the "born of conviction" principles, one of the state's leading newspapers spelled them out for readers. Owned by the Hederman family, staunch segregationists and leading laymen at First Baptist Church, the *Jackson Daily News* closely followed the developments of the story, reporting the controversies within the churches prompted by the manifesto. The editors often buttressed these news items with editorials and other stories connecting church integration with social integration in general. For instance, the day the newspaper printed Bishop Marvin Franklin's official response to the ministers' statement, it also reprinted a thirty-year-old article about Bishop Warren A. Candler, a former bishop from Georgia. Bishop Candler was addressing the impending merger of the Northern and Southern branches of the Methodist Church, but the editors of the *Jackson Daily News* felt "the article [was] of special interest at this time." In the piece, which the newspaper printed in its editorial section, Bishop Candler argued that segregation worked to the advantage of both blacks and whites, concluding that "national and racial lines are ordained of God."[33] Toward the end of the same issue, the editors alerted their readers to activities in Chicago, where delegates to the National Conference on Religion and Race were meeting. Under the headline, "Church Groups Urge Militant Mixing," the article detailed the aims of the conference, saying, "Its purpose is to galvanize America's religious bodies in 'courageous and effective action' against segregation, discrimination and prejudice in all areas of life." The next day, the *Jackson Daily News* reported on Dr. Martin Luther King Jr.'s speech to delegates at the National Conference on Religion and Race under a similarly titled headline, "Church Mix Drive Pleasing to King." In the article, Dr. King explained what churches and synagogues could do to achieve an integrated society. Dr. King gave a list of activities and issues that religious groups should tackle, but at the very top of the list was an unambiguous proposition: Churches must "remove the yoke of segregation from their own bodies by eliminating all racial barriers in worship."[34]

In March, two important meetings of Methodists in the South offered contrasting messages in response to the issues raised by the twenty-eight. The Southeastern Jurisdictional Council of the Methodist Church held its annual meeting in Memphis in early March and there addressed a variety of concerns, including the issue of "freedom of the pulpit." Sidestepping the underlying issue of integration, the council voted unanimously to affirm "the right and duty of every Methodist pastor and every layman to express what he believes to be the mind of Christ on every social issue of the day."[35] Although the resolution merely endorsed the official position of the Methodist Church, it stood in contrast to the positions of some Mississippi churches and MAMML, which put limitations on the speech of ministers.

Later that month, the leaders of MAMML called on fellow Methodists to meet in Jackson, their first conference since the release of the "born of conviction" manifesto. President Lester said that the purpose was to seek ways to restore "conservative Methodist control" to the church. Threatening to utilize the powers granted by the 1960 church property bill, he added, "There must be a united effort to salvage our church property and structures." About 450 Methodists attended the meeting at a Jackson hotel and heard speeches from leading pro-segregationist laymen before affirming several resolutions. John Satterfield, past president of the American Bar Association and general counsel for MAMML, compared black and white rates of "illegitimacy, venereal disease, and intelligence and aptitude tests," concluding that "segregation of the races in the Christian spirit is best for both races."[36] Dr. Medford Evans countered the assertion that integration was somehow inevitable, pointing to the Methodist Church's own experience as proof. Despite the fact that "the bishops, the seminaries, and the literature are committed to intetration [*sic*] . . . there is very little integration. Why? Because integration is virtually impossible in the established American way of life." The assembly of Methodists adopted resolutions opposing "any attempt from whatever source to integrate our churches." Warning of a potential schism within the church, they declared, "The threat to integrate our beloved church has seriously impaired its membership growth." Once again, they asked congregations throughout the state to announce their positions on integration.[37]

In mid-April, the bishops of the Methodist Church affirmed two new resolutions on race relations at a meeting in San Francisco, California. Though it remained unclear why, Bishop Marvin Franklin was not in attendance at these sessions. One resolution spoke directly to the controversy among Methodists in Mississippi, encouraging Christians to affirm the brotherhood of man and to support "ministers and laymen who take leadership for the sake of an inclusive church."[38] The bishops approved another resolution reminding fellow Methodists they were a connectional church that "proudly claim[s] all peoples among our membership, all races under our banner." The bishops endorsed efforts of ministers and laypeople who were striving to improve race relations, adding more explicitly that "particular emphasis [be] given to the right of all people, of all races, to enjoy full citizenship in this nation and every nation under God." The resolution ended by specifying that they were not sanctioning any particular method of attaining these goals, but merely wanted to express their concern that "we be Christian in this and all other relationships in life."[39]

The "born of conviction" statement and its aftermath were not the only affairs on the minds of the Methodist bishops meeting in San Francisco, but the bishops' resolution constituted a direct rebuke of the leadership of Bishop Marvin Franklin and a rebuttal to the arguments of the segregationist laymen in the Mississippi Conference. Though the bishops' statement surely comforted Dr. Selah, Rev. Furr, and Dr. Clark, all three understood they had already crossed the line and departed too far from the narrative of uniformity in Jackson. Yet for the moment, they vowed to weather the storm and await the decision of the annual Mississippi Conference in May. Dr. Selah promised himself that if black visitors tested his church's closed-door policy, and ushers in fact turned them away, he would resign immediately.

Though no black activists presented themselves for worship at Galloway Memorial Methodist or any other Protestant church in the two years following the Freedom Rides, local activists were becoming more organized and active by early 1963. The Jackson movement was entering a new stage and would commence direct action tactics that included attempting to worship at the white churches of the state's capital city.

[4]

"There Can Be No Color Bar in the House of God"
SPRING 1963

Beginning in December 1962, a group of Tougaloo College professors and black ministers, under the leadership Medgar Evers, field secretary for the NAACP, coordinated a boycott of downtown businesses in Jackson. By encouraging the community to avoid the economic center of the city, where thousands of African Americans worked and shopped, the movement aimed to end racial discrimination in hiring and to improve treatment of blacks as consumers. Moreover, since members of the segregationist Citizens' Council owned or worked at many of these downtown businesses, movement leaders intended to cripple the power structure of the city. While adults led the movement, students from Jackson area colleges and high schools formed the bulk of the rank-and-file, participating in strategy sessions and spreading the word by distributing leaflets and organizing support in black churches. The success of the boycott was difficult to gauge, but by May 1963, broad support for the boycott in the black community convinced movement leaders that Jackson was ready for a more aggressive campaign. Moreover, despite the physical violence against marchers in Birmingham in recent weeks, Birmingham officials had finally agreed to create a biracial commission and end racial discrimination in local businesses.

Jackson movement leaders hoped to replicate in Birmingham the success of direct action in Jackson. Evers, with the support of John Salter, a professor at Tougaloo, and Rev. Ed King, Tougaloo's chaplain, wanted to expand the scope of the boycott to include more direct action, namely sit-ins and mass demonstrations. In early May, they pushed the Jackson NAACP board of directors to adopt a resolution that promised marches, picketing, and any other legal means if racial segregation did not end in the city. The resolution, which the head office of the NAACP quickly endorsed, urged city officials and business leaders to join in biracial negotiations in order to prevent an escalation of their campaign. Mayor Allen Thompson, with images of the Birmingham protests fresh on his mind, announced that he would not meet with movement leaders and pledged to prevent unlawful demonstrations. With discussions between the city officials and the NAACP at an impasse, Jackson movement leaders turned to one of the few lines of communication that they felt was still available to them, white ministers. While many in the movement saw a Birmingham-like confrontation in Jackson as inevitable, movement leaders wanted to exhaust all options before they initiated massive demonstrations and sit-ins.

Rev. Edwin King, a key member of the movement's strategy committee, was in a unique position in the white church community. On one hand, he was a white Mississippian, born and raised in Vicksburg and a graduate of Millsaps College, a Jackson liberal arts school affiliated with the Methodist Church. Based on relationships forged in his youth, in college, and in seminary in Boston, he knew many church leaders in the Jackson area, particularly Methodist ministers. Yet to many King was an agitator. In early 1963, he arrived back in Mississippi to take a position as dean of students and chaplain of Tougaloo, a predominantly black college on the northern outskirts of Jackson that produced many of the leadership and student volunteers in the Jackson movement. Before his return to the state, his reputation as a liberal minister and civil rights activist was well documented. In 1960, Montgomery, Alabama, police arrested him twice for disorderly conduct, once as he ate with other white men at a black-owned restaurant and a second time as he ate with a black minister at a white-owned restaurant. His actions were not lost on local Methodist leaders, who, in 1961, put off King's ordination by designating him "on trial."

While the "born of conviction" statement and its aftermath escalated tensions in many white churches, disagreements over church integration in early 1963 encouraged black ministers and the leaders of the Jackson movement. Even though Rev. King viewed the twenty-eight ministers' statement as "mild," he recognized that it "had been the strongest stand taken by any white group in the wake of the Ole Miss disaster." The white church community was finally showing signs of asserting some leadership in the state. Throughout the spring, Rev. King kept in contact with Jackson ministers with whom he had established friendships in his youth and as a student at Millsaps. Rev. King knew some of these men to be moderate or liberal on racial issues. They included several ministers on the faculty at Millsaps, Galloway's ministers, and Dr. Roy Clark, the pastor of Capitol Street Methodist.

Dr. Selah specifically told Rev. King to keep him informed "about all that was happening."[1]

During Holy Week, Tougaloo students discussed a plan to attempt to attend—and potentially integrate—a white church in Jackson. While Rev. King and the students had often considered such a tactic since Rev. King's arrival at Tougaloo, this was the first time the activists developed a specific plan. Intending to overlap with visits to white churches in Birmingham, some students expressed their desire to try to attend Galloway on Easter Sunday. As the largest Methodist church in the state and the place of worship for many outspoken segregationists, it seemed like an appropriate place to point out the immorality of segregation and the oneness of mankind. Furthermore, the conflict between local church policy and national church pronouncements was particularly acute at Galloway, where the official board maintained a closed-door policy to which their ministers were not committed. In keeping with their prior arrangement, Rev. King notified Dr. Selah of what could be the first test of Galloway's closed-door policy. Dr. Selah told him, "He very much wanted an integrated church but was afraid that the Negro students might not be admitted and that they might even face violence." Dr. Selah also expressed concern that a visit by Tougaloo students might damage progress he was trying to make by working within his congregation. Although he did not oppose church visits as a tactic, timing was crucial. Dr. Selah saw the upcoming Mississippi Conference meeting in May as a bellwether. Not only were delegates electing representatives to the following year's general conference, the fates of many of the twenty-eight ministers who signed the "born of conviction" manifesto and other ministers would be an issue. He therefore asked Rev. King to encourage the students to delay their visit until at least after May, which they agreed to do.[2]

For the time being, movement organizers and participants were willing to let the ministers try to steer their congregations toward integration rather than force a confrontation. The showdown between interracial visitors and white churches in Jackson would have to wait. On Easter Sunday in Birmingham, two white Protestant churches, First Baptist and First Presbyterian, admitted black visitors, while three other churches turned them away. The church visits in Birmingham served as backdrop to the incarceration of Dr. Martin Luther King Jr., who spent the end of Holy Week writing his "Letter from a Birmingham Jail" to white religious leaders in the city. Reflecting on the events in Birmingham, Rev. King saw a clear cause and effect; with the door closed to communication in many of the churches, African Americans took their protests to the streets.[3]

By May, the boycott of Jackson businesses was in its sixth month, and local NAACP leaders believed that it was time to initiate direct action. In a letter to the national office of the NAACP, John Salter explained, "The great majority of Negro people in the Jackson area are supporting the boycott and, from another standpoint, a community—previously unorganized—is now becoming structured in a 'movement' sense." In order to "crack this mess wide open in Jackson," Salter made the case that "we must have direct action and much of it—we have definitely reached that stage." On Sunday, May 12, the board of directors of the Mississippi NAACP approved a resolution to "end all state and local government-sponsored segregation in the parks, playgrounds, schools, libraries and other public facilities." The movement promised to employ "all lawful means of protest—picketing, marches, mass meetings, litigation, and whatever other legal means we deem necessary." The national office endorsed the effort in Jackson and pledged monetary support if needed.[4] On Monday, Mayor Thompson responded to the resolution by denouncing its source, telling a group of businessmen that he would refuse "to talk with any member of the NAACP, CORE, or any other outside agitator as such." He was only open to meeting with "responsible leaders of the Negro community," adding, "We can give these outside agitators the worst beating they have ever had."

At the time, political leaders in the capital city followed events in Birmingham closely and worried that a similar confrontation might occur soon in Jackson, yet significantly, they reasoned that any disturbance could only come from the outside. An investigator for the Sovereignty Commission checked with his informants and issued a report on May 16, declaring that local movement leaders "are bluffing when they threaten demonstrations in Jackson and in the near future due to their weakness and lack of leadership." The investigator concluded, "If we have trouble in Jackson or Hinds County . . . it will be after the Negro leaders that are active in Birmingham and other cities . . . complete their missions there and then come to Jackson, Mississippi to lead any demonstrations that might occur here."[5] Mayor Thompson and other white leaders clearly doubted the resolve and strength of the Jackson movement. They believed that the local African American community would only question its status if prompted by some external source.

Curiously, later in the week, several white Baptist ministers received mimeographed copies of the NAACP's desegregation warning. While it is not clear who sent the copies to the ministers, they did not come from anyone at the local NAACP. Yet the effect of the letters was clear. One of the ministers who received the NAACP's resolution, Rev. Jim Shanahan of Parkhill Baptist Church, interpreted it to mean, "The Negroes apparently considered the churches a part of the 'public facilities' they sought to integrate." Furthermore, the resolution prompted the superintendent of missions for the Hinds County Baptist Association, Dr. J. Clark Hensley, to mail a letter to all the Baptist ministers in the county, suggesting that each church "evolve a plan in the event that they want to integrate our churches." In his autobiography, Dr. Hensley explains that because of his position, he was in contact with government officials, including the Federal Bureau of Investigation (FBI), and frequently relayed information to his pastors. While the timing is unclear, deacons at two Baptist churches in Jackson, Calvary, and Woodland Hills, did formulate a plan some time in May and adopted closed-door policies. The deacons at First Baptist discussed the issue at their May 14 meeting, but took no decisive action.[6]

After Mayor Thompson decided to reject the Jackson movement's latest demands to meet with a biracial committee and begin the dismantling of racial discrimination in public facilities, Medgar Evers went on local television to appeal to the "consciences of many silent, responsible citizens of the white community." In a speech that centered upon the discrimination African Americans faced on a daily basis in Jackson, Evers still argued, "There are white Mississippians who want to go forward on the race question." He not only appealed to white Mississippians' "sense of justice and fair play," but he pointed out that "their religion tells them that there is something wrong with the old system." While television broadcast the speech throughout the state, Rev. King hoped that Evers's appeal would hold particular sway with white ministers. At this juncture, he felt that "the action of the white church leadership was the one possible force which might still be activated for change in Jackson." He sensed that white ministers and denominational authorities did not appreciate the urgency of the situation, believing that a Birmingham-like confrontation could occur at any moment. If he could just get white ministers in the same room with local black ministers, then a chain reaction might occur. The black ministers would impress upon the white ministers the black community's resolve. Then, the white ministers "might just be able to influence their denominational officials to start something, anything."[7]

Evers and Rev. King did not realize that there was a behind-the-scenes effort underway on the part of some white religious leaders in Jackson to avert another Birmingham. White Protestant ministers met together frequently as the Jackson Ministerial Association, and the Protestant and

Catholic bishops often assembled in unofficial gatherings, but there was no formal citywide organization that brought together Catholic, Protestant, and Jewish religious leaders. Yet in the years following the *Brown* decision in 1954, a group of Jackson clergy that was more moderate or even liberal on social issues maintained an ongoing dialogue, often meeting informally at the instigation of Rabbi Perry Nussbaum of Temple Beth Israel.[8] Rabbi Nussbaum was involved in a variety of civil rights activities, such as the Mississippi Human Relations Council, but he was reluctant to take the lead among his fellow clergymen. He felt that "this race relations problem was basically a Christian problem and not only was it basically a Christian problem, but it was primarily a Protestant problem." Rabbi Nussbaum saw that his primary duties lay with his own congregation, and he did not want to become "a surrogate to Christian responsibility." Though he concluded that the meetings amounted to little more than "a spate of words that go around and around and around," the clergy developed a camaraderie that helped sustain them in the late 1950s and early 1960s. He counted Dr. Selah as his "own personal insurance," for as long Dr. Selah could survive at the helm of Galloway, Rabbi Nussbaum believed he could remain at Temple Beth Israel.[9] Dr. Clark, one of Rabbi Nussbaum's friends and an attendee at many of these unofficial gatherings, recalled that Rabbi Nussbaum persisted in trying to convince the group to issue a strong collective statement on race, as leading ministers in other cities facing desegregation efforts had done. Yet most of the ministers, like Dr. Clark, reasoned that the time was not yet right for such overt action.[10]

In mid-May, as tension began to build in Jackson, white religious leaders and clergy attempted to formulate a plan that would prevent the type of violent confrontation seen in Birmingham. On May 16, the city's white bishops met at St. Andrew's parish house to discuss how they could be most helpful in resolving the escalating crisis.[11] They decided that the first course of action would be to arrange a meeting with Mayor Thompson. Bishop Richard O. Gerow of the Natchez-Jackson Diocese of the Roman Catholic Church called Mayor Thompson, who tried to avoid meeting with the group, but finally relented and agreed to meet with the bishops the next morning. On May 17, the bishops and the mayor met for nearly two hours. The bishops tried to reassure the mayor that they would work with him in finding a solution, and that they would cooperate in preserving order. Moreover, they promised to keep him informed of any additional steps they took. Yet they were unable to reach their ultimate objective, to come up with a concrete plan for the city's that would forestall NAACP demonstrations.

Mayor Thompson explained, "We have had a happy city until these outsiders agitated our people," declaring that he would not discuss anything with the NAACP or the Congress of Racial Equality (CORE). With the mayor unyielding, the bishops decided to arrange a meeting the next week with other white ministers in the city. Bishop Gerow wrote in his diary that they hoped this meeting might lead to a larger one with black clergy and potentially lay leaders as well.[12]

For his part, Bishop Gerow struggled to lead his own diocese while remaining within the constraints of Jim Crow. He was reluctant, for example, to desegregate the Catholic school system he oversaw for fear that doing so would violate Mississippi's mandatory segregation statutes. Yet when it came to other aspects of his position, those he did control—such as the attendance policies of local parishes—Bishop Gerow consistently supported equality. On several occasions in the 1950s and early 1960s, when individual Catholics objected to the seating of black visitors in white Catholic parishes, he instructed his pastors to keep the church doors open. In a 1951 letter to his priests, he urged, "Remember that the parish is a general church and may be attended by anyone no matter what his race." When his priests asked him to clarify whether segregated seating was an appropriate measure, he said no, that the duty of the pastor was to "eliminate this abuse and to make our people realize that there is only one race recognized by Almighty God, and that is the human race."[13]

Even before meeting with African American ministers, Bishop Gerow was sympathetic to their aims. He wrote in his diary that "although the war between the states abolished slavery a hundred years ago, even up to today the Negro in the South has been 'kept in his place' as a caste inferior to the dominant white race." He expressed shock at Birmingham's violent reaction to peaceful demonstrators and remained committed to helping prevent a clash in Jackson. The night of the unproductive meeting with Mayor Thompson, he met with Father Gasper of Christ the King Parish, one of the city's two black Catholic congregations. They discussed the current racial situation in Jackson, and Father Gasper explained that African Americans in Jackson "have long felt deeply hurt at the injustices which have been inflicted upon the people of their race and at the indignities they have suffered." As a result, Jackson's blacks "have organized themselves under the NAACP and are determined that this unjust attitude toward them must cease." Father Gasper added that the black ministers of Jackson were united in their determination to cooperate with the NAACP and end inequality.[14]

As planned, the bishops and white ministers gathered for lunch at the Walthall Hotel on May 23 and decided to seek a meeting with local black ministers. Bishop Allin organized the interracial meeting, which took place the next morning at Farish Street Baptist Church.[15] Unlike the unofficial ecumenical gatherings held in the previous decade, informal interracial meetings of Jackson's ministers were rare in Jackson's recent history, though some of the wives of ministers were part of the interracial group United Church Women. Some Jackson clergy attempted to establish biracial communication in secret, most notably the meetings in 1961 at the parish house of Rev. Edward Harrison that followed the first sit-ins in the city. With a larger round of demonstrations and sit-ins looming, the white and black clergy decided that the timing was right to come together again.

On the morning of May 24, an assembly that included representatives from all the major black and white religious groups in the city convened at Farish Street Baptist Church. In addition to the bishops and white clergy who attended the meetings in the last week, two white Baptist leaders, Dr. Chester L. Quarles and Dr. William P. Davis, joined the group for the first time. Dr. Quarles served as executive secretary-treasurer of the Mississippi Baptist Convention, and Dr. Davis was president of Mississippi Baptist Seminary and secretary of the state convention's Department of Work with Negroes. About twenty black ministers and movement representatives, including Rev. King, were also present. The ministers told each other of their efforts so far to meet with Mayor Thompson to formulate a plan of action to begin desegregating city facilities and institutions. The black ministers informed their white counterparts that they had elected a small group to represent them in consultations with the mayor, but he rebuffed those men in favor of a few hand-picked men he knew would side with him. After hearing from the black ministers, Rev. King felt that the white clergy sensed the unity within the black community in the push for change. Moreover, he saw that the white ministers understood the need for more of an effort on their part to influence the white business community and city officials. Bishop Gerow echoed King's sentiment privately in his diary, recording that he recognized the immediate concern of the black ministers was "the fact that they were deprived of all chance of communication with the city officials." Since the mayor refused to meet with the black representatives, the white ministers suggested that they could try to convince leaders of the Jackson Chamber of Commerce to serve as mediator. Keeping their promise to inform Mayor Thompson of any new developments Bishop Gerow, Rabbi Nussbaum and a few other white clergy went to the mayor's office, where the president and secretary of the Chamber of Commerce happened to be meeting. The mayor invited them in, and the religious leaders explained to the two Chamber leaders their hopes of resolving the crisis. Mayor Thompson agreed to meet with some of the black ministers, and one of the Chamber men promised to bring together his directors for a meeting with white clergy. Both the mayor and the president of the Chamber of Commerce set their meetings for the following Monday, May 27.[16]

While these discussions among the religious leaders of the city marked a dramatic shift away from the passive attitude of the past, Jackson movement leaders recognized that it would probably not be enough. Salter believed that the discussions with city leaders were futile, concluding, "Direct action in the streets was the only real solution."[17] As the clergy met in interracial discussions, Rev. King, Evers, and Salter came to an understanding that now was the time for protests. In consultation with the black ministers in the movement, especially Rev. Leon Whitney of Farish Street Baptist Church and Rev. G. R. Haughton of Pearl Street African Methodist Episcopal (AME) Church, the movement's strategy committee decided they would begin massive demonstrations and sit-ins if the mayor refused to change his position.[18] With the Jackson Chamber of Commerce and mayor's meetings set for Monday, they agreed to commence direct action on Tuesday, May 28.

On Monday morning, a delegation of a dozen white ministers who had been involved in interracial discussions over the last week held a meeting with the board of directors of the Jackson Chamber of Commerce. The week before, the Jackson Chamber of Commerce publicly aligned itself with Mayor Thompson's positions, saying that businesses should be able to choose whom to employ or serve, and that demonstrations or civil disobedience would only delay any positive resolution.[19] At this meeting, Bishop John Allin spoke on behalf of the other white clergy, explaining the position of the black ministers, who needed to establish some level of communication with city leaders. Dr. Roy Clark pointed out that the white ministers tried to avoid identifying themselves with either side, but instead tried to act as a bridge between the two. The directors asked the ministers several more questions and then directed them to leave as the chamber went into executive session. The white ministers left without receiving any indication of change on the part of the Chamber of Commerce, though some directors seemed optimistic that the meetings with the mayor would prove more consequential. In the next day's *Clarion-Ledger*, the religious leaders learned that the directors declined to take up the ministers' request that they help keep open "the lines of communication between the races." Whether the Citizens' Council or the mayor had the Chamber of Commerce's hands tied, the group clearly did not want to make the first move. That afternoon, white and black religious leaders assembled at Farish Street Baptist Church and awaited the return of the group meeting with the mayor. Unlike the movement leaders, who did not expect the mayor to alter his position, the clergy seemed to share the business leaders' optimism that the mayor, black ministers, and movement representatives would come to an agreement that could prevent another Birmingham.[20]

The meeting with Mayor Thompson began at 2:00 p.m. at city hall. Eleven representatives from the Jackson movement, all but two of them ministers, were present. Rev. King tried to attend in his capacity as a college chaplain, but the mayor insisted he leave, so as to avoid making this a biracial meeting. King later wondered how his "'liberal whiteness' integrated the meeting and the Mayor's 'traditional whiteness' kept it safe, pure, and segregated." Also present at the meeting were six African American men handpicked by the mayor to counter the contentions of movement representatives about the racial problems facing the city.[21] After cordial introductions, Mayor Thompson read a lengthy prepared statement indicating that his position remained unchanged, that he would not create a biracial committee, and that no amount of protests and boycotts by "paid agitators and organized pressure groups" would change his mind. The response by movement representatives was short and direct. Rev. E. A. Mays, speaking for the others, said, "I don't believe, from the speech you gave, that there is anything in it that will coincide with the things that we have in mind." The representatives left and returned to Farish Street Baptist Church to inform the others in the movement and the assembled religious leaders about what transpired.[22]

Like the meeting the previous Friday, the gathering at Farish Street Baptist Church included the heads of all the major religious groups in Mississippi. While the interracial gathering was unique in itself, it was equally significant that these particular men were there, since most of the black and white ministers did not really know each other.[23] In contrast to their hopeful attitude earlier in the day, the ministers now expressed surprise that the meeting with the mayor failed to yield anything positive. Dr. Clark recognized the long-term objectives of the ministers and the local movement, which were communicated to the group, but he recalled that most of the discussion centered on the power structure Mayor Thompson operated in and how best to work with it. The black ministers understood as much, and therefore pressed for what they saw as the most meaningful demand—the establishment of a biracial committee—for if the mayor agreed to it, African Americans in Jackson would have a "recognized structure in the community in which they had the status to present their positions." Rev. King suggested that the white ministers take out a full-page advertisement in the newspapers signed by all the men at the meeting. While the white religious leaders recognized that demonstrations were now close to being realized, the ones who spoke up wanted more time to try to work behind the scenes. Others expressed the more practical concern that it would likely take a while to come up with a statement with which they could all agree. Yet they soon realized that they had to produce something, for a crowd of police and newsmen was gathering outside the church in anticipation of some sort of public announcement.

For Rev. King, who now understood that these white religious leaders would not take a strong stand, what mattered most was for television and newspaper cameras to capture the symbolic significance of the meeting, with white and black ministers working together to address the racial problems in Jackson. The content of a statement did not matter as much as the pictures that the press would broadcast across the state and nation. White viewers would clearly see their bishops and denominational leaders discussing problems in an interracial setting, something the mayor refused to do. Their religious leaders would be seen laboring toward a resolution in a spirit of brotherhood and equality, in contrast to their political leaders' defiance and inability to recognize that a problem even existed.

Yet Rev. King also understood that such an interracial picture would require a miracle, for "these churchmen had had years of experience at avoiding any direct application of Christianity to the major problems of Mississippi."[24] While the black ministers chose Rev. S. Leon Whitney, the pastor of Farish Street Baptist Church (who also attended the meeting with Mayor Thompson), as their spokesmen, the white religious leaders debated their next step and then decided that there would be no white spokesman. As Rev. Whitney went out the front door of the church to speak with reporters, the white bishops and religious leaders slipped out a side door and departed without the press seeing them.

Though the ministers failed to reach an agreement, the meetings led to other interracial gatherings of clergy through the summer and had a pronounced effect on the white ministers who attended. Rev. Hulan recalled, "The best thing that came out of the meetings with the ministers both white and mixed was the admissions of mutual concern and prayers, and a new spirit of at-one-ness across denominational and racial lines under the Holy Spirit." As a result of the meetings, Dr. Clark began to realize "that the white people had no understanding whatsoever of the pre-suppositions upon which the Negroes were working." Though the meetings failed to produce many tangible results, the main long-term benefits were improved communication and "learning to talk between us." Moreover, the meetings enriched his contacts within the white community, as well.[25] Bishop Allin wrote a press release the day after the meeting, acknowledging that informal interracial discussions had taken place. In the statement, which he issued as acting secretary for the white ministers, he explained the intention of the meetings: "Our only effort has been to seek some means to aid men of good will of both races to establish some effective lines of communication." Bishop Allin admitted that the discussions produced little progress, but he hoped that Jackson citizens could solve their own problems.[26] Yet, by the time anyone was able to read the statement, it was too late—the sit-ins, picketing, and violence aimed at peaceful demonstrators were well under way.

The direct action phase of the Jackson movement commenced on Tuesday, May 28, and continued through the end of the following week. On the first day, two coordinated protests occurred. The first was a picket along a business section of downtown Capitol Street, where students and teachers from Jackson area colleges carried signs saying, "Jackson Needs a Bi-racial Committee." The police quickly arrested five demonstrators, including Jeannette King, Rev. King's wife, and Margrit Garner, the wife of a Tougaloo professor and a member of Galloway.[27] Meanwhile, Tougaloo students and faculty began a sit-in at the Woolworth's lunch counter nearby. As the police stood outside the store, Anne Moody, Pearlena Lewis, and Memphis Norman sat on their stools and bowed their heads in prayer while a growing white mob hurled racist insults at them. Joan Trumpauer, who felt called to transfer from Duke to Tougaloo after her experience in the state as a Freedom Rider, and Salter and Lois Chafee, two white Tougaloo professors, then joined them at the counter. Someone in the mob threw the three black students on the floor, with Norman receiving the worst injuries: A twenty-six-year-old ex-police officer pulled Norman from his chair and stomped him repeatedly in the face and head. A plain clothed policeman arrested them both. Rev. King, wearing his clerical collar, stood behind the mob to observe and telephone Evers with updates. After the students informed him they were not yet ready to leave, he went outside to see if the police would intervene. Captain Ray, cognizant of the Supreme Court's recent decision nullifying arrests during the 1960 sit-ins, told King that the police could not interfere with a sit-in, since Woolworth's was a private store, and the manager had not yet requested the police to step in. After making phone calls to Evers and Dr. Dan Beittel, Tougaloo's president, King sought out someone he felt could get the police or mayor to act: a white minister. A few blocks away, Methodist ministers and laymen from across the state were gathering at Galloway for their annual conference. Since it was lunchtime, the chance of reaching anyone would be slim, but he tried anyway. King called Galloway in the hopes of convincing Rev. Furr or someone else to gather other white ministers and come down to the store, but he could not reach anyone. Meanwhile, the integrated group at the lunch counter sat resolutely amidst a mix of obscenities, racial slurs, and splatters of ketchup and mustard. When the mob proceeded to pick up articles from the store they could use as projectiles, the manager finally intervened and announced on the public address system that the store was closed. As everyone left Woolworth's, Salter, with his face bleeding and clothes stained with condiments, said to Captain Ray, "Fine brand of Christianity you practice in Jackson."[28]

The nation-wide media coverage of the violence at Woolworth's provoked a temporary change of heart in Mayor Thompson. That afternoon, he reassembled the group of ministers with whom he met the day before, and informed them that all segregated signs in public accommodations would come down, that he would hire blacks for various city positions, and that he would soon initiate a biracial committee. While this plan did not address all of the demands of the movement, it was enough for movement leaders to decide to suspend demonstrations while they waited to see if the mayor followed through with his initial promises. Nearly a thousand triumphant people attended a mass meeting that night at Pearl Street AME Church to hear from white and black leaders and local ministers, a few of whom reported on their meeting with the mayor. But this jubilation did not last long, for shortly thereafter, the mayor announced that he made no concessions to the ministers.[29] To the leaders, the reason for the mayor's reversal was obvious: "The whole heritage of Mississippi, and the Citizens Council machine that was so enmeshed with the political-economic structure throughout the city and the state, had brought its full weight to bear." Salter and the other leaders spread the word that demonstrations would continue.[30]

The city's political and economic structure utilized its own forms of massive resistance to the escalating civil rights campaign. Rather than desegregate, nearly all of the downtown lunch counters, including Woolworth's, simply closed down. During the next week, Jackson police arrested over six hundred for picketing and attempted sit-ins, most of them high school and college students. With increased participation of Jackson's black citizens came increased violence and police brutality. On the night of the Woolworth's sit-in, someone threw a Molotov cocktail into the carport of the Evers home. Upon arrival, the police dismissed the incident as a prank. One officer said, "It was just some people having some fun probably." The day after the Woolworth's sit-in, students at Lanier High School gathered at lunch to sing freedom songs. The police, who patrolled the city's schools, anticipating some type of demonstration, responded by beating several students and parents who arrived to help their children.

This police brutality convinced movement leaders that it was now time for Jackson ministers and other adults to get directly involved and risk arrest. On Thursday, May 30, over a dozen black ministers, students, and faculty at Tougaloo— included Rev. King, Salter, and Bill Hutchinson—conducted a kneel-in on the steps of the Federal Building on Capitol Street. As Hutchinson, a white pre-ministerial student and speech and drama professor at the college, later wrote, the purpose of the pray-in was to "commemorate Memorial Day, to pray for peace throughout the world, and to pray for justice and reconciliation among the races in Mississippi and throughout the rest of the world." Since the building was government property and housed several federal offices, such as the post office, the FBI, and the federal district court, leaders hoped that if arrested, they could appeal to their contacts in the Justice Department. In front of a large crowd of hostile white people, newsmen, and at least one hundred policemen, the officers arrested the fourteen for "breach of peace." In what had become customary practice for detaining civil rights protestors, the Jackson police brought in black prisoners from the city jail to haul King and the others away.[31] Yet, what peace King and the others breached was unclear. As he told the police, their intention "was to exercise their rights of religious worship and free speech guaranteed by the Fourteenth Amendment to the Constitution of the United States." On Friday, May 31, Jackson police arrested over four hundred students as they participated in a mass march on Farish Street. Salter and Evers observed, as police clubbed many of the students and fired shots over their heads. The police then took the students to makeshift jail cells at the livestock area of the State Fairgrounds.[32]

Demonstrations and massive participation by the black community declined over the next several days as the national NAACP stepped in to shift the direction of the movement, wanting to concentrate more on voter registration. On Sunday, June 2, New York NAACP staff members who had arrived in Jackson when demonstrations began effectively removed Evers and Salter from future strategy sessions. The protests financially strapped the NAACP, for they contributed $64,000 in bail funds during this first week. But as one historian emphasizes, the NAACP never seemed committed to the tactic of civil disobedience.[33] Moreover, the Mayor promised to accede to some of the movement's demands if the mass demonstrations ceased. In a meeting with black leaders on Friday, May 31, he agreed to hire black policemen and school crossing guards, and pledged to improve job opportunities for African Americans in city government positions. Yet Mayor Thompson remained adamant that he would not appoint a biracial committee.[34]

Punctuating these shifts in direction, a judge from Hinds County Chancery Court awarded the city an injunction on Thursday, June 6, prohibiting the movement from coordinating future demonstrations or acts of civil disobedience. Jackson officials had made the move after learning that the NAACP intended to request a federal injunction against police interference with demonstrations. Although the court order directly named twelve individuals, including Medgar Evers, John Salter, Rev. King, and Dr. Beittel, its language was broad enough to include anyone "in active concert with them." The injunction also named specific organizations, such as the NAACP, the CORE, the people of Tougaloo, and "all other persons in active concert with them."[35] The combination of the NAACP's withdrawal of support and the city's injunction effectively ended massive direct action for the immediate future.

In addition to listing the protest activities that occurred in the previous week, the injunction barred an activity that had not occurred: kneel-ins at churches. Individuals were now prohibited from "engaging in acts and conduct customarily known as 'kneel-ins' in church in violation of the wishes and desires of said churches." City officials told the *Clarion-Ledger* they felt that the defendants were planning kneel-ins at local churches.[36] Earlier in the week, Jackson police passed on the rumor to investigators at the Mississippi Sovereignty Commission that local activists would hold sit-ins at white churches. On Sunday, June 2, one of the investigators drove to Tougaloo to see for himself if integrated groups were organizing for the purpose of driving downtown to engage in kneel-ins. He noticed that cars leaving campus contained small children and reasoned that they were en route to their own churches. A group of students and an unidentified white man confronted the investigator near the gate and barricaded his car, but then let the investigator proceed after the group apparently saw that he was armed.[37]

While downtown Jackson was consumed with various protests, white mobs, and a heavy police presence during the last week of May, Methodist ministers and laymen convened at Galloway for their annual conference. One of the key items on the agenda was the election of delegates for the Southeastern Jurisdictional Conference and the 1964 General Convention in Pittsburgh. The same day that students were beaten and harassed inside Woolworth's, conference attendees a few blocks away elected four men "considered to be among the most conservative in the Conference on racial matters" on the first ballot.[38] One of the four was John Satterfield, long-time general counsel for MAMML and outspoken opponent of integration. The next day, attendees elected more like-minded men to lay and clerical positions in the two conferences, signaling, as the *Clarion-Ledger* reported, a "victory for strong conservatism."[39] One of the casualties was Dr. Stafford, who was voted out as conference lay leader. His consistent defense of the "born of conviction" signers and support for "moderate statements on the racial issues and Methodism" over the last five months did not endear him to a majority of conference delegates.

Also on the conference agenda was a vote on the status of Rev. King. In keeping with the procedure for other Methodist ministers, King requested that he be given full contact with the conference. Since 1961, he had been technically "on trial," meaning that he had to await official assignment while the Board of Ministerial Training and Qualifications verified his acceptability as a minister. During the conference, the board recommended that King's "on trial" status continue, but the ultimate decision rested with a special session of conference ministers convened by Bishop Franklin. For Rev. King, the timing could not have been worse, for these ministers met the day after police arrested him and a dozen others for praying together on the steps of the Federal Building. Although he had only been back in Mississippi for five months, widespread media coverage of his leadership in the Jackson movement and his recent arrest convinced a slim majority that he had "exceeded his just duty as chaplain to the Tougaloo students."[40] The ministers voted eight-nine to eighty-five to discontinue "without prejudice to his character and that his ministerial status be that of a local elder, and his membership to be placed in a church of his choice." This result did not surprise King, but his abandonment by his mentors and colleagues in his home conference did. While King's immediate concern was his own status, the larger significance of his expulsion during the violence occurring elsewhere downtown was also on his mind. He wrote on his copy of the conference program, "[How] can this conference walk away from Jackson condoning what is going on?" Barred from the white conference, he promptly received an offer from Bishop Charles Golden to join the Central Jurisdiction. He gladly accepted, finding a home in the black jurisdiction.[41]

Glad to retreat from the disquiet of Jackson, Dr. Selah served as the guest preacher at the South Georgia Conference for the first week of June. In one of his sermons, he told his fellow Methodists, "When we subvert or deny justice to any human being, we crucify the Son of God afresh." Applying this specifically to the situation in Jackson, he told the local press that May- or Thompson should appoint a biracial committee and work to settle the issues peacefully. He believed in the goodwill of the people of Jackson and loved his members at Galloway, even if he had to stand firm and tell them when they were wrong. He said that the church members were "sweet-spir- ited," and that most "want me to state my conviction," though he guessed that "90 percent of the people . . . probably disagree with me on this." He acknowledged that some members quit coming to Galloway after he de- fended the twenty-eight, but added that others who did not belong to the church started attending recently, and that church giving had not suffered.[42] Though recognizing the chasm between Galloway's pulpit and pews over the issue of race, he gave no public indication that he would do anything other than to try to weather the storm at his church.

Privately, however, Dr. Selah prepared for the possibility that he might have to resign. At some point in spring 1963, he began carrying a printed statement in his pocket that he would read aloud to the congregation if his ushers turned away any African Americans from his church.[43] Dr. Selah would explain to his congregation that though they did not always agree with him, he had consistently maintained, "There can be no color bar in the church of God." He would tell them that he did not invite the black visitors to come, but would not see them turned away from a Christian institu- tion. He would conclude by telling the congregation that he loved them, but would have to resign.[44]

Meanwhile, a group of white and black ministers met in Jackson on June 6 for the first time since the beginning of the direct action phase of the movement. Bishop Gerow reported that everyone realized little was being accomplished by their attempts "to bring about better race relations and more justice for the Negroes." Nevertheless, the white ministers appreciated the cordial relationships they were building with their black counterparts, feelings that the black ministers were reciprocating.[45]

Further north, a different kind of assembly convened, one that would prove to have lasting consequences for events in Jackson and throughout the state. In New York City, leaders from the NCC gathered and promised a more vigorous involvement in civil rights activities throughout the country. They passed a resolution declaring, "The Church of Jesus Christ can make no compromise with discrimination or segregation on the basis on race."[46] On June 7, the general board of the NCC declared there was a full-scale crisis on the issue of civil rights, pointing to inaction by Christians and churches as a major factor in precipitating the dilemma. Their report specifically addressed segregation and exclusion in the church, pointing out that because "many churches are closed to Negroes and other ethnic minorities," and "church institutions discriminate," the church itself is therefore "not free from sin on this serious issue." The board took several actions, one of which was to urge "every communion and all units of the National Council of Churches to examine their structures and practices in order to eliminate discrimination and injustice within the church." To implement the recommendations, and to signal that the NCC was no longer content simply to issue declarations, the NCC created a new agency, the CRR. The NCC enabled the new group to encourage demonstrations and other direct action, to lobby on behalf of new civil rights legislation, and to mobilize the resources of the churches "in order to put their own house in order by desegregating all of the institutions of the church." At the time, and for the next few months, efforts to desegregate church institutions centered on a pilot program developing integrated churches in Northern cities that would serve as models for others.[47] The NCC did not know it then, but the task of organizing and assisting in efforts to desegregate churches would prove to be a crucial mission for the CRR.

As Jackson movement leaders considered their next course in light of the injunctions against them, they did not debate whether or not to discontinue direct action. While the NAACP's action effectively ended mass demonstrations, movement leaders and students discussed smaller, targeted protests. Knowing that they would surely be arrested, the only issue now was what to target. Evers, King, and many of the students were particularly intrigued by the inclusion of kneel-ins in the list of activities prohibited in the injunction, even though none had ever been attempted in Jackson.

Two months earlier, movement organizers and participants had considered kneel-ins at white churches as a strategy to protest racial discrimination. Tougaloo activists talked about visiting Galloway during Holy Week, but Rev. King was content to give Dr. Selah more time to make progress within his church. Yet they kept the idea of church visitation or kneel-ins alive through the spring, waiting for the proper time to utilize the tactic.[48]

Like other acts of civil disobedience the movement utilized, kneel-ins would make segregation an issue for people who would otherwise ignore it. For King and Evers, kneel-ins would target a specific group, for they wanted to "bring the segregation issue to the conscience of white Christians." Although they expected church ushers from most churches to turn them away, they hoped that some "just might be a little upset at the reality of closing the doors of the Christian church." Before Rev. King and Memphis Norman departed for a fundraising and speaking trip in New York City over the weekend, Rev. King, Evers, and some students decided a group would try to attend Sunday worship services at First Baptist Church. For Rev. King, other than demonstrating on the Capitol steps, "the next best place to show the hypocrisy and vital interrelation of Mississippi Religion, Mississippi Politics, and the Mississippi Way of Life was First Baptist Church." What also made First Baptist symbolic was the fact that Governor Ross Barnett was a Sunday school teacher there.[49]

On Saturday night, after more students volunteered to participate in the visits, Evers and the students decided to expand the list of targeted churches by several more, including one where they did not expect to be turned away. At each, if they were not allowed in, they would try to engage in conversation with the ushers until they were asked to leave. In the morning, integrated groups would simultaneously attempt to enter First Baptist, Calvary Baptist, Capitol Street Methodist, and the Catholic Cathedral of St. Peter the Apostle. In the evening, groups would attempt to enter Woodland Hills Baptist and Broadmoor Baptist. Evers, who would drive the group of students trying to attend First Baptist—and clearly violating the injunction—fully expected to be arrested.

On Sunday, June 9, twenty-two African American students participated in the first visits to white churches in Jackson. By the end of the day, churches had turned away seventeen of them. Despite a police presence at most of the churches involved, no arrests were made. Ushers at the Catholic Cathedral of St. Peter the Apostle were the only ones to admit a group of students, which was not a surprise. Though St. Peter's did not have any active black members, African Americans had attended the church regularly.[50] At Calvary Baptist, the state's largest Baptist church, long-time member Dick Barnes was the deacon stationed on the church steps. Even though he opposed a recent vote by the deacons to enact a closed-door policy, it was his duty to tell the students that they could not come in.[51] As at Calvary, ushers at Woodland Hills Baptist turned away the black students because of the closed-door policy the deacons adopted at the last monthly meeting.[52]

One of the ushers told Anne Moody and three other students that Woodland Hills was a "private house of God, and you are not welcome." At First Baptist, the head deacon told four students, "In view of the tension present today, I believe your presence would disrupt the worship of all our people." The Jackson paper noted that the governor arrived just as the deacon confronted the students, but "went on into the church without taking note of the incident."[53]

After First Baptist turned back the four students, they walked a block to Galloway. Although this side trip was not part of the original plan, the students thought, given Rev. King's earlier conversations with Dr. Selah, that they might be more successful in attending worship services there. Yet, as at other white Protestant churches on this Sunday, the Galloway ushers refused to let them enter. During the first choral anthem, Rev. Furr informed about Dr. Selah what had occurred outside. At the conclusion of a shortened sermon on "The Spirit of Christ," Dr. Selah pulled a prepared statement from his pocket, one he had been carrying for weeks in the event that his ushers turned away black visitors. He told his congregation he loved them and then repeated what he had said countless times before, "There can be no color bar in a Christian Church." He explained that he did not invite African Americans to try to attend worship there, and even admitted, "Their coming is a bit embarrassing to me." Nevertheless, he reiterated that he could not stand seeing them turned away from a Christian institution, and so he would have to ask the bishop for another assignment. Rev. Furr then stepped up to the pulpit and also tendered his resignation, saying he "c[ould] not willingly serve a church that turns people away."[54]

While ushers at Calvary Baptist, Woodland Hills Baptist, and Galloway Methodist, in accordance with their closed-door policies, refused to admit the African American students, ushers at First Baptist, Capitol Street United Methodist, and Broadmoor Baptist turned away the students without the sanction of an approved church policy. Yet it did not take long for First Baptist and Capitol Street Methodist to endorse and continue the policy initiated by their ushers. The same day as the first church visits, the deacons at First Baptist proffered a resolution endorsing their ushers' actions, which passed without dissent in a standing vote. The statement began with a familiar refrain, asserting that the current protests were disrupting the "splendid relations" blacks and whites had experienced for years. Doubting the sincerity of blacks presenting themselves to worship at the church in the midst of the demonstrations, the resolution left no ambiguity regarding the attendance policy, saying that the church would "confine its assemblies and fellowship to those other than the Negro race."[55] Significantly, deacons at First Baptist had considered proposals to clarify the church's racial policy on at least four occasions since the 1954 *Brown* decision. Most recently, deacons discussed potential policies during meetings on January 8, 1963, a week after publication of the "born of conviction" manifesto, and on May 14, two days after the state NAACP issued its desegregation warning to the city. Yet the deacons had refrained from bringing a close-door resolution before the congregation until African Americans attempted to attend worship services there on June 9.[56]

The following day, the official board of Capitol Street affirmed the actions of its ushers by closing its church doors as well. On several earlier occasions, the executive committee had discussed what the ushers would do if African Americans presented themselves for worship. Dr. Clark and committee decided to wait and deal with the situation when it actually occurred, reasoning, "It would be better to face the issue when it came rather than anticipating it and taking a decision that might be more restricted than the one we could get when we actually faced it."[57] Now that African Americans had tried to worship at Capitol Street, the executive committee met to draw up a policy. Members of the committee expressed doubts that the black students came there to worship sincerely, and the committee reasoned that even if the ushers did seat them, that there were so many people in the church opposed to admitting African Americans that there might be violence. At a minimum, admitting the black students would surely divide the congregation and cause a substantial loss of membership. Recognizing the direction of the official board, Dr. Clark insisted that the committee avoid the type of exclusionary language employed by other churches, like Galloway, that specified the church as whites only. In the end, the committee voted, and the official board affirmed, that the church would decline to seat African Americans "at this time," leaving open the possibility of revisiting the issue when the racial climate was more amenable.[58]

Though Dr. Clark disagreed with the decision of the committee and the board, he, unlike Dr. Selah and Rev. Furr, had to remain in the pulpit, at least for now. He had felt that he could serve if the church "gave the opportunity for me to witness to my position and to feel that I could creatively work toward the goals which I have." Yet the recent actions of the board merely confirmed what he had decided earlier in the year, that his ministry at Capitol Street was nearing its end. With the adoption of the closed-door policy, there "was no possibility for creative involvement," and Dr. Clark sensed that he "had reached the point where the only basis upon which you can stay is complete capitulation."[59] He paid a visit to Bishop Franklin to make sure that their previous understanding was still in place. Earlier in the year, Bishop Franklin promised Dr. Clark that he could leave his post at Capitol Street as soon as Dr. Selah retired. When this occurred, Bishop Franklin aimed to transfer someone to the Galloway pastorate promptly, and then send Dr. Clark to the church previously led by Dr. Selah's replacement. Bishop Franklin assured him that the exchange would still occur, but he added that it might take a few more months.[60]

Broadmoor Baptist, on the other hand, never voted to prohibit African Americans from worship services, something that makes the actions of the ushers on June 9 even more curious. Rev. David Grant, Broadmoor's pastor during this time, wrote in his autobiography that he personally "kept the church from ever officially voting on forbidding other races to attend our church services," feeling that African Americans would eventually "be allowed to attend and that it would be more difficult to reverse a decision than to make one." Regarding the racial tensions at the time, he admitted that he "had the responsibility of doing what I believed to be right, but at the same time I had to protect the unanimity of the church."[61] In contrast to the stance taken by Dr. Selah and Rev. Furr, Rev. Grant believed that defending the will of the majority was just as important as upholding his convictions. He prevented the deacons from enacting an official policy, but there is no evidence that he forestalled his ushers from barring black visitors.

If the immediate goal of the church visits was to appeal to the Christian consciences of white moderates, then it was clear that, after Sunday, achieving this objective would take some time. While all of the Protestant churches targeted that day turned African Americans away, the visits sparked conversation and debate within churches, forcing members to confront the segregation within their sanctuaries. No longer was segregation something they only encountered in the secular aspects of their daily lives, when they took their children to a whites only school or ate at a whites only restaurant. Even though members attended churches that had maintained all-white memberships during their lifetimes, this segregation was not obvious until African Americans tried to attend. The church visits made segregation more conspicuous in each local congregation, now revealed as another space where activists confronted Jim Crow.

When Rev. King returned from New York, movement activity seemed to be at a standstill. While the church visits opened up a new alternative to mass protests, many in the movement feared arrest, especially now that it was unclear whether or not the NAACP would continue to provide bail money. On Tuesday, June 11, the Jackson movement held a poorly attended mass meeting at New Jerusalem Baptist Church. In a room beside the sanctuary, Evers and Rev. King discussed Sunday's church visits and the state of the movement. While Rev. King tried to allay Evers's worries about Dr. Selah and Rev. Furr's future, Evers seemed strengthened by the two men's actions. He told him that "what they said, what they did—refusing to preach in a segregated church—now that has made me feel better than anything in this whole movement in many days."[62] Evers then said, "I'm sorry I didn't get to know them. I'd like to talk to men like that. And now they will have to leave Mississippi. I'm sorry it all happened like this." Rev. King assured Evers that he would tell Dr. Selah and Rev. Furr that he had asked about them. When some students then came in and told Rev. King they were ready to leave, he said, "See you at the office tomorrow, Medgar, good night."[63] That was the last time they spoke. Later that evening, Evers was murdered by a sniper as he got out of his car in own his driveway. Medgar Evers's planning and participation in Sunday's church visits were among his final protests against racial injustice. Fully aware of the late leader's commitment to cracking open the doors of segregation by visiting white churches, Rev. King vowed to continue what Evers began.

[5]

"I Began to Have a Little Hope"

JUNE 1963

As word of the murder of Medgar Evers filtered through the Tougaloo campus and the black community in Jackson, it became clear that his killing had awakened people's activism. On Wednesday, June 12, street demonstrations, including some involving black ministers and others who had expressed reservations about direct action in the past, commenced throughout the city. Jackson police were ready, arresting dozens and clubbing hundreds more. The police brutality heightened national interest, as newspapers and the evening news broadcast images of the demonstrations, but the violence also served to quell interest within the NAACP on future demonstrations in the city. Some local leaders wanted daily demonstrations, sensing that students and the black community in general wanted more mass direct action. Yet when it was announced that Evers's funeral would be held on Saturday morning, NAACP staff effectively postponed mass demonstrations when they spread word that if police arrested anyone on Friday, they would probably not be bailed out in time to attend the funeral. Nevertheless, everyone agreed that there would be a march immediately following the funeral.[1]

Meanwhile, Mayor Thompson met again with a group of black ministers and promised that if they halted demonstrations, he would make some concessions, such as hiring black policemen, but he remained firmly against appointing a biracial committee. He told the group that such a committee would become a "tool of pressure groups" since, in his estimation, most African Americans living in Jackson were content and outsiders were to blame for causing unrest. As proof, Mayor Thompson offered the group of ministers an opportunity to select five black Jacksonians to live in any other city in the United States for a month, all on the city's expense. As Mayor

Thompson argued, "Let them try and find a job, a place to live, try to get along and raise a family, and then see if they still think they have things so bad here in Jackson." The ministers told the mayor, "The demonstrations will continue here until the goals of the Negro community for equality are accomplished."[2] The day after meeting with movement leaders, Mayor Thompson received his affirmation when the US Supreme Court upheld the chancery court injunction banning civil rights demonstrations in Jackson. With that victory in hand, lawyers for the city filed a motion to make the temporary injunction permanent.[3]

Thousands attended the funeral at the Masonic Temple auditorium, including people from across the state, NAACP and church leaders from across the country, and a delegation from the Southern Christian Leadership Conference (SCLC). In the audience, Dr. Martin Luther King Jr., Rev. King, John Salter, movement activists, and many people just now moved to action sat or stood as they listened to the eulogies. Rev. King remembered that there were only a few white ministers present. He recognized only one, Rev. Wofford Smith, the Episcopal chaplain at the University of Mississippi. Some he did not recognize were part of a six-member delegation sent by the NCC's week-old CRR. As one historian notes, the commission's attendance at the funeral was their first official act and represented the first step in their growing involvement in Mississippi.[4] Also in attendance was Rev. John Morris, the head of the Atlanta-based Episcopal Society for Cultural and Racial Unity. Rev. Morris was one of a dozen white Episcopal priests police arrested in Jackson two years before during the Freedom Ride effort. Reflecting on the content of the eulogies, Salter and Rev. King remember hearing much praise for the NAACP and not enough about their friend Medgar Evers. Myrlie Evers wrote that the funeral was not what Medgar would have desired; neither was it, she wrote, "at all what I wanted." She added that she "wondered how many of the people had come to pay a final tribute to Medgar and how many out of curiosity or simply to be seen."[5]

As planned, thousands marched from the Masonic Temple to Collins Funeral Home on Farish Street a few miles away. Led by heads of the NAACP and SCLC, the mourners walked the route silently, but when those at the front reached their destination, the hundreds still walking began singing and then turned back, moving toward Capitol Street, the street targeted by boycotts and protests during the preceding months. The police presence was strong, and once officers began trying to disperse the crowd, a few protesters started throwing stones and bottles. That was enough to unleash the familiar attack dogs and clubs. Activists reported hearing shots fired above their heads. Rev. King and Salter had gone into a nearby office to try to alert other leaders—and particularly Dr. King—to what was happening on the streets. But they were spotted through a window by the police, who sprang inside, struck Rev. King, and arrested them both. News accounts reported that there were more than two dozen arrests and that bottle and brick throwing injured fourteen policemen. Moreover, these accounts said that two white Tougaloo professors led the "riot." A *Los Angeles Times* article named King and Salter as the instigators.[6]

The funeral procession and the spontaneous protest the day of Evers's funeral marked the final mass demonstrations of the Jackson movement. While King and Salter sat in jail cells, the strategy committee of the Jackson movement met to discuss what to do next. The black ministers and NAACP leaders voted to allow King and Salter to remain on the committee, despite a vocal effort by some to remove the two men, but they decided to discontinue any future demonstrations. The Supreme Court had affirmed the city's injunction, and most were frightened by the violence that occurred earlier in the day, regardless of who incited it. Moreover, efforts by the Kennedy administration to convince Mayor Thompson to meet some of the movement's demands were finally proving fruitful.

The morning after the assassination of Medgar Evers, President John Kennedy telegrammed Bishop Gerow to invite him to a meeting of religious leaders at the White House the following Monday. The president wanted a private meeting with the bishop on a day when he was assembling several hundred clergymen from across the country for the purpose of discussing the racial situation and soliciting support for the civil rights legislation he had proposed on national television the night of Medgar Evers's murder. Bishop Gerow immediately accepted and sent word that he wanted to include Bishop Allin and Father Bernard Law in the meeting. On Sunday, June 16, Attorney General Robert Kennedy telephoned Bishop Gerow to discuss the situation in Jackson. In their brief conversation, Bishop Gerow told the attorney general about the interracial ministers' meetings and their efforts to reach out to Mayor Thompson and the Jackson Chamber of Commerce. Attorney General Kennedy explained that he wanted to be sure that they include a prominent black minister from Jackson in the meeting with President Kennedy the next day, and he arranged for Rev. Leon S. Whitney to make the trip. The attorney general sent a telegram to Rev. Whitney, who hastily made plans to fly to the capital.[7]

Rev. Whitney served as pastor of Farish Street Baptist Church and vice president of Mississippi Baptist Seminary for Negroes. He had remained active in local civil rights and interracial efforts since taking the pastorate in 1958. Jackson police dispatched their attack dogs on him and arrested him during the demonstrations surrounding the 1961 trial of the Tougaloo Nine. Rev. Whitney currently served on the board of the Mississippi Council on Human Relations and, in the past month, he hosted most of the interracial clergy meetings at his church. As his widow later recalled, he was articulate and tended to keep his cool. She felt these attributes explained why his fellow ministers usually selected her husband as their spokesman and leader in discussions with the mayor and white leaders.[8]

On Monday, June 17, the interracial delegation from Jackson met first with Attorney General Kennedy at the Justice Department. As Bishop Gerow wrote in his diary, Kennedy wanted to know "the story, as we had to tell it, of Jackson," and they each shared their views for about an hour. Kennedy asked them to reconvene after lunch and present him with recommendations that they would then present to the president. The two bishops and Rev. Whitney met and, according to Bishop Gerow, decided that they should be modest in their recommendations, as that opportunity would "be the beginning of the opening of the door, and that later greater rights might be opened up to them." They came up with a list of proposals encouraging Mayor Allen Thompson to continue discussions with the local black leaders and to implement some of the ideas the mayor had already agreed to, such as hiring black policemen. They pushed for President Kennedy to talk directly to Mayor Thompson, saying that the president should "express sympathy with the Mayor," and that he should "comment that he knows the Mayor wants Jackson to be an ideal city." They returned to Attorney General Kennedy's office and discussed the recommendations for another forty-five minutes and then departed for the White House.[9]

In one of the large halls in the White House, several hundred leading clergymen from throughout the country assembled to hear from President Kennedy and to discuss the current racial crisis. President Kennedy gave a brief speech, stressing that since the race question was primarily a moral one, it was the duty of religious leaders "to bring this moral aspect of the question to the people—that our method should be to attain a peaceful adjustment to lead the people properly." He then gave the ministers an opportunity to speak and assigned Dr. J. Irwin Miller, the president of the NCC, the task of organizing a statement for the group. When the president left the hall, the Jackson delegation departed as well, and met in a separate room with the attorney general and the president. They discussed the situation in Jackson and the ministers' recommendations for about an hour.

Bishop Gerow wrote in his diary that the president "received [the recommendations], studied them, asked questions, listened to our comments and showed himself intensely interested—and deeply concerned over the racial conflict throughout the country." President Kennedy left the room to call Mayor Thompson and discuss the ministers' ideas.[10]

President Kennedy and Mayor Thompson spoke on the telephone for about ten minutes. After the president asked "whether there's anything that we could do to make the situation less . . . critical down there," Mayor Thompson first told the president what a "wonderful" and "marvelous" fellow he was, and then attempted to explain the situation in Jackson from his standpoint. The mayor told the president, "We have frankly almost everything under control," but urged him to let the courts, rather than Congress, decide the future of desegregation. Mayor Thompson also asked President Kennedy to again say publicly, as he did during the Birmingham marches, that "intimidations won't work." The mayor explained, "People listen to you and if you would just tell 'em to stay out of this because they're using these young children . . . and that's where your trouble comes." After hearing Mayor Thompson's views, President Kennedy interjected, saying that when he talked to the Jackson clergymen, "there seemed to be two or three things that didn't seem to me to be too unreasonable." Mayor Thompson explained that the city was in the process of upgrading the positions of some truck drivers in the sanitation department and preparing to hire black policemen and school crossing guards. Yet on the question of a biracial committee, Mayor Thompson remained resolute, declaring, "I just can't do that right now." They discussed the specific timetable for hiring black municipal employees, and then ended the conversation on a friendly note. Mayor Thompson said he was about to give a speech with Governor George Wallace and wanted to assure the president that he was not to get his feelings hurt "about anything anybody says that I say." President Kennedy responded by giving him "full permission to denounce me in public as long as you don't in private."[11]

On Tuesday, June 18, Mayor Thompson, meeting with a group of black ministers, said that the city would follow through with the proposals suggested by President Kennedy. The mayor agreed to upgrade the salaries of black employees in the sanitation department and to hire a few black policemen to patrol in the black community and black crossing guards for black schools. Moreover, he agreed to continue to meet with black ministers and leaders. In return, the mayor expected all demonstrations and mass marches to cease.[12] Thompson's plans included no concession to desegregate public facilities and businesses or to form a biracial committee. Although his promises fell short of the ministers' original demands, the ministers prevailed upon a majority at a mass meeting at the Pearl Street AME Church to accept the mayor's proposal. Rev. G. R. Haughton told the audience to "accept this as a beginning," while still leaving open the possibility for future demonstrations. For his part Mayor Thompson boasted that the "siege" was over, that he did not compromise nor "surrender any rights of white citizens."[13]

Rev. King and Salter were unable to attend the meeting with the mayor or the mass meeting at the church because they were at Baptist Hospital recuperating from a serious car accident. On Tuesday morning, on the way back to Tougaloo from a meeting with their lawyer, Jack Young, who informed them that the police were going to charge the two with "inciting a riot," King and Salter were hit head-on by another car, which had veered into their lane. The car that hit theirs had been forced into their lane by another car, one alleged to have been driven by a Vanderbilt student who was the son of a member of the Jackson Citizens' Council. Just before the wreck, Salter remembered thinking how odd it was that they were not being followed by policemen, which had always been the case wherever they drove in the city.[14] Both men sustained injuries requiring immediate surgery. King's injuries permanently scarred one side of his face.

Despite the disillusionment that followed Evers's murder, the recent violence and police brutality, and the apparent disintegration of the Jackson movement, there was one event that signaled a degree of positive change for activists in Jackson. On Sunday, June 16, as a train carried the body of Medgar Evers to the nation's capital, where he would be buried at Arlington National Cemetery, a group of black students visited several white churches, just as they had done under Evers's leadership the previous Sunday. As before, police maintained a presence around most of the downtown churches. Bishop Gerow, who was on his way to the airport to attend the meeting with the president, saw a motorcycle policeman outside of the Cathedral of St. Peter the Apostle. He went up to the officer and told him that African Americans were welcome at the church, and that he should not interfere in any way with their entrances. The policeman responded that he was there merely to keep order, not to interfere.[15]

On this Sunday, Rev. King coordinated the visits. He knew that arrests were likely, given the tension carried over from the previous day's demonstration and the simple fact that any attempted visit would still violate the city's injunction. But just as before, one of the purposes behind the visits was to stir the consciences of white Christians. Moreover, the church visits targeted white ministers, who, especially in the last few weeks, he said, "were unable or unwilling to confront their people with the religious and moral significance of what was taking place in Jackson." Despite being turned away the week before from all the Protestant churches they visited, Rev. King hoped that "these churches, in shock over Medgar's murder, might actually open their doors and let blacks and whites pray together."[16]

The shock of the assassination of Medgar Evers did prompt one congregation, Temple Beth Israel, to open their doors officially, though the temple had yet to be visited by black activists. Rabbi Nussbaum, a native Canadian, had led the synagogue since his arrival in Jackson two months after the Supreme Court's *Brown* decision in 1954. Though he regarded himself as a liberal in social matters, the rabbi resolved to dedicate himself to serving his congregation and developing relationships between the Jewish and Christian communities. He spearheaded ecumenical efforts and maintained close friendships with other like-minded ministers. Like these fellow clergymen, his sermons on racial moderation were often at odds with the sentiments of many members of his congregation. In 1957, when he learned that the local B'nai B'rith lodge invited a member of the Jackson Citizens' Council to speak at a meeting, he denounced the lodge and the Citizens' Council from the pulpit, arguing that racial discrimination was inconsistent with the teachings of the Hebrew Bible. The next year, after a wave of bombings hit synagogues and Jewish institutions throughout the South, he wrote an admonishing column in the temple bulletin, "It Could Happen Here." A copy of his essay ended up in the Jackson newspapers, prompting several temple members to lead an unsuccessful effort to prohibit him from speaking in public without the board's approval. Then, in 1961, Rabbi Nussbaum was one of the few local clergymen who secretly ministered to jailed Freedom Riders. Though he disagreed with the riders' tactics, he reasoned that he had an obligation to visit his fellow Jews, especially after receiving panicky appeals from some of the riders' parents. In addition to counseling individual prisoners, he brought them provisions and held brief worship services. At the time, he believed he might leading the first interracial worship service in Mississippi. The recent exodus of Methodist ministers who held moderate views on race—most notably "his personal insurance," Dr. Selah—left him especially doubtful about his own future.[17] He heard of Evers's murder while he was in Atlantic City attending a rabbinical conference and immediately wired his board of trustees, who were set to meet in a few days, urging them to adopt a resolution that their temple's services would be open to all. Though some, like the board's president, felt insulted that the congregation needed to specify that they were "open," several racially conservative members were reluctant to extend what amounted to an invitation for African Americans to attend the synagogue. Nevertheless, the board overcame their disinclination and approved the open-door resolution.[18]

At morning and evening services on June 16, ushers turned away groups of black students at First Baptist and at two churches that activists had not targeted the week before, First Christian Church and Central Presbyterian Church.[19] The Tougaloo groups clearly meant to extend the reach of their campaign to include other denominations represented in Jackson. The pastor of First Christian was Rev. Roy Hulan, the presiding leader of the Jackson Ministerial Association and a participant in interracial discussions, including meetings of the Council on Human Relations and the interracial ministers' meetings in May. His wife, Polly, was active in United Church Women, a local interracial women's fellowship. Like Dr. Selah, Rev. Hulan had been laboring to guide his church toward greater inclusiveness ever since his lay board adopted a closed-door policy in 1961. Yet no African Americans had tested that policy until this Sunday, when a group of ushers told two black students, Anne Moody and Carrie Lopsky, that they could not enter. One of the ushers read a prepared statement, explaining that it was not safe for them to attend the church at this time, and that the church was "a church of Christ, not a place for publicity." A few of the church members who were near the entrance tried to reassure the young women that not everyone in the church approved of the exclusion policy. One older white woman even told the ushers that she and her family would volunteer to be seated next to the black students. When the ushers refused to budge, the woman told the ushers and the young women, "God is the judge of us all. Who else can judge where we worship." The ushers then threatened to call the police, so Moody and Lopsky walked away.[20]

In the two years since adoption of the rule, Rev. Hulan had consistently protested the decision to close the doors. He voiced his conviction once again during this service. The denial of entry of blacks to worship services at other Jackson churches the previous Sunday and the murder of Evers provided the immediate backdrop for this Sunday's sermon, "When Men Are at Odds." His message centered on Paul's letter to Philemon, in which Paul instructed his friend to forgive his runaway slave and accept him as a brother in Christ. For Rev. Hulan, Paul was showing that "men naturally at odds are transformed into brothers when they are individually drawn into the Body of Christ." Applying Paul's example to the current situation, Rev. Hulan saw blacks and whites at odds, with the African American believing that he is a "follower of Christ without receiving the love of his fellow Christian," while "the white man in many areas wants to maintain the status quo." He ended his sermon with an emphatic declaration: "To deny any person, on account of race or color, access to the House of God—not my house, not your house, not First Christian's house, but God's House—is an un-Christian act. This I believe." Rev. Hulan certainly meant his words to be more of an admonition than a rebuke, for he had no warning that African Americans would attempt to worship in his church that particular Sunday. At the end of the service, someone informed him that ushers had in fact denied entrance to two young African American women.[21]

Ushers also barred the entry of two young black men from Central Presbyterian Church, the first Presbyterian congregation the activists attempted to visit in Jackson. The two men walked up the steps to a group of ushers and shook their hands, asking if they could attend the worship service. They insisted that they were not there to cause trouble. One of the ushers replied that the church leaders did not think it advisable to admit them and offered to transport them to a black church. Earlier in the week, the church's session had selected a few elders to stand guard, giving them wide latitude in preventing the entry of unwelcome visitors. Recognizing the resolve of the greeters, the young men explained that they did not want any trouble and then shook the ushers' hands and climbed into a nearby taxi. Yet the church visit was not without incident, as one of the ushers descended the steps to shove a television cameraman before other ushers intervened. A larger group of black visitors returned that night, but the ushers turned them away, too.[22]

For the second Sunday in a row, a group of six black students returned to First Baptist, where the congregation had voted the week before to designate themselves whites only. The group attempted to attend the night worship service. Because they seemed more persistent than they had been on the previous Sunday, a local sheriff assisted the head deacon in barring the visitors.[23] Nevertheless, as on the previous Sunday, police declined to arrest any of the activists.

While the students left the premises after church officials and police denied their entry, Rev. King and other activists felt that any attempted church visit could still constitute activity that could lead to an arrest. Since the escalation of the direct action campaign in late May, police arrested movement participants for what seemed more innocuous behavior. Moreover, a June 6 injunction against civil rights activists further clarified and expanded illegal activities. The county court order enjoined activists "from engaging in acts and conduct customarily known as 'kneel-ins' in churches in violation of the wishes and desires of said churches." The members of First Baptist made their "wishes and desires" explicit in their vote the week before. Moreover, the injunction also prohibited "trespassing on private property after being warned to leave the premises . . . congregating on the streets or public places as mobs . . . and . . . performing acts calculated to cause breaches of the peace."[24] On this second Sunday of attempted church visits, Rev. King and the student visitors perceived that the police were establishing a precedent, refraining from arresting black visitors as long as they left church property after being turned away.

While the lack of arrests confirmed that church visitation could continue to be a constructive strategy for protesting segregation and disquieting white Christians, movement participants had another reason to feel optimistic. Four African American women attended morning worship at St. Andrew's Episcopal Church, the first white Protestant church to open its doors in Jackson. Like the ministers at Galloway Methodist, Capitol Street Methodist, and First Christian, the new minister at St. Andrew's, Rev. Christoph Keller Jr., was a voice for moderation and reconciliation. He became rector in October 1962, just a few weeks after riots took place at the University of Mississippi.[25]

Rev. Keller took the position at St. Andrew's following the stormy tenure of Rev. Edward Harrison, who resigned the pastorate after weathering several incidents involving race. In the late 1950s, Rev. Harrison stood firm in maintaining a controversial Sunday school curriculum that, in some lessons, openly advocated integration. In the summer of 1961, Rev. Harrison provoked more derision after he served communion to a group of jailed Freedom Riders. Though he explained that he was merely serving the sacraments to fellow Episcopal priests, he drew special attention to himself because he was the city's only white minister the media reported to have met with the imprisoned activists.

Meanwhile, local newspapers also reported that Rev. Harrison had been conducting biracial meetings of citizens and clergy at the St. Andrew's parish house, just as local civil rights activists commenced the first sit-ins in Jackson at the downtown library. The meetings came to light after Bill Clark, a parishioner and head of the local chapter of the John Birch Society, posed as a New York Times reporter and recorded a telephone call with Jane Schutt, one of the white women attending the biracial meetings. Clark helped lead an effort to convince the vestry to unseat Rev. Harrison from the pulpit. When that failed, Clark and a few others tried to oust him from his position as ex-officio chairman of St. Andrew's School.

Rev. Harrison resolved to continue his ministry at St. Andrew's, but another bizarre incident in 1962 proved to be the last straw. In May 1962, an Episcopal priest from Texas gave an address at a Citizens' Council dinner in Jackson on "Why Integration is Anti-Christian." The priest presented the audience with a telegram allegedly authored by Rev. Harrison, in which Rev. Harrison urged him not to come to Jackson. An investigation confirmed that the telegram was a forgery, but calls for Rev. Harrison's dismissal continued, and he resigned in early September 1962, just a few weeks before James Meredith integrated the University of Mississippi. Rev. Harrison's successor, Rev. Keller, shared his commitment to racial tolerance, but the two men differed in style. As one member recalled, God sent Rev. Harrison to us to shake things up, while he sent Rev. Keller to love us.[26]

Yet one crucial distinction between Rev. Christoph Keller and his counterparts at Galloway, Capitol Street, and First Christian was that he presided over a church where a clear majority of lay leaders affirmed his vision of racial moderation. His wife, Caroline, recalled that once they arrived at St. Andrew's in October 1962, Rev. Keller immediately set out to build a relationship of trust with his vestry before he began speaking forcefully from the pulpit. As Rev. Keller later remembered, the church was "uneasy and divided, and not always unanimous in their opinion of how racial conflict should be addressed," but the "parishioners and specifically the lay leadership of St. Andrew's never wavered in their support of our efforts to bring some measure of harmony and openness to the racial problems confronting us."[27] The leadership of one individual in particular—the warden, Sherwood W. Wise—proved crucial the morning of June 16. Wise was not publicly known as a moderate on racial matters. In fact, within his capacity as president of the Mississippi Bar Association, he testified to a US Congressional committee the year before in defense of Mississippi's literacy tests and other voting requirements that effectively disenfranchised African Americans in the state. Later in the week, he and other presidents of Southern bar associations were set to meet with President Kennedy and lobby him to oppose the civil rights legislation pending before Congress. Yet Wise supported Rev. Harrison through the pastor's tumultuous ministry and endeavored, he believed, to "help bring some peace and order into our thinking." When a friend encouraged Wise to join the Citizens' Council, he declined, even though the offer was accompanied by a threat that if he wanted to continue to work and succeed in Jackson, he needed to become a member. Wise cited the examples of Bishop Allin, Rev. Harrison, and Rev. Keller while he served as warden of St. Andrew's. When demonstrations began in Jackson and churches began preparing for the potential arrival of black visitors, Wise followed Rev. Keller's lead because, he said, "I knew he was right and the time had come when people of good will must speak out, even though this might carry some risks."[28]

Because of the leadership structure of Episcopal churches and the relationship that Rev. Keller had established with his church leaders by June 1963, he was able to instruct his vestry that the church must admit African Americans who presented themselves for worship. When lay leaders had discussed this possibility after the demonstrations began in Jackson, some pointed out that the motive of the activists would not be to worship. According to Caroline Keller-Winter, Rev. Keller told his vestry that if he had to examine the motive of every one of them, then they would be in real trouble. He said, "If they come to demonstrate, then they can stay to worship."[29] Though a few discussions became testy, only a couple of vestry members objected to the prevailing view, which was that the ushers would seat the black visitors because St. Andrew's had seated African Americans since the church's founding in the nineteenth century. John Fontaine, one of the vestry members present at these discussions, later recalled that the real issue was how to be civil about seating the black visitors without being too effusive.[30]

As a matter of church policy, Rev. Keller maintained the power to reject or admit anyone for worship, but in practical terms, as in other churches, the decision ultimately rested with whoever was greeting people at the church doors. Rev. Keller told reporters later that he did not know in advance that African Americans would attempt to worship at St. Andrew's, but the ushers seemed to know that the visitors were coming this particular Sunday.[31] One clue may have been the presence of media cameramen and "Thompson's tank" outside before the service. Upon seeing the anti-demonstration vehicle parked adjacent to the church and in front of the governor's mansion, Wise confronted the driver and ordered police officers to leave, which they did. Sensing that black visitors might walk up the church steps in a matter of minutes—and not knowing what he was supposed to do if that occurred—one of the ushers, twenty-six-year old John Anderson, asked his warden, "Mr. Wise, what are we going to do?" Wise put his hands on Anderson's shoulders and replied very simply, "John, we are going to seat them." For Anderson, who admitted later that at the time he regarded the activists as "troublemakers", the resolve and example that Wise provided at that moment was crucial to understanding why the church admitted the black visitors. Wise knew he had the support of Rev. Keller, but he also knew that some members of the church would not agree with the admission of African Americans. Yet he remained confident that he was taking the right stand, reasoning that it was in accord "with tradition and practice that had existed at St. Andrew's from the beginning."[32]

Four young women arrived in two separate groups, and each carried a Bible in her gloved hands. Jeanette King dropped off Camille Wilburn and Emma Joffrion, whom ushers greeted. Wise told them they were welcome to come in, but the assembly of cameramen needed to stay outside. A few newsmen entered St. Andrew's as well, but without their cameras. King then went to pick up Anne Moody and Carrie Lopsky, whom ushers had just barred from worshiping at First Christian. Since the first group apparently succeeded in entering St. Andrew's, Moody and Lopsky asked for King to drop them off there as well. With the services already underway, there was no one to greet them outside. When they entered the vestibule, the ushers asked the newcomers to sign the guest registry and then seated them right behind the other two women. Although a newspaper reported, "Some eyebrows were raised," there were no disorderly incidents or noticeable acts of hostility toward the black visitors.[33] In his homily, Rev. Keller directly addressed the racial problems in Jackson and the recent murder of Medgar Evers. He pointed out that in contrast to achievements in such endeavors as space travel, there were no concurrent achievements in human relations. The only developments in the latter field were "fear, tension, suspicion and a tragic death in the community." As the young women walked out of the church, they met Rev. Keller. He recalled later "the fear and determination expressed in the face of one of these women as I shook her cold and trembling hand at the door of the church." Rev. Keller tried to reassure the women and invited them to visit again. Moody felt "he said it as if he meant it, and I began to have a little hope."[34]

The opening of a white Protestant church in Jackson—and St. Andrew's in particular—was a pivotal moment for many of those involved, and it received substantial national press coverage. For Anne Moody, who had never worshiped and prayed in a white church before, and who thought "God would strike the life out of [her]" as she sat in the pew at St. Andrew's, the welcoming attitude of the parishioners and Rev. Keller imparted a degree of optimism. Owing to the leadership of Wise and guidance of Rev. Keller, Anderson began to reconsider his opinion of the activists as troublemakers.

As an usher, he accepted the black women into the church that Sunday and immediately recognized the whole event as a "pivotal, transforming experience." For Rev. Keller, it was "a turning point in the life of St. Andrew's and Mississippi as they moved toward more harmonious racial relations and compliance with the Civil Rights legislation subsequently enacted."[35] The event also garnered widespread publicity, as both the *New York Times* and the *Los Angeles Times* published articles about the church visits, accompanied by photographs of the students descending the steps of St. Andrew's after shaking hands with Rev. Keller.

While the open doors at St. Andrew's Episcopal Church represented a limited accomplishment for the movement, in a week during which a sniper murdered their leader and police amplified their suppression of protests against racial injustices, the opening of a Protestant church nonetheless represented a victory. Moreover, given the result of the June 18 mass meeting, where a majority of black ministers and movement participants voted to accept the mayor's modest concessions and end massive demonstrations, any crack in the door that shielded Jackson's segregationist structure encouraged activists who favored continued direct action. With their options now limited to small-scale protests and the threat of arrests still lingering, Rev. King and many of the student activists saw church visits as an increasingly attractive strategy for exposing the immorality of racial segregation. As Rev. King later summarized, that church visits would be a way to remind white Christians that they "cannot escape thinking about the problems of segregation even on Sunday morning . . . that every single aspect of your Southern Way of Life is under attack."[36] Movement activists placed primary importance on registering voters and working on community development programs, but they understood that visiting white churches would make manifest a social system that white church members previously did not have to confront on Sunday mornings. The visits, they hoped, would spark discussions and debates, causing white Christians to consider whether or not segregation was consistent with their faith.

"The Christian Church Is Down the Road"

SUMMER 1963

As the school year came to a close and the summer heat began to en-velop Mississippi, some students and other activists worked in and around Jackson on voter registration drives and educational and anti-pov-erty programs. Among their activities was an interracial work camp based at Tougaloo College that planned to offer out-of-state and international students the opportunity to join with Mississippi students in a variety of civil rights and outreach programs.[1] The work camp convened under reli-gious auspices, with the World Council of Churches (WCC) and the World Student Christian Federation (WSCF) jointly sponsoring the program. Rev. Pharis Harvey, a white Methodist divinity student at Yale and a staff mem-ber of an affiliate of the WSCF, led the project. For most of July and the beginning of August, the students completed service tasks around campus, helped out in the offices of civil rights groups in the region, and attended seminars and workshops connecting Christian principles to various issues facing the country. Rev. Harvey tried to gather different perspectives on so-cial issues for these discussions, even inviting someone from the Mississippi State Sovereignty Commission to speak. Beyond educating the students and helping them develop activist strategies, Rev. Harvey had a fundamental vision for the work camp. Though only two out of the twelve students were African American, he wanted the camp experience to be as interracial as possible. He and the participants therefore insisted that they must do ev-erything together, including going to church. Rev. Harvey and the students were particularly intrigued by the church visit campaign that Evers and Rev. King had initiated earlier in June.[2]

The twelve students in the work camp came from a variety of religious backgrounds, and some had little experience in civil rights activism. Rev.

Harvey grew up in Oklahoma in a totally white community, but married a Mississippian, a liaison that resulted in problems with her relatives once the couple became activists. As a seminary student at Yale, where SNCC was active, Rev. Harvey participated in dialogues with civil rights leaders such as Stokely Carmichael, wanting to become more involved in the movement. Leading the work camp was his first movement activity beyond the Yale community.[3] Lisa Anderson, one of the white students, was not active in the movement; neither was she particularly religious before she attended the work camp. Anderson grew up in New Jersey and was a rising senior at Cornell University. A few years before, she participated in an experiment in international living in Sweden, and her brother had recently volunteered with the American Friends Service Committee at a work camp in Italy. Her primary interest in coming to the work camp at Tougaloo was to do volunteer work in the United States.[4] In contrast, Ivory Phillips, one of two black students at the camp, had been active in the Jackson movement before participating in the program. A native of Rosedale, he was a rising senior at Jackson State. After the camp, he planned to continue work on voter registration in his hometown and then teach at Immaculate Conception in Clarksdale. During his time in college, he attended mass meetings and rallies of the Jackson NAACP and worked some with Medgar Evers. He was the only black male in the group. The other African American in the group was Thelma Sadberry. A native of Jackson, she had just graduated from Tougaloo in May.[5] Though most of the students were white, Dr. Phillips remembers the group as being geographically diverse, with a few from the South but the majority coming from other parts of the country.

Significantly, the decision to try to attend worship at white churches in Jackson did not arise out of any conscious effort to continue something that local activists started, and the tactic was not derivative of the larger local strategy to foster interracial communication among Christians. Rev. Harvey acknowledged that local activists such as Rev. King guided their thinking and aided them with particular strategies with local churches, but he saw their church visits as part of the purpose of the work camp to carry out an interracial program. Additionally, he and Phillips recalled a general feeling among the twelve that they wanted to make a Christian witness to the local churches. For the students, it was religiously imperative that they, a group under the auspices of the WCC, be allowed to worship together. The mostly white group attended various black churches together, yet they knew that it was a different matter entirely to attempt to worship at a local white church, even though only two of them were African American.[6] Anderson remembered that Rev. Harvey brought up the idea of church visitation during one of the first devotionals, announcing that Professor Garner invited the group to attend his church, Galloway. Rev. Harvey asked the students whether they were willing to go, and if so, whether they were willing to be arrested. After some discussion, all agreed to the first question, but decided that they should try to avoid arrest if possible.[7]

On three consecutive Sundays in July, groups of work camp volunteers attempted to attend worship at eight white churches. They returned to several of the churches that students targeted June 9 and June 16. Integrated groups attended Christ the King Catholic Church and St. Andrew's Episcopal Church. St. Andrew's, the only white Protestant church to admit African Americans so far, continued to admit black guests. Anderson recalled that when they went to St. Andrew's the first time, there was a heavy police presence. Since Phillips was well aware of Jackson police tactics—particularly their habit of ticketing activists for minor traffic offenses—he insisted that Rev. Harvey park the car and pay the meters on either side of the car as well. The policeman nonetheless recorded their license number. Inside St. Andrew's, Rev. Keller and several parishioners extended a cordial welcome to the visitors, though Anderson noted several quizzical looks and comments such as, "I see we have visitors." Rev. Pharis wrote at the time that a small group of elderly ladies jeered at the group as they exited the church.[8] Yet their experience at St. Andrew's was mostly free of incident compared with what happened at other Protestant churches.

At First Baptist Church, where Gov. Barnett led a Sunday school class, black visitors continued to be turned away. On July 21, ushers refused to admit three young women: one white, one Japanese, and one black. Ushers told the students, "We would prefer that you not come in here because of the strained relations in Jackson."[9] This was one of the last times African Americans attempted to visit any Baptist churches in Jackson during the campaign. In order to open the doors at the churches, especially those whose ministers condoned or even defended their churches' exclusion policies, King understood that a degree of top-down influence would have to occur—something inherently difficult among the churches of the Southern Baptist Convention. Unlike the hierarchical or connectional structures of other Protestant churches targeted by the students, churches that were obliged to adhere to synod or conference directives, the localized, congregational structure of Baptist churches ensured that they would not have to answer to the Southern Baptist Convention or Baptist leaders. Only individual Baptist church members held the keys that would open their own doors.

Yet even if Baptists in Jackson did look to their denominational leaders for guidance, they would certainly see a mixed message regarding individual churches' inclusion policies. In May, for instance, an African American applied for membership at First Baptist Church in Houston, Texas, a church whose pastor, Dr. Rev. K. Owen White, was president of the Southern Baptist Convention. After a group of black students was turned away in 1962, Dr. White specifically instructed his ushers to admit everyone who came to worship, regardless of race. Yet he did not seek a change in the screening policy for membership, which excluded blacks from membership in the church. The ushers began admitting African Americans and, on May 19, 1963, one of them stepped forward when Dr. White gave the invitation. At the time, Dr. White told the man that the church would have to change its membership policy in order for him to join. After Dr. White met privately with the man twice leading up to the decision, Dr. White concluded that the man "wanted to see if he could join the church where the president of the Southern Baptist Convention is pastor." On June 12, just a few days after the first church visits in Jackson, First Baptist of Houston announced it was denying the black man's application for membership. The official statement to the press echoed the rationale given by ushers at First Baptist in Jackson: "In the light of existing conditions and in the best interests of the Lord's work, the church feels it wise to continue the present policy in regard to reception of members." The church continued to admit African Americans to worship but denied those who sought membership, with the result that representatives from CORE began picketing First Baptist. The black men and women carried signs that read "Is God Black or White?" and "How Can A Christian Church Be Segregated?" Significantly, Dr. White followed the standard set by the previous president of the Southern Baptist Convention, Dr. Herschel H. Hobbs, who also denied membership in his Oklahoma City church to an African American because he questioned the man's motivation.[10] White Baptist churches in Jackson did not follow the two men's prescriptions precisely, for Jackson churches refused to even allow African Americans to enter their sanctuaries for worship. Yet the exclusion policies of the Jackson churches did follow the rationale of the two presidents, questioning the motives of all African Americans seeking to worship at their white churches.

In the Jackson area Baptist churches, those members who opposed their churches' closed-door policies sensed they were vastly outnumbered. At Woodland Hills Baptist Church, where students did not return after the June 9 visits, a church member later recalled that the Citizens' Council was especially well represented among the deacons and membership. After

George Purvis told his fellow deacons at Woodland Hills that he would not be a part of the "welcoming committee" guarding the doors in case black visitors showed up, he knew he would not win reelection. He did not run again.[11] And students never returned to Calvary Baptist Church, where Dick Barnes had to enforce a closed-door policy that he opposed. Dr. Joe Tuten refrained from commenting on racial issues from the pulpit during this time, avoiding a subject that caused his predecessor, Rev. Luther Joe Thompson, to be forced out in 1960. Yet the pastor's silence did not preclude one member, Mary Hendrick, from using her position as a young-adult Sunday school teacher as a pulpit, constantly speaking out against her church's closed-door policy. While the years have not diminished the emotional pain she and her husband experienced during this time, she joked afterward that her students probably got tired of their lessons always centering on the same verse from Galatians where Paul writes, "There is neither Jew nor Greek, there is neither bond nor free, there is neither male nor female: for you are all one in Christ Jesus."[12]

At Galloway, the fallout from the first church visits continued, as members confronted the loss of their two pastors. After eighteen years as Galloway's senior pastor, Dr. Selah returned to his home state and alma mater to serve as vice president of Central Methodist College in Fayette, Missouri. His associate, Rev. Furr, a native Mississippian, accepted a transfer to the Southern California—Arizona Conference. Both men finalized their transfers just five days after they announced their intentions to leave Galloway.[13]

In the succeeding months, Dr. Selah received hundreds of letters from bishops, ministers, and people from different faiths across the country expressing admiration for the stand he took. Dozens of those letters were from members and former members of Galloway, sharing private thoughts about race that they could not share publicly. Verna R. Wood confessed that Dr. Selah "had made [her] feel differently about the whole mess, and I am the lousiest Christian of them all." Carroll Brinson expressed regret over his decision to resign, but admitted, "No real progress will be made in bringing about a permanent harmonious relationship between the two races until more people in this feel and act as you do." Francis S. Harmon, a Galloway member in the 1920s and a leading Methodist layman in New York City, felt inspired by Dr. Selah's actions. Rather than return to his former church when he visited Jackson a few weeks later, Harmon pledged instead to "seek out a Negro church where I am welcome in a personal effort to put into practice the Christian fellowship so much needed at this time." In the meantime, Harmon wrote a series of trenchant letters to the editor to the

Clarion-Ledger and the *Jackson Daily News*. He wrote to tell his former Jackson neighbors that if they wanted to maintain closed church doors, then they must cancel all contributions to Christian missions overseas. It would, he said, be illogical "to help finance Methodist missionaries to convert non-believers and to receive them into Methodist fellowship when they cannot participate in Sunday morning worship in the church providing the money." Members of other Jackson churches wrote Dr. Selah as well. Ann Hewitt of Fondren Presbyterian Church wondered whether the ushers at her church would do the same as those at Galloway, but felt confident that her pastor, Dr. Moody McDill, "will act as you did if a similar situation arose."[14]

Galloway's official board approved resolutions thanking Dr. Selah and Rev. Furr for their service. In response, Dr. Selah explained his decision, reminding the board of his consistent disapproval of the board's racial policy since the adoption of the June 1961 resolution barring African American visitors. When ushers turned away the students on June 9, he wrote, "I felt in conscience that I had to ask for another assignment. It broke my heart to do this. But a man must live with himself and his conscience."[15] Rev. Furr's response to the board was more direct: "I suppose you . . . can be forgiven for such extravagant lies. In any case, it was good to receive."[16]

On June 10, when Galloway's official board held its monthly meeting, board members once again affirmed the church's closed-door policy, tabling a motion brought by two members to open worship services to African Americans. Additionally, board members adopted a resolution requesting Bishop Franklin to appoint ministers who would preach sermons consistent with the beliefs of the congregation.[17] This type of restriction clearly kept several potential candidates from expressing interest in the post. According to Dr. Roy Clark, pastor of Capitol Street Methodist Church, the circumstances surrounding Dr. Selah's resignation added to Bishop Franklin's difficulty in finding a replacement. If a minister agreed to come to Galloway, it would look like he wanted to turn African Americans away and would tolerate a situation that Dr. Selah could not, even if the minister himself opposed the closed-door policy.[18] While only the bishop could appoint replacements, members of the board met with candidates and felt confident that their preferences would meet the approval of Bishop Franklin. In early August, Hugh Smith, chairman of the Pastoral Relations Committee, and Nat Rogers, chairman of the official board, met with Dr. William Jefferson Cunningham and proposed that he fill Dr. Selah's position.

To the board, Dr. Cunningham must have seemed an appropriate candidate. For the previous eight years, he had served with distinction as pastor of St. John's Methodist Church in Memphis, Tennessee. At the time, western Tennessee, including Memphis, was in the North Mississippi Conference, and Dr. Cunningham was therefore under Bishop Marvin Franklin's jurisdiction. Moreover, Dr. Cunningham had close ties with the state as a native Mississippian, as a graduate and trustee of Millsaps, as a former pastor at three Mississippi churches, and as a past president of the board of education of the North Mississippi Conference. Yet in other respects, the board's interest in Dr. Cunningham was peculiar. His son-in-law was Rev. Jerry Trigg, the young pastor of Leggett Memorial Methodist Church in Biloxi and an outspoken opponent of segregation. During a public debate in downtown Jackson a year earlier, Rev. Trigg rebutted accusations of communist leanings in churches from Myers Lowman, who traveled around the state speaking on behalf of the State Sovereignty Commission. Additionally, Rev. Trigg was one of chief architects of the "born of conviction" manifesto.[19] His son-in-law's candidness on race notwithstanding, Dr. Cunningham made clear to Smith and Rogers that he "would have to take the same stand Dr. Selah had taken." But he added that while he "was not in agreement with the racial policy, if I came I would understand it and try to work creatively with the people toward the Methodist ideal of the church." After the meeting with the two men from Galloway's board concluded, Dr. Cunningham felt that the matter was over and "had no reason to expect the invitation to be considered further."[20]

Yet the courtship of Dr. Cunningham continued. In contrast to Dr. Cunningham's assessment of the meeting, Rogers and Smith "were impressed with [Dr. Cunningham] as a man and as a Christian minister" and recommended his appointment to the official board. Smith reported to the board that Dr. Cunningham understood the racial policy of Galloway but would not come to the church "as a crusader on controversial matters." He explained that Dr. Cunningham shared Dr. Selah's views on race, but added, "Most Christian ministers think the same about this matter." The first week in August, the Pastoral Relations Committee and the official board voted unanimously to request that the bishop appoint Dr. Cunningham to Galloway. For his part, Bishop Franklin did not need any convincing, for he had already told Dr. Cunningham at the Methodist assembly at Lake Junaluska in North Carolina that he was "ideal for the place."[21] While the bishop's prodding and a desire to return to a church and city he loved were at the forefront of his mind, Dr. Cunningham also felt "the moment of truth had come." He knew that taking the helm at Galloway could present some hardships, but he felt that if he "turned this down—no matter that prominent ministers in other states had already done so—I would be haunted for the rest of my life by an inner voice saying that when my crucial opportunity came, I turned it away." Dr. Cunningham accepted the offer, effective September 2, and told the *Clarion-Ledger* that he looked forward "eagerly to the inspiring challenge at Galloway."

As the church awaited his new appointment, Dr. M. L. Smith, former president of Millsaps, served as interim pastor. In addition, Dr. Selah's predecessor at Galloway, Dr. Clovis C. Chappell, returned and preached reassuring sermons to the congregation. The Sunday after Dr. Selah and Rev. Furr resigned, Dr. Chappell spoke to an overflowing crowd. According to members John and Margrit Garner, many of the conservatives Dr. Selah alienated over the years now returned, knowing that Dr. Chappell would not offend their sensibilities. In Dr. Chappell's first sermon, he preached mostly on the power of prayer, but then he addressed the issue on everyone's mind, saying, "I know you are all wanting to know if I am on your side." He then stated, "No sir. I'm not. I'm on the Lord's side." While the Garners viewed Dr. Chappell's statement as "meaningless sidestepping," most of the congregation expressed relief, responding to it with "a big laugh."[22]

As Dr. Chappell and other visiting ministers—including Bishop Franklin—preached to the congregation in June and July, ushers continued to reject black visitors through varying means. One Sunday, an usher informed an integrated group that Galloway was only open to members and their guests.[23] On another Sunday, a Galloway usher told another group, "This is a Christian church and we intend to keep it that way."[24] The usher's retort spoke to the perception by many white church people that the activists were not sincere in their desire to worship at that particular church, that the sacred space was being corrupted by agitators in an attempt to score political points. Exposing a gulf in perceptions that would last the duration of the church visit campaign, ushers and other segregationist church people failed to understand that the contrast between a worship activity and protest activity was a distinction they had created, one that never existed in the minds of the church visitors. The visitors may have been activists or protestors in a conventional sense, but the attempts to enter all-white churches were attempts to uphold basic biblical teachings and the denominational beliefs and policies of those very churches, a decidedly theological and moral objective. On another level, the usher's statement was a sad but revealing commentary on his and other segregationists' conception of Christianity at the time, one that implied the entrance of a black visitor and two local citizens publicly renowned for their civil rights activism would somehow debase a holy assembly. "Christian" now meant "whites only." Though the integrated groups were not welcomed inside, Rev. Harvey secured a one-on-one meeting with Bishop Franklin. He came away with the impression that Bishop Franklin was torn internally, that he knew the right thing to do and even wanted to do the right thing, but did not feel strong enough to withstand the pressures against him.[25]

Integrated groups from the work camp were also turned away from four additional churches during the month of July. One group, after being rejected by ushers at Galloway, walked to Capitol Street Methodist, though it is likely that the students did not even reach the church steps. The *Clarion-Ledger* specified that policemen, not ushers, turned back the work camp volunteers. A police officer told the students that they had "no business" there.[26] The church's pastor, Dr. Clark, was in the waning days of his decade-long ministry at the church. Based on the arrangement made with Bishop Franklin, Dr. Clark would transfer to the church that had just been vacated by the new pastor at Galloway. Now that Dr. Cunningham was set to transfer to Galloway in September, Dr. Clark knew his new destination: St. John's Methodist Church in Memphis. He preached his final sermon at Capitol Street in late August.[27]

Work camp volunteers also tried to worship at West Capitol Street Church of Christ and First Presbyterian Church, where ushers turned away groups of students on July 21. First Presbyterian was the state's largest Presbyterian congregation and had maintained a closed-door policy for years. After renouncing their denomination's vote to affirm the *Brown* decision and to encourage the lowering of racial barriers in local churches in 1954, the church's pastor and elders continued to direct the church on a rigidly segregationist course. In the late fifties when the General Assembly's Council on Christian Relations pushed for desegregation throughout the denomination, the session of First Presbyterian voted to withhold funds to the committee overseeing the council and called for the council to be abolished, declaring that the denomination should not take "any action with reference to current social, political and economic problems." When that effort failed, the church's pastor, Dr. John Reed Miller, continued to condemn the integrationist pronouncements of the Council on Christian Relations.[28] By the early 1960s, Dr. Miller publicly associated himself with several pro-segregationist and conservative causes in Jackson. He developed a close friendship with William J. Simmons, the administrator of the Citizens' Council and a chief advisor to Governor Barnett. The same day that religious leaders from Jackson met with President Kennedy to resolve the city's racial crisis in June

1963, Dr. Miller gave the invocation at a dinner of the Southern Unpledged Electors, where Alabama governor George Wallace was the featured speaker. The governor's speech came just a week after he reluctantly submitted to federal authorities enforcing a court order requiring desegregation of the University of Alabama. As Dr. Miller sat at the head table, Governor Wallace urged attendees to defeat President Kennedy in the following year's election for setting up "a military dictatorship for the protection of Negro rights." [29]

Before integrated groups attempted to worship at First Presbyterian, Rev. Harvey contacted Dr. Miller, telling him to expect the students. When the students arrived, they saw policemen in the area and a group of about six ushers blocking the door. The ushers told the integrated group it could not enter. When the students asked why, one of the ushers said, "We don't want trouble" and threatened to call in the police. Rev. Harvey recalled a poignant, but in hindsight humorous exchange with a tall usher that was similar to what a group had heard recently at Galloway. After the usher insisted that the group was not welcome, Rev. Harvey asked if this was a Christian church. The usher replied, "No, the Christian church is down the road." [30] When rejected by all-white churches, students would usually worship together and provide visible testimony of the oneness of mankind at the predominantly black New Hope Baptist Church, the home congregation of one of the work camp students, Thelma Sadberry.

Assessing the effects of the church visits in his report to the World Council of Churches' Commission for Ecumenical Voluntary Service Projects, Rev. Harvey concluded that the visits "contributed to the movement toward an open society," and "helped both the work campers and the various congregations involved examine the Christian faith in regard to their congregational life." Yet the most significant aspect of the church visits was "the increasing JOY we found at the few opportunities that were afforded us to enter the House of God in praise and prayer, and the real sense of celebration, of thanksgiving for these high moments when we sat with other Christians in common worship." [31] On a more personal level, the church visits helped Rev. Harvey appreciate the depths of the divisions in the church. So often, he thought about the role of the church reforming society without recognizing the need to reform the church. [32]

The church visits in July had a variety of effects on the work camp participants as well. Karen Pate returned to her hometown Prairie City, Oregon, and talked in her Methodist church about the visitation campaign and the exclusion policies of some white churches. Her experience highlighted the problem of racial discrimination within her church's own denomination, something that the congregation would continue to follow with interest in the succeeding months.[33] For Ivory Phillips, who was already active in the Jackson movement, the interracial facet of the work camp left a lasting impression. He was struck by the fact that ten white students who were not even from Mississippi were willing to witness to what they saw in scripture. The example set by Rev. King also had a profound effect on him. As he recalled thinking, here was a white Mississippian who had just been severely injured because of his convictions, and he still remained genuine and resolute.[34] Lisa Anderson Todd, on the other hand, had not been an activist before she arrived at the work camp. Her participation in the church visits forced her to confront whether or not she would commit herself to the civil rights movement. She remembered the key questions before her at Tougaloo: Was she willing to participate in some sort of demonstration, and if police arrested her, would she agree to refuse bail? Police did not intervene to detain her or any of the others in their attempts to worship at white churches in Jackson, but she considered her role in the visitation campaign a first step in her involvement in the movement. A few days before she left Tougaloo, she and other volunteers met Fannie Lou Hamer in her home. This experience was another seminal moment for Lisa Anderson Todd, because after seeing what Hamer was going through, Todd questioned how she could go through her own life normally. When Todd left Tougaloo, she registered voters in Greensboro, North Carolina, attended the March on Washington in late August, and returned to Mississippi the next year for the Summer Project.[35]

In addition to the churches targeted since June and a few new Protestant churches, the work camp volunteers tried to attend worship services at Trinity Lutheran Church, the largest Lutheran church in the state. Here, the church visits set off a contentious six-month battle within the church, and then between the church and its synod over the issue of racial discrimination. The church's pastor was Rev. Wade Harold Koons, who, like Dr. Clark and Rev. Hulan, had served as pastor in Jackson for a decade. The three were part of a small group of like-minded ministers who worked behind the scenes to try to steer the church community toward racial moderation in the 1950s and early 1960s. Though unknown to the public, Rev. Koons was another white Jackson clergyman who helped minister to jailed Freedom Riders in 1961. He attended the interracial ministers' meetings earlier in the year, including the first meeting on May 23. Yet unlike most of his fellow ministers, he was not from the Deep South. He was born in Sycamore, Ohio, and served churches in Ohio, New York, and West Virginia before coming to Jackson. Until the civil rights demonstrations in May and June 1963, black visitors to Trinity Lutheran were a common occurrence. In 1955, Trinity's church council, the congregation's lay board, affirmed the right of black visitors to worship at any services there. Tougaloo students attended the church throughout the 1950s, and a black personal care assistant accompanied a handicapped member on many Sundays.[36]

Despite Trinity's open-door policy, church members acting on their own barred black visitors from attending worship on several Sundays in June and July. On June 30, when an integrated group presented themselves for worship, a church member blocked their entry. He told Rev. Koons, "Something special was going on and visitors could not be admitted," referring to recent announcements throughout the local media of church visitation attempts at white churches in Jackson. This action prompted the church council to reconsider the congregation's attendance policy at their next meeting. On July 1, the church council voted to reaffirm Trinity's open-door policy. Dissatisfied with the result, segregationist members of Trinity circulated a petition asking the church council to put the matter to a vote by the entire church. At a special session of the church council on July 9, Rev. Koons advised the council that the petition was out of order, but the council voted to call a referendum on August 25 in which all members would decide whether or not to allow African Americans to worship.[37] In the meantime, advocates for both sides prepared for the vote by bringing in outside leverage. Complicating the situation was the fact that Rev. Koons was on vacation on the Sundays when black visitors tested the church's policy.

On July 21, twelve black and white work camp volunteers attempted to attend worship at Trinity, the first time an integrated group tried to enter since a church member turned away students on June 30. The July 21 team included a white Lutheran pastor and his wife from Tucson, Arizona. Despite the Church Council's recent reiteration of the congregation's open-door policy, a group of church members again took it upon themselves to bar the couple's entry.[38] The vice-president of the church council, Fred Patton, was deeply disturbed that a few men acted in violation of the council's policy by prohibiting black visitors on two Sundays following the July 1 resolution. In advance of the impending church-wide vote that would resolve the issue, Patton contacted Dr. Raymond D. Wood, the president of the Southeastern Synod of the Lutheran Church of America (LCA), to see if he could provide support for those church members who wanted open doors. At the annual synod meeting in May, which Patton attended as a delegate, the synod adopted a resolution recommending, but not mandating,

that churches "make no restrictions on the basis of race in the membership, the worship, and the outreach of service of our congregations." The
synod urged Lutheran churches to "do now what is possible . . . to eliminate discrimination in their own lives by developing an inclusive ministry,
and striving for racial justice in the communities where they 'witness.'"[39] Dr.
Wood wrote Patton a response to his letter, which Patton then forwarded to
all the members of Trinity. He asserted that the synod, which encompassed
Mississippi, Alabama, Georgia, and Tennessee, was "encouraging our pastors and congregations to welcome all races to Lutheran services and activities." He said that he knew of only a few churches that maintained closed-
door policies, but stressed there were many more that welcomed black
visitors. He pointed out that he knew of only one family in the entire synod
who left their church because of its open-door policy. Dr. Wood concluded
his letter by reminding Patton that statistics should not be the focus, for the
church should only do "the Christian thing . . . to do what Christ would do
under the circumstances." The synod's president believed that Christ "would
welcome all."[40]

In addition to circulating a copy of Dr. Wood's letter to all of Trinity's
members, Patton wrote his own. Making a considerably more impassioned
plea than the president's, Patton told his fellow members that by turning
away blacks from worship—and recognizing that these visits were broadcast on television and reported in newspapers—"We have set an example
to thousands of our white children that the Christian way to judge human
beings is by the color of their skin." He also directly countered his opposition's argument that church visitors did not really come to worship. He
concluded, "Even if the motivation was a completely evil one, and we do
not think any of our members believe their intent is really evil, then is it not
the purpose of our church to accept sinners with the hope that exposure to
Christ's teachings will reform them?"[41]

The Sunday after Trinity's members received Patton's circulars, including
a reminder that the position of the church council was to admit African
American visitors, the doors temporarily swung open. On July 28, an integrated group led by Rev. Harvey, the work camp's leader, successfully attended the early worship service and the adult Sunday school that followed.
A few members reported to Rev. Koons later that the group was "cordial,
quiet, and receptive in every way."[42] Anderson Todd remembered feeling especially welcome at Trinity, as the ushers seemed excited to see the visitors,
and the visiting minister specifically told her afterwards that the integrated group had an emotional impact on the congregation. Phillips, the lone

African American in the group, felt that it was almost inconspicuous. Rev. Harvey was not sure why the church allowed them in this Sunday, but he noted that a different crew of ushers was at the doors. One man in particular invited the members of the group to remain for Sunday school, which they did. Yet when the same group of students returned the next Sunday on August 4, a different set of men barred their entrance. In his report to the WCC, Rev. Harvey noted that the usher who allowed the students to enter and invited the group to Sunday school the week before must have done so at some personal risk, for the next Sunday the usher had a pained look and was unable even to speak with the students. Members told Rev. Koons, who was still away, that police swarmed the area that Sunday, and that segregationist members of the church guarded the doors.[43]

The successful entrance into Trinity Lutheran on July 28 infuriated Fritz Schluetter, a church member who contacted an investigator at the Mississippi State Sovereignty Commission the next day. Schluetter expressed his hope that Erle Johnston, the Sovereignty Commission's director, could provide the congregation a letter rebutting Dr. Woods and Patton ahead of the upcoming vote, and do anything else that could help prevent the integration of the church. For good measure, Schluetter identified by name all of the people involved that he could remember, including the two ushers who admitted the integrated group.[44]

In mid-August, Schluetter received a reply from the Sovereignty Commission's director, which he then circulated to other members of the church. Johnston began by countering Patton's assertion that the visitors were probably genuine or should be welcomed anyway as sinners needing Christ's direction. He argued that integrated groups were not sincere: "It is far more likely they are trying to prove a point or to make martyrs of themselves with the assistance of a few liberal members of your congregation." In addition, he reminded Schluetter of the church property law the Mississippi legislature had enacted a few years before; Johnston interpreted the statute to mean that a church is considered private property and belongs solely to the individual congregation. He concluded by reasoning that since blacks have their own churches, "nothing could be accomplished by opening the doors of your church to Negroes."[45]

In addition to furnishing the pro-exclusion forces inside Trinity Lutheran with a rationale for barring African Americans from the church, the Sovereignty Commission also looked into the visitors themselves. Sovereignty Commission investigator Virgil Downing spent three days in late July checking into the identity of the white volunteers at Tougaloo. Downing's activity report specifically identified Rev. Harvey, but not the others. Either unaware or unconcerned about the additional activities of the work camp volunteers, Downing wrote simply that these white individuals "are in Mississippi to sponsor integration of the white churches in Jackson."[46]

A few days before the congregational vote, all the members of Trinity Lutheran received an ominous letter from one of Jackson's two city commissioners, D. L. "Lock" Luckey Sr., a church member. His son, D. L. Luckey Jr., served on the church council. In the letter, which Luckey wrote on official city letterhead, he said that he was trying to stay out of the controversy but ultimately determined, "It has come to a point where one must show his color." He urged his fellow members to vote against "mixing," though he went on to say that the vote was irrelevant, since the city of Jackson considered such mixing to be a disturbance and thus a breach of peace. According to Luckey, even if a majority of the congregation favored open doors, integrated groups would still be arrested and charged with breaching the peace. Additionally, he suggested that Rev. Koons could face arrest, for "anyone, regardless of their official capacity, interfering with any officer of the law performing his duty will also be handled according to law." Commissioner Luckey reasoned that any arrests for breach of peace would hold up in court because the offense had been used effectively so far to deter local efforts by activists to desegregate public facilities.[47]

The members of Trinity Lutheran met in a special congregational session on August 25 to decide whether to allow African Americans to worship with them. The group of twenty-five members who presented the church council in July with the petition to call the meeting worded their resolution broadly—to Rev. Koons's mind, they did so to confuse people. The petitioners included Schluetter and George Mori, a member who was also on the executive committee of the Southeastern Synod. Rather than stating their true intentions and wording the policy as other churches had, the petitioners inverted the resolution to read, "Trinity Lutheran Church of Jackson will allow members of the Negro race to attend any or all of its activities." Though Rev. Koons tried to follow parliamentary procedure, he quickly realized that the meeting was turning into a farce. He noticed that Mori and Schluetter succeeded in bringing in all possible members, many of whom were not in good standing according to Rev. Koons. He reported to Dr. Franklin Clark Fry, the president of the Lutheran Church in America, that segregationists booed people who spoke out for the resolution, and that "the hissing and cursing by a woman was conduct not short of blasphemy in the House of the Lord." The segregationists would not even permit Rev.

Koons to speak. A motion to present an alternative resolution stating that the church would not discriminate on the basis of race and would admit all visitors to worship failed. When the members finally did vote on the original resolution, the vote was lopsided, 108 against the resolution to open doors and 42 in favor.

After the meeting, a church member told Rev. Koons, "I heard those same statements, the same hissing and booing in Germany as a little girl of five years." Rev. Koons called Dr. Raymond Wood later that day to inform him about the meeting, and Dr. Wood concluded that the "congregation had done nothing except waste its time," since the vote to reject the resolution was not exactly a vote to establish a new policy. Rev. Koons wrote Dr. Fry to explain the dire situation in Jackson, expressing fear that "anti-clergy and anti-church feeling" might spread to other churches and cities throughout the South. Though he firmly believed that he "c[ould] not close the door of the House of God to anyone who comes in a normal manner to worship or pray," he concluded pessimistically that Jackson was just not ready for an integrated congregation.[48]

Despite the confusion over what exactly church members accomplished at the August 25 meeting, segregationists clearly felt victorious. In a memo written a few days later, Johnston noted the Sovereignty Commission's role in the vote. He wrote that the commission "worked with a group opposing the integration and the Director wrote a letter outlining reasons for retaining segregation and gave it to the committee to be used as the committee wished." While one cannot precisely gauge the extent to which leverage from Director Johnston and the State Sovereignty Commission mattered in the church-wide vote to bar black visitors, it is important to appreciate the significance of the commission's involvement. Under Gov. Barnett, the commission had returned to its original mission created by the legislature in 1956: to investigate and compile dossiers on civil rights activists, in addition to offering "friendly persuasion" to counter pro-integration forces.[49] The commission had become increasingly watchful of activities on the campus of Tougaloo since 1961, when students from the college led the first sit-ins in Jackson and white students began attending Tougaloo. Commission staff members gathered information and speculation about Tougaloo professors and students, often sharing their research with leaders of the Jackson Citizens' Council. The presence of white people on the Tougaloo campus—especially students from Millsaps College and the work camp volunteers—became a particular concern in the preceding months. The commission even hired an informant from within Tougaloo who would visit the commission office with weekly reports on civil rights activities occurring on campus.⁵⁰

Yet by backing the effort to close the doors at Trinity Lutheran, the commission's director used the power of his office, a state agency, to help thwart the integration of a religious institution. Since there is no evidence of Sovereignty Commission intervention up to this point with any of the other churches that reconsidered their visitation policies, one must ask why the commission intervened at Trinity Lutheran. Part of the answer lies in the simple fact that a church member requested the director to become involved by providing a letter to "discourage and slow down" the integration movement within the church. In attempting to understand why Johnston was so eager to take up Schluetter's request, however, it is important to consider how much was at stake in the August vote.

When the church visits began on June 9, all of the white Protestant churches turned away black visitors. Yet the following Sunday, there was a crack in what had been a solidly all-white Protestant church community: St. Andrew's Episcopal admitted four black women. Despite being consistently turned away from most churches, however, the church visits continued unabated. St. Andrew's remained the only Protestant church open to black visitors until July 28, when Trinity Lutheran briefly allowed integrated groups to worship with the congregation. Some observers would judge the church visit campaign so far as a resounding failure, for only two white Protestant churches out of the dozen visited opened their doors, and only one of those consistently did so. The church visitors themselves no doubt felt increasingly discouraged, as ushers or policemen repeatedly barred their entrance into worship services. Yet, some segregationists must have sensed that they were in danger of losing control of their churches. Moreover, they understood that once their churches succumbed to the forces of integration, the logic that buttressed other aspects of their all-white society would be jeopardized. In the case of Trinity, the future of the church was clearly up for grabs. On one side, the head of the church council, the church's pastor, and the president of the regional synod called for open doors. With ecclesiastical support unavailable, backers of a closed-door policy turned to one of the key enforcers of racial discrimination in Mississippi, the state government. Johnston willingly intervened because he recognized that the church visits succeeded in integrating one church and were on the verge of succeeding at another church. As the director of a state agency responsible for sustaining segregation, he hoped to prevent another victory for the activists.

The involvement of the Sovereignty Commission in the affairs of a Jackson church is therefore one way to consider the effects of the church visit campaign through the summer of 1963. The church heightened the visibility of Jim Crow in the city's Christian congregations, forcing white church members to confront segregation in a facet of their weekly routine in a place that had been unchallenged as a sanctuary for racial purity. In September, students returned to Tougaloo for the fall semester. Many of them had recently traveled with Rev. King to the nation's capital to participate in the March on Washington.[51] When students resumed church visits in September, it became clear that pro-segregationist forces were not content merely to turn away the students as they had done before. After the Citizens' Council announced a campaign to "save Jackson churches from integration," police suddenly began arresting the integrated groups of church visitors. Like Erle Johnston of the State Sovereignty Commission, the Citizens' Council and their police allies understood they were in danger of losing their churches to integration.

[7]

"Saving the Churches from Integration"
AUGUST-OCTOBER 1963

B y the end of the August 1963, a few church doors were beginning to crack open—and beginning to crack open the city of Jackson. Defying an injunction that gave the police the ability to arrest those engaging in kneel-ins on church property or participating in any type of demonstration, integrated groups had sought entrance to thirteen different white congregations in Jackson on various weekends throughout the summer. Two of those churches, St. Peter's Roman Catholic and St. Andrew's Episcopal, regularly permitted black students to worship with the white members, while one church, Trinity Lutheran, temporarily opened their doors to integrated groups but then closed them again. Ushers at the rest of the churches, often backed up by policemen, turned the activists away. The police refrained from making arrests, despite their apparent power to do so owing to the June injunction. In the two months since the beginning of the campaign, the church visits forced many Jackson congregations to consider the issue of segregation in a Christian context and precipitated internal disputes over the churches' racial polices. Those controversies had already caused the resignation of ministers in two Methodist churches, and a similar dispute was threatening the pastorate at a third Jackson church.

After nearly a decade as minister of First Christian Church, Rev. Roy S. Hulan's status suddenly became uncertain following the barring of two black women from worship services on June 16. Though unaware of what his ushers had done outside the church doors, that Sunday Rev. Hulan delivered a sermon centered on the brotherhood of man. He specifically denounced the exclusion of anyone from the house of God on account of race. After sensing no reaction from his congregation, he delivered a much more impassioned and, by his own admission, furious message the

following week. He later confessed that his anger was not directed at anyone in particular, though many did take it personally. For his part, he said
he resented "what had happened in a church where I had been preaching
the gospel of reconciliation for nine years." He condemned his flock for not
understanding Christ's teachings and for not even conducting themselves
as a Christian body, since "the Church of Jesus Christ has no color bars at
its doors." Additionally, Rev. Hulan responded to the rationale—that they
obviously did not sincerely come to worship—for barring the two young
women from the morning service. Rev. Hulan countered, "It is not for us to
judge. Many people come to the church every Sunday. No one stops them
and asks, 'Do you come to worship or not?' I am sure that many come from
quite different motivation, but they come, and are admitted." Though most
in the congregation did not react positively to his plea, it certainly made an
impression on some members. Dr. Carl Brannan, a friend of Rev. Hulan and
an elder in the church, was particularly struck by Rev. Hulan's insistence
that by enforcing a color bar the congregation forsook any claim to being a Christian church.[1] It is not clear whether the elders wanted to bolster
their previous moves or sought to deflect responsibility, but later that week,
they decided to put the church's exclusion policy to a church-wide vote. The
closed-door policy adopted in 1961 and reaffirmed earlier in 1963 had been
approved only by the board of elders and the general board. They set the
congregational vote for July 22.[2]

   As First Christian prepared for the vote, some members began an effort
to replace Rev. Hulan. While he was out of town, the elders held a meeting
in which the chairman presented ballots on the subject of whether or not to
keep Rev. Hulan as pastor. A few elders objected to the proceedings, since
Rev. Hulan was not present. When the elders met again with Rev. Hulan in
attendance, a majority gave him a vote of confidence. Yet from then on, Rev.
Hulan's position as minister became increasingly tenuous. On July 22, the
church voted overwhelmingly, 213 to 25, to forbid African Americans from
attending worship. Emboldened by this action, a group of members then
circulated a petition requesting the elders to put Rev. Hulan's status before
a church-wide vote as well. Ninety members signed. By church rules, the
elders had to act on the petition, and they agreed to set a congregational
meeting to vote on August 26.[3]

   Privately, Rev. Hulan admitted that the vote would go against him. While
his sermons since the first church visits provoked this effort to remove him
from the pulpit, he recognized that this was just the latest in a series of conflicts on human rights in which he stood apart from a significant segment

of his congregation. Rev. Hulan believed strongly in ecumenicalism, cham-
pioning the NCC when some of his members dubbed it a communistic
organization. Ever since his arrival in 1954, he had sought more catholic
dialogue in Jackson, as evidenced most recently by his participation in
Rev. King's interracial ministers meetings in May. Moreover, he recognized
that some members objected to his active involvement with Tougaloo College. First Christian had supported Tougaloo since 1954, when the college
merged with the Southern Christian Institute, a Disciples of Christ mission.
Unlike many of his members, who never felt comfortable with their role
as financial sponsors, Rev. Hulan embraced the relationship as an extension of Christian brotherhood. He frequently came to campus to speak at
chapel services and attend graduation ceremonies and meetings of the Mississippi Council on Human Relations. Much to the chagrin of many in his
church, he invited Tougaloo faculty and administration officials to attend
First Christian.[4] Rev. Hulan's personal connection to the college never wavered, even when the campus became a focal point for civil rights activity
in the state. From his perspective, his recent statements on race represented
the tipping point for many of his members, who resented his consistent association with Tougaloo and ecumenical groups.

As Rev. Hulan awaited his fate, the elders moved to preempt the August
26 vote by asking him to step down. At an August 15 meeting they prevented
him from attending, the board of elders adopted a resolution calling on him
to resign, citing a "schism" and arguing that it was their duty to "restore harmony, and to reconcile differences within the congregation." Recording his
reaction later, Rev. Hulan pointed out, "In inviting the minister to withdraw
the elders are inviting the wrong person. Why not invite the group of members originating the schism to withdraw?"[5] On August 20, he mailed a letter to all the members, declaring, "I have never been more confident in the
rightness of my stand than I am at the moment." Explaining his decision to
proceed with the church-wide vote, he reasoned, "For me to resign voluntarily now could be taken as an indication of a lack of conviction concerning what I believe, or unwillingness to take the consequences of preaching
the full gospel." He reminded his congregation that the church's covenant
assured the minister freedom of the pulpit, which he felt he was being denied. Rev. Hulan declared the ultimate issue to be one of loyalty, "loyalty
to Christ, loyalty to His Church, and loyalty to the Brotherhood in which
I have spent my life and ministry." He concluded by urging the church to
forget its differences with him and commit their lives anew to Christ and
the church.[6]

The Sunday before the congregational vote, Rev. Hulan delivered a sermon developing the issues he raised in his letter to the members. He preached from the fourth chapter of Luke, focusing on a key verse in which Jesus quotes from Isaiah, saying, "I have come to set at liberty those who are oppressed." Calling Jesus "*the* great Emancipator," Rev. Hulan proclaimed the four freedoms of faith: the freedom from sin and condemnation; the freedom of Christian brotherhood to worship in a community of believers; the freedom to interpret scripture guided by the Holy Spirit; and the freedom of the pastor to preach without restraint. He again explicitly stated that because of the freedom of brotherhood, "We have no right to invite or to debar any person from the Lord's table because it is Christ's invitation and not ours."[7]

On August 26, the congregation of First Christian voted 172 to 92 to ask for their pastor's removal. At the time, Rev. Hulan observed that a sizable portion of the church was filled that day with people he rarely saw, and some he did not recognize at all. Evidently, those wanting his removal lobbied families who had not attended the church recently, or indeed, at any time during his tenure to show up for the vote, a tactic evidently similar to one used at Trinity Lutheran the day before during a congregational vote on attendance policy. Rev. Hulan's son, Richard, estimates that the tally was about 50-50 among active members. He says that his father had no misgivings about his decision to take a stand. While Rev. Hulan regretted that he would never again act as the pastor of a large church in a major city, he had his self-respect. Following his dismissal, the Hulans left Jackson to return to Kentucky, where he accepted a new call and preached his first sermon at Cynthiana Christian Church on December 15.[8] With the exits of Dr. Selah, Rev. Furr, and Dr. Clark, Rev. Hulan's departure now marked the fourth time a Jackson pastor left a church over the issue of race, as black visitors subsequent failed attempts to attend worship at the respective churches made clear. Still, Rev. Hulan held the distinction of having been the only one effectively forced out of his pulpit by his congregation.

During the first week in September, new ministers arrived at Galloway Memorial and Capitol Street Methodist. At Galloway, Dr. Cunningham preached his first sermon, while a few blocks away, Rev. Seth Granberry ascended the pulpit at Capitol Street Methodist, replacing Dr. Clark. Rev. Granberry's new associate was Rev. Joe Way, who had transferred from the Meridian area earlier in the summer. One indication of the range of views regarding race and moderation within the congregation was Rev. Way's status as was one of the twenty-eight signers of the "born of conviction" manifesto. At this time, he was the only such pastor active in the city.[9]

Meanwhile, religious and political forces outside the state continued to discuss the issue of segregation and the church's role in sustaining it. At their annual meeting in New York, the WCC came out with their strongest statement yet about segregation in the church. The WCC, which had sponsored the summer work camp at Tougaloo, declared, "Only by removal of racial barriers can churches themselves faithfully preach the Gospel."[10] The issue of racial barriers in public accommodations was being considered by policymakers in Washington, DC, where Congress reconvened after the August recess, just days after the largest civil rights demonstration in American history. To "summarize" the Civil Rights Act of 1963 for readers, in May 1964, the Clarion-Ledger turned to John Satterfield, the outspoken segregationist and newly elected delegate to the Methodist General Convention in Pittsburgh. He published two lengthy essays on consecutive Sundays in early September, trying to demonstrate how the new law would provide "unlimited federal control of individuals, businesses, and the states."[11]

While most of the students had not yet returned to Tougaloo for the fall semester, several faculty and a few students tried to attend white churches during the first few weeks in September. On September 8, Professor Clarice Campbell, who had recently arrived at the school to take the social science position vacated by John Salter, wanted to worship at Galloway with another white faculty member and a Nigerian ministerial student. Even though the men guarding the doors were informed that the student was a clergyman from Nigeria, he was black, so the ushers turned the integrated group away.[12]

Rejected from Galloway, the three then went to First Unitarian Church. Though no integrated groups had attempted a visit there before, the new minister of First Unitarian, Rev. Donald A. Thompson, was an advocate for racial tolerance. As a non-Southerner and a former labor organizer, Rev. Thompson clearly stood apart from other white ministers in Jackson. Upon arriving in the city, he became involved with the Mississippi Council on Human Relations. His stand for integrated worship services was unambiguous, but some in the church were uneasy about the attention that they might receive. Ushers welcomed Campbell and the other two men inside, but one member told them they should not publicize their visit, since the authorities are watching them and since Unitarianism "is not a popularly accepted religion in this region." In the ensuing months, African Americans continued to attend First Unitarian, and by 1965, the church counted six blacks among its membership. That same Sunday, a group from Tougaloo was also admitted at a Presbyterian church whose minister had contacted Rev. King to request that the students attend. While ushers stood watch at other churches, this minister "met the students on the steps, and, waving the half dozen policemen on, ushered the students into the church."[13] With the admission of African Americans into these two churches, the church visit campaign had now successfully integrated four Jackson churches.

While the campaign began as an attempt to stir the consciences of white moderates in general, it intended to reach the hearts of the ministers in particular. For Christians well versed in biblical principles of spiritual equality, brotherhood, and love for neighbors, "to turn Negroes away from the white churches was harder to justify than from schools or movies." Yet since the murder of Medgar Evers, who led the first church visits, only three Protestant churches consistently seated African Americans. Rev. King had hoped that "these churches, in shock over Medgar's murder, might actually open their doors and let blacks and whites pray together."[14] Three months after Medgar's assassination, Rev. King had a similar hope after more bloodshed occurred, this time inside a black church two hundred miles away.

On Sunday, September 15, which was youth day at the Sixteenth Street Baptist Church in Birmingham, Alabama, a dynamite explosion near the outside wall of the church killed four girls and injured twenty-three more African Americans who were in the basement attending Sunday school. The lesson that morning was on "the love that forgives." The church bombing capped off the city's first week of school desegregation and punctuated a series of racially motivated bombings that had taken place in the city over the last several years. Yet up until this time, no one had been killed.[15] The murder of children in a house of God shook the country and caused some to place blame on Christians themselves. The editors of the *Mississippi Methodist Advocate*, for instance, encouraged "Christians to beg forgiveness of Almighty God for their sins of prejudice, of discrimination and violence against their fellow Americans," and expressed hope that "perhaps the death of four little girls will awaken the nation to the folly of racial injustice."[16]

For Rev. King, the connection between closed white church doors and bombed-out black churches was axiomatic, for "surely the path from the locked and guarded white sanctuaries led to the bloody rubble, to the stained glass window of the Good Shepherd with the face of Christ blasted away." The night of the bombing, Rev. King led an integrated group back to Galloway, thus far the most visited church. The group included several students who had returned to campus, where orientation was set for Monday and classes were slated to begin the next week. Rev. King and the students thought, "In the aftermath and soul searching which must be going on after Birmingham, there might be some new opening or attitude in the white churches." While a group of Galloway men and women refused to allow the Tougaloo group inside to attend evening service, they did engage one another in conversation about the church bombing that morning. Rev. King recalled that the students talked about "the dead children, of their hopes that Mississippi could somehow work things out without all the violence and bloodshed of Birmingham." As the group guarding Galloway spoke, Rev. King sensed their attitudes had changed, as they appeared to be shocked and "no longer so sure that blocking the doors of their own church was quite 'the Christian thing to do.'" Nevertheless, they would not let the visitors enter. [17]

While Rev. King and the Tougaloo activists saw the Birmingham bombing as an opportunity to intensify their visitation campaign, the forces hoping to keep the church doors closed were just as emboldened to maintain the status quo. Through the summer and fall, segregationists used a variety of justifications to exclude African Americans from worship services, though questioning the sincerity of the visitors became the most frequent excuse. In practical terms, this reasoning seems disingenuous, for in order to remain consistent, a church would have to query everyone before he or she entered in order to gauge true motivations. Rev. Christoph Keller said as much to his vestry at St. Andrew's Episcopal when a few members objected to black visitors on the grounds they did not come to worship. Yet to those who favored closed-door policies, it seemed logical to prejudge the intentions of the black visitors. White church people felt they knew who the others were: They came from Tougaloo College, the center of civil rights activity in the state, and they were apparently led by Rev. King, someone already publicly marked as an agitator and lawbreaker. The visitors also seemed eager to publicize their interactions on the church steps, as evidenced by the presence of news media during some of the visits. If the students really wanted to worship God, they could do so, either back on campus or in their own all-black churches. [18]

In addition to doubting the sincerity of black visitors, segregationists employed other justifications borrowed from political discourse, particularly rebuttals to the civil rights bill currently working its way through Congress. Some focused on the principle that churches were private property, just like any business that happened to cater to the public. For instance, when ushers at Woodland Hills Baptist turned away Anne Moody on June 9, they told her that Woodland Hills was a "private house of God." While the ushers may not have realized the legal significance of their statement, a recently enacted state law set up the process whereby individual church members could gain the property rights to their building. In the 1960 decree, usually referred to as "the church property law," legislators empowered members of certain congregations to take possession of their property if they wished to break away from their denomination.[19] Even though the legislature meant for the bill to apply to churches wanting to secede, state government officials interpreted it to mean that churches were considered possessions of their local congregations, regardless of their churches' connections to specific denominations. For example, when Erle Johnston, head of the Mississippi State Sovereignty Commission, cited this logic in explaining his understanding of the legal position of an individual church in the state, he argued that a church is private property, just like any store or restaurant. Since the building itself was financed by the local congregation, members had "the legal and moral right to determine who uses it."[20] No one would dispute Johnston's point, yet he went a step farther, suggesting that the individual congregation was the church owner, not the denomination or even some combination of the two. The church members should therefore decide who "uses" the church, not some outside entity.

Additionally, those justifying the exclusion of black visitors often said that the outsiders' presence would disturb worship, and thus result in a "breach of the peace" that the June injunction specifically forbade. To be sure, both sides acknowledged some instances of indubitable disruption. On at least one occasion, Rev. King and the students knocked heavily on the outside doors of Galloway while worship continued inside and members received communion. Yet examples of actual disturbances were the exceptions rather than the rule. But segregationists felt that the mere presence of African Americans in the midst of a white church would disturb the worship service and represent a breach of the peace. When First Baptist turned away black students on June 9—even before that church officially voted on its closed-door policy and before actual disturbances had occurred—the usher simply told the students that their "presence would disrupt the worship of all our people."[21] In other words, the issue was not the sincerity of worship, but the fact that participation of an African American in worship would disrupt the racial purity inside the sanctuary. Dr. Cunningham, the new senior pastor at Galloway, later focused on this issue when he summed up the rationale behind his church's closed-door policy:

What were these faithful men guarding? It was the "time-honored tradition," as the resolution plainly stated. It was not religion they were
guarding. The resolution had said nothing about religion. It was the
"separation of the races," the Southern mystique, which the board
had said overwhelmingly it hoped would "never be impaired." But the
"time-honored tradition" of "the separation of the races" had itself become a religion.[22]

The "time-honored tradition" of "separation of the races" provided the peace
that the presence of African Americans would breach.

While the ushers utilized various rationales for excluding black visitors
throughout the summer of 1963, they began to receive support from one
of the primary public forces laboring to sustain segregation in Mississippi
and throughout the Deep South, the Citizens' Council. In the year since
the group suffered an unambiguous defeat with James Meredith's admission into the University of Mississippi, the Citizens' Council had seen its
grasp on Jackson slip as well. While still enjoying influence in all branches
of state and local government, the Jackson Citizens' Council leaders were
dismayed about recent concessions made by Mayor Thompson in the wake
of boycotts, sit-ins, and marches. Mayor Thompson agreed to hire six black
police officers, though those patrols would be limited to the black sections
of the city. Yet for the Jackson Citizens' Council executive committee, the
hiring "of these negro police men was unwise . . . and the idea should only
be regarded as an experiment." The leaders reasoned that the mayor's decision only created a new set of problems, since it opened the possibility that
the black policemen would "be permitted to utilize the police clubhouse
with their families," and would be allowed to "attend the policemen's ball
and other social functions with their families." Additionally, the executive
council felt that the admission of several African Americans into the main
downtown public library could "not be tolerated." [23] If allowing even token
integration of a public facility a block from the governor's mansion was not
deflating enough, the fact that this library had been the site of the state's first
sit-in two and a half years before gave its opening added significance. Now,
the executive committee recommended either closing the main branch, or
removing "all chairs, tables, etc. . . . in order that it may remain open for the
use of both races—on a stand-up basis." [24]

Additionally, the opening up of several Protestant churches to black
visitors alarmed the leaders of the Jackson Citizens' Council. In an August newsletter to council members, the executive committee expressed

gratitude that only a few churches had admitted "negro demonstrators," adding that "in view of the numerous assaults upon our Churches each Sunday this is an excellent record." Yet, pointing to "a 'secret group' within one of the churches" that permitted African Americans to enter without church-wide approval, they warned council members that "integration doesn't just happen—in every case it is an 'inside job.'"[25] The newsletter urged members to "take immediate steps to remove this 'Secret Group' from positions of authority and save their Church from integration." Moreover, the executive council pointed out that "several candidates for our Legislature have the backing of one or more 'secret-groups' dedicated to school and Church integration," so members should "be sure that these would-be integrationists are defeated!"[26] Whether it was the integration of a school or a church, for the leaders of the Citizens' Council, the mechanism for change was the same. The will of the majority was being thwarted by a determined minority.

Since Jackson Citizens' Council meetings and rallies were open to the public, and no record of their membership from the early 1960s exists, it is difficult to quantify precisely the degree of council influence within Jackson churches. Nevertheless, it is significant that individuals inside and out of many of the churches perceived a heavy Citizens' Council presence. Of the churches targeted up to this point, one council leader recalled that he and other leaders and members filled crucial lay positions at First Baptist, Galloway, and First Presbyterian. Additionally, former members at Calvary Baptist and Woodland Hills Baptist also recalled a vocal Citizens' Council presence among the deacons at their churches.

For Dr. Cunningham, the Citizens' Council held special sway at Galloway. During his first official board meeting in September, he realized the extent to which pro-council sentiment prevailed when no one objected to the distribution of Citizens' Council literature by John Wright to other board members. During his tenure at Galloway, Dr. Cunningham concluded that "no major decisions were made in board meetings that did not square with the Citizens' Council," and that "without a doubt a prime factor in creating the closed door policy at Galloway was the powerful Citizens' Council backed by the awesome might of the State Sovereignty Commission."[27]

From the outside, Rev. King and his student volunteers perceived that the Citizens' Council was behind the effort to keep the church doors closed, and was trying to solidify control over all the churches. A summary of this stage of the campaign, written a few months later, cited one familiar threat apparently utilized by the council in local churches. With local banks being well represented in positions of leadership in the Jackson Citizens' Council, lay leaders who had their own businesses were suddenly told that they would not receive any more loans unless they kept their church doors closed. Students also indicated that some council members were transferring memberships from one church to another so that exclusion policies would prevail.[28] While this evidence does not provide a complete picture of the Citizens' Council's presence in Jackson churches, significantly, a range of individuals nonetheless believed that the council exerted a strong influence over many churches in the city.

In an interview over forty years later, W. J. Simmons, the administrator for the Citizens' Council in the early 1960s acknowledged the influence the council maintained in many Jackson churches, but he could not recall specifically what the group did to "save their churches from integration." He recalled that the other issues on the table, particularly school desegregation in the state and the lobbying against the passage of Pres. Kennedy's civil rights legislation, stood out.[29] While Simmons was speaking in hindsight, the newsletters of the Jackson Citizens' Council at the that time continued to focus on the efforts to integrate local churches, thus demonstrating council leaders' concern about the steps of white Jackson churches becoming a battleground over segregation. In one important sense, it was one of the few local battlegrounds. As Rev. King pointed out, conversations between integrated groups and church guards were the only meaningful interracial discussions occurring in the city at that time.[30] Significantly, the August newsletter only mentioned one church that needed to be saved from integration, indicating that Citizens' Council leaders felt other churches were not yet in danger of opening their doors. Yet by late September, the dynamics had clearly shifted. Two more Jackson churches, one of which had turned away visitors back in June, now opened their doors.[31] Moreover, the September 15 church bombing in Birmingham that killed four girls provoked near-universal horror and strengthened the resolve of those trying to end racial injustice. The attempted worship at Galloway the night of the bombing indicated that groups from Tougaloo had no intention of stopping the church visits. If anything, with all the students returning to Tougaloo for the first time since early June, this effort demonstrated that a more intensive and sustained campaign of church visits was possible.

Six days after the Birmingham church bombing and three days after classes restarted at Tougaloo, the Jackson Citizens' Council demonstrated how significant the church visit campaign had become by clarifying their plan to "save these churches from integration." Acknowledging the developments of the last month, leaders of the Citizens' Council pointed out, "There have been instances of additional churches admitting negroes since our last newsletter," and added that council felt that "it is time to come forward with a positive plan of action." The council implored its supporters to remember, "Mixing of the races certainly does *not* have the backing of the majority of the congregation in *every single case*." (emphasis original) Recognizing that some would perceive council involvement as meddling in the internal affairs of individual churches, the group's leaders defended their proposal by pointing out, "The matter of church integration has become a concern to many of our members." The council announced a series of meetings with lay leaders representing various denominations, which would lead to a more comprehensive strategy "to eliminate church integration entirely." In the meantime, the council urged its members to contact the information and education committee of the Jackson Citizens' Council if they had any problems with efforts to integrate their own churches.[32]

To bolster the new Citizens' Council plan, the following day the front page of the *Clarion-Ledger* gave theological support to church segregation, printing a two-thousand word broadside titled "The Role of the Lord's People: Evangelization, Not Equalization, Said to Be Task of the Church." Written by Dr. Clay Cooper, president of Vision, Inc., the essay emphasized the principle of submission before the law, and noted the apparent absence of notions of social equality in Christ's teachings. Rather than laboring for the equalization of mankind, Christians should endeavor to "avoid entanglement in worldly disputation," just as "our apostolic predecessors" did. For if "they lived with the status quo, for the sake of Christ and His kingdom, then we also can and must." For the Hedermans and other segregationists, upholding the status quo by maintaining closed church doors was now more crucial than ever.[33]

For Rev. King and others working to end the segregationist hold on white churches in Mississippi, the meaning and timing of the Citizens' Council announcement was clear. Rev. King felt that in the "wake of the Birmingham tragedy, the soul of the white Christians had been touched," and the Citizens' Council feared that they were losing control of the churches, that the climate would permit the churches' closed-door policies to change. Hazel Brannon Smith, editor of the *Lexington Advertiser* and Jackson's weekly *Northside Reporter*, interpreted the pronouncement to mean that the Citizens' Council was "going to take over the job of preventing the integration of Jackson churches." While God and the minister guided churches before, she wrote, "the Citizens' Council intends to replace both as the power in the church in Mississippi."[34]

The Citizens' Council pronouncement did not alter the strategy of Rev. King, who was determined to renew the church visit campaign after the Birmingham bombing. Moreover, Tougaloo students were back from their summer break, and many were enthusiastic about continuing the weekly visits. Joan Trumpauer, one of the student leaders, arrived back on campus with the mindset that church visitation should be one of the tactics the movement should employ. Because of her previous arrests, she worried about participating as a visitor. She therefore decided to take a behind-the-scenes role as a coordinator for the effort. Once Rev. King and other adults decided upon which churches to target, she recruited participants and organized drivers, aiming to have someone—sometimes herself—act as a spotter, remaining at a distance and observing the encounters.[35] While no one at Tougaloo knew precisely what the council meant by its pronouncement, other than intensifying the pressure on lay leaders to preserve the racial purity of their congregations, soon it became clear that the campaign was entering a new phase.

Just as the Jackson Citizens' Council announced its plan to "save these churches from integration," the church doors at Trinity Lutheran suddenly swung back open. Ushers at Trinity admitted an integrated group on September 22, much to the surprise of the students and segregationist church members who thought that lopsided vote on August 25 clarified the church's stance. Following the congregational meeting that shot down a resolution to maintain an open-door policy, the church council instructed its ushers on September 2 to tell black visitors who presented themselves for worship of the new policy at Trinity Lutheran dictating that African Americans could not enter. The council directed ushers to add that the council "regrets the decision very much and hopes that it will be changed in the future." Yet on September 22, for reasons that are unclear but likely included the influence of Rev. Wade Koons and lay leader Fred Patton, ushers admitted two female students, one black and one white, into the late morning worship service.[36]

Given the ushers' actions, especially against the backdrop of the Citizens' Council's announcement, segregationists within Trinity proceeded with more drastic action. Someone again notified state authorities, this time the Mississippi Bureau of Investigation. A case report by the bureau specifically blamed Rev. Koons for letting the integrated group in on September 22. Moreover, demonstrating the extent to which the investigators were willing pressure on the Koons family, the case report indicated, "Rev. Koons' wife, Katherine Koons, is presently teaching school at the Poindexter School" and "[it] is believed that she is probably indoctrinating the minds of her pupils with the NAACP doctrines." When the case report reached the desk of Erle Johnston, director of the Sovereignty Commission, he wrote a letter to the superintendent of schools informing him of the Koons's racial views. Johnston passed on the rumor that Mrs. Koons "is indoctrinating some of the students with beliefs contrary to ours."[37] Then on September 24, five Trinity members co-signed and sent Rev. Koons a letter asking him to resign. Fritz Schluetter, the letter's author, reminded him that it was customary to change pastorates every five to six years, but added, "Recent and current events have contributed and aggravated the already existing feeling of dissatisfaction to many of our members until they have expressed the feeling that it is almost unbearable to attend services." Rev. Koons sent a copy of the letter to Dr. Raymond Wood, president of the Southeastern Synod. Wood, knowing that a majority on the council backed Rev. Koons, advised him that he should call a special meeting of the church council to expose the conspirators and to settle the issue definitively. The meeting occurred several days later with Dr. Wood in attendance, and a motion asking Rev. Koons not to resign passed eight to four.[38]

As the Tougaloo activists made preparations for visits to seven churches on October 6, Rev. King learned directly for the first time that Jackson police might arrest black visitors. On Saturday, October 5, he called several ministers whose churches would be targeted the next day to tell them they "were not going to try to trick them and sneak into their church by surprise," and to "put a burden on their conscience because with this knowledge came responsibility and made it harder for the ministers to plead that they had no idea what was being done by their usher-guards." One of the ministers he talked to was Rev. Granberry, the new pastor at Capitol Street Methodist. The two men knew each other quite well, for Rev. Granberry had served at Rev. King's church in Vicksburg when he was in high school. In fact, Rev. King found Rev. Granberry to be instrumental both in his decision to pursue the ministry and, ironically, in what he later wrote were his "first questions about segregation that came as a result of my developing loyalty to the church and the teachings of the national Methodist Church through the youth leaders of the Mississippi church." Yet when it came to the issue of a minister's role in the segregated South, Rev. Granberry preferred not to challenge the status quo. He accepted the position of pastor at Capitol Street knowing the church's closed-door policy and resolving to work within its limitations. But unlike Dr. Selah or his predecessor, Dr. Clark, he never publicly voiced his disapproval of the policy.[39] He told Rev. King that regardless of his personal beliefs on race, he could not take a stand one way or the other, because it "would only divide the congregation and cause trouble, hostility, pain, and turmoil." He felt that as a pastor, he needed to maintain the open contact and trust of those in his congregation so that he could continue to fulfill his pastoral duties. In an interview years later, Rev. Granberry's son, Seth Granberry Jr., said he believed that his father was indeed trying to steer his church away from a policy of exclusion. Yet a core group of lay leaders remained adamant, preventing the integration of Capitol Street. As Seth Granberry Jr. concluded, his father's hands were tied if he wanted to stay.[40]

Late that Saturday night, Rev. Granberry and Rev. King talked for an hour about their convictions and discussed what would happen the next day. Significantly, October 6 was World-Wide Communion Sunday, when churches from around the United States and the world joined together in a symbolic communion service demonstrating unity and "rising above the boundaries of nation and denomination by remembering together the boundless love of God." Rev. Granberry told Rev. King he had no control over what would occur on Sunday, that ushers would turn away students in keeping with the church's closed-door policy adopted before he arrived at the church. While Rev. King fully expected ushers to deny the students admittance, he wanted some assurance from Rev. Granberry that students would be allowed to engage the ushers in dialogue, and to pass out copies of Martin Luther King Jr.'s "Letter from a Birmingham Jail" to any member who would receive them outside the church. According to Rev. King, Rev. Granberry cautioned him, "This time the Jackson city police might arrest the students." Despite the state's anti-demonstration statutes and the June injunction prohibiting acts of civil disobedience that resulted in any "breach of peace," including kneel-ins, Jackson police had maintained a presence outside the churches, but refrained from arresting any visitors. Given this four-month precedent, Rev. King told Rev. Granberry that he "did not believe any arrests were probable."[41] At the time, Rev. Granberry's warning did not seem significant, but it was the first time any minister or usher said anything about possible police intervention.

On Sunday, integrated groups of students sought entrance at seven Jackson churches. Ushers turned the students away from all of the churches except St. Peter's Roman Catholic, which had consistently admitted black students since the first church visits in June. Students returned to Capitol

Street Methodist, First Christian, Galloway Methodist, and Trinity Lutheran, but also tried to attend worship at two churches that had not yet been
targeted, Fondren Presbyterian and Our Redeemer Lutheran.

Fondren Presbyterian's long-time pastor was Dr. J. Moody McDill, who
attended the interracial ministers meetings in May and who, during his long
tenure at the church, had become a consistent voice for racial tolerance in
the city. Some members recalled that within the context of Jackson's closed
society, Fondren was known as "the liberal church," for unlike many of the
other Protestant churches in the city, no outspoken or militant segregationists attended Fondren.[42] Dr. McDill felt that he had given enough of a theological foundation for human equality during his ministry, and that most of
his members would accept black visitors. So at some point in the early fall,
he contacted one of the adult Tougaloo leaders requesting a visit from the
group. This message was relayed to Rev. Bill Hutchinson, a white Tougaloo
instructor in speech and drama who was ordained a Presbyterian minister
over the summer. He and his wife and daughter had been members of Fondren since they arrived in Jackson the year before. The Hutchinsons had
joined both Tougaloo and Fondren the previous fall, but they immediately
felt ostracized within the congregation because of their connection to the
college. Rev. Hutchinson was reluctant to get involved in the civil rights
movement locally when he first arrived, feeling that his duty was to teach.
Yet as his students became involved and he saw the violence directed at
them, he knew that he could not stand on the sidelines any longer. He accompanied students to an attempted visit to a white Baptist church in the
spring, and police arrested him as part of the May 30 kneel-in at the Federal
Building downtown. At Dr. McDill's suggestion, Rev. Hutchinson agreed to
accompany a black and a white student, but fearing for his family's safety,
his wife and five-month-old daughter stayed at home.[43]

As at other Jackson churches, in session meetings throughout the summer lay leaders at Fondren Presbyterian debated whether or not to admit
black visitors, but they had not yet officially decided what to do. In late September, the elders received a request from the diaconate that the session
formulate a written policy regarding the seating of African Americans, and
the session tried to do so over the next two weeks. At one meeting, the session held a preliminary vote on a draft that would encourage black visitors to try to attend church elsewhere, but that "if the conscience of such
individuals still lead[s] them to request admittance to the service, they will
be seated." It passed six to four, but the elders delayed a final vote until the
full session was in attendance. At another meeting (coincidentally, an hour

before black students attempted to attend morning worship on October 6), elders discussed a different proposal that would prohibit individuals or groups who came "for demonstration purposes, such as having a photographer or police present or having notified the church that they are coming." Yet as with the policy they reflected upon the week before, they tabled the amendment until a meeting of the full session.

When Rev. Bill Hutchinson and the two students arrived that morning, there no specific attendance policy was in effect, though the only vote taken indicated a slim majority did want the doors open. Rev. Hutchinson felt it was a particularly appropriate Sunday to bring guests since, like other churches in the city that day, Fondren was celebrating World-Wide Communion Sunday. To the shock of Dr. McDill and many others present, including the state's secretary of treasury, William Winter, some of the church's deacons acted on their own initiative and refused to let Rev. Hutchinson, a church member, and his student guests enter.[44]

Ushers at Our Redeemer Lutheran Church also turned away an integrated group. Our Redeemer Lutheran was part of the Missouri Synod, a more conservative Lutheran denomination than the Lutheran Church of America, with which Trinity Lutheran was affiliated. One of the ushers read a prepared statement explaining the church's justification for excluding the group. The rationale was familiar. By a majority vote, the statement read, the members of Our Redeemer Lutheran determined, "Any group not accustomed to attending the regular services of our church would interfere with the spirit of reverence and dignity of such services." Additionally, the statement pointed to "present day tensions and misunderstandings among various groups of people," and the fact that "there is a Negro Congregation of like faith and order in our city where such sincere Christians can worship and serve." The usher then indicated that he would call the police if the visitors did not leave the premises. Wanting to avoid a possible confrontation, the integrated group departed.[45]

Three Tougaloo students arrived at Capitol Street Methodist Church after being followed from the gates of the college by a police car. One of the students, Julie Zaugg, an exchange student from the Chicago area, was white, while the other two, Ida Hannah and Bette Anne Poole, were African American. Hannah was the only native Mississippian in the group, having grown up in Leake County just north of Jackson. She learned racial difference, as many other Southern African Americans did, as a young girl. Hannah recognized discrepancies between her schooling and that of white children with whom she played. For instance, she discovered that her textbooks were her friends' discarded schoolbooks, and that the subjects she was learning did not correspond to those of her white counterparts. She met Medgar Evers when he set up an NAACP youth chapter at a junior college she attended, but it was not until his murder that she vowed to actively join the movement. Hannah transferred to Tougaloo in September 1963 as a sophomore and quickly began participating in the church visit campaign, feeling that if the two races could worship together, then they could understand each other better.[46]

Bette Poole, like Julie Zaugg, counted Chicago as home, but Poole was born in Texas and lived for a while in Mississippi. As a young child, she first encountered racism when she saw how frightened her mother was of a white policeman in Texas. Her father, a Baptist preacher who died when she was nine, always reminded her that nobody was better than she, a lesson she continued to struggle with as she traveled back and forth between the different worlds of Chicago and the South. She experienced racism on those trips, saw demonstrations on the television as young girl, and resolved to be one of the freedom fighters. Now Poole was a rising senior at Tougaloo and a committed activist in the Jackson movement, having participated in the boycotts and demonstrations, the first church visits in June, and SNCC voter canvassing in Jackson over the summer.[47]

The Capitol Street bulletin announced the special program for World-Wide Communion Sunday. When the time came for the "Examination of Conscience," the bulletin stated that the minister would lead the congregation in a responsive prayer taken from the Gospel of Matthew, saying, "The first commandment is . . . thou shalt love the Lord thy God with all thy soul, and with all thy mind, and with all thy strength. The second is this: Thou shalt love thy neighbor as thyself. There is none other commandment greater than these."[48] As Poole, Hannah, and Zaugg approached the church steps, an usher met them on the sidewalk and asked them what they wanted. They told him that they "came to worship," to which he replied, "You are not welcome." At this point, a policeman, who, according to Rev. Granberry was there to direct traffic, came over to the students and the usher. He told the students to move along, since they were not welcome. After the women pointed out that this was World-Wide Communion Sunday, the policeman told them, "You have other nigger churches to go to." According to Poole's testimony, the officer gave the students two minutes to leave, but then grabbed and cursed at her. When the three turned to leave, after only a few second the policeman said, "You waited too long," and motioned to the other police officers who were parked across the street. The policemen then grabbed the women, pushed them into a police car, and told them they were under arrest. As the students left the premises in police cars, the officers still had not informed the three of the charges against them.

Jackson police questioned the group that afternoon, and a municipal court judge tried and sentenced them the next day. During the interrogation, one of the officers tried to question their motivation for trying to attend Capitol Street Methodist and pulled out a church offering envelope. He threw it at them, saying, "Why didn't you just use this?" Unbeknownst to the officer, the envelope was especially designated for World-Wide Communion Sunday and bore a picture of five hands of five different colors. One of the three detainees seized the opportunity and pointed at the envelope, answering, "That's exactly what I was trying to do." Even though the three never stepped off the sidewalk and never raised their voices, the police charged them with breaking two Mississippi statutes, trespassing and disturbing divine worship. Significantly, Jackson authorities did not cite or utilize the June injunction in the charges, but instead relied upon state laws, one of which—outlawing trespassing—city officials employed when charging demonstrators in late May. With no lawyer present at the trial or during any part of the questioning the day before, the students pled no contest. They were sentenced to one year in jail, and bond was set at $1,000 each, the highest sentence and bond yet for a civil rights demonstrator in Mississippi.[49] Though the judgment was consistent with the dictates of the recently enacted state anti-demonstration statutes, the broader meaning of Mississippi justice for dissenters was all too apparent. As the next issue of the *Mississippi Free Press* pointed out, the white men accused of bombing Sixteenth Street Baptist Church three weeks earlier were given a three-month jail sentence and fined $100 each.[50]

Unprepared for the arrests, Rev. King hurried to try to get the women out of jail and to investigate why police took them into custody in the first place. With the arrests occurring outside a Methodist church, Rev. King tried contacting Bishop Franklin, but he was out of town. Bishop Franklin later pled with Rev. King to stop the visits, insisting that the protestors had proved their point and were now just bringing bad publicity on the Methodist Church in Mississippi. Rev. King spoke with Rev. Granberry and various lay leaders to ask them to intervene, but they deflected responsibility. Rev. Granberry gave Rev. King more details from his conversation with the police earlier in the week, saying, "I wasn't asked, I was told if ya'll came and were not admitted you'd be arrested."[51] In effect, Rev. Granberry was telling Rev. King that the church had not asked for the arrests, and there was nothing he could do because the police acted on their own. With Methodist leaders in Mississippi declining to help get the young women out of jail, Rev. King turned to denomination leaders in New York and Washington, DC, who were already at work trying to understand the situation in Jackson and taking steps to bail the students out.

Ann C. Brown, general secretary of the Woman's Division of Christian Service of the Board of Missions of the Methodist Church in New York City, learned of the arrests just as many others had, reading of it in the Monday edition of the *New York Times*. She telephoned a friend, Bess Arrington, a member of Galloway Memorial Methodist, who told her what she knew of the incident, and then telephoned Thelma Stevens, chairman of staff of the Christian Social Relations of the Woman's Division. Brown and Stevens then called Dr. A. Dudley Ward of the General Board of Christian Social Concerns (GBCSC) of the Methodist Church and J. Moore of CRR, neither of which knew about the arrests in Jackson. Brown and Stevens made contact with Rev. King, who explained that the three students did not think they were taking part in any sort of demonstration, and were not part of the NAACP or any other civil rights organization. He told the Methodist leaders that the students decided upon church visitation because they wanted to do "some small thing to show how they felt . . . as they did not want to do anything to lead to arrest." Rev. King added that the three simply wanted to attend World-Wide Communion Sunday. Satisfied that their motives were pure, the Methodist leaders now resolved that the denomination was accountable and must furnish the bail money to get the three students out of jail. Brown felt that "this was peculiarly a Methodist responsibility and more peculiarly a Woman's Division responsibility" because of the Woman's Division's own "Charter of Racial Policies" and because the three Tougaloo students were women. Brown and Stevens talked with other members of the Woman's Division administrative committee and voted to share the $3,000 bond with the GBCSC. Each group pledged $1,500 of the total. The irony of the situation was immediately clear to Professor Clarice Campbell, who wrote, "This might suggest an interesting pattern whereby every denomination would assume responsibility for raising bail to release persons who find themselves in jail for having tried to worship in its particular denomination."[52]

Grover C. Bagby of the GBCSC explained the involvement of his division in securing bond money for the three women in a newsletter, concluding that all Methodists "must face squarely the fact that this kind of arrest should never have been possible in the first place." He acknowledged that some

Methodists were likely unsympathetic to the tactic of kneel-ins, where black activists tried to gain access to churches where they were not wanted. Even so, Bagby believed that the activists did not create the problem; kneel-ins were a response to prejudice, a problem that already existed. In addition to citing bigotry as a source of the dilemma, Bagby argued that Methodists and other Christians had lost sight of the true nature of the church. While many regarded their church as a private institution that held the right to choose with whom it would associate, a rationale sustained partly by the enduring segregation in the structure of the Methodist Church itself, Bagby maintained that the "Church is of God." Since God did not favor one man over the other, Christians could not act "as judges of our fellow men as to their fitness to attend 'our' churches." He urged his fellow Methodists to resolve the contradiction between the prejudicial structures within the church and official pronouncements in the most recent Methodist Church *Discipline* that the "House of God must be open to the whole family of God."[53]

Brown, Ward, and Bagby consulted with each other and with John Pratt, the attorney for the CRR, about steps they needed to take beyond providing bail. They agreed that a representative needed to go to Jackson and stay through the weekend to observe the church visits. The three Methodist leaders also decided they would call a few sympathetic Methodist bishops. With the next Council of Bishops gathering scheduled for Detroit, Michigan, in mid-November, they felt that the bishops could push through a special appeal for help in Jackson.[54]

Predictably, the October 6 arrest of three young women trying to enter a whites only church received extensive news coverage in the city and throughout the country. The *Clarion-Ledger* emphasized the students' apparent unwillingness to move off the church grounds, reporting, "Police were called when they refused to leave." The *Mississippi Methodist Advocate* called the arrests "a tragedy of errors," expressing shock that the arrests occurred on a day that "has been set aside by the Christian World for people of all creeds and nationalities to unite in observing Holy Communion." In contrast to the account given in the *Clarion-Ledger*, the editors of the *Mississippi Methodist Advocate* blamed the police, since the women never stepped on church property and "the Church did *not* call the police and the Church did *not* place a complaint of trespassing or disturbing public worship." (emphasis original)

In addition to receiving coverage in Mississippi periodicals, the arrests of the students attracted national attention for the first time since the church visit campaign began in June. Hannah's parents found out about their

daughter's arrest by hearing her name read by David Brinkley on the evening news. The *New York Times* wrote a short summary of the arrests and
the other attempted visits that Sunday. With two of the students, Poole and
Zaugg, calling Chicago home, the arrest received extensive coverage in the
Chicago Daily News in the ensuing weeks. The October 8 edition led with
the front page headline, "They Went to Church—So Two Chicago Co-eds
Get Year in Dixie Jail." Reporter Nicholas von Hoffman gave updates on the
women and interviewed Rev. King, who expressed complete surprise at the
arrests. Rev. King noted, "This hasn't happened even in Birmingham."[55]

The three young women remained in jail for two nights before they were
released Tuesday, October 8. Owing to the conversations she had with the
policemen and cellmates, Hannah recalled her incarceration as the most
soul-searching part of the experience. One of the jailors seemed especially
moved by their witness, confessing to them how vital African Americans
were to his own upbringing and how sorry he was about this aspect of his
job. Hannah also remembered being locked up with a prostitute to whom
they tried to minister. Most of the time, Poole and Hannah tried communicating from their segregated cells with Zaugg by praying and singing freedom songs.[56] Seeking legal counsel for the students, Rev. King contacted
three lawyers, R. Jess Brown, William Kunstler, and Arthur Kinoy. Brown
was one of only a handful of black lawyers in the state at the time and,
according to Rev. King, the only local black lawyer not beholden to the
conservative tactics of the NAACP. Just one year earlier, Brown waged a
prominent legal battle against the state that ultimately succeeded when his
client, James Meredith, enrolled in the University of Mississippi.[57] William
Kunstler and Arthur Kinoy, both from New York, were veteran civil rights
attorneys, having recently defended the Freedom Riders and downtown
Jackson picketers. Kunstler was currently trial counsel for the SCLC. All
three eagerly agreed to litigate the students' appeal.

In addition, the CRR stepped in to offer legal assistance. John M. Pratt,
the new counsel for the commission and a recent graduate of Union Theological Seminary, began strategizing with William Kunstler and Arthur
Kinoy, and set up a new fund that paid for the bail and legal costs of those
arrested in Jackson. Though the CRR focused most of its efforts in lobbying
for passage of a strong civil rights bill, currently stuck in the House Judiciary Committee, they took a special interest in aiding civil rights workers
in Mississippi. One of the commission's first acts after its creation in June
was to send a delegation to the funeral of Medgar Evers. The CRR followed
this by sponsoring a group of ministers and laymen to travel to Clarksdale

in July to make contact with white church people, and to try to mediate between the local movement and white city officials. On August 16, Pratt secured the release of fifty-seven people who had been imprisoned since June, when they were arrested during a voter education and registration drive in Leflore County, Mississippi. This marked the first time the NCC stepped in to provide bail money in a civil rights case.[58] Pratt believed that all Protestant denominations had a stake in the efforts of the church visitors in Jackson, reasoning, "Since the Christian faith declares that all persons are equal in the sight of God, the churches should take the lead in doing so." As a practical matter, Pratt argued, "As long as a church opens its doors to the public, it should be just as ready to admit persons, regardless of color, as any public lunch counter, theater, or hotel."[59]

With William Kunstler's prodding, the lawyers and defendants decided to shift their legal strategy away from a focused appeals process that would likely delay a final decision for years. Instead, Kunstler resolved to take the initiative immediately and employ a sort of "legal direct action."[60] On Friday, October 11, the lawyers, with the backing of the NCC, filed a sweeping lawsuit in federal court, seeking an injunction against any future arrests and prosecutions of church visitors, and arguing that Sunday's action denied the women the right to the free exercise of religion guaranteed by the First Amendment. The complaint said that the women sought to enter "a place of public worship, so that they might quietly and peacefully take part in divine worship." The attorneys specifically asked the court to declare unconstitutional Mississippi's "interference with divine worship" statute. The suit alleged that the municipal judge denied the arrested women the right to due process because he deprived them of appropriate counsel during Monday's proceedings. Moreover, the complaint argued that the stiff sentences they received amounted to cruel and unusual punishment. To the plaintiffs, the defendants in the case—Governor Ross R. Barnett, Mayor Allen Thompson, the chief of police, the municipal and city prosecutors, and the sheriff and county attorney of Hinds County—constituted a cabal denying the students their constitutional rights. The suit, therefore, sought two types of relief: a federal injunction against state interference with the free exercise of religion, and a restraining order against future arrests and prosecutions. A hearing was set for October 21 before the newly appointed federal judge for the Southern District of Mississippi, the arch-segregationist Judge W. Harold Cox.[61]

While the Tougaloo activists reassessed what occurred in front of Capitol Street Methodist on October 6, trying to remember what transpired minute-by-minute, a key question remained unresolved. Why did the police intervene and arrest the integrated group this time, when they could have been making arrests all along, by invoking either the mayor's injunction or the state's anti-demonstration statutes? The more they recalled their experience, the more the three women and Rev. King determined that the events leading up to the arrests that Sunday were really no different from what had occurred most of the earlier church visits. The police could have charged previous groups with trespassing and disturbing divine worship just as easily as they charged the three on October 6. The crucial question, therefore, was simple: What changed?

In the days and weeks after the October 6 arrests, Jackson activists began to receive partial answers. They immediately perceived that either the Citizens' Council specifically, or more broadly, the segregationist power structure in Mississippi stepped in to encourage police intervention. In an interview with a reporter from Chicago, Rev. King attributed the arrests to the Citizens' Council's plan to "save these churches from integration."[62] He based this belief on his own observations and on what Rev. Granberry told him before and after the Sunday visits: that the police were acting on their own accord in making the arrests. In the ensuing days, Rev. King would receive more evidence confirming his suspicions.

Local attorney Francis B. Stevens, the associate conference lay leader for the Mississippi Conference and an early defender of the "born of conviction" ministers, expressed horror at the arrests and set out to investigate the matter himself. Stevens interviewed the three students, Rev. King, and as many other principals as he could. Though he sympathized with the aims of the Tougaloo activists, he did not support the weekly visits, believing the effort was undermining efforts by moderates like himself to help steer the church through this tense period. After probing the matter for a few days, he determined, "The arrests were caused by a change in policy of Mayor Allen Thompson," who previously felt content to leave the matter with the individual churches. Yet when the visits continued, "segregationist leaders put pressure on the mayor to arrest the visitors anytime they failed to heed the admonition of an officer to 'move on.'" Now the mayor, a member of the Methodist Church, was determined to end the visits regardless of how much the national church spent on bail. Stevens relayed to Methodist Church authorities a conversation between Mayor Thompson and Rev. Granberry, in which the mayor bluntly asserted, "Methodists can raise one quarter million dollars as bail money if they want to. We don't care. I have all the money of the city behind me." Stevens told Rev. King his conclusions, and Rev. King then passed them along to William Kunstler on October 9. Kunstler felt confident enough in the explanation to add Mayor Thompson and other government officials as defendants in the lawsuit. For his part, William J. Simmons could not remember, years later, if the police intervened because of pressure from the Jackson Citizens' Council. Yet Simmons did say that council leaders encouraged police to enforce breaches of the peace, and that the Jackson police "very well could have been influenced" by the council to make arrests.[63]

While presumed pressure from segregationist leaders helps explain the timing of the sudden arrests, the Jackson police were certainly aided in their willingness to arrest church visitors by the fact that this type of intervention was not unprecedented. No government official had previously arrested activists outside of churches in Mississippi, but police in Georgia and Virginia had arrested African Americans outside various white Baptist churches earlier in the year. In January, police arrested three students who had been turned away from a Baptist church in Albany, Georgia, while in June, just as the church visit campaign began in Jackson, police in Atlanta arrested a white minister who refused to leave the steps of First Baptist. In July, police in Prince Edwards County, Virginia, arrested twenty-two African Americans after they sat down on the steps outside Farmville Baptist Church.[64]

These arrests gave Jackson police some direction in utilizing local statutes to arrest African Americans trying to attend worship services at white churches. Yet significant differences existed between the tactics of the church visitors in Jackson and those employed by their counterparts in other cities, distinctions that made the grounds for arrest in Jackson more precarious. Most importantly, the church visitors in other cities clearly invited arrest by treating their protest as a sit-in, choosing to remain on or near the premises of the targeted church after ushers turned them away. The methods of these activists in Georgia and Virginia therefore more closely fit the characteristics of a "kneel-in." In contrast, activists in Jackson up to this point aimed to engage church ushers and members in dialogue. When the ushers insisted that they leave, the activists complied. Moreover, the church visitors in Jackson deliberately avoided any type of behavior that the police or church officials could interpret as constituting a disturbance of divine worship or disorderly conduct. Therefore, in addition to leaving the scene, the integrated groups made sure they spoke quietly and avoided obstructing members' entrances into the church.

As in other cities, one of the goals of the Jackson activists was to highlight segregation in the church as a way of tugging at the hearts of white

Christians. Additionally, the church visits were part of a larger effort to rid cities of segregation in all its aspects. Yet in Jackson, activists were less interested in confrontation and brinksmanship than they were in opening channels of communication. In the last four months, Rev. King and the Jackson activists felt they were making progress, given the fact that more churches were open then than had been open in June. Even in the closed churches, activists and white church members exchanged points of view without police interference. The arrests of October 6 therefore signified a new phase of the campaign, one in which government authorities would not tolerate even minor interracial dialogues on church steps.

"We Knew Strength and We Knew Peace"

OCTOBER 1963

The October 6 arrests of the three young women in front of Capitol Street Methodist Church ended the four-month-long détente between activists and the Jackson police. Since the end of the mass demonstrations and the beginning of the visits of integrated groups to white churches, city authorities had refrained from intervening during the weekly confrontations at local churches. Though a police presence was continuously felt—officers tailed activists traveling to the churches and maintained a watchful eye on the activists as they engaged members on the steps of churches—up until October 6, the police stood back and allowed ushers to function as the enforcers of segregation. Yet unlike church visitors in many other cities, the activists in Jackson continued to show up at a variety of white churches Sunday after Sunday, even when most church doors remained closed. The segregationists and the activists both recognized the stakes. White churches needed to remain committed to sustaining segregation if the seemingly closed society were to prevail. When a few churches indicated their unwillingness to continue along this path, the Citizens' Council, and then the police, stepped in.

A few days after the arrests, Rodney Shaw, a staff person with the GBC-SC, arrived in Jackson to lead a previously scheduled annual conference of the Christian Social Concerns Institute. Beginning October 12, about twenty Mississippi Methodists participated in workshops. Shaw reported that he had to devote considerable attention to defending the actions of the GBCSC in providing half of the bail money used to gain the release of Ida Hannah, Bette Poole, and Julie Zaugg from jail earlier in the week. When the Mississippians asked Shaw why the board intervened at all, Shaw turned the question back on them, asking why they did not try to get the women out of jail. He said Mississippians could take care of the situation, someone from the outside could intervene, or the three students could stay in jail "as their reward for trying to attend a Methodist church." Though Shaw did not sense that he won over any in the group, he felt satisfied that he at least had defended the board's actions well and clarified their reasoning for the laypeople.[1]

While Tougaloo students and faculty planned for visits the next Sunday, several Capitol Street Methodist members encouraged Rev. King to return. Two of them were ordained Methodist ministers who worked at Millsaps College. Rev. Jack Woodward served as director of religious life at the college and led the college-age Sunday school at Capitol Street. He opposed his church's closed-door policy and freely discussed his convictions during his Sunday school lessons.[2] Another was Dr. Lee Reiff, a minister and professor of religion at Millsaps. Dr. Reiff specifically told Rev. King he would like to risk arrest on Sunday by attempting to enter his own church with the women. Knowing that Dr. Reiff and his wife might lose their jobs if police arrested them, Rev. King reasoned that he would rather have someone on the inside to help steer the church toward positive change. Another source of encouragement came from Capitol Street's assistant pastor, Rev. Joe Way. He and Rev. King had been roommates for a semester at Millsaps, and Rev. Way and, unlike his superiors, particularly Rev. Granberry and Bishop Franklin, Rev. King recalled that Rev. Way "wanted the church to open the doors and he believed that the anguish and debate brought to the congregation by the church visits was a good thing and should continue." He promised to remain in contact with Rev. King and to advise him about the proper timing for any more visits.[3]

In addition to these men, another individual inside Capitol Street, Martha "Marti" Turnipseed, came forward to offer her support. She was the daughter of Rev. Andrew Turnipseed, a prominent Methodist minister from Alabama who became embroiled in a similar controversy over race in the late 1950s. While serving as district superintendent for the Alabama-West Florida Conference, he, along with other ministers in Mobile, signed a petition encouraging the city counsel to desegregate public buses. Pressure from segregationist laymen mounted for his removal, and the bishop finally demanded that he transfer elsewhere. Owing to her activism, his daughter Marti met a similar fate in April 1963. After participating in a sit-in at a Woolworth's lunch counter in Birmingham, she was expelled by officials from Birmingham-Southern College. She transferred to Millsaps and found a church home at Capitol Street Methodist. When the police released the three from jail on Tuesday, October 9, Turnipseed and a few other Millsaps students traveled up to the Tougaloo campus to meet with them. As a youth and Sunday school leader at Capitol Street, Turnipseed was particularly upset over the arrests. She informed Rev. King that, like Dr. Reiff, she was willing to go to be arrested in front of her own church. Yet, as he told Dr. Reiff, he felt that the movement needed people who could be effective witnesses inside the church. Ultimately, Turnipseed invited Zaugg to visit the church and speak to the Sunday school class led by Rev. Woodward. They hoped the church youth would be able to see she was not the communist rabble-rouser that arch-segregationists made her out to be.[4]

Immediately following the arrests in front of Capitol Street Methodist, Rev. King began receiving telephone calls from fellow Methodist ministers from across the country. Alerted by word of mouth and by the extensive news coverage, particularly in Chicago, these concerned ministers offered to help in any way they could. Two of the first calls came from former classmates of his at Boston University School of Theology, Rev. Woodie White and Rev. Stanley J. Hallett. Rev. White was a black Methodist minister who served an all-white church in Detroit, while Rev. Hallett was a white Methodist minister and staff member at the Church Federation of Greater Chicago. Rev. White later recalled discussing the strategy of the campaign with Rev. King during these telephone conversations. Both men worried that, with arrests beginning, the safety of the students was in jeopardy, and the campaign itself was in danger of becoming too localized an effort. Rev. King thought that one way to resolve both issues would be to invite pastors to accompany the students on their church visits. Since it was too risky to involve local black clergy, the clergy would have to come from the outside. The presence of outsiders, and especially ministers, could help provide protection for the students and bring more national attention to the effort in Jackson.[5]

When Rev. Stanley Hallett phoned Rev. King, he called on behalf of a group of Chicago-area ministers associated with the Chicago Inner City Methodist Ministers' Fellowship. He told Rev. King that he and other ministers wanted to come to Jackson to bear witness with the Tougaloo activists in their church visit campaign in the coming weeks. Rev. Hallett specifically offered to come to Jackson that Sunday and to try to attend worship with the three women at Capitol Street Methodist. While it did not seem to represent a key moment in the campaign—for some non-Mississippians participated in the campaign during the July work camp—the decision to encourage out-of-state ministers to come to Jackson was a pivotal one nevertheless.

In the battle over perceptions, the ministers knew that segregationists and even some racial moderates would interpret their involvement as constituting another invasion by "outside agitators." Yet the ministers did not regard themselves as "outsiders," since they were Methodist ministers merely hoping to attend a Methodist church. In their theological understanding of the Christian church, there was no such thing as an "outsider."

In addition to altering the composition of those participating in the campaign, the decision to include non-local activists also opened the campaign up to the possibility of conflicting goals and strategies that might shift the nature of the campaign itself. While the Tougaloo activists envisioned their campaign as a local effort to test the convictions of white Christians across denominational lines, the Methodist ministers had a more specific, though not necessarily incompatible, purpose in mind: integrating the Methodist Church.

For both practical and strategic reasons Rev. King gratefully accepted the offer of support from Rev. Hallett and other Methodist members. For Rev. King, the offer of assistance from his fellow ministers "was the best possible news for me."[6] Yes, Rev. Hallett was an outsider, but he was a Methodist minister. How could a white Jackson usher doubt the sincerity of a white Methodist minister wanting to worship at a Methodist church? Moreover, unlike Dr. Reiff or other local church people who were sympathetic to the campaign, Rev. Hallett would not suffer many repercussions, if any, back home if the police arrested him. Rev. King, Rev. Hallett, and the group inside Capitol Street then formulated a plan whereby a few white students from the movement, including Zaugg, would attend Sunday school with Turnipseed. Directly confronting what often served as the excuse for closed doors, the accusation that the students were not sincere about worshipping, the women would then be able to explain to the class that their motives were genuine. After class, together with anyone else who wanted to come with them, they would join the black students, Dr. Reiff, and Rev. Hallett in trying to enter from the outside.[7]

On Sunday, October 13, integrated groups attempted to worship at five Protestant churches. At Capitol Street Methodist, Zaugg and another white Tougaloo student, Dolores Dunlop, attended Sunday school with Turnipseed and explained the goals of the church visits. After Sunday school, the three of them, along with a few more white students from the class, went outside and joined Poole, Hannah, Dr. Reiff, and Rev. Hallett on the church steps. Rodney Shaw, who was still in town leading a workshop, observed from a spot nearby. Rev. Hallett introduced himself to the six ushers as a

Methodist minister and announced that the group would like to come into the church and worship. An usher began pointing at the white students and adults, saying that they could come in, but then pointed at Poole and Hannah, telling them that they could not enter. Rev. Hallett asked the chief usher whether everyone in the church felt the same way, and the usher replied, "No, but most of them do." Rev. Hallet then asked if the group could read scripture and say a prayer, and the usher consented. Rev. Hallett read a section from Acts, chapter 22, about Paul's conversion experience and then, after being prompted by one of the students, he read the passage on love from I Corinthians, chapter 13. The group then bowed their heads and said the Lord's Prayer, with some of the ushers awkwardly joining in. Rev. Hallett then asked the usher if they could come in, and the usher suggested that they go to the black Methodist church down the street. Rev. Hallett replied, "I am sure they would receive us, but why won't you?" The ushers did not respond, so Rev. Hallett thanked them for their courtesy, saying he simply wanted to speak with them as fellow Christians, and then he and the group walked off.

The integrated group had remained on the church steps for about thirty minutes by their estimation, but curiously, the police did not budge from their post nearby. Shaw wrote that he saw a layman, whom he identified as the president of the Methodist Men's Club at Capitol Street, gesturing at the policemen, urging them to come over and arrest the visitors. Unlike the previous week, though, the group left the church grounds unmolested.[8]

As the integrated group departed, Shaw stepped forward and introduced himself to the Capitol Street ushers. They immediately asked him what he thought of the incident that just took place, and he responded that he did not come to judge or to bring answers, but said they should always ask what Christ were He was standing there. The ushers explained that Christ would not want people to agitate at a church if they were not interested in worshipping. Then Shaw tried to reason with the ushers as he had done with the attendees at the Christian Social Concerns Institute he was leading. He explained how he just been in the Jackson airport, one of the few truly desegregated spaces in the city, and pointed out how, even through blacks were present, there had been no disturbances. He asked, "Why is it there is no disturbance when Negroes are present at the airport, which does not advertise the presence of God, but there is a disturbance when Negroes appear at the church which does advertise that God is present?" He added, "So we must ask ourselves whether the disturbance is caused by their coming or by our turning them away?" The ushers answered by insisting that the students were professional agitators, being paid to "put on this show." Shaw tried to talk with them more, but could tell that the spirit of goodwill had passed, so he walked away.[9]

Ushers and deacons also turned away integrated groups at St. Luke's Methodist and Trinity Lutheran. At St. Luke's, Professor Campbell tried to attend the service with some of her students. After she insisted that they were not there to cause trouble, just to worship, the man guarding the doors told them he did not want to discuss the matter. As police stood by, the group left the premises. At Trinity, as happened the Sunday before, ushers refused to let the students enter. Rev. Koons openly advocated open doors, and despite an August congregational vote to close the doors, some students had been allowed to worship there on various Sundays. Whether or not black students were admitted seemed to depend more on who was guarding the door than on the August congregational vote.

While three churches turned away black visitors on October 13, the police, despite being present at all of the churches, did not make any arrests. Since the attitude of the minister and ushers at Capitol Street Methodist had not changed, the only difference seemed to be the presence of an out-of-state Methodist minister, Rev. Hallett. At the time, Rev. King interpreted this new development as a reestablishment of the "'status-quo' of the period before the arrests," when the groups maintained the "'right' to have conversations and interracial dialogue, at least, without police interference."[10] What Rev. King did not know was that the restraint police exhibited on October 13 may have been due to the influence of Rev. Granberry of Capitol Street. Rev. Granberry told Shaw that he informed the ushers and others on the official board after the October 6 arrests that he supported the admission of everyone who wanted to come. Yet Rev. Granberry did give the ushers wide latitude in judging the motivations of the visitors. He made clear to the ushers that they should ask the police to intervene only if the group seemed more interested in being arrested than in attending a worship service. Rev. Granberry explained to Shaw that he was not in a good position to provide effective leadership on the matter because he had only been at the church for six weeks, and many church members resented his presence.[11]

With the arrests the previous week apparently an aberration, there were additional reasons for the Tougaloo activists to feel optimistic that Sunday. At St. James Episcopal Church, where integrated groups sought to worship for the first time, ushers welcomed the black students into the morning service. Consistent with their actions at St. Andrew's Episcopal Church throughout the summer, ushers at the city's Episcopal churches now invariably granted entrance to any black student seeking to worship. Moreover, ushers at a Lutheran congregation, most likely Our Redeemer Lutheran Church, admitted an integrated group into their morning service, despite having turned away another group the week before. When handed the order of worship, the students found that it included a written apology for being denied entry the week before.[12]

Now the Tougaloo students could depend on six white churches in Jackson to serve as counterexamples to those who maintained closed-door policies. On October 13, Professor Campbell wrote that the day's developments demonstrated "the much-touted campaign of the Citizens' Council to prevent integration of the churches was given a bit of a setback." She concluded, "The gains here, though small, are significant."[13] At this juncture, Rev. King sensed that "the students were willing to keep coming every Sunday for months and months—and to keep asking their embarrassing questions and discussing race relations with the white church people." He believed that if the campaign continued, "The quiet white moderates would begin to speak," and that if they "began to support any kind of change in racial patterns in Jackson, even (or, perhaps, especially) at the Church—then the door was open, not just the church door, but the door to the possibilities of moderate, gradual change in all Mississippi."[14] In early June, no African Americans were permitted inside white churches in Jackson. Now, after four months, six of the twenty-two churches that had been visited admitted black visitors, exposing a breach in what once was a bulwark of the city's segregated society.

Rev. Hallett and other Chicago-based ministers, however, remained concerned primarily with how the exclusion policies in Methodist churches in Jackson affected the denomination overall. Though police refrained from arresting the integrated group in front of Capitol Street Methodist or any of the other white churches on October 13, the fact that the city continued to prosecute the three arrested women—and that a Methodist church would continue to bar anyone, even when accompanied by a Methodist minister—was especially inexcusable. Rev. James M. Reed, vice president of the Inner City Methodist Ministers Fellowship in Chicago, and pastor of an integrated Methodist church, the Parish of the Holy Covenant, immediately promised that an additional group of ministers would travel to Jackson for visits the following Sunday. He told one of his local papers he feared that racial problems in the Mississippi Methodist Church could upset the planned merger between the Methodist Church and the Evangelical United Brethren (EUB) Church. Rev. James Neuman, a pastor of an EUB church in Chicago, echoed Rev. Reed's concern: "Speaking only for myself, I don't think I could vote to join a segregated church."[15]

Yet not all of the Chicago-based Methodist clergy agreed with the effort to join the church visit campaign in Jackson, including the bishop. Recognizing that Methodist ministers under his charge were enlisting others to go to Mississippi, Bishop Charles W. Brashares mailed a letter to all his pastors in the Rock River Conference. He denounced the exclusion policies of the Jackson churches, calling the situation "a tragedy which belittles American democracy and Christian witness around the world." Even so, he discouraged ministers in his conference from participating in the Jackson church visit campaign. Though the incidents in Mississippi were embarrassing to Methodist churches elsewhere, he argued that his ministers should focus on their witness in Chicago. He explained, "Any shortcomings in the churches of Chicago have a bad influence in Mississippi" and urged the ministers under his care to "make the church to which we belong here a witness of our fellowship in Christ."[16]

Rebuffing their bishop's pleas, Rev. Reed and five other Methodists from the Chicago area traveled to Jackson later that week. Joining Rev. Reed were Revs. Gerald E. Forshey, Elmer Dickson, Don Walden, and James Buckles, all ordained within the Methodist Church. The layman in the group was Lee Rayson, an attorney from Tinley Park, Illinois, and president of the Methodist Student Union Board at the University of Chicago. He read about the World-Wide Communion Sunday arrests and immediately called Rev. Reed, who had just gotten off the phone with Rev. King in Jackson. Rayson eagerly told Rev. Reed, "I want to go with you, and I'll drive."[17]

Rev. Forshey was then enrolled as a graduate student at the University of Chicago, but until June he had served as pastor of a predominantly black inner city church in Chicago, Armitage Avenue Methodist Church. In August, he was part of the CRR delegation sent to Clarksdale, Mississippi, to aid in direct action protests and discussions with local leaders. As with many other white ministers active in the civil rights movement, he was particularly concerned with how the Christian church, and especially his denomination, failed to confront the central problems facing contemporary society, a view he expounded upon in a newsletter. Just as the church declined to challenge Hitler, and church pews in Germany remained empty in the succeeding decades as a result, he believed that the church in America would become irrelevant unless it addressed basic human rights issues. The church now had an opportunity for immediate action, a *kairos*, to purify itself and to help obtain civil rights for all. For Rev. Forshey, the church "must

pass through the eye of the racial needle, or it shall not enter into the kingdom of heaven." Like many other ministers, he first learned of the Jackson
arrests from coverage in one of the Chicago newspapers. Upon reading the
account, his wife, Florence Forshey, simply asked, "What are you going to do
about it?"[18]

Rev. Dickson was pastor of Hope Methodist Church in Westchester, Illinois. He heard about the arrests at a meeting of the Interracial Council
of Methodists of Metropolitan Chicago (ICM), a recently formed group of
black and white ministers from the Methodist Church and the EUB who
strove to make the church more inclusive on all levels. He grew up in Riverside, an all-white suburb of Chicago, where issues of racial justice seemed
distant. He credited his rearing in the church with instilling a biblical understanding of justice. In seminary, he recalled one event that exposed
some hidden racism in his own life. On a trip with some classmates, he
became apprehensive when he had to share a bed with a black man. Later,
when he became a pastor in Chicago, he resolved to confront these feelings. Learning of the arrests in Jackson and the efforts by his fellow Chicago
ministers to participate in the campaign, he wanted to avoid feelings of self-
righteousness. The visits had already caused turmoil inside the churches
and the Methodist Church, but he felt confident that God called him to be a
part of the Jackson witness.[19]

Rev. Walden, like Rev. Forshey, felt particular concern over the larger implications and meaning of the arrests. Pastor of Chicago Lawn Methodist
Church, he wrote that he and the group "went to Jackson as members of
the family of Methodists, deeply concerned by what seemed to be a serious
undermining of the foundations of our family." He did not believe accounts
of the circumstances surrounding the arrests when he read about them in
the *Chicago Daily News*, so he decided to investigate further and collect as
many details as possible. He went to Jackson to "continue our inquiry into
the facts of such a seemingly incredible incident at a Methodist Church."[20]

Just as Rev. King had previously sought to contact ministers whose
churches would be targeted the next day—and in keeping with the investi-
gatory bent of some in the group—these men immediately set out to speak
with local Methodist ministers and denominational leaders. They were
unable to reach Dr. Cunningham of Galloway or Bishop Franklin, but did
meet with Rev. Granberry, Rev. Frank Dement Jr. of St. Luke's Methodist,
and Dr. Leggett Jr., district superintendent of Jackson for the Methodist
Church. The Chicago ministers reported that in the meetings on October
19, "there was very little real conversation" with Dr. Leggett. Dr. Leggett later

told a Chicago reporter, "I begged them to go home." Like the ushers who turned away integrated groups in the past, Dr. Leggett doubted the sincerity of the visitors. He said, "I felt in my heart it was a publicity stunt." He explained, "A white man was murdered by a Negro the other day, and just a few weeks before a white woman was raped by a Negro in a cabin; I told them it would not be advisable for them to participate in any integration." He also took offense at the ministers' contact with Rev. King, telling them Rev. King was "an emotionally disturbed rabble-rouser."[21]

According to Rev. Walden, who recorded details of the conversation, Rev. Granberry pleaded with them not to come, predicting more arrests and possible violence if they found themselves incarcerated. He told the three he feared the repercussions of welcoming African Americans inside the church, for not only would the church pews be empty the following Sunday, "We wouldn't be able to get bank credit; the only way we can keep going is to respect the customs of the South." Moreover, he promised that if they came on October 20 with an integrated group, police would arrest them. He admitted he and his lay leaders told the police they did not want blacks worshiping at their church, and the police agreed to arrest any more integrated groups that presented themselves on the church steps. Though he expressed concern for the ministers' safety, he specifically declined to intercede on their behalf in the event of police brutality.[22]

In a sworn statement given later, Rev. Granberry said he tried to impress upon the ministers that since they intended to bring "Negro people into our congregation, they would under these circumstance present themselves as agitators at the door of our church." He defended the official board's policy to maintain closed doors, saying, "At least for the time being, under the pressure that are [sic] present in our social order, no Negroes would be admitted to attend public worship services."[23] Moreover, he told the ministers that if they conducted some sort of service on the steps of Capitol Street Methodist, as Rev. Hallett had the week before, they would be violating denominational law. He pointed out that according to paragraph 943 of the *Discipline of the Methodist Church*, only he had the right to hold services within the bounds of the church to which his bishop assigned him. Rev. Granberry indicated that he had already written a letter to Bishop Brashares of Chicago protesting the actions of one of his ministers, Rev. Hallett, the week before.[24]

Overall, the Chicago ministers tried to present themselves as fellow Methodists confronting the same issues as their colleagues in Jackson. Rev. Walden sought to communicate the oneness of the church, with problems "so common to us all that what is done in Chicago Methodism affects

Mississippi Methodism and vice versa." Yet after talking to the white Jackson ministers, Rev. Walden understood their mindset more clearly. For these Jackson Methodist clergymen, the term "outsider" had less to do with geography than with "opinions on race that are in opposition to the prevailing mores of the culture."[25] Afterward, he remained pessimistic: "I cannot say we were successful in communicating our concern about the oneness of the church," because "to our brother Methodist pastors we were northern meddlers, more of those people deterring the alleged progress which the church had been making until all the recent outside agitation began."[26]

Saturday night, the group from Chicago met with Tougaloo student activists at Rev. King's house and made preparations for the next day's visits. Following a plan that would become routine in succeeding months, Joan Trumpauer and other Tougaloo activists held orientation sessions for the visiting ministers, usually at the Kings' home on campus. Despite the warning from Rev. Granberry, this particular weekend the ministers seemed confident that the police would not arrest them since they were Methodist ministers seeking to enter Methodist churches. Nevertheless, the Tougaloo activists, who bore the brunt of police brutality a few months before, insisted on preparing for the worst. Trumpauer and others instructed the ministers on how to remain calm in the face of verbal or physical abuse, and coached them on how to curl one's body into the "non-violent crouch." Rev. King remembered that in this particular session, they joked about whether or not to even carry Bibles, since they could "easily be turned into weapons."[27]

The Chicago ministers planned to join students and church members attempting to worship at three Methodist churches, Capitol Street Methodist, Galloway Memorial Methodist, and St. Luke's Methodist. Student groups had targeted Galloway Memorial and Capitol Street since the beginning of the church visit campaign in June, while they had tried to attend the morning service at St. Luke's for the first time just a week earlier. In addition to the routine of arriving at the churches in time for worship, two of the ministers and Joyce Ladner, a student and movement leader at Tougaloo and president of the United Campus Christian Fellowship, arranged to try to go to Sunday school at Galloway with member John Garner, a white physics professor at Tougaloo. Professor Garner noticed that since the visits began, ushers guarded the doors to the sanctuary before worship services, but not the doors to the education building during the Sunday school hour.[28]

John and Margrit Garner joined Galloway when they arrived in Jackson in 1962. Conscious of their outsider status—Margrit was from Switzerland

and John was from Illinois—the Garners hoped to develop relationships within the white Methodist community. They did not come to Tougaloo to become activists, but gradually joined the local effort because of their increasing awareness of the gap between white and black in Mississippi and their ties to movement people at Tougaloo. Margrit participated in many of the movement meetings and activities earlier in the year, and picketed Woolworth's in May, triggering an arrest by the Jackson police. John began to recognize the disparity between his own life as a white man and the daily sacrifices in the lives of African Americans, a discrepancy revealed most clearly by the murder of someone he had just been getting to know a few months before, Medgar Evers. When the Garners joined Galloway, church leaders steered them to one of the more open-minded adult Sunday school classes. Though there were some vocal conservatives in the class, there were other also like-minded Methodists with whom the Garners developed friendships, such as two Millsaps College professors, Dr. T. W. Lewis and Dr. Robert Bergmark.[29]

Recognizing the possibility that police might arrest the group at Galloway owing to the presence of Ladner, the group decided it would be best for Margrit Garner to stay away this Sunday. Any arrest now would constitute her second that year, and combined with the possible arrest of her husband, could empower state authorities to remove their son, Stephen, from their custody.[30] If the four successfully attended the adult class, just as when Zaugg attended the college-age Sunday school at Capitol Street with a church member, they aimed to discuss their motives with the class, hoping to impart their sincerity in wanting to worship at the church because of their Christian convictions. Yet unlike the week before, the presence of Ladner inside Galloway would integrate the Sunday school, thus breaching the church's closed-door policy.

Integrated groups also planned to visit Trinity Lutheran and Fondren Presbyterian, two churches whose ushers had turned away students in the past over the objections of their ministers.[31] Rev. Koons of Trinity and Dr. McDill of Fondren were both trying to steer their congregations toward racial inclusiveness. After members of Trinity voted down a resolution to open the doors in late August, Rev. Koons continued to admonish the congregation and, on at least one Sunday in September, integrated groups succeeded in attending morning worship at Trinity. He resisted calls for his resignation, but he also seemed unable to prevent the actions of a determined group of laymen who, acting as ushers at Trinity, turned away black and white students on October 6 and 13. Unlike Trinity, Fondren had not yet adopted a restrictive attendance policy, though the church's elders had discussed such a move in the preceding months, and a group of deacons there turned away an integrated group on October 6.[32] The autonomous actions of the deacons prompted Dr. McDill to announce during services the following week that he would resign if ushers continued to bar blacks from entering. Like others who had already left their pulpits because of their churches' racial policies, Dr. McDill had served as the long-time pastor of his congregation and was well respected by an overwhelming majority of church members.[33] Sunday's attempted visits at Fondren would therefore test the resolve of both Dr. McDill and his deacons.

On Sunday morning, October 20, integrated groups of Tougaloo students and faculty and six out-of-state churchmen fanned out across Jackson, trying to attend five churches that had previously turned away black students. The *Clarion-Ledger* later observed that this was the "biggest attempt to date to crack racial barriers at places of worship."[34] At Trinity Lutheran, Marveline Faggett, Ruth Moore, and Dolores Dunlop arrived in time for the 8:30 worship service. As Moore later explained before a judge, she and the others went there simply to attend church, believing, "There is one church and that's God's Church. If we are all Christians, we can worship together."[35] The students later reported to Rev. King that there were two groups of men outside. One group they recognized had previously welcomed them inside was now standing at the door. Then another group rushed toward them, exhibiting hostility. Deputy Police Chief John Lee Ray and Officer J. D. Griffith followed the students as they engaged with members of the latter group, who announced that Trinity was a segregated church. Rev. Wade Koons reported later that L. P. Roberts, who rejected the first integrated group on June 30, now ordered the police to arrest the three for trespassing on private property. Deputy Chief Ray testified later that the students "made no indication that they were going to leave," so he and Officer Griffith stepped in to arrest the three women. Contradicting Rev. Koons's testimony, Deputy Chief Ray explained that no church member from Trinity Lutheran asked the police to intervene.[36]

About forty minutes later, Rev. Buckles, Rev. Dickson, Ladner, and Professor Garner arrived at Galloway shortly before Sunday school began. Rev. Dickson later remembered that he and Rev. Buckles "were obviously concerned, and even scared, but not deterred from making the racial witness that we all believed came out of the prophetic resources of both the Old and New Testaments." The four proceeded into the education building through a side door, having encountered no one guarding the doors outside. Yet once inside, they quickly attracted the attention of an usher and other lay leaders. The usher, who was actually a friend of Garner's, was the first to spot the group. He rushed to meet them and announced that the white men in the group could stay but the black woman, Joyce Ladner, was not welcome. Rev. Buckles immediately asked to see Dr. Cunningham, whom they had been unable to reach the day before. As a fellow Methodist minister, Rev. Buckles understood that in Methodist churches only ministers maintained the authority to ask any visitors to leave. The usher asked the group to leave, and when they still refused, he walked away. After about a minute, he returned with a group of about four other men. One of the official board members again asked the visitors to leave, but the group still insisted on seeing Dr. Cunningham first.

At this point, a policeman entered the education building and approached them, having been summoned from the parking lot outside by someone who saw the integrated group enter the building. Garner later wrote that the board member motioned to the police officer, who then asked the group if they still refused to leave, even though a member of the board of stewards had asked them to do so. Garner then responded, explaining to the officer that he and his wife were members at Galloway, and the other three were his guests. Moreover, two of the guests were Methodist ministers. The officer then pronounced them under arrest for breach of peace. The four were then led into an unmarked police car and delivered to the city jail by 9:30. The Jackson police later replaced the breach of peace charge with disturbing public worship and trespassing.[37]

For Garner, the arrests that morning defied logic. He wrote at the time, "There was not a loud word spoken during our arrest. As for public worship, Sunday school did not even start until we were in jail. How my guests and I could be arrested for trespassing in my own church I do not understand." Neither Dr. Cunningham nor Rev. Clay Lee, the new assistant minister at Galloway, appeared during the incident. Dr. Cunningham later wrote that he did not learn of the situation until after church, which would have meant more than two hours later, since the arrests occurred before Sunday school. Some Galloway members who were sympathetic to the integrated group's situation told Rev. King that they informed both ministers at the time. Either way, Rev. King doubted that it was possible for either minister to be ignorant of what occurred.[38]

At Capitol Street Methodist, for the third week in a row Hannah, Poole, and Zaugg arrived in time for the morning worship. As happened the week before when a white minister, Rev. Hallett, accompanied them to the church steps, two of the Chicago ministers, Rev. Forshey and Rev. Walden, joined the three young women. From a distance, a group of sympathetic Capitol Street Church members joined Rev. Jim Reed and Leland Rayson, a Chicago attorney, in observing the integrated group as they approached the church doors. Rather than risk more arrests, Rev. King wanted Rev. Reed and Rayson to be able to accurately describe anything that occurred.[39] Nicholas Von Hoffman, a reporter from the *Chicago Daily News*, detailed the exchanges among the integrated group, the ushers, and the police. A group of fifteen ushers stood on the steps, and one of them stepped forward to announce, as before, that the ministers and Zaugg were allowed inside, but the two black women were not. Rev. Forshey, acting as spokesman for the group, sought to clarify, asking, "We are not welcome at a Methodist church?" The chief usher just repeated his earlier statement. Rev. Forshey then said, "Then we are not welcome in a Methodist church." The usher elaborated, explaining, "Because of the prevailing tension, we will have to ask you to leave." He added, "You are on a church property." A police officer then stepped in to say, "They have asked you to move on." Rev. Forshey responded to this intervention, telling the policeman, "Please stay out of this. Let us Methodists solve our problem." The officer was insistent, declaring, "You are on church property and they have asked you to leave." Rev. Forshey then tried to hand the chief usher a note addressed to Rev. Granberry, but the usher declined it. The policemen then escorted the integrated group away and on to the city jail.[40]

Accounts of the exchange from the Capitol Street ushers and policemen differed. According to the ushers, the ministers and students refused to leave and insisted on conducting a religious service on the church steps, as they had the week before.[41] The administration of the service—readings from scripture and a recitation of the Lord's Prayer—the week before, regardless of its brevity, infuriated Rev. Granberry and likely contributed to the police intervention now. Rev. Granberry pointed to a certain section of the Methodist *Discipline*, which forbade pastors from holding religious services within the bounds of another pastoral charge unless permitted to do so by the pastor in charge.[42] Deputy Police Chief J. L. Ray later testified that when the integrated group approached the church doors, one of the ushers, W. H. Phillips, read a proclamation on behalf of the church's official board. When Rev. Forshey became "argumentative," Phillips then looked at Ray and said, "I turn the situation over to you." Deputy Chief Ray, who arrived at Capitol Street thirty minutes before after talking with Hoffman and Bishop Franklin, explained that he stepped in to make the arrest in

order to "preserve the peace." Deputy Chief Ray specifically stated that neither Phillips nor anyone else from Capitol Street asked him to arrest the
visitors.[43]

Professor Campbell drove Rev. Reed and Martin Palmore, a black Tougaloo student, to St. Luke's Methodist in time for the 11 a.m. worship. He
and Palmore approached the steps of St. Luke's and engaged the ushers in
conversation, but the ushers remained resolute in keeping them out. Rather
than provoking church officials into calling on the police by insisting on
staying on the church steps, Rev. Reed and Palmore walked away. Unlike the
previous Sunday, the police were not present. Professor Campbell speculat-
ed, "St. Luke's members asked them to stay away or . . . there weren't enough
police to go around to all the churches." Across the street at Fondren Presbyterian, Rev. Hutchinson, Trumpauer, and Connie Shepherd, a black student leader, arrived for the morning service. Ushers there had barred them
two weeks earlier, prompting the pastor, Dr. McDill, to threaten to resign
if Fondren continued to forbid entry to African Americans. Rev. Hutchinson wrote Dr. McDill and the session a letter questioning how one could
defend turning away Christians on World-Wide Communion Sunday. He
also spoke directly with Dr. McDill, who encouraged him to try again. This
Sunday, a man at the church doors greeted the visitors, but then queried
their sincerity: "Have you really come to worship?" When they again stated
their intentions, he said that they could come sit with him and he escorted
them inside. Dr. McDill gave another pointed sermon to his congregants
touching on the racial turmoil in Jackson churches. Professor Hutchinson
later remembered this as "one of the most moving and meaningful worship
services I had ever attended."[44]

In all, police arrested twelve individuals on October 20 in front of Jackson churches, including five black Tougaloo students, four white Methodist ministers, one white Tougaloo professor, and two white students. For
three of the students, this was the second arrest for trying to attend worship
services. Despite the uniqueness of each of the attempts and the varying
statuses of the visitors, who ranged from a member of one church in which
he allegedly trespassed, to ministers within the particular denomination in
which they trespassed, police charged everyone with trespassing and disturbing divine worship. Just as they had on October 6, Jackson police set
bond at $500 per charge, which amounted to $1,000 for each of the twelve
individuals arrested.[45] Yet the police clearly did not demonstrate the same
restraint they maintained the previous week, which Rev. King and others
in the movement had attributed to the presence of outside white ministers.

This time, the presence of many more out-of-state ministers seemed to engender an even higher degree of resistance from the ushers and the police.

Eleven of the twelve remained in jail in segregated cells for five more days. Fortunately, Rev. Granberry's earlier warning of violence against the prisoners never materialized. Soon after police fingerprinted them, the individual interviews began. Rev. Dickson recalled that while the officers questioned Rev. Buckles, he began hearing loud noises in the next room and feared that the police were beating him. For a moment, he felt genuine fear, but also resolution, for "we were making a historic witness that had the potential of being a part of the sea change that came in American society." To his immense relief, Rev. Buckles emerged from the interrogation unscathed. Professor Garner wrote that he and his fellow prisoners "were treated well" and "were allowed to see our lawyers when necessary and were able to make phone calls." His wife, Margrit, talked with Dr. Cunningham the afternoon of the arrests, pleading with him to do something about the fact that police detained a church member on church property. She hoped that at least he would visit her husband in jail, just as he would any other church member. Despite her request, Dr. Cunningham never met with Professor Garner or any of the others who found themselves in jail for trying to attend Sunday school in his church. Dr. Cunningham later wrote that after speaking with Margrit Garner, he "went posthaste to the city jail" and tried to "effect the release" of those arrested, a statement indicating that he went to the jail and spoke with the police, not those arrested.[46]

The jailed ministers also had difficulty convincing local Methodist leaders to visit them. Rev. Forshey wrote Bishop Brashares, his bishop in Chicago, asking if he could try to persuade either Dr. Leggett or Bishop Franklin to come to the jail and celebrate Holy Communion for them, but neither did.[47] Dr. Leggett told a Chicago reporter later in the week, "To bring the sacrament in such surroundings would be a sacrilege." Moreover, he echoed the familiar charge levied by segregationists, referring to the Chicago ministers as "agitators from outside the state." He believed that the ministers "came to Mississippi to go to jail and they would have been disappointed if they didn't land there." Personally, Dr. Leggett admitted, he favored segregated churches in Mississippi, for "the great majority of Mississippi Methodists do not believe in integration," and integrated services "would destroy the churches over which I preside."[48]

The jailed ministers did see many other visitors that week, including the Chicago men police did not arrest, and groups from Tougaloo who brought daily care packages and words of encouragement. Rev. Reed brought Rev.

Dickson his Bible and Methodist hymnal. They sang together and read from the Book of Acts. As Rev. Dickson remembered, the ministers felt they "were almost reliving the apostles' experience in first century jails."[49] Much to the surprise of Rev. King, the police allowed him to visit the prisoners. On one occasion, Rev. King led the jailed ministers in a celebration of Holy Communion, with a cell serving as the chapel, a hardened breakfast biscuit as the loaf, and a prisoner's tin cup containing contraband as the wine. Reflecting on the moment later, Rev. King recalled, "There was a kind of awe . . . kneeling before some small crucifix in a tiny chapel in the side aisle, waiting, in no hurry, to walk back into the great building around us. We knew strength and we knew peace."[50] While Jackson's district superintendent for the Methodist Church viewed such a service as blasphemy, these Methodist ministers saw it as the utmost expression of piety. They were bound by their faith and their unity and their conviction that God's table was open to all.

[9]

"Betraying Jackson"

LATE OCTOBER–EARLY NOVEMBER, 1963

While the arrest of the three Tougaloo students on October 6 initiated a new phase of the church visit campaign, one in which ushers and police intervened to prevent open interracial dialogue on church steps, the involvement and ultimate arrest of out-of-state ministers on October 20 marked another shift in the local movement. With twelve of the fifteen arrests so far occurring at Methodist churches, Methodist ministers and laypeople now journeyed to Jackson for the specific purpose of exposing the contradiction between the stated ideal of the denomination that the House of God was open to all, and the reality that individual congregations excluded black visitors and tolerated or even encouraged police intervention. They hoped to draw more attention to this incongruity so that the Methodist hierarchy would intercede, or so that the upcoming general conference in Pittsburgh in April 1964 would mandate desegregation throughout the bodies of the Methodist Church, including those at the congregational level. Since activists had not yet succeeded in cracking open any of Jackson's Methodist churches, and now that there was no guarantee that church or city officials would put up with any more interactions on church steps, Rev. Ed King and the local activists recognized that change would likely come from the top down. They therefore welcomed help from the outside for the first time, even though doing so clearly altered the focus of the campaign. They would continue to attend the Episcopal, Catholic, and Presbyterian churches that were open, but the spotlight now honed in on the closed-door policies of Jackson's Methodist churches.

Though non-Mississippi ministers and laypeople now joined the Jackson activists on their weekly visits, they did not intend to gain control of the local campaign. In fact, the out-of-state groups went to great lengths to ensure that they deferred to the leadership of Rev. King, and they understood the unique role of the students in the effort. For instance, Rev. Reed, who coordinated the Chicago-area ministers and others wanting to become involved in the campaign, wrote up an information bulletin. He urged his fellow ministers and laypeople to put themselves "in the hands of the Tougaloo people for training, advice, and strategy," and to "let them indicate the way in which you can most effectively help the cause." If they found themselves arrested, he instructed, they should remain in jail until bail was raised for all, including the students. He and Rev. Martin Deppe, pastor of Mandell Methodist Church in Chicago, set up the Methodist Evangelical United Brethren Freedom Fund to help raise money for bail and to cover legal fees. Since police would be arresting Tougaloo students along with the ministers, Rev. Reed specified that the ministers should also cover bail for the students, since "they have no financial resources, only courage."[1]

Visiting ministers arranged for financial assistance to cover all their costs, including their potential arrests, before they arrived in Jackson in part because national Methodist Church organizations were no longer stepping in to provide bail money. Though leaders at the Woman's Division of Christian Service of the Board of Missions of the Methodist Church, one of the two original sources of aid, supported the aims of the Tougaloo activists and the ministers who accompanied them, they were now dealing with substantial fallout caused by their actions in early October.

In the month since supplying $1,500 of the $3,000 to get Poole, Hannah, and Zaugg out of the Jackson jail after their October 6 arrests, the Woman's Division had received a barrage of letters and resolutions from Methodist women in Mississippi blasting the decision to aid the three students and pledging to withhold funds from the national group. As part of the Board of Missions of the Methodist Church, the Woman's Division supported mission work in the United States and funded missionaries working abroad. Ann C. Brown, general secretary of the Woman's Division, and J. Fount Tillman, president of the Woman's Division, received a total of eighty-six letters from Woman's Society groups from Mississippi condemning the Woman's Division's assistance to the three women, with many of the letters containing multiple signatures. About half of the correspondence came from women and Methodist church groups in Jackson. Brown and Tillman did not report receiving a single letter from a Mississippi resident supporting their decisions. Much of the criticism centered on the fact that none of the three girls were Methodists and the belief that they had broken the law. At least one writer repeated a charge often propagated in the *Clarion-Ledger*,

"There is some real Communist infiltration at Tongaloo [sic]." In addition to protesting the action of the Woman's Division, some reported that local Methodists were withholding funds from charities associated with the Woman's Division. For instance, workers at Jackson's Bethlehem Center, a downtown youth center that received money from Methodist Women's Societies in Jackson, pled with the Woman's Division to help them out because their funds were completely dried up by the end of October, and they had little assurance of local support in the future given the Woman's Division's action.[2]

In their written response to these letters, leaders of the Woman's Division did not back down from their decision to help the three students get out of jail. In a letter forwarded to all Methodist Women's Societies in Mississippi outlining her rational, the Woman's Division president reassured these women that the source of the funds did not come from pledge money or mission work, but from a special general contingent fund of the administrative committee. Nevertheless, she devoted most of the letter to outlining how Christians should think about the current racial crisis. As a Tennessean, she reminded her audience that she was a fellow Southern layperson, but explained that it was her experience as a missionary that gave her an even greater perspective on the issue of race in the church. She told her readers that the Chinese, Indians, Latin Americans, and Africans that she knew identified with people of color in the United States and were constantly asking her if it was true that churches in America turned away African Americans. Converted Christians abroad were having difficulty reconciling what she and other American missionaries were telling them about fundamental Christian beliefs with what they were hearing about what Christians were doing in churches in America. She pointed out her own struggle as a missionary in Africa in 1957 during the crisis at Central High School in Little Rock, Arkansas, when communists took to the airwaves in Africa asking people if they still believed in the American style of government. She sought to make it clear that while assigning dissenters the "communist" label, segregationists were in fact tools of communist efforts. She concluded simply, "The race question must be settled at home if our Christian message is to be effective [abroad]."[3]

With the second set of arrests marking a new pattern on the part of the police, some local and national editors stepped up their attacks on the actions of churches and police in Jackson. The Chicago-based and liberal-leaning religious magazine, the *Christian Century*, saw the decisions of local churches, not police, as the fundamental concern. Unlike the police, who

"have done precisely what is expected of them," the local church "has des-
ecrated its sanctuary by closing it to Negroes and whites that together seek
God and Christian fellowship within its doors."[4] Still, local religious and lay
editors saw the behavior of the police as particularly ominous. Father Bernard Law, editor of the *Mississippi Register*, expressed more concern over
what he saw as the "police power" that was "overstepping its bounds to an
alarming degree." Citing the letter that the city commissioner sent to his
fellow members at Trinity Lutheran— suggesting that even if the church
voted to open the doors to African Americans, the police would still intervene to enforce the segregation policies of the city—Father Law concluded
that this state of affairs was "nothing short of shocking." He admitted that
even if he was misinterpreting what the Jackson official meant, the recent
actions of Jackson police did not "inspire confidence in the commitment of
the city and police officials of Jackson to the system of separation of Church
and State."

Like Father Law, Hazel Brannon Smith, editor of the *Northside Reporter*,
appeared particularly concerned about the arbitrariness of police intervention. Alluding to the recent arrests at Galloway, which involved a police officer entering the church and arresting a church member and two ministers
affiliated with that particular denomination, she asked rhetorically if this
was "not the action of a police state?" While she affirmed the right of "every
Mississippi Church [to] be able to form its own worship and admission
policies," she argued, "These are questions to be resolved by Christians and
the churches with their God, without help or interference from the local
police or the Citizens' Councils."[5]

Immediately following the second set of arrests on October 20, Rev. King
and the other activists labored to get more information from those detained
so they could discuss legal strategy with their lawyers. Fortuitously, their
New York lawyers planned to arrive that afternoon. Just a few hours after
Sunday's arrests, William Kunstler and Arthur Kinoy flew into Jackson.
There was a hearing set for the following day concerning the first arrests.
They quickly learned that not only were the three women they originally
represented back in jail for repeating the same offence, nine others were incarcerated as well.[6] Leland Rayson, the Chicago attorney who observed the
arrests at Capitol Street Methodist, and Jess Brown, a local black attorney
who defended the Tougaloo activists in the past, joined Kunstler and Kinoy
in preparing motions for the proceedings scheduled for the next day. Working well into the night, they located a Reconstruction-era law that would
potentially enable them to remove the cases against the church visitors to

federal courts, where the defendants might stand a better chance of winning. According to the United States Civil Rights Act of 1866 and Title 28, Section 1443 of the United States Code, a defendant could remove a case from a local or state court to a federal court if the local officials denied a defendant their civil rights. The lawyers now hoped this overlooked law—originally used to combat "black codes" during Reconstruction—could help fight discrimination in what activists regarded as the Second Reconstruction.[7] Since the arrests of the Tougaloo Nine and the Freedom Riders in 1961, movement activists had to contend with segregationist legal officials in the Mississippi courts, including the new local federal judge, William Harold Cox. Beyond the state, especially in the Fifth Circuit Court of Appeals in Atlanta and the United States Supreme Court, there were more men who, according to Rev. King, served with "honor, integrity, and a commitment to justice and the Constitution."[8] Yet employing this legal tactic also meant they would have to delay efforts then underway to get the twelve immediately out of jail. The attorneys felt that if they paid bail to the city, this action could potentially damage their legal efforts to transfer their cases to federal court.

On Monday morning, October 21, the four lawyers appeared before Judge Cox to introduce the new set of motions and to add those arrested the day before to the original complaint. They asked him to sign a writ of habeas corpus, which would acknowledge federal jurisdiction over the twelve prisoners. Leading the attorneys from the city and state's side was Thomas Watkins, a life-long member of Galloway. Caught off guard by the petition to transfer the cases to federal court, Watkins objected, and Judge Cox adjourned the court until later in the afternoon to give Watkins and the other attorneys time to respond to the lawyers' motions. Both Watkins and Judge Cox admitted before the court that neither had ever heard of the code Kunstler cited.[9] When the court finally reconvened later in the day, Judge Cox began by hearing on the original motion filed two weeks earlier. For several hours on Monday and then again on Friday, October 25, the court heard testimony from all sides of the controversy, including that of the mayor, the arresting officers, the ministers of the churches involved in the arrests, and the twelve defendants. Today, the testimony (available only in newspaper coverage and records kept by Kunstler, Watkins, and Rev. King) helps clarify the nature of the relationship between the police and the churches and the motivations of the activists.

Mayor Thompson and the arresting officers emphasized that the police arrested the activists because the city felt bound to enforce segregation in establishments that wanted separation of the races. The congregations of all the churches where arrests occurred—Capitol Street Methodist, Galloway Memorial Methodist, and Trinity Lutheran—maintained closed-door policies, either through a church-wide vote, or through a decision from their lay boards. Significantly, however, the city officials stressed that no member or leader at any of the churches specifically asked the police to intervene, either verbally or through some sort of signal. When asked if he had intended to "utilize whatever means you had officially at your disposal" to "perpetuate or adhere to that policy" of racial segregation within a church, the mayor responded, "That's right." He added that he conferred with several unidentified ministers in his office, and that he would use five hundred policemen, if necessary, to assist churches wanting to remain segregated.

Yet the mayor could not completely distance himself from his actions, since he, like attorney Watkins, was a member of Galloway. Officer Joseph Griffith, the policeman who made the arrests at Galloway the day before, testified that none of the ushers or other church officials requested him to intervene. Deputy Chief J. L. Ray, who was somehow present at all of the arrests at the three churches the day before, concurred that no one from the churches ever asked the police to detain the activists. He testified that he stepped in to make the arrests at Capitol Street Methodist "when the situation became argumentative and the group refused to leave." An usher had looked at him and said, "I turn the situation over to you," but for Ray, that did not necessarily mean that the usher asked him to make the arrest.[10] Since the churches maintained closed-door policies that the activists clearly understood at the time, the ushers and other church officials did not specifically have to ask the police to intervene. The police interceded on the church's behalf, absolving it of any responsibility for directly initiating the arrests. The church's accountability merely rested with whether or not they had a closed-door policy, something the police felt was purely a church matter.

During cross-examination and oral argument, the city attorneys elaborated on the police's motives in arresting the integrated groups. Rev. King took notes during the proceedings and recorded a poignant statement from one of the attorneys. Responding to the issue of whether church policy toward visitors figured into police intervention, one of the city's lawyers divulged what their side previously implied: "The [Methodist] *Discipline* and the teachings of the Methodist Church does not matter. So long as we know one person doesn't want a Negro in his church the police will feel free to intervene."[11] Watkins later elaborated on the city's position in arresting the integrated groups in an essay responding to the litigation. Significantly, he never acknowledged that the injunction of late May, which forbade all forms of protest in Jackson, including "kneel-ins," had anything to do with the city's decision to intervene. Rather, he wrote, "The state and city allow each church to make its own decision as to whether it will operate on an integrated or segregated basis." Only when a church expressed its desire to remain segregated did the police "protect the right of such church to operate . . . without physical violence or forced intrusion by persons who have been advised that they are not welcome but who refuse to recognize the right of a particular church to exclude them."[12] With regard to the incidents at the three churches on October 6 and 20, no one alleged "physical violence" beyond argumentation, and only one venue, the Sunday school class at Galloway, could qualify as the site of a "forced intrusion"—although even with that visit, the four visitors were merely fortunate enough to successfully sneak inside through a side door. Yet the essential part of the segregationist motivation was clear: The city did not need an injunction, for the police only acted to enforce segregation in particular churches in order to preserve order, regardless of whether or not the church specifically requested such help.

When Rev. Koons and Dr. Cunningham took the witness stand, they made it clear that the instigation for the arrests did not come from them. Rev. Koons actually volunteered to take the stand on behalf of the students arrested at Trinity Lutheran, while Dr. Cunningham only indicated his willingness to appear in court after the defense lawyers indicated they intended to ask him to take the stand. Rev. Koons testified that he welcomed all to worship at his church and would only support arrests if the individuals involved were truly disruptive. He specifically objected to the arrests at Trinity Lutheran on Sunday, saying that none of the three women disturbed any church members before or during the worship service. Dr. Cunningham testified that he did not ask Mayor Thompson or the police for any assistance in maintaining racial segregation at Galloway Memorial. Later, Dr. Cunningham remembered being asked by Kunstler whether any lay leaders at Galloway maintained an agreement with the police to arrest integrated groups attempting to enter. He recalled responding with a laugh, saying, "Of course not!"[13]

Rev. Granberry did not take the stand, but issued an affidavit through the attorneys for the city. In both content and tone, he departed significantly from the testimony of Dr. Cunningham and Rev. Koons, who distanced themselves from the actions of the police. Most of the affidavit concerned discussions between Rev. Granberry and the Chicago ministers on October 19, the day before the second round of arrests. He explained to them that the church maintained a closed-door policy and, if they arrived with any black guests, would consider them agitators. Yet his affidavit never indicated what would happen next: Because they were agitators, the police would detain them for trespassing and disturbing divine worship. He therefore never addressed the issue of direct collusion between himself and the police, or between any of his ushers and the police.[14] Still, in contrast to his counterparts, he never objected to the police intervention. For Rev. King, the statement by Rev. Granberry made it clear that "now the church seemed more willing to let the police do their dirty work." When the two of them spoke just before and after the first arrests at Capitol Street Methodist on October 6, Rev. Granberry told him that there was nothing he could do about the arrests, since neither he nor any other church official asked the police to intervene. On October 6, Rev. King understood this rationale to mean that church leaders were trying to remain neutral, or at least present themselves as guiltless bystanders. Yet when arrests were again made at Capitol Street Methodist on October 20, Rev. King believed that Rev. Granberry could no longer plead innocence. He concluded that Rev. Granberry's previous claims of religious neutrality had turned to acquiescence in the face of a growing police state.[15] By instructing the police that the matter was now in their hands, church officials physically and legally conceded authority to the police. What began as a state of detachment evolved into a state of consent.

To buttress their arguments against the defendants, city attorneys called to the stand Rev. B. K. Hardin, pastor of Boling Street Methodist Church in Jackson. Tougaloo activists had not visited his church before, not only because it was a small church and thus lacked the strategic value of the Methodist churches hat were visited, but because Rev. King and the students likely understood the futility in any attempted visit there. Rev. Hardin was an outspoken critic of integration in the community, and served as the chairman of the clerical advisory committee of MAMML, which had just announced a "litigation fund" to support a possible suit against the NCC and other groups for "interfering with freedom of worship" in Jackson churches.[16] Rev. Hardin's testimony before Judge Cox affirmed Rev. Granberry's position about the status of visiting ministers to churches outside their own jurisdictions, saying that they had no ministerial rights outside of their respective areas. He argued that individual Methodist churches controlled their own policies regarding attendance and membership, and that the Methodist Church in general was not "open."[17] Although his statements were virtually indistinguishable from Rev. Granberry's, Rev. Hardin testified in person on behalf of the city, the only local white Methodist minister to do so.

When the defendants took the stand before Judge Cox, their testimony emphasized two points. The first was a statement of fact, that from their vantage point, the police went out of their way to help churches maintain segregation. For instance, Poole, who was detained outside Capitol Street Methodist on October 6 and again on October 20, said that during the first arrest, a policeman repeatedly interrupted when an usher tried to say something. After giving the young women a time limit in which to leave before provoking arrest, the policeman then became "emotional and excited and angry" and called them back over and placed them under arrest.[18]

Yet much of what the defendants discussed concerned statements of belief and intention. Since the church visits began, the most consistently repeated argument against their admission was that the visitors had no sincere interest in attending the church. Since they were activists, opponents accused them of just trying to prove a political point. As attorney Bob Nichols argued during Monday's proceedings, the groups on October 6 and October 20 "met earlier and mapped the church attempts as a plan"; it was clear that "the group did not have the purpose of worshipping in mind." When the defendants testified, they wanted to counter this assertion and, once again, define the meaning of the church visit campaign. Asked why she wanted to attend Capitol Street, Poole explained that it was "part of my religious belief that a church shouldn't segregate or discriminate and the churches are open to all people." Ruth Moore, one of the black students arrested at Trinity Lutheran on October 20, testified, "There is one church and that's God's church and if we are all Christians then we can worship together." Professor Garner stated his belief that "if anybody wants to come and worship in my church this is wonderful and I would accept anyone who wanted. He wouldn't even need to be a Christian." While Garner and the students defended their actions based on their Christian convictions, the ministers who testified focused most of their statements on Methodist principles and policy. Rev. Forshey affirmed a statement uttered many times before by Dr. Selah, that "there is no color line in the Methodist Church," adding that any attempt to restrict attendance based on race was "against the official law of the Methodist church." Addressing the charge of trespassing, he explained that, as a Methodist minister, "I could not trespass on Methodist property."[19] His decision to come to Jackson was not based solely on his Christian beliefs, but he felt personally compelled to affirm basic principles and rules of his denomination.

At the end of Monday's hearing, Judge Cox denied the motion for *habeas corpus*, which would have given custody of the defendants to federal authorities. He also declined to immediately decrease the $1,000 bond on each of the defendants, saying that it was not excessive. He told the defendants, "It looks as if you people came down here looking for trouble. I think you found it."[20] As for the other part of the suit—the injunction that sought to prohibit any more arrests on grounds of the constitutional guarantee of freedom of worship—Judge Cox set a hearing for Friday, October 25.

Fully prepared for such a result on the motions regarding federal custody and bail, given the judge's previous rulings, Kunstler and the other attorneys immediately filed a petition with the Fifth Circuit Court of Appeals. On Thursday, October 24, Kunstler appeared in Atlanta before a panel of three appeals court judges, asking them to reduce the bail and to grant a mandamus order under the 1866 Civil Rights Act, which would enjoin Judge Cox to take custody of the defendants. The judges ruled in favor of the twelve activists, ordering Judge Cox to "forthwith issue the writ of *habeas corpus* directing the custody of the petitioners be given to the United States Marshall." They also ordered him to set bail at the hearing the next day in Jackson.[21]

At the hearing back in Jackson on Friday, October 25, Judge Cox initially refused to issue a writ of *habeas corpus*, but later in the afternoon, he took custody of the prisoners and turned them over to the United States commissioner for a bail hearing. At this point, eleven of the twelve—all except Garner— remained incarcerated. On Tuesday, Garner paid the city his $1,000 bail based on the two charges, having received the money from the church his parents attended in Wilmette, Illinois. While other churches in the Chicago area contributed enough funds to release the others earlier in the week, Kunstler and the other lawyers insisted that the defendants try to remain in jail while they pursued their cases in court. Although their defense involved a rather complicated set of legal issues and procedures, the lawyers felt that if all of them paid their bail, they would endanger the effort to turn custody over to federal authorities. Once they were in federal custody, the commissioner changed the blanket set of charges that the police originally issued to all twelve. For the seven students, the charges and the bail remained the same. The commissioner released them each on payment of $500 on each of the charges of trespassing and disturbing divine worship. He released Garner and the four ministers on their own signature on the trespassing charge and $500 on the charge of disturbing worship. Despite having been released already, the new bail still had legal ramifications for

Garner, who now hoped to recoup the original $1,000 he already paid to the city on Tuesday.[22]

In addition to the legal proceedings that took place the week after the second round of arrests, there were new developments at Fondren Presbyterian Church. After deacons admitted an integrated group for worship services on Sunday, Dr. McDill called a special meeting of the session on Tuesday to give each elder a chance to share his opinion on the recent visits. After a discussion and a prayer, they adopted what can only be described best as a quasi-open-door policy. After beginning with a statement of principle that all sincere worshippers were welcome, the resolution then abruptly acknowledged the reality that some church people objected to the presence of certain visitors. The policy characterized insincere visitors as "individuals who may create controversy," though the statement never explained exactly who was included. Unlike the closed-door resolutions reaffirmed by Galloway in January and adopted by First Baptist in June, which explicitly excluded all blacks from entering, Fondren's policy never racialized the potential visitors.[23] Instead, the resolution objected to anyone who might upset the sensibilities of church members. If the deacons proved unpersuasive in their efforts to sway the unwanted guests, then the visitors would be admitted inside, and deacons would "try" to seat them in the balcony. As a committee drafted resolution, the policy contained inconsistencies and ambiguities likely reflecting the difficulty of formulating a statement that could satisfy a majority on the session and Dr. McDill, who pledged to resign if they voted to prohibit African Americans. With the new policy, Fondren continued to maintain open doors, but the church's deacons would now try to dissuade certain individuals from entering and potentially relegate them to the balcony if they did come into the church. Nevertheless, the policy did not permit deacons to turn away African Americans, a significant departure from the policies at other churches in Jackson and one that the session at Fondren considered on October 6.

On Friday evening, October 25, the toll of the bells of Woodworth Chapel on the Tougaloo campus announced the arrival of the newly freed group of church visitors and beckoned the community to the chapel for a rally. As the capacity crowd sang freedom songs, the twelve gathered at the podium, flanked by Kunstler, Rayson and Rev. King. Each of the jailed students and ministers gave a testimonial of his or her experiences during the last five days. Ladner spoke of the significance of the group's actions to the overall freedom movement and the particular meaning of the campaign to her, a native Mississippian. She shared her disappointment in the white churches of Jackson and declared being arrested in a church was the worst thing she could imagine. Yet she remained determined to risk more arrests, for "this was the generation of Black people who had to stand up and fight." Kunstler urged the activists not to give up on the legal system, vowing to continue the fight to make the federal government responsible for ensuring justice in Mississippi. He then thanked the Tougaloo activists for sharing the movement with him, saying, "Without you as my clients and my friends, I would never have known how deeply I could feel about people and ideals." The rally ended, as all freedom rallies did, with the whole group linking arms and singing "We Shall Overcome."[24] The long week of church visits, arrests, jail time, and court hearings was over, but Sunday was just around the corner. Another opportunity for the activists to demonstrate their convictions awaited.

For the third week in a row, a different group of white ministers from Chicago joined African American students in attempting to visit Methodist churches in Jackson. This group of four included two Methodists and two who were ordained in the EUB, a small, mostly white denomination that was set to merge with the Methodist Church the following year. All knew one another through the ICM. Rev. J. Preston Cole served as chaplain of the Methodist Foundation at the University of Chicago, and Rev. David J. Twigg was pastor of Humboldt Park Methodist Church. The two EUB ministers were Rev. Richard J. Tholin, who taught at the Evangelical United Brethren Seminary, and Rev. Sheldon Trapp, who pastored Lane Park EUB Church. Rev. Trapp's involvement in the campaign took on even more significance because his wife was the daughter of a EUB bishop. The practice of segregation in the various institutions of the Methodist Church complicated the upcoming merger of the two denominations, and Rev. Tholin felt he needed to "support, as we enter union, those strong and vocal forces within Methodism trying to preserve the integrity of the church in the midst of the racial crisis." As he explained years later, the EUBs "had very few blacks, so it was difficult to convince people that there was a problem." Like many other ministers in Chicago, Rev. Tholin kept abreast of developments down in Jackson. After hearing of the arrest of five Methodist Chicago area ministers on October 20, he and others in the ICM decided they must continue the witness, or it would "allow segregationists to believe that they could use the police power of the state to enforce segregation without any protest." Rev. Tholin concluded, "When the police power of the state is used to arrest Christians quietly attempting to enter a Christian church to worship, they must not be left to stand alone."[25]

The Chicago ministers arrived in Jackson on Saturday, October 26, and immediately went to King's house on the Tougaloo campus. Rev. Tholin remembered that when they walked in, students and others present were already singing and making preparations for the next day's visits. As Rev. King talked to the group, Rev. Tholin was struck by the distinctly evangelical symbolism involved in the church visit. He would be ascending the church steps to bear witness to their convictions just like he would in an altar call; the decision to demonstrate his commitment to his God was his alone.[26] They made plans to go in two groups to the two large Methodist churches, one to Galloway and the other to Capitol Street. Each group would consist of a black student, a Methodist minister, and an EUB minister. A third group of students would try to attend Trinity Lutheran. Unlike the visits the week before, the Methodist and EUB ministers now intended to try a tactic similar to the one employed by Rev. Hallett two weeks before. If ushers turned the integrated groups away, they planned to leave the property, making sure the black students returned safely to the car. Then the white ministers would go back to the church steps to pray. As Rev. Tholin explained, by returning to the church, the ministers would "bear a silent witness to the unity of the church and to protest its brokenness."[27]

Additionally, the ministers from Chicago wanted to come to Jackson to discuss the racial crisis with local clergy. One of the ministers they spoke with was Rev. Keller, the rector of St. Andrew's Episcopal Church. Though St. Andrew's had remained open to black visitors since June 16, Rev. Keller reported that church members were under heavy pressure to close the church to African Americans. He said his laypeople were being told they were "betraying Jackson." Rev. Keller indicated that the church would not close, and that he was working to give members a theological basis for their responses to segregationists. Significantly, though, Rev. Keller did not tell the men to try to stop future visits by integrated groups, or that the visits were undermining his efforts to guide the church toward racial reconciliation. Rev. Tholin got the impression that Rev. Keller felt the visits had been worthwhile, and that the contact between outsiders, students, and church members at St. Andrew's should continue.[28]

On October 27, which was the Methodists' Reformation Sunday, the two groups arrived at Galloway and Capitol Street. Professor Clarice Campbell once again acted as chauffeur, driving Rev. Tholin, Rev. Twigg and a black student to Galloway. There they engaged a few of the ushers in conversation, but owing to the official board's closed-door policy, the ushers refused to let them enter.[29] Rev. Tholin recalled speaking with a young white man who pointed to the mayor and a few other prominent church members who were standing at the top of the steps with the ushers. In keeping with the plan, the black student then returned to the car, while the two ministers remained on the steps in prayer. This time the police refrained from arresting the ministers. Deputy Police Chief J. R. Ray told the *Clarion-Ledger* that police did not make any arrests at Galloway because "they were not called," a very different explanation than the one he had given in court just a few days earlier. [30] Although the ministers did not understand completely why the police did not intervene, Rev. Tholin reasoned that Dr. Cunningham's testimony that he did not ask police to arrest the activists must have been a factor. Because the ushers and the police stood aside, Rev. Twigg and Rev. Tholin remained on the church steps until after the service ended and were able to bear witness to the members of the church, who asked why they were there. [31]

At Capitol Street Methodist, Rev. Cole, Rev. Trapp, and a black female student employed the same strategy as the group who went to Galloway. After an usher refused to let the integrated group enter, the student left the property. The usher then told the two ministers they could now enter the church, since they were both white. The ministers declined and instead knelt in prayer on the church steps. The usher insisted that they could worship inside but could not worship on the steps. When the ministers continued to pray aloud, the usher grabbed one of the ministers by the arm and told them to get off church property. The ministers complied and descended the steps, only to kneel once again on the sidewalk by the church. Chief Ray explained that, at this point, "the police were called" and he "arrested the ministers after first requesting, then ordering, them to leave."[32] Police charged the two with disturbing divine worship and breaching the peace. Since the arrests occurred on the sidewalk, not the church steps, the police seemed disinclined to charge the two ministers with trespassing. Combined with the arrests the previous Sunday, the arrest of Rev. Cole and Rev. Trapp brought the total of white ministers detained for trying to attend whites only churches in Jackson to six.

Meanwhile, a car with three students noticed that a police car and a paddy wagon were trailing them as they drove towards Trinity Lutheran. When they arrived at the church and saw an additional police car parked beside the sanctuary, they decided not to get out and headed back to campus. In a written statement, Eli Hockstadler, one of the three students, explained, "Since we had come to worship, not to be arrested, and knowing that an integrated group of three girls were arrested there the previous

Sunday, we were afraid to even attempt to attend the service for fear of being arrested."[33]

The two ministers police did not arrest at Galloway, Rev. Tholin and Rev. Twigg, then met with Dr. Cunningham and Rev. Granberry to discuss why their ushers continued to turn away African Americans from their churches. Reflecting on these discussions and the racial situation in Jackson a few weeks later, Rev. Tholin reasoned that white churches excluded African Americans for the same reason that Mayor Allen Thompson refused to appoint a biracial committee in the city. If he did so, whites would have deal with any given African American "as a man within the community." Similarly, to admit that African Americans were equal before God, whites would have to accept them as members of the community. Rev. Tholin concluded simply: "The police power of the state was marshaled to keep churches segregated because accepting the Negro to worship would mean accepting him fully as a man, and because the church is a captive to its culture on this issue."[34]

Upon returning to Chicago, Rev. Tholin, Rev. Trapp, and a few others affiliated with the EUB circulated a petition urging the commissions dealing with the proposed union of the Methodist and EUB denominations to rethink the merger, citing the matter of racial segregation. In the statement, the ministers made clear that they did not oppose the merger, but asserted that the commissions on union needed to fully investigate and expose the issue of discrimination within the denominations before completing the plan of union. The EUB ministers confessed "the prejudice that exists in our own congregations," and recognized that "the EUB Church is just as sinful and possibly more so than other churches."[35] Though the EUB did not have any churches in the South and did not experience the same degree of disruption over race that the Methodists were undergoing, the ministers acknowledged the steps they needed to take within their own congregations in the North to become more inclusive.

The following weekend, the cycle began again as three more Methodist ministers arrived from the Midwest to accompany black students attempting to enter Jackson churches. One was Rev. Edgar L. Hiestand Jr., a minister serving a Methodist congregation in Maywood, Illinois, a Chicago suburb. The segregated structure of the Methodist Church had concerned Rev. Hiestand since his teenage years. As a student at Northwestern, he led his fraternity brothers in visits to worship services at black churches. During his first appointment in a church in Wheaton, Illinois, he instituted exchanges with black Methodists, urging them to come to his church and

speak. Rev. Hiestand recently arrived in Maywood with specific instructions to continue the integration of the church his predecessor initiated.
Rev. Hiestand carried on the task of reaching out to the black residents in
the neighborhood of the church, and the church gradually became majority
African American during his tenure. Like many Methodist pastors in the
Chicago area, he heard about the Jackson church visit campaign and the
arrests through local media coverage and the network of ministers, including his friends Revs. Reed and Deppe, and felt he needed to take part in the
witness to demonstrate his commitment to interracialism back home.[36]

The other two ministers who arrived for the November 3 visits were
from Wisconsin. Rev. Arthur M. North served as pastor of Berlin Methodist
Church, and Rev. Barry Shaw led Wautoma Methodist Church, about a half
hour away. Both believed in a desegregated church, but unlike Rev. Hiestand
and most of the other ministers who travelled to Jackson to take part in the
witness, the two did not really see themselves as activists. They ministered
in towns with very few African American citizens, and race was simply not
a central concern in their local ministries. Moreover, unlike many of their
counterparts, their decisions to come to Jackson were rather spontaneous.
Rev. Shaw received a call from a Chicago minister urging him to make the
trip, but he still was not convinced. He told Rev. North about the call and
cited the potential for the trip to be like a spiritual life retreat. Rev. North
was not especially interested in going, but he promised that if Rev. Shaw
decided to go, he would take part as well so that Rev. North would not have
to go alone. Acceding to the friendly pressure from his friend in Chicago,
Rev. Shaw decided to go on Friday, and he and Rev. North immediately set
out by car for Jackson.[37]

The three had all arrived by Saturday, and they immediately set out to
talk with as many local ministers as they could. Though the three came to
Jackson to participate in the campaign, Rev. North and Rev. Shaw, unlike
Rev. Hiestand, also wanted to treat the weekend as a fact-finding mission,
aiming to hear all sides of the segregation issue. Earlier in the week, they
had read in the *Chicago Daily News* that Bishop Franklin and Rev. Granberry specifically asked out-of-state ministers to come talk to them in order to
understand the whole picture in Jackson. Over the course of the weekend,
the three succeeded in securing separate meetings with a variety of Jackson
ministers and authorities and, over forty years later, the visiting ministers
still had specific memories of many of these conversations.

Police Chief Ray, who was a member of Capitol Street Methodist, tried to
get them to understand that Jackson police were merely trying to keep order

when they intervened on church steps. He wanted to maintain the peace in those churches that wanted to allow blacks to attend, and he aimed to keep the peace outside of churches that wanted to forbid black visitors. While his explanation was rather predictable, the ministers recalled being stunned by their discussions with Bishop Franklin and Dr. Leggett. Bishop Franklin seemed uninterested in offering any leadership on the matter, telling them emphatically that he was just trying to hold the church together until he retired in April. Rev. Shaw recalled feeling threatened by Dr. Leggett, who told the ministers they had no business interfering with the churches in Jackson. The visitors were especially struck by the language of Dr. Leggett and Rev. Granberry, for both men wanted to talk more about the ruinous legacies of the Civil War and Reconstruction than about the integration of the Methodist Church. For Rev. North, the conversation with a non-Methodist, Dr. J. Moody McDill of Fondren Presbyterian, made the strongest impression. Dr. McDill explained how many of his close friends, men who were trying to guide their churches toward moderation, had to leave Jackson because black activists appeared on the church steps and forced the ministers to take a stand one way or the other. Dr. McDill argued that the immediate effect of the campaign so far was that it had left a leadership vacuum in the state. After talking with Dr. McDill, Rev. North started to consider whether the church visit campaign was actually doing more harm than good.[38]

In planning for Sunday's round of visits, Rev. King and the ministers decided to apply the same tactic as had been used the week before. Though Jackson police arrested two ministers when they returned to kneel on the steps of Capitol Street Methodist after the black student who accompanied them left the church property, the strategy seemed to shield the student from potential arrest, something local activists desired for the student's safety and because of the financial burdens of bail money and legal fees. Another more practical concern during this time of year was that the students should be studying for exams rather than being incarcerated. The ministers traveling to Jackson expected to find themselves in jail and understood that they needed to secure bond funding before they travelled to Jackson.

On Sunday, November 3, Rev. North, Rev. Shaw, Rev. Hiestand and a black student intended to go to Capitol Street Methodist, but instead a student driver mistakenly dropped them off at a church nearby, First Baptist. There they encountered the usual convocation of two dozen ushers at the top of the church steps, but in contrast to what occurred on prior Sundays, Rev. North and Rev. Shaw resolved not to provoke arrest by kneeling or remaining on church property after church officials turned them away. Rev. Hiestand reluctantly acceded to the change in tactics. Rev. North remembered one of the ushers being particularly cordial, saying he was working to open up the church, and that a recent vote suggested that church members were moving in the same direction. Rev. Hiestand recalled the ushers being cordial to the white ministers, but not the black student. One usher told the student to worship "at the Negro Baptist church over there." As police stood nearby, the ministers talked with the ushers for at least another half hour before realizing that they were at the wrong church.[39]

Rev. Hiestand went around the corner to Galloway, while Rev. North, Rev. Shaw, and the student proceeded down the street to St. Andrew's Episcopal Church. Worship services at both churches were already well underway. Rev. Hiestand stood outside talking with the ushers at Galloway, while the others went into St. Andrew's and sat in the back. When communion started, Rev. North recalled that many parishioners demonstrated their disapproval of the outsiders' presence by simply leaving. One of the ushers came up to them and whispered to Rev. North that because of the tense situation, it would be helpful if the integrated group refrained from going to the front and partaking of communion, which they agreed to do.

That evening, the three ministers finally went to that morning's intended destination, Capitol Street Methodist. Rev. King wanted the three ministers to go in and kneel at the alter the entire service, but Rev. North and Rev. Shaw, who were beginning to question the value of the visits, expressed doubt over the usefulness of such an overt demonstration. Rev. Hiestand, on the other hand, remained committed to the witness effort and vowed to make some sort of visible testimony to the fact that the church did not welcome all people. When they entered the church, Rev. Granberry spotted the three and asked them to help serve communion to the congregation. Rev. North and Rev. Shaw agreed to do so, but Rev. Hiestand did not. As his fellow pastors administered the sacrament to the members of Capitol Street Methodist, Rev. Hiestand remained in the pew and refused to even take communion.[40]

As a result of their experiences in Jackson that weekend, Rev. North and Rev. Shaw reached strikingly dissimilar conclusions about the effectiveness of the church visit campaign from those of Rev. Hiestand and their counterparts who preceded them to Jackson. In a three-page report that detailed their observations for an upcoming meeting of the Council of Bishops of the Methodist Church, they argued that the weekly visits— particularly the ones involving groups from Chicago and elsewhere—were hardening the positions of segregationists and setting back the goal of integration in Mississippi. They contended that the "outside pressure groups" were "creating havoc within the Mississippi Methodist Churches, for they force the integrationists to identify themselves, which, in practice, always works to the advantage of the segregationists." Citing the exit of Dr. Selah and the withdrawal of funds for the WSCS, the ministers reasoned that the church visit campaign was cutting off effective communication between integrationists and segregationists by "closing the doors to witness and turning friends into enemies." They also doubted the motives and approach of Rev. King and other participants in the church visit campaign. They believed that Rev. King suffered from "a severe persecution complex" due to his expulsion from the Mississippi Conference earlier in the year because of his "long record of aberrant behavior." The two ministers contended that other church visit participants, particularly those from the North, showed "signs of serious disturbances," for it remained unclear whether "their witness is truly out of love for the Body of Christ or serving personal needs and deficiencies."

Disputing another central claim of local civil rights activists, Rev. North and Rev. Shaw maintained, "Reports of police harassment and brutality in Mississippi are grossly exaggerated," rationalizing that even if the accounts were true, they would not be surprising, given the strong emotions involved and the "baiting tactics" of the demonstrators. Though the two ministers offered stinging indictments of the witness campaign, they concluded that the individuals most responsible for the racial controversy in Methodist churches in Jackson were the denomination's two local leaders, Bishop Franklin and District Superintendent Leggett. Based on their own conversations with these two men and other local ministers, Rev. North and Rev. Shaw judged Dr. Leggett to be a "firm advocate of segregation," and decided that Bishop Franklin was "probably undecided about his own personal convictions, but, in practice, acts as a segregationist because he is dominated by J. W. Leggett, Jr." Since other white churches and denominations in Jackson remained open to African Americans, they felt that white Methodists might accede to effective top-down leadership on the racial issue.[41] While the two ministers refrained from advising the Council of Bishops to take a particular stand on the situation in Jackson, their first-hand observations and analysis offered a rebuttal to the underlying motivations and tactics of the local activists and their Northern supporters in the church visit campaign.

Though the effort to integrate white churches in Jackson had accelerated and taken on added meaning in the month since the arrests began and the

arrival of Methodist ministers from elsewhere, the witness campaign occurred within the context of a new push to highlight voting discrimination.
On October 6, the same day that police first arrested church visitors at Capitol Street Methodist, the Council of Federated Organizations (COFO) held
a statewide convention in Jackson and officially launched the "Freedom
Ballot Campaign," which had already been in the works for a month. COFO
and other civil rights activists intended to organize the state's disenfranchised and provide them the opportunity to vote in an election that paral-
leled regular statewide elections scheduled for November 5. Though it was a
mock election, organizers hoped that with a large turnout, they could demonstrate to white Mississippians and others that African Americans in Mississippi would vote if they could. The COFO convention elected NAACP
activist Aaron Henry as their candidate for governor and, a week later, Rev.
King agreed to make the ticket biracial by adding his name to the ballot as
a candidate for lieutenant governor. For most of October and the days leading up to November 5, Rev. King and Tougaloo activists fanned out across
the state to turn out the vote, holding rallies and setting up polling stations.
Ultimately, eighty-three thousand cast their ballots in the "Freedom Ballot
Campaign." Though this was well below the goal of two hundred thousand
votes, the numbers were nonetheless significant, given the brevity of the
campaign and the intimidation and harassment from authorities and white
supremacists that organizers had endured in the last month.[42] Meanwhile,
a majority of white citizens voted to "Stand Tall with Paul," and elected as
governor Paul B. Johnson Jr., the man who confronted federal marshals the
year before in an attempt to prevent James Meredith from enrolling at the
University of Mississippi.

A few days later, on November 9, another contingent of out-of-state
ministers—all from the Detroit area—arrived in Jackson with the intention
of attending several of the local white Methodist churches.[43] As one of them
later recalled, the chief motivation of the group was a commitment to the
ideals and constitution of the Methodist Church, which held that Methodists should be able to worship at any Methodist church in the country. All
of them were part of a group they called the "Dirty Thirty," which broadly
aimed to further the process of integration in their conference and in their
own churches. One of the chief issues at the time was the process of ministerial appointments. Many downtown churches that chose to remain in
their original locations rather than move to white suburbs were becoming interracial because of the ongoing desegregation of the structure of
the Detroit Conference, and because of the city's changing demographics.

The ministers were primarily concerned that Methodist authorities were depriving these inner-city churches of effective leadership, because they would often move more experienced pastors to more affluent and white suburban churches and appoint younger, greener ministers to the interracial churches.[44]

One of the ministers who came to Jackson this weekend, Rev. Paul Lowley, served as an associate pastor in an interracial, inner-city church undergoing this transformation. Like a few of the other young Methodist ministers from the Midwest who joined the witness effort in Mississippi, he had attended seminary at Garrett Biblical Institute in Evanston, Illinois. Though the school was not especially liberal at the time, it employed some socially liberal professors. One of these teachers, Rev. Tyler Thompson, had a profound effect on Rev. Lowley and his understanding of confrontation and garnering attention during periods of social unrest. While in seminary, Rev. Lowley joined CORE and participated in several demonstrations and pickets of local businesses. He put his understanding of community organizing into action while serving in his first appointment in Detroit, where he soon heard about the arrests at Methodist churches in Jackson. With a few of his friends and fellow ministers making the trip, Rev. Lowley decided to join as well. He did not intend to get arrested, but instead wanted to engage the white Methodists in Jackson in dialogue in order to reason with them. In addition to his strong feelings on race, he felt that because the Methodist Church was a connectional denomination, it was simply indefensible to turn Methodists away from a Methodist church.[45]

Though each of the groups was unique in its own right, the involvement of two of the men in this particular group gave this visit added meaning. Rev. Archie Rich was an African American, so for the first time in the campaign, a black Methodist minister would attempt to worship at a white Methodist church in Jackson. Moreover, the inclusion of Rev. Richard Raines Jr. added an important name to the group. He was the son of Bishop Richard C. Raines, the presiding bishop of the Indiana area of the Methodist Church and Vice Chairman of the CRR. To ensure that churches under his tutelage were aware of his position on racial policies, Bishop Raines wrote all his pastors in early September, reminding them of the 1960 *Discipline* denouncing discrimination on the basis of race, culture, or religion. He instructed his pastors to be certain that all visitors "be received cordially and seated insofar as possible where he or they choose," and he advised the official boards to discuss how they could work to affirm human dignity in their churches and communities.[46] Moreover, Rev. Raines had two brothers who were Methodist ministers, as well as vocal advocates for civil rights. One brother, Rev. John Curtis Raines of Long Island, participated in the Freedom Ride campaign in 1961 and was jailed in Little Rock, Arkansas. Another brother, Rev. Robert A. Raines of Germantown, Pennsylvania, was a leader in the fight to desegregate the denomination and was slated to come to Jackson in two months to lead a devotional retreat of ministers in the Mississippi Conference. Though not as prominent as his father or even his brothers, Rev. Richard Raines tried to lead his own congregation toward greater inclusiveness. Just before he arrived at Whitfield Methodist, the church relocated to Dearborn from inner-city Detroit, where the church was becoming surrounded by a black neighborhood. When Rev. Raines posted a note on the church's message board stating, "All races are welcome," a church official removed it and took away the key to the board. Though discouraged, Rev. Raines became even more involved with other young Methodist ministers in an effort to further the process of integration in the Detroit Conference. When he heard about the church visit campaign in Jackson at one of the meetings of this group, he quickly enlisted.[47]

On Sunday, November 10, Rev. King accompanied Revs. Rich and Lowley as they tried to attend one of the morning services at Galloway Memorial. Though all three were Methodist ministers, ushers objected to the entry of Rev. Rich because of his race, and the three left the premises. Rev. Rich and Rev. Lowley then joined the rest of the group at Capitol Street Methodist. Before they arrived, Rev. Richard Raines and Rev. Al Bamsey entered the church through a side door and, except during the singing of hymns, the two ministers knelt in silent witness at the railing in the front of the church throughout the entire service. This was a new tactic, one intended to be a poignant one. As Rev. Raines later recalled, they aimed to present "the incongruity of saying yes to one person and no to another person based upon race." No one bothered them as they knelt at the rail, and only a few church members confronted them after the service. Rev. Bamsey later remembered being struck by the fact that the language of the sermon sounded so normal—except that it did not pertain to African Americans.[48] Outside, ushers barred the integrated group of Rev. Rich, Rev. Lowley, and Rev. Charles Sutton from going in, but permitted the men to discuss the situation for about a half hour. Rev. Lowley recalled that a large group of ushers met the ministers at the bottom of the steps, and that one of the ushers acted as spokesman. He pointed at each of the ministers and said, "You can come in and you can come in." Then, pointing at Rev. Rich, he said, "But you can't come in." When Rev. Lowley asked why Rev. Rich could not worship with them because they were all Methodist ministers and, more fundamentally, because they were all human beings with equal rights, he received a reply that stunned him. The usher pointed to Rev. Rich and said, "That man is not fully human." A man dressed in Sunday clothes and identifying himself as the police chief stepped forward and asked the ministers to follow him. He told them to get in their car and drive behind him to the police station. The three did not know if they were being arrested, but they did as Chief Ray instructed. When they arrived at the police station, he told them he thought they were in danger at Capitol Street Methodist, that the crowd was becoming too hostile. Police did not arrest or charge them with anything, and Rev. Lowley remembered Chief Ray as completely cordial and understanding. Rev. Lowley reasoned at the time that someone—perhaps even Bishop Franklin—specifically asked the police not to arrest any visitors because of the Council of Bishops meeting in Detroit in a few days. That evening, the ministers went back to Galloway, where ushers again refused to allow the group to enter because of the presence of Rev. Rich. Utilizing the tactic they employed that morning at Capitol Street, two of them went in through a side door inside and spent some time afterwards talking with Dr. Cunningham.[49]

Though the Methodist ministers hoped to sway the consciences of white Methodists in Jackson by bearing witness to their Christian beliefs on the steps of churches, they were beginning to realize that the churches were not interested in altering their exclusion policies, and—at least at Galloway— he congregation was becoming even more entrenched in its closed-door policies. The day after attempted visits by the Detroit group, at the regular monthly meeting of the official board, lay leaders at Galloway once again affirmed the church's attendance policy and clarified the procedure for rejecting black visitors. This was the first meeting since the initial arrests at Galloway, which included the jailing of a member of the church, and the first board meeting since, during subsequent visits, the excluded ministers remained on the church property after being turned away. The chairman of the official board read a statement affirming that Galloway intended to remain "a segregated church," since a majority of the board and of church members supported the exclusion policy. Addressing rumors that the church might be in the process of opening the doors, he stated unequivocally, "There is no such plan and there is no inclination on the part of our Ministers or the Officials of the Church to make any move that would be against the majority." The statement went on to spell out the procedure for turning away certain visitors and seeking the aid of the police, specifically addressing the type of tactics that out-of-state ministers had utilized within the last several weeks. Not only were African Americans forbidden from admission to church services, they could not stand or remain on the property of Galloway during any church service. Though the statement instructed ushers to try to avoid any arrests, it maintained, "Police assistance will be requested only when our officially designated representatives are unable to cope with problem situations." Alluding to the conduct of the Garners and other dissenting members of Galloway, the chairman indicated, "All members not officially assigned to deal with demonstrators are requested to ignore these activities and not to engage in discussions or become otherwise involved."[50]

A month after Jackson police began arresting integrated groups on the steps of churches, and five months after the visits began, the campaign had yielded mixed results in its effort to open the city's white churches. Though Rev. King and the Tougaloo activists hoped that the presence of Methodist ministers might help prod churches into moderating their positions, no Methodist churches admitted the groups. As proven on November 10, Methodist churches would not even admit an ordained Methodist pastor if he were black. Even in some of the churches that had admitted the students, such as St. Andrew's Episcopal and Fondren Presbyterian, actions during the last month showed that the activists were far from welcome. Yet the campaign created a space that opened dialogue between Northern and Southern Christians. Out-of-state ministers came to witness on church steps, but they also came to talk about the racial crisis with church people and their ministers. Additionally, because of arrests during the last month, the campaign caught the attention of Methodist ministers and laypeople throughout the country, who saw Jackson as the primary battleground in an effort to desegregate the denomination. The arrests in front of Methodist churches in Jackson provided Methodists nationwide with a clear and unambiguous reminder that local congregations continued to flaunt the ideals of the denomination. Activists aimed to highlight this fact ahead of the upcoming general conference, but during the week of November 11, they turned their attention to a meeting of the country's Methodist bishops in Detroit.

[10]

Behind the "Magnolia Curtain"

NOVEMBER–DECEMBER 1963

By mid-November 1963, Jackson activists and their supporters had several reasons to feel optimistic about the effectiveness of the church visit campaign. Following the arrests on October 20, police refrained from intervening and incarcerating integrated groups for two consecutive Sundays. Though arrests generated national support and underscored the persistence of discrimination within churches, police interference had inhibited constructive dialogue on the church steps and seemed to galvanize the voices of opposition inside the churches. Many church people equated the integration effort with "outside agitation," a perception that gained even more traction with the arrival and arrests of out-of-state ministers. The police restraint on the first two Sundays in November therefore opened a space for discourse among the Tougaloo students, their clerical allies, and the white Christians of Jackson.

Another reason that Jackson activists felt more sanguine was that their effort seemed to be galvanizing Methodist support for definitive desegregation of the denomination. Many black and white Methodists had labored since the union of the Northern and Southern churches in 1938 to integrate all the structures of the denomination, but until the Jackson church visit campaign, no Methodist had ever been arrested for trying to do so. The weekly exclusion of African Americans from white Methodist churches in Jackson accentuated in unambiguous terms the problem of segregation within the Methodist Church. When presiding and retired bishops of the church met in Detroit for three days, concern over racial discrimination—brought to their attention largely by the Jackson campaign—became predominant.

As the bishops of the Methodist Church convened at a hotel in downtown Detroit for their biannual meetings on November 12, Methodist ministers descended upon the city as well to testify to their outrage over the arrests in Jackson and to lobby the bishops to take a strong stand in favor of complete racial integration of the church. About sixty ministers and seminarians, including Rev. King, Rev. Reed, and many others directly associated with the Jackson church visit campaign, held a prayer vigil at the historic Central Methodist Church, near the hotel. Central Methodist was the state's first Protestant congregation, and in the last few decades it had become known for the liberal social activism of its clergy. One of the church's five pastors, Rev. Sutton, participated in the latest witness in Jackson, and its senior pastor, Rev. James Laird, spearheaded local efforts to instigate interracial ministerial appointments in the Detroit Conference. Meeting there, the ministers made plans to picket the next day just outside the room where the bishops planned to meet to pressure their superiors into making a powerful statement.[1]

Yet not all of the ministers agreed with the approach of Rev. King and his supporters. Rev. Arthur North, who joined in the witness and talked with a variety of Jackson clergy and authorities just over a week before, travelled to Detroit to explain to anyone who would listen how the visit campaign was tearing the church apart in Mississippi, actually undermining the cause of integration. Together with Rev. Shaw, who had gone to Jackson with him, he coauthored a memo describing the experience there. Rev. North deposited copies of the document in the hotel mailbox of every bishop and talked informally with several bishops, including some from abroad. He tried to explain to them that quiet progress was being made inside the churches. He recalled years later that much of his lobbying centered on correcting misrepresentations about the situation in Jackson made by Rev. King and his allies. He felt that Rev. King was gaining too much ground by distorting facts. At one point, when Rev. King addressed the group and explained how the Ku Klux Klan tried to murder him in a car accident in June, Rev. North confronted him directly, complaining that there was no evidence to support such an accusation.[2]

On November 13, the ministers waited outside the bishops' meeting room. Many wore arm bands with the symbol "20–20," referring to the section of the Methodist *Discipline* that declared that Methodist churches open to all. They had cancelled their planned demonstration when they learned that the bishops were indeed preparing a statement on race. Inside the meeting room, all of the presiding and retired bishops of the Methodist

Church discussed the implications of segregation in churches and debated the precise language of their announcement. The day before, they assigned the message committee to draw up a statement, which they now considered. One bishop argued that the closing of churches to African Americans harmed Christian mission efforts everywhere, saying that it was a "blow to evangelism all over the world." Another advised the group to specifically name and condemn Capitol Street Methodist Church in Jackson for its policies, which he felt were a "blot against the house of God." A few Southern bishops urged them to downplay the finger-pointing and to avoid any wording that others could interpret as an endorsement of the tactics of the church visitors in Jackson. Bishop Franklin pleaded against criticizing any individual church by name and tried to get his fellow bishops to understand that the ministers coming to Jackson were "hurting and not helping." The bishop of Georgia, who also had to contend with several recent attempts to integrate white churches in his conference, seconded Bishop Franklin's opinion, arguing that the church visits amounted to "irresponsible meddling." He counseled more "prayer, patience, and intelligent negotiation."[3]

The secretary of the Council of Bishops presented a sample of letters he received from concerned Methodists urging more vigorous action by the bishops. One was from a Nashville, Tennessee, resident who was currently serving as staff person at the General Board of Evangelism in Norway. He explained that he was at a Methodist Youth Camp in Norway when the youth there saw pictures on the television of Methodist churches in Jackson turning away African Americans. He reported that the young Norwegians "were greatly upset," and concluded sharply, "I believe that the image of Methodism in the United States is being greatly hurt by this television picture."[4] The bishop also produced a letter from Rev. James Nixon, who wrote on behalf of the ministers planning to convene in Detroit. Though the ministers knew that the bishops would, at a minimum, reaffirm their San Francisco statement from earlier in the year and the positions articulated in the 1960 *Discipline*, the ministers wanted the bishops to clearly communicate their position on the right to worship in a Methodist Church, a right that Methodists in Jackson so explicitly denied. In what Rev. Nixon and the others termed "An Anguished Appeal to the Council of Bishops on Freedom of Worship," they summarized the arrests in October and argued that the closed church doors violated church beliefs, including the Methodist Social Creed. Not only was the denial of the right to worship "offensive to the Christian conscience," it was a "betrayal of [the church's] Master." The ministers believed, "The Methodist Church cannot be a redemptive element in culture when it practices the same segregation as the society it would redeem." They urged the bishops to assume leadership on the issue of freedom to worship, ordering all churches to open their doors, and supporting those who would need to implement change on the local level.[5]

After two and a half hours, the bishop of Texas emerged from the meeting room and read the amended statement to the protesting ministers. He announced that the document reflected the unanimous opinion of all the bishops, including Bishop Franklin of Mississippi and other white Southern bishops. The bishops affirmed, "The Methodist Church stands for the equal rights of all racial, cultural, and religious groups," and then addressed the principal concerns of the assembled ministers and seminarians. The bishops stated that the "Methodist Church is an inclusive church," and that they therefore urged all pastors "to receive all who are qualified and who desire to be received without regard to race, color or national origin." Moreover, the bishops condemned any attempt to deny someone membership or the ability to worship in any congregation because of race. Pointedly referring to the events in Jackson, the bishops held that "to move to arrest any persons attempting to worship is to us an outrage."[6] By asserting that only pastors maintained the authority to admit visitors, they were explicitly disavowing the power of lay boards that voted to close church doors. Later in their statement, the bishops affirmed the right of oppressed minorities to protest and assemble in public, as long as demonstrations were orderly. The declaration represented the strongest statement yet by Methodist bishops on the issue of open doors and inclusiveness, and the sixty ministers responded with applause outside the Michigan Room. As Rev. King remembered, he and others "thought something significant had happened."[7]

While the bishops continued to discuss other business in closed session, the ministers reconvened at Central Methodist and began to examine the wording of the bishops' statement. Many of the ministers quickly realized that their applause at the hotel had been a bit premature, and they began composing a response. In their reply, the ministers praised the bishops for trying to overcome the "leadership vacuum" that "helped produce the present crisis in which we find the precepts of Jesus flaunted, the Church silent on crucial issues, and a situation in which we have expressed more concern for the unity as an institution than for unity in Christ." They argued, "Where there is effective and forthright moral leadership at the top . . . the undecided are encouraged to take a positive position, and those who support a segregated church and society are impeded in their efforts to threaten." The ministers then asked the bishops for tangible action that would break down racial barriers in the denomination. Their first two recommendations directly concerned the situation in Jackson. Step number one was to send an unambiguous appeal for all the Methodist churches in Jackson to open their doors now. Step number two was to endorse the church visit campaign, specifically the actions of those Methodists who tried to worship at whites only churches. The other proposals addressed larger issues, such as the abolition of central jurisdiction, the full integration of all institutions of the church, and the endorsement of more social action by the denomination, including providing bail bonds and legal defense for civil rights activists. Their final recommendation seemed simple enough but directly concerned the dissemination of the bishops' statement into places like Jackson. They suggested that every local church hear the full text of the statement of the bishops.[8] The ministers embraced the ideals in the declaration of the Council of Bishops, but they decried the lack of specificity in its implementation.

Disappointed with the adequacy of the bishops' statement, the ministers who had come to Detroit immediately organized a new group, Methodists for Church Renewal (MCR), to keep up the pressure on Methodist leaders for complete integration of the denomination. Though the individuals within MCR articulated a broad set of social objectives, the concern over racial justice within the church remained paramount. As Rev. Deppe later remembered, MCR came into being because of the October arrests in Jackson and the bishops' ineffective response to it.[9] With the general conference in Pittsburgh just a few months away, MCR aimed to push the denomination to end volunteerism in desegregation of the church. Along with Rev. Reed and others in Chicago, MCR also intended to help send more ministers to Jackson to participate in the witness. Rev. Laird, host of the Detroit assembly, agreed to chair MCR and locate the group's headquarters at his church. The steering committee of MCR included ministers and professors who had followed the situation in Jackson since the arrests on World-Wide Communion Sunday. Rev. James D. Nixon of Detroit and Rev. John M. Badertscher of Cleveland, Ohio, for instance, were already making plans to travel to Jackson the very next weekend.[10]

In order to test whether Methodist churches in Jackson planned to alter their exclusion policies after the strong proclamation made by their bishops, and to see if Bishop Franklin intended to put into action the ideals he affirmed by signing the statement, Rev. King, Tougaloo students, and ministers from Detroit and Cleveland made preparations for another round of visits the following Sunday, November 17. The students in particular recognized the value in continuing the campaign now that it was finally gaining national attention. In a campus newsletter published that week, student activists declared, "What began as an activity of secondary importance during the civil rights demonstrations of last summer, has become one of the most important aspects of the Jackson Movement." The newsletter reprinted the bishops' statement and pointed out that the campaign had the attention of the Methodist Church hierarchy and the NCC.[11]

Aiming to send as direct a statement as possible to the white Methodist community in Jackson, the Tougaloo activists and the ministers and laymen from Detroit and Cleveland who accompanied them decided to target the four largest Methodist churches in Jackson: Galloway Memorial, Capitol Street, St. Luke's, and Broadmeadow, a suburban church activists had not yet attempted to enter. The group of visitors included seven pastors from the Detroit area and two ministers and two laymen from Cleveland, Ohio.[12]

For the second consecutive Sunday, the visits to white churches would include African American ministers. This weekend there were two. Dr. Charles E. Morton was a distinguished Baptist pastor, so he joined the campaign as the first non-Methodist minister to take part in the witness. His participation was also unique because he was a native Southerner. Dr. Morton was born in Bessemer, Alabama, and attended Morehouse College in Atlanta. He taught at black colleges in New Orleans and in Fayetteville, North Carolina, where he became active in the NAACP and in local political campaigns. In September, he had accepted the pastorate at Metropolitan Baptist Church, a large, predominantly black middle class church in Detroit, and quickly became friends with Rev. Nixon, who enlisted him in the trip to Jackson. Though he was not a Methodist, Dr. Morton joined the church visit campaign simply because he wanted to be sure that "Methodists were acting according to the Discipline of the church," and "acting as Christians."[13]

Rev. Woodie White served as senior pastor of East Grand Boulevard Methodist Church, a mostly white congregation. When he became associate pastor of the church two years earlier, the event marked the first biracial ministerial appointment in the history of Methodism in the state.[14] Though he became involved in a youth chapter of the NAACP as a teenager in New York City, his hometown, Rev. White's real education about Southern race relations occurred while he attended Paine College in Augusta, Georgia, in the 1950s. Unlike most of the other ministers who went to Jackson as part of the witness, Rev. White knew Rev. King very well. The two were roommates their first year at the Boston University School of Theology and had traveled often to Rev. White's home in New York City. As they became close, Rev. White saw Rev. King as someone totally different from the stereotypical

white man from Mississippi that he envisioned. He later recalled how Rev.
King struck him as "clearly the most committed person I had met personally who was involved in the struggle of race in the South." The two men had
been in constant contact during the month following the first arrests and
discussed the role of non-students in the campaign. They shared concerns
about the safety of the Tougaloo students, should they continue the campaign unassisted, and also worried that the press and others were seeing the
exclusion policy of churches in Jackson as too localized an issue. Rev. King
thought that one way to ensure the safety of the students as well as bring
public attention would be to invite pastors to accompany the students on
their church visits.[15]

Like his colleagues in Detroit, Rev. John Badertscher was at the forefront of an effort to address the problems facing downtown Methodist
churches in Cleveland. Inner-city churches there and in Detroit were losing members to white suburban churches and had trouble integrating into
the increasingly black communities that surrounded them. His district superintendent had recently appointed him head of a new group designed to
build links of cooperation and support between inner-city congregations
and the more prosperous suburban churches. In order to develop these
ties, he wanted African Americans to see the denomination—and Methodists in Cleveland especially—in support of integration. When he received
a call from Rev. Deppe asking him to take part in the Jackson witness, he
quickly enlisted and pledged to arrange for others in the area to join him.
At an October meeting of his district leaders, Rev. Badertscher made the
case for a group to make the trip to Jackson on behalf of the Cleveland
District. Though some at the meeting expressed reservations, saying that
ministers should tackle segregation at home first, Rev. Badertscher's position prevailed, and the district superintendent even promised to provide
money for bail if the group found itself in jail. Rev. Badertscher argued that
Northern cities, especially Cleveland, were just as segregated as Southern
cities. Yet he hoped that his participation in the witness in Jackson would
call attention to the problem of segregation in the Methodist Church in
Cleveland. He believed that "the scandal of a segregated structure . . . left
the white and black Methodist churches institutionally isolated and without public credibility in their advocacy for racial justice." He successfully
recruited another young Methodist minister, Rev. Ken Houghland, and two
laymen, Robert Meeks and Ed Craun, to join him. Meeks was a seventy-
year-old retired schoolteacher, while Craun was a head salesman for a local
company and one of the more high profile and theologically conservative

laymen in the district. For Rev. Badertscher, the presence of Craun likely swayed the vote of the Cleveland District in favor of the trip and gave the witness added legitimacy.[16]

The groups from Detroit and Cleveland arrived in Jackson on Saturday to receive instructions from Rev. Ed King and the student activists and to try to make contact with local clergy whose churches they would target the next day. Discussing strategy, they resolved to apply more pressure on the churches than had been employed the previous two Sundays. Rather than walking away from the church after ushers refused them entry, Rev. King and the ministers decided they would present themselves for admission and remain in quiet prayer, even if police stepped in to arrest them. As Rev. Badertscher recalled, the members of "white churches needed to be made aware of the evils being committed in their name."[17] After the ministers received their assignments for the next day, three of them called on Rev. Frank Dement Jr., pastor of the church they would attempt to visit the next day, St. Luke's Methodist. Rev. Dement invited them to his home on Saturday night and tried to dissuade them from coming. He explained the attitude of the church, that St. Luke's took a position that no black people could worship there and that if they came, police would arrest them. When Rev. White pointed out the position of the denomination as stated in the *Discipline*, that Methodist churches should be open to all, Rev. Dement countered that the statement was just a resolution, not a church law. He encouraged the group to go back home and take care of race problems in the North.[18]

On Sunday, November 17, integrated groups of ministers, laymen, and students arrived for morning worship at four Methodist churches. At Galloway Memorial, Rev. Houghland, Craun, and Herman Glass Jr., a Tougaloo student from Louisville, Mississippi, ascended the church steps and greeted the ushers. Rev. Houghland presented them with a letter from his bishop in Cleveland defending their effort and stating the policy of the denomination to admit fellow Methodists. One of the ushers responded, "You can debate your point and we can debate our point and we won't settle anything. If you want to worship together, there is a Negro church on Lynch Street." As the ushers stepped away, the three men bowed their heads in prayer. At one point, a white woman entering the church went over and shook their hands. When police arrived, the ushers again presented the letter from their bishop. One of the police officers said, "You settle that with the bishop in this conference, not your conference." After they refused to leave the church steps, the police arrested the three men and charged them each with trespassing and disturbing divine worship.[19]

Nearby, four of the white Detroit ministers attempted to attend worship at Capitol Street Methodist. One of them, Rev. Robert Willoughby, had arrived earlier and attended the college age Sunday school class with two white students. After Sunday school, he met a colleague out front and they presented themselves to the ushers for admittance. The ushers agreed to let them enter, as long as they signed a mimeographed statement agreeing to abide by the order of worship and to refrain from making any disturbance during the service. Church officials at Capitol Street clearly wanted to avoid the type of display that occurred the week before, when two Methodist ministers knelt at the railing in the front of the sanctuary throughout the entire service. The visitors submitted to this new requirement and walked inside, as Rev. Nixon and Dr. Morton approached the church from the left side.

John Pratt, the counsel to CRR, stood across the street to observe. While the two ministers were still on the sidewalk, a large group of ushers rushed down the stairs and confronted them. One usher asked, "What do you want here?" Rev. Nixon replied, "We have come to worship God." Another usher raised a hand that held a sheet of folded white paper, which to Rev. Nixon appeared to be some sort of signal to the policemen across the street. Rev. Nixon then announced that he had a copy of the statement of the Council of Bishops he wanted to read. The spokesman for the ushers told the ministers that they were not interested in hearing it, insisting that the two men were not going to worship there. When one of the ushers tried to grab Rev. Nixon's arm, Rev. Nixon and Dr. Morton dropped to their knees and began praying on the sidewalk. At this point, Rev. Nixon heard a paddy wagon approaching and then saw a policeman approaching the head usher. The officer asked the usher, "Do you prefer charges?" and the usher nodded and said, "Yes." When the two ministers saw black trusties heading toward them to escort them to the wagon, the ministers stood up and walked to the vehicle, submitting to their arrest. After the service, Rev. Willoughby and Rev. Bailey emerged from the church and greeted Rev. Granberry. A number of Capitol Street members and Millsaps students approached them as well and said that they were glad to see them.[20]

The pattern of arrests of integrated groups this Sunday continued at two more Methodist churches. Rev. Badertscher and Marvin L. Palmore, a Tougaloo student from Picayune, attempted to worship at Broadmeadow Methodist. Unlike the other Methodist churches targeted this Sunday, Broadmeadow was being approached for the first time by activists trying to attend worship services. Though it is not clear why activists had avoided the church up to that point, Broadmeadow clearly lacked the same strategic importance. It was a newer, suburban congregation, and activists perhaps saw the futility trying to open it because Broadmeadow's pastor, Rev. Charles Duke, was an avowed racial conservative. Earlier in the year, for instance, in response to the "born of conviction" controversy, he had given a sermon in which he told his congregation, "I do not accept intergration [sic] as an advancement for the Negro and I do not accept segregation as discrimination against the Negro." [21] As Rev. Badertscher later remembered, the whole episode on November 17 was over "with stunning swiftness." Ushers met the two visitors on the steps, and one of the ushers read a prepared statement. When Rev. Badertscher and Palmore insisted they were not interested in leaving, police stepped in and arrested them. One of the officers asked Rev. Badertscher, "Have you Yankees come down here just to stir up trouble with our nigras?" Rev. Badertscher answered, "No sir, I don't think taking a friend to church is stirring up trouble." They were on their way to jail before the congregation had sung the opening hymn. [22]

At St. Luke's Methodist, which activists had attempted to enter on two previous occasions in October, when they met with no police interference, Rev. White, Rev. Donald Hall, and Meeks, a white seventy-three-year-old layman from Cleveland, arrived for the morning service. A car dropped the three off right in front of the church, and as they were about to step off the sidewalk, two men stopped the group. One of the men asked what they wanted, and the ministers and layman said that they came to worship. One of the local men, now identifying himself as the chief usher, said that the three "were not wanted." The other local man said they were "agitating and trespassing." Rev. White asked if this was a Methodist church, and explained that he did not understand how he, a Methodist minister, Rev. Hall, also a Methodist minister, and Meeks, a Methodist layman, could possibly be accused of trespassing at a Methodist church. Rev. White asked how they could be agitating when all they wanted to do was worship. These arguments did little to convince the head usher, who told the men that their status as a mixed group indicated they were agitators. One of the ushers then signaled for policemen, who left their squad car and came over to where the group stood. The usher informed the policemen that he did not want the three men there, and that they refused to leave. A policeman asked them if they understood what the usher demanded, and said that if they did not leave, they would be arrested. Rev. White again said that all they wanted to do was worship together. The policeman asked the usher if he wanted to charge the three, and he said yes. As was the case with the other seven arrested that day, police charged the three men with trespassing and disturbing worship, though it was unclear to them whether they were even on church property, and they were not loud or disruptive at any time.[23]

If the church visits of November 17 represented a test of how Methodist church people in Jackson would respond to the principles espoused by their bishops a few days earlier, then the churches clearly indicated their unwillingness to accept the precepts of their denominational leaders. Ushers at all four Methodist churches called in the police, who arrested a total of ten visitors. Police intervention resulted in the first mass arrests outside Jackson churches in a month, and brought the total to twenty-seven arrests since police first stepped in on October 6. Though police intervention at the churches was not guaranteed each Sunday, policemen established a clear pattern of direct involvement. Police maintained a watchful eye at each of the churches, but kept their distance until a church authority requested their help, either orally or by a signal. Ushers were becoming increasingly reluctant to engage the visitors in any substantive dialogue. Denied the opportunity to worship or to make their witness verbally, the church visitors testified to their convictions silently, by standing or by kneeling in prayer. These physical testimonies now took on added meaning because these church visitors had the implicit backing of the Council of Bishops. Though the bishops stopped short of endorsing their effort outright, the bishops clearly denounced closed church doors and offered support to activists who conducted orderly demonstrations to protest racial oppression.

All ten of those arrested were accused of trespassing and disturbing divine worship, and ordered to pay a $500 bond for each charge. Upon arriving at the jail, police officials segregated the ministers and laymen into separate cells based upon race. All of the ministers remained in jail for the rest of the week, while one of the laymen at Central Methodist Church in Detroit, who headed a credit union, organized bail for the Detroit team. The district superintendent of the Methodist Union of Cleveland put up the bail for the Cleveland group. Rev. White recalled this as a particularly harrowing experience, because for the first time since arriving in Mississippi, he was not with his colleagues. Until Dr. Morton arrived in his cell, Rev. White was all by himself. For Dr. Morton, the organization of the entire jail was intriguing. He remembered how the black trustees would pass notes back and forth to them. He got the sense that the black trustees were doing something to other white prisoners' food and wanted to be sure that the food intended for them reached its proper destination. The white ministers and laymen kept busy reading, singing hymns, sharing stories of their respective arrests, and receiving a few visitors.[24]

One of their guests was Francis Stevens, the former conference lay leader and a member of Broadmeadow Methodist Church. Stevens was especially distressed by the first arrests at Capitol Street and had personally investigated the situation a few weeks before, concluding that Mayor Allen Thompson ordered the police to intervene because of pressure he was receiving from segregationist leaders. Now, Stevens confronted arrests at his own church. He told the men from Cleveland that he disagreed with the policy of his official board, but also opposed the approach employed by the Northern ministers in their attempt to open his church doors. He wanted the visitors to see the futility of their effort, since the church visits "merely hardened the resolve of segregationists and antagonized laymen who were then in doubt as to what policy they ought to follow." Stevens appreciated the intention of the ministers and laymen, but he nevertheless felt that the witness campaign was doing more harm than good.[25]

Though the church visit campaign and the arrests at Jackson churches had garnered national media attention at various times since June, the significance of the arrests at Methodist churches in Jackson in the context of the statement on race made by Methodist bishops in Detroit captured the attention of the editorial cartoonist for the *Los Angeles Times*. The day after the newspaper detailed the arrests on November 17, the *Times* published an illustration by Bruce Russell, the longtime and Pulitzer Prize-winning cartoonist for the paper. In his drawing, titled "Way of the Cross" at the bottom of the cartoon, Russell depicted the doors of a brick church with a large sign in the foreground. Where the viewer would expect to see the name of the church, Russell wrote "Jackson, Mississippi church," and where the title of the upcoming sermon would normally appear, he inscribed, "Sermon . . . 'Come unto Me' ALL EXCEPT YOU KNOW WHO!"[26] The cartoon succinctly summarized the situation in Jackson. Russell did not specifically name the church because he did not need to, since all but a few white churches in the city banned African Americans. The title of the sermon pointed to the failure to follow Christ's teachings, while also suggesting that the chief culpability for denying admission to African Americans belonged to the ministers themselves. The absence of people from the cartoon emphasized the lack of humanity in the whole affair and hinted at the end result, that a church continuing to preach exclusion would become irrelevant, isolated, and uninhabited.

With the Methodist churches in Jackson showing no interest in abiding by the stated ideals of their bishops, Tougaloo activists prepared for another round of visits the following Sunday. Four white ministers from Ohio had already made plans to participate in the witness after being contacted by Rev. Hallett, who helped organized the trips of out-of-state ministers to Jackson, and Dr. C. Everett Tilson, a leader in the recently-formed MCR and a professor at Methodist Theological School in Delaware, Ohio. Rev. Hallett enlisted Rev. Al Tomer, a pastor in Kenton, Ohio, and a friend since seminary, who then pledged to recruit three others. As Rev. Tomer explained in a letter to Rev. King, he and a few others were working to end discrimination in Kenton. He felt strongly "that we must try to help keep people from cutting themselves off from God by cutting themselves off from their Negro brothers." Rev. Tomer made a number of calls, not all of which were well-received, but three others, Rev. Richard Teller of Tipp City, Rev. John Wagner of Richwood, and Rev. John Collins from the Cincinnati area, agreed to join the witness. The four men drove out of Ohio on Friday, November 22, but shortly after crossing the state line into Mississippi, they learned over the radio the news that would set the mood for the entire weekend and the weeks ahead, that President John F. Kennedy had been assassinated in Texas.[27]

All four ministers maintained a commitment to social justice based upon Christian convictions, but none of them really saw himself as a civil rights activist before they came to Jackson. Their participation in the witness resulted from earlier experiences that shaped their views on race. Rev. Teller first saw with his own eyes the institutionalization of racial inequality while completing basic training in 1945 in Macon, Georgia, where the extreme poverty of rural blacks truly shocked him. He developed a religious basis for understanding the struggle of African Americans while attending Union Theological Seminary and studying under men like Reinhold Niebuhr. During his first appointment to a white Methodist church, in Portsmouth, Ohio, he initiated a pastoral exchange with a local black Methodist church on several Sundays and led efforts that succeeded in integrating a public swimming pool. When he told his lay leaders in Tipp City about his intention to join the Jackson church visit campaign, they supported him simply because he felt so strongly about integration.

Revs. Tomer and Wagner did not receive much encouragement from their lay leaders. Rev. Tomer's official board members were clearly unenthusiastic about his plans, though they agreed not to stand in his way. Several Kenton residents came up to him and told him not to interfere in someone else's affairs. He received a letter from a businessman who said he disagreed with his approach, but included fifty dollars to help cover trip expenses. When Rev. Wagner told his congregation about his intentions, only two members supported him, a physician and a farmer. The two men promised to secure his bail money so he would not have to worry about it. Even without the backing of his church, Rev. Wagner felt he had been at the church long enough to build up a level of trust so that, at a minimum, his congregation respected his judgment.[28]

On Saturday, the four visiting ministers secured meetings with the ministers of the two churches they planned to attend the next day. The four met with Rev. William Leggett III, pastor of Christ Methodist and son of the District Superintendent William Leggett II, and Rev. A. E. Dyess of Wesley Memorial. Tougaloo activists had not yet attempted to enter either Methodist church and felt that the ministers might avoid arrest by visiting churches where policemen were not likely to be present. Rev. Wagner and Rev. Tomer later reported to Joan Trumpauer that they did not find Rev. Leggett to be as rabidly segregationist as his father. With the president's murder overshadowing their conversation about race and the South, they found him to be genuinely concerned. Rev. Leggett told the ministers that he had long wrestled with the racial question, but believed that as a pastor, he needed to "meet the people where they were and try to lead them gradually to where they should be." As he saw it, even discussing the possibility of integration would split the church and separate him from his congregation, for his official board had already voted to prohibit any African Americans or other agitators. Rev. Leggett said he hoped the two ministers and their black companion would not come, but the two ministers promised that they would be peaceful in their witness the next day. For the Ohio ministers, Rev. Leggett represented the tenuous position of moderates in Mississippi, who "desire progress to be made on this problem but do not dare to speak or act for fear of the consequences." Rev. Tomer wondered if moderates could have changed the racial climate in Mississippi if they had spoken out sooner. Years later, though, the memory that remained most vivid for Rev. Teller and Rev. Tomer was of a book they saw right behind Rev. Leggett on a shelf in his office, Dietrich Bonhoffer's classic *The Cost of Discipleship*. Though they did not ask Rev. Leggett about the book, they remained confounded that someone could read it and not appreciate its applicability to the current situation in Jackson.[29]

Meanwhile, Rev. Collins and Rev. Teller met separately with the pastor of Wesley Methodist. Rev. Teller later recalled the firm belief of Rev. Dyess that Mississippi practiced segregation, and that was the way it was going be. Rev. Teller also sensed that the president's murder was deeply unsettling to Rev. Dyess, especially since it occurred in a Southern state.[30]

In addition to talking with the ministers of the churches they would try to attend the following day, the four ministers arranged a meeting with Louis Hollis, executive director of the Jackson Citizens' Council and the superintendent of Sunday school at First Baptist Church. None of the previous visiting ministers tried such an approach, but the Ohio group remained committed to the idea that this was as much a fact-finding mission as it was an effort to encourage local activists and bear witness to equality in the Methodist Church. Hollis explained to the ministers the aim of the Citizens' Council, to "maintain states rights, constitutional government, and racial integrity." He insisted that the Citizens' Council worked to "head off violence," causing Rev. Tomer to wonder if Medgar Evers's murder was a means of preventing further violence. Hollis maintained that Mississippi did not have a race problem, and that any problems the state did have were due to people not following the system of segregation. Rev. Tomer then asked Hollis what happened if someone "got out of line" and began acting like an integrationist. Hollis responded very frankly, saying that locals "did whatever was necessary." Rev. Tomer left the meeting feeling that the Ohio team "had been in contact with a modern version of the vigilantes, a group largely responsible for having drawn a Magnolia Curtain around the state of Mississippi as it strives to go its own way, alone."[31]

Saturday night, the Ohio ministers attended a play on the Tougaloo campus and spent time meeting the student activists, some of whom would join them the next day in trying to worship at white churches. Though the school decided to go ahead with the play despite the president's assassination, it also held a vigil to mourn his passing. Rev. Wagner later remembered the "moving quiet and sadness" of the evening, which in fact represented the mood for the entire weekend.[32] They spoke with student activists, wanting to know what the movement meant to them and what their families thought about their involvement. Trumpauer spoke of the three months she spent in Parchman Prison after her arrest as a Freedom Rider. One of the other students talked about the physical abuse he suffered at a lunch counter sit-in, and how his participation in the civil rights movement gave "a new sense of meaning ... to his life and to his faith." Another discussed threats that various white people made to his family because of his activism. Hearing the stories and joining the students in freedom songs, Rev. Tomer felt he was "in an entirely different world from that of the white persons we had visited during the day." These black and white activists faced the threat of violence daily, but "their response was only to witness quietly and more determinedly to their convictions." He saw that "God was at work in their midst, and that somehow, they were the wave of the future." The ministers stayed at Rev. King's house that night and, later in the evening, Rev. Wagner heard a series of gun shots that he thought at the time issued from someone going after squirrels. The next morning, he asked Rev. King about the sounds, and Rev. King explained that guns shot into the various houses on the Tougaloo campus were a regular occurrence. He showed Rev. Wagner a steel plate outside his baby's window, which only made Rev. Wagner more nervous.[33]

On Sunday, November 24, the ministers joined students in attempting to worship at Christ Methodist Church and Wesley Methodist Church. According to the plan worked out with Rev. King the day before, the adults would accompany a black student to the church, walk the student back to the car after ushers turned them away, and then try to enter the church and sit in the front pew and kneel during the service. The ministers understood that Jackson police might arrest them no matter what they did, but they resolved to leave if ushers prohibited them from entering or demanded they get off church property. Though police intervention in the preceding month and a half was rather haphazard, policemen did seem to be establishing a pattern of arresting visitors since the court hearings in late October. In the last several weeks, Jackson police had stepped in if the visitors refused to leave church grounds, and once when a church official clearly requested officer involvement.

At Wesley Methodist, the church visit went according to plan. Rev. Collins, Rev. Teller, and two black students walked up to the church entrance, where ushers promptly refused them admission. Rev. Collins and Rev. Teller explained they were Methodist ministers and that the two young men were confirmed Methodists as well, but the ushers insisted the black students were not welcome. The ministers then told the students to go back to the car and return to pick them up in an hour. Rev. Collins and Rev. Teller walked back to the church, went inside, and sat in a pew about five rows from the front of the church. Except for singing the hymns and reciting the Creed, the two ministers knelt in their pew for the entire service. Rev. Teller recalled that during the announcements, Rev. Dyess rose to talk about the president's assassination. He explained how firmly he believed that segregation was the only answer for Mississippi, but also how appalled he was at something one of his children said after returning home from school on Friday. The child told her parents that when the teacher announced Kennedy's death, the fourth graders erupted in applause. Rev. Dyess simply said, "If this is the kind of hatred our ways are producing, then we had better re-examine our lives." After the service, a woman came up to Rev. Collins and Rev. Teller and told them how glad she was to see them there. Rev. Teller reasoned that she must have been with one of the Methodist women's organizations and understood their effort. The two ministers greeted Rev. Dyess, who told them how grateful he was that they did not make any kind of disturbance. The ministers then walked past a few policemen, who had not been present when they arrived an hour earlier, and got into the car where the two black students were waiting to drive them back to campus.[34]

Meanwhile, Rev. Tomer, Rev. Wagner, and a black female student arrived at Christ Methodist well before morning worship. They walked up to the front door, where eight churchmen met them. One of the ushers greeted them with "strained friendliness" and explained that the church's official board voted not to admit "Negroes or agitators." The ministers walked the student back to the car and then stood by the parking lot—clearly identifiable as ministers because of their clerical collars—so members would see them as they went toward the church. Once the service began, the two walked back to the front entrance to talk with the ushers who remained outside. The ushers asked why they were doing this, and the ministers tried to assure the men they were not communists or self-righteous Yankees; they simply wanted to "witness to the fact that in Christ we are all brothers and sisters who cannot reject one another because of the color of our skins."[35] Moreover, the church itself "belonged to Christ and ... He alone had a right to set standards of admission to His worship." When one of the ushers asked where in the Bible it says that troublemakers should be encouraged to take part in the life of the church, one of the ministers mentioned Christ's cleansing of the Temple. The two ministers talked with the ushers for about twenty minutes before one insisted that they leave the church property, which they did. As they left, the ministers thought about the church bulletin they obtained the previous day when they met with Rev. Leggett. Looking at the order of worship, the ministers could not help notice the incongruity of what was happening on the two sides of the church doors. As ushers blocked an African American and two Methodist ministers from entering, members of Christ Methodist inside sang a familiar hymn:

> In Christ there is no East or West,
> In Him no North or South.
> But one great fellowship of love
> Throughout the whole wide earth.[36]

While the Ohio ministers went to the Methodist churches, three black students attended morning worship at St. Andrew's Episcopal. The congregation had consistently admitted African Americans since the church visits began in June, though the Tougaloo activists sensed that many church members opposed their presence. Though ushers admitted the group and seated them in the back pew, some members continued to demonstrate their disapproval. When one of the students, Camille Wilburn, who was Episcopalian, went up to the front to take communion, two white girls next to her at the rail left without receiving the sacrament. After the service, a woman who had confronted the visitors on previous Sundays asked Wilburn "why she came where she wasn't wanted."[37] Rev. Keller and lay leaders like Sherwood Wise were trying to steer the congregation towards moderation, but even they could not prevent individual acts of spitefulness. Though technically open and desegregated, St. Andrew's continued to wrestle with the consequences of the continual presence of African Americans in the congregation.

Sunday afternoon, the ministers ate in the Tougaloo cafeteria and discussed the morning's events with the students. Reporters from the *New York Times* and other newspapers were there to talk about reactions to Kennedy's assassination. Reflecting the divergent perspectives of being constantly inside the movement versus participating as activists for just a weekend, the students and the ministers held two distinct views on this day. Considering both the president's shocking murder and the visits, Rev. Wagner felt especially sad and un-heroic. He wrote to Rev. King a few days later, saying, "There is a kind of weight we now carry around in us, not only because of the death of the President but because of your particular situation in Mississippi." He added that Rev. King and the other student activists "have given us a burden which we do not wish to be rid of," and that he hoped to "bear it in a meaningful and helpful way."[38] Trumpauer, however, felt markedly better about the church visit campaign than she had just a few days before. Friday, the day of the assassination, was "a bad day," as she succinctly wrote in a letter to movement supporters, and she "was pretty discouraged about the prospects of these ministers." Yet November 24 was "a wonderful Sunday." Through the witness of the Ohio ministers and her fellow activists, she emphasized, they "reached people without arrests or overt bitterness." She concluded that she "felt better about the churches than I had in a long time." She wrote Rev. Wagner personally, echoing these sentiments and saying that what he and the other Ohio ministers were able to accomplish "was one of the highpoints of the church visits." For Trumpauer, this was the first Sunday in a long time that had a "Sunday feeling."[39]

With students out of town for the Thanksgiving holiday, the church visit campaign resumed the following weekend. As a new contingent of ministers arrived in Jackson from out of state, representatives of most of the Protestant and Orthodox denominations in the United States convened in Philadelphia for the triennial general assembly of the NCC. In addition to voting for a resolution advising congressmen to discharge the civil rights bill out of the House Judiciary Committee immediately, the general assembly affirmed what Robert Spike, executive director of the CRR, described as the "most comprehensive and explicit statement on what total desegregation of the church would mean." Prohibition of African Americans from most churches in Jackson, and the commission's leadership in the legal effort following the twenty-seven arrests, were clearly at the forefront of the representatives' minds. On December 6, the general assembly issued a series of recommendation in a "Call to the Churches for Action to Meet the Crisis in Race Relations." At the very top of their list was a demand that "all Christian Churches should in fact be open to all regardless of race and should publicly so declare." With church desegregation fundamental to integration, the general assembly advised its member churches to begin calling pastors and staff people of other races and to develop interracial and ecumenical gatherings among churches. For Spike, the resolution and the "fervor" with which the representatives adopted the recommendations was confirmation of the commission's civil rights activities by church leaders.[40]

On Saturday, December 7, two white ministers and one black minister arrived on the Tougaloo campus to join students the next day in the witness. Unlike most of the other out-of-state Methodist ministers who preceded them, two of these men were from the South, and the third pastored a church in Memphis. The two white clergy were Rev. A. W. Martin, a pastor in Whites Creek, Tennessee, and Rev. Bill Wells, the state director of the Methodist Student Movement of North Carolina in Greensboro. Rev. Martin and Rev. Wells did not know each other, but both knew the third member of the team, Rev. James Lawson, pastor of Centenary Methodist Church in Memphis.

Rev. Martin was a native Tennessean and the son of a Methodist minister and seminary professor. His wife, Beatrice Williamson Martin, grew up on a farm in Neshoba County, Mississippi, and understood the context of the racial controversy in the Mississippi Conference. Earlier in the year, her father, Andrew Williamson, led an effort in his church to defend its pastor, who one of the twenty-eight signers of the "born of conviction" manifesto. The Martins met while teaching at a school in Puerto Rico affiliated with the

Women's Division of the Methodist Board of Missions, an experience that "reinforced our basic beliefs in fairness with something approaching blindness to the color of the skin of our students." Yet it was their experience in graduate school at Vanderbilt University in the early 1960s that proved to be the catalyst for their involvement in the civil rights movement. Upon arriving in Nashville in late 1959, the couple sought out and became friends with a fellow student Beatrice's brother knew, James Lawson. When Vanderbilt expelled Lawson for suggesting he would disobey unjust and un-Christian laws, the Martins organized student protests. They took part in several more sit-ins in Nashville and remained in touch with Lawson as he completed his degree at Boston University and began pastoring a church in Memphis. Shortly after the arrests at Capitol Street in Jackson in early October, Rev. Martin called Rev. Lawson and suggested that the Jackson witness needed an all-Southern delegation. For Rev. Martin, the Northern ministers were helpful but were too easily labeled "outside agitators." Rev. Martin promised to pick Rev. Lawson up on the way to Jackson, and Rev. Lawson promised to call another white friend of his, Rev. Wells, to gauge his interest.[41]

Rev. Bill Wells grew up in a segregated Southern town and, like Rev. King, began to question racial assumptions after becoming more involved in youth organizations through the Methodist Church. Rev. Wells was from Wilson, North Carolina, a city with an even proportion of whites and blacks. Yet, other than house servants, he did not have any personal friends who were African Americans prior to his involvement in the Methodist youth programs. After being elected president of the Methodist Youth Conference of Eastern North Carolina, he attended national conferences with other presidents and developed a friendship with Lawson. They maintained contact through their seminary years and early ministries. When Rev. Lawson called his friend to see if he could come to Jackson for the December 8 witness, he explained that most of the outside help up to this point had come from the North, and he and Rev. King wanted more Southern ministers to join the effort. Years later, Rev. Wells recalled that he agreed to make the trip simply because Rev. Lawson asked him. He really did not want to go and admitted to being scared, but he determined that God was speaking to him through Rev. Lawson.[42]

Rev. Lawson was well known to the Tougaloo students and even to the Jackson authorities. As a leader in the Fellowship of Reconciliation in Nashville in the early 1960s, Rev. Lawson led non-violent workshops that Rev. King and other civil rights activists attended, and he participated in several direct action campaigns. In 1961, Jackson police arrested him together with

other Freedom Riders at the downtown bus terminal.[43] Rev. Lawson continued to mentor movement leaders when he took the helm of Centenary
Methodist Church in Memphis in 1962. Rev. King had been trying to get
Rev. Lawson to come to Jackson for weeks and was glad to see him when he
finally arrived.

On Sunday morning, Rev. King received a call from Rev. Joseph Lowery
of the Central Jurisdiction that, in Trumpauer's estimation, "changed everything." Rev. Lowery told Rev. King that Bishop Franklin had agreed, within
the next two weeks, to meet with Bishop Charles Golden, who oversaw the
black Methodist churches of Tennessee, Alabama, and Mississippi within
the Central Jurisdiction. As it was explained to Trumpauer, Bishop Franklin
was under an ultimatum to come up with a plan to open all the Methodist
churches in Jackson, or else several bishops would join the witness effort and
actively encourage ministers under their charge to join in the church visit
campaign as well. This behind-the-scenes work was enough to convince Rev.
Lawson to reconsider the value of attempting to worship at a white Methodist church this particular Sunday, so he left to return to Memphis.[44]

Rev. Wells and Rev. Martin went ahead with their plans to worship at
Capitol Street Methodist. Before they arrived, they agreed they would just
try to join in the worship service and refrain from using the tactic employed recently. They would not try to enter the church and kneel in the
pew throughout the entire service as a visible witness. Instead, they intended to be as inconspicuous as possible. They decided not to even wear their
clerical collars or identify themselves as ministers, and they would not arrive with a student. They aimed to participate in the worship service, even
making arrangements to meet with Rev. Granberry afterward. Yet when
they arrived at Capitol Street, they quickly realized they were not welcome.
After parking the car, Rev. Martin recalled, he saw a man writing down the
car's license tag number. When the pair of visitors was on the sidewalk in
front of Capitol Street, about to ascend the church steps, a group of men
rushed down to meet them. The ushers began asking why they came to
this church, and specifically wanted to know if they planned to go to the
front and kneel during the service. The two ministers explained that no,
they just wanted to take part in the worship service like everyone else. One
of the ushers then said, "I'm sure then that you won't mind signing this
statement that promises that you won't interfere with the service." Rev. Martin and Rev. Wells agreed with the wording on the card, but as a matter of
principle did not want to sign anything like this. They remained in front of
the church talking with the ushers for about twenty minutes, then they left.

The ministers still wanted to go to a church and determined that the only church they knew they could enter unimpeded would be a black church. The two white ministers then went to attend worship at the nearest black church they could find. They reported being "received warmly."[45]

That afternoon, the two met with Rev. Granberry, who had also heard about the behind-the-scenes efforts to open the churches. He told them he heard that eight bishops were thinking about coming the following weekend. He said he knew he could not turn away a Methodist bishop, but did not feel that he had control over what would occur on his church steps. He was seriously considering another option, simply closing the church and canceling services on Sunday.[46]

Fortunately for Rev. Granberry, the bishops did not participate in the church visit campaign in Jackson the following weekend, though they did not rule out coming in the future. Bishop James K. Mathews of Boston and Bishop Golden originally intended to join the witness on Sunday, December 15, and even told a reporter from the New York Times of their plans, but they decided against the trip at the last minute. They had discussed making traveling to Jackson for several weeks and tried to enlist other Methodist bishops to meet them there as part of one large witness. But now, Bishop Mathews explained their change of plans by saying this was not right time for them to go. Years later, Bishop Mathews wrote in his autobiography that they aborted the trip because support from a number of other bishops never materialized. For Mathews, it was essential that other bishops unite with them and the church activists in Jackson in a large joint witness, but as he wrote, "none [was] prepared to do so."[47]

While Methodist bishops postponed their trip to Jackson, the leader of another denomination, the Lutheran Church in America, decided it was time to deliver an ultimatum in person to the members of Trinity Lutheran Church. In the two and a half months since an integrated group succeeded in attending worship services at Trinity, segregationists had patrolled the periphery of the church on Sundays, barring the entry of African Americans. Rev. Koons reported that city commissioner Luckey, a member of the church, evidently ordered the regular city police to stay away and replaced them with motorcycle policemen and armed plain clothed policemen each Sunday. News of the situation at Trinity shocked other Lutheran ministers in the South. Some of them called on Dr. Franklin Clark Fry, president of the LCA, to intervene. One minister asked Dr. Fry if there was a way to force members who objected to the open door policy of the denomination to forfeit their memberships. He reasoned that if these dissenting members were allowed to remain and keep the door closed—and potentially succeed in forcing the pastor out—"then the Church will have lost the most important battle before it today." Dr. Fry replied that he was powerless to require dissenting members to resign because of the denomination's firm policy of congregational autonomy. But Dr. Raymond Wood, president of the Southeastern Synod, decided that he would pay a visit to Trinity Lutheran Church on December 8 and speak before the congregation.[48]

Dr. Wood began his message by congratulating the congregation on its growth and service to the city, but he devoted most of his talk to explaining what the church needed to do to right themselves in the eyes of the denomination. He summarized all the recent decisions and pronouncements made by various Lutheran bodies that clarified the denomination's stance on race and attendance policies. He discussed the most recent synod vote that decided, "Our churches are not our possessions but houses of God," and that congregations should "do now what is possible to eliminate discrimination." Dr. Wood said he spoke on behalf of the denomination and announced his unequivocal support for Pastor Koons and his efforts to eradicate the vestiges of segregation at Trinity. He then asked that the congregation take two steps toward the goal of eliminating racial discrimination. The congregation should rescind the actions taken at the August 25 meeting and any other action in direct contradiction of the various statements and positions of Lutheran Church bodies. Secondly, he urged church members to ban the practice of allowing certain men to interfere with the attendance of others, and therefore to admit any person to worship services. He concluded, "I urge this, not simply because your membership in the LCA and the Southeastern Synod requires it. I urge this because it is right." Dr. Wood then offered a prayer and welcomed questions. Rev. Koons wrote Dr. Franklin Clark Fry that, at this point, "the pro-segregationists broke loose in the most discourteous manner one could imagine." When one of the members asked what would happen if the church failed to follow his proposals, Dr. Wood pointed them to the by-laws of the LCA, which clearly indicated that the congregation would be suspended or excluded from membership in the denomination, subject to a vote before the synod.[49] Though Dr. Wood did not give them a timetable to take the actions he proposed, he and church members understood that they would settle the matter on or before January 19, the day of the annual congregational meeting of Trinity Lutheran.

Though Bishops Mathews and Golden declined to join the Jackson church visit campaign on December 15, a group of four ministers from New

York City followed through with their plans to participate in the witness. In the preceding months, many of the New York East Conference pastors kept abreast of developments in Jackson through the network of the MCR. One of the pastors, Rev. John A. Collins of Jefferson Park Parish in Manhattan, was from Chicago and remained in touch with several of the Chicago-based ministers who were assigning the various delegations weekends to participate in the Jackson witness.[50] He agreed to put together a team for mid-December, contacting two black Methodist ministers, Rev. Melvin Williams and Rev. F. Herbert Skeete, and his good friend, Rev. David P. Ver Nooy. Rev. Ver Nooy was president of the New York East Conference Board of Christian Social Concerns, whose parent group, the GBCSC, had provided bail for some of those arrested in October and for other civil rights activists. The New York delegation traveled to Jackson under the auspices of their conference's Board of Christian Social Concerns, which paid for their travel expenses and commissioned them to seek out local Methodists to assess the situation before going ahead with an integrated visit to churches on December 15.[51] Like the groups that came to Jackson for visits on November 10 and November 17, aiming to testify to the interracial face of the Methodist Church, this group was a mix of black and white ministers. Like some of the ministers who preceded them, all four were dedicated civil rights activists involved in local issues in New York City, and three of them already had the arrest records to show for it. In July, police in New York arrested Rev. Williams, Rev. Skeete, and Rev. Ver Nooy, who were walking on a picket line as part of their protest of discriminatory hiring practices of black construction workers in Brooklyn.

Rev. Skeete was born in Harlem but grew up in Barbados, his parents' native country. Until he returned to the United States for college and seminary, he had not really experienced racial segregation, as African Caribbeans in Barbados were in the majority, and the schools he attended were integrated. The reality of racial prejudice in the Northeast grabbed him, as he later recalled, and he became actively involved in civil rights efforts while in seminary at Drew University and during his first pastoral appointments in New York City. Rev. Ver Nooy, a native of an all-white town in central New York, became more aware of the struggle of African Americans through his ministerial assignments, all three of which were in interracial churches. His first appointment, in the late 1950s, was to a predominantly white church in a black neighborhood that became a majority-black church by the end of his tenure. By 1963, he served an interracial church in Brooklyn and, with Rev. Skeete, Rev. Williams, and Rev. Collins, became involved in two important local civil rights issues, the integration of public schools and ending discriminatory hiring practices in the city. Years later, he recalled that he accepted the invitation to go to Jackson mostly out of respect for his friend Rev. Collins, who was organizing the trip, and because he felt obliged to participate because of his membership on the conference's Economic and Social Relations Committee.

Rev. Collins served in the inner city, a white pastor in a predominantly black church in East Harlem. Unlike the others, he also had experience within the movement in the South. Following the sit-ins in Greensboro, North Carolina, in 1960, he and other seminarians at Union Theological Seminary formed the Student Interracial Ministry, which began sending white theological students to black churches in the South and black students to white churches. The summer of 1960, he worked at an AME church in Talladega, Alabama, where, in addition to helping with the ministry at the church, he made contact with several white clergy in an attempt to jump-start dialogue.⁵²

As on some of the previous weekends, the ministers sought out local people to fully explain the situation in Jackson. Before they departed New York, Lanier Hunt, a member of the New York East Conference Board of Christian Social Concerns and a native Mississippian, secured meetings for the New Yorkers with a variety of white Methodists that he knew in Jackson. One of these meetings was particularly important. On Saturday, the team met with a large group of Galloway lay people and their ministers inside the church, an event that lay leaders or police would not have tolerated on a Sunday morning. At a latter meeting, Rev. Collins tried to appeal to the historic nature of Galloway Memorial, urging members to summon the greatness of the congregation in order to be a force for positive change in Mississippi. According to Rev. Ver Nooy, the members responded that they could not control the situation, that to ask for police to stop arresting integrated groups altogether was asking too much. Members said they needed more time before the church could open the doors, but declined to set a specific timetable. Nevertheless, the laymen told the ministers that police would not be present this particular Sunday. In their report to the New York East Conference Board of Christian Social Concerns, the New York ministers relayed the sentiments of the white Methodists in Jackson who feared that the desegregation of the Methodist Church structure would provoke secession. They also cited the sentiments of the lay people at Galloway, who said they recognized that closed church doors were wrong, but stressed they were having difficulty opening them. Galloway members pointed to the fact that the city's segregationist mayor was an active member, and that allowing black visitors to attend the church would be terribly embarrassing to him. They worried that open doors would ruin the church, as many members would leave and take their financial resources with them. For their part, the ministers tried to communicate their sympathy for complex situation faced by members of the Jackson churches, but "tried to say that their actions affect us, and that in a very real sense we were not outsiders, but insiders, and that we are all part of one church."

While the meetings gave the ministers a sense of the perspective of some in the white community in Jackson, the discussions also encouraged the Jackson activists. Professor Campbell pointed out that the meeting with the laymen from Galloway was a sign of progress, since it was the first time that laymen met separately with visiting ministers, and since the meeting was itself racially integrated. Trumpauer wondered why Dr. Cunningham included the lay leaders in the meeting, sensing that Dr. Cunningham may have been trying to demonstrate to his churchmen that he was in no way "selling out." Nevertheless, she reasoned, "It means that we reach more people."[53]

In addition to meeting with some lay people from Galloway, the New York ministers met with Rev. Dement of St. Luke's Methodist and Rev. Granberry of Capitol Street. The New Yorkers found both men to be cordial and sincere, but one exchange was the especially memorable for Rev. Ver Nooy. At one point in the conversation, Rev. Granberry brought up the Civil War and Reconstruction, as he had on previous occasions with other Northern ministers. Rev. Granberry remained angry about the behavior of Union soldiers who burned down Jackson, reducing it to "chimney town." He told the ministers, "Look what your ancestors did to my ancestors." Rev. Skeete then seized the opportunity, saying, "Remember what your ancestors did to my ancestors. But the Christian faith is about forgiveness." Rev. Granberry then got up and hugged Rev. Skeete and said, "You're a good old boy." As Rev. Ver Nooy remembered years later, in other contexts Rev. Granberry's statement to Rev. Skeete would have seemed offensive. At the time, though, Rev. Granberry and the others were touched.[54]

The visiting ministers also spent time with representatives of the black community, including Bishop Golden, who came to Jackson but decided not to try to attend a white church. Speaking to Rev. G. R. Haughton of Pearl Street AME and Alan Johnson of Pratt Memorial Methodist, and spending time with the youth of both churches, the New York ministers got a sense of the feelings of Jackson's black residents. The New York delegation felt that the African Americans appreciated their witness, even telling the ministers, "The visits were making possible some limited contact between white and Negro leadership." Based on these conversations with blacks and whites in Jackson, in its report to the conference the delegation offered a succinct rebuttal to the fundamental assumptions of Mayor Thompson, the Citizens' Council, and other segregationists in the city. They simply concluded, "There was a complete misunderstanding of the conviction and determination of the Negro community."[55]

The ministers promised their board of Christian social concerns in New York that they would evaluate the conditions in Jackson before going ahead with integrated visits. After meeting and praying about the matter Saturday night, the four ministers decided to proceed with the visits the next morning. In doing so, they wanted to "avoid any misunderstanding by white leaders in Mississippi" that they "could not accept a situation in the church that is intolerable." Moreover, they aimed to demonstrate their support to local civil rights leaders in Jackson and to keep up the pressure on the city's white churches. As a matter of courtesy, they called Dr. Cunningham and Rev. Granberry, informing them of their intentions. Rev. Granberry asked Rev. Ver Nooy to help lead a prayer during the worship service, but only if Rev. Skeete did not join in. Rev. Ver Nooy reiterated that he planned to come with Rev. Skeete. The four ministers wrote in their report that they specifically asked Dr. Cunningham and Rev. Granberry to come to the doors of their churches to assure that police would not make any arrests. According to the New York ministers, Dr. Cunningham and Rev. Granberry both declined. Dr. Cunningham wrote years later that this statement was inaccurate, that at no time did anyone ask him to intercede in front of the church.[56]

At Galloway, Rev. Collins and Rev. Williams arrived shortly before the 11 a.m. worship service. As she had done many Sundays before, Professor Campbell dropped the ministers off. As they were about to ascend the steps, they saw a group of men coming down the steps, and so they stepped back on the sidewalk. They knew that police might arrest them, so they wanted to try to avoid the additional charge of trespassing. They explained to the ushers that they were both Methodist ministers and wanted to participate in worship at this Methodist church. One of the ushers told Rev. Williams that there was a black Methodist church down the street that would welcome him, but that he was not allowed to enter Galloway. The two said, "No thank you," that they had come to worship together. The ministers then said they would just stand where they were in prayer. Rev. Collins recalled that some church members passed gave them hostile looks, but others looked sympathetic, and a few came up to them and offered their gratitude for the ministers' witness. Rev. Collins then saw one of the ushers signal the police officers who were standing nearby, and Police Chief Ray came over and arrested Rev. Collins and Rev. Williams, charging them with trespassing and disturbing divine worship. The ministers asked Chief Ray how he could arrest them when the minister of the church did not want them arrested. Ray responded, "Do you run your church?" The ministers understood clearly what he was implying, that the lay boards, not the ministers, controlled the churches in Jackson.[57]

Meanwhile, Rev. Skeete and Rev. Ver Nooy arrived at Capitol Street. Before they could step onto the bottom stair in front of the church, a group of men rushed down to them. One of the ushers looked at Rev. Ver Nooy and said that he could come in, then looked at Rev. Skeete and told him to go to the black church down the street. When the two revealed they were both Methodist ministers, the ushers were unmoved, threatening to bring in the police who were waiting nearby if they refused to leave. Being denied the opportunity to worship inside the church, the two ministers asked if they could remain where they were in silent protest. The ushers said no and signaled to the police. While still on the sidewalk, the ministers then dropped to their knees, and one of the policemen said they had two minutes to move on. When the ministers still would not budge, the officers pulled them up and placed them under arrest on the now customary grounds of trespassing and disturbing worship. On the way to the jail, the arresting officer and Rev. Ver Nooy had a brief exchange. The policeman told the two ministers that the thing locals objected to most was outsiders coming down to tell them how to live their lives. Rev. Ver Nooy asked the officer if he was a Methodist, and he said no, he was a Baptist. Seizing the opportunity for a pointed retort, Rev. Ver Nooy responded that since he was a Baptist, the officer was actually the outsider. As ordained Methodist ministers, Rev. Ver Nooy and Rev. Skeete could hardly be considered interlopers.[58]

The four ministers from New York remained in jail for the rest of the week, while their supporters back in New York organized bail and their attorneys tried to get the cases removed to federal court. Their conference, the New York East Conference, arranged with the Women's Division of Christian Service of the Methodist Church to secure bail. The Women's Division had helped supply bail money for other civil rights cases, including the first arrests at Capitol Street in October. While in jail, Rev. Skeete recalled having an experience similar to that of the other black ministers who had found themselves incarcerated a month earlier. The other black prisoners and the black trustees were sympathetic to the new internees' cause and treated them well. In fact, Rev. Skeete remembered being more worried about the safety of his white friends. Rev. Collins and Rev. Ver Nooy passed the time playing battleship and exchanging lectures on law and sociology, their respective interests. They were in adjoining cells and were able to communicate through a hole in the wall where a brick had come loose. Chief Ray met with them several times and, as Rev. Collins later recalled, seemed much more reasonable and understanding than the ushers they encountered on Sunday. But unlike their predecessors, the New York ministers received a visitor who had declined visit other ministers in jail, Dr. Cunningham of Galloway. Dr. Cunningham met at least once with each of the two white ministers, and Rev. Skeete recalled meeting with him and Rev. Williams every morning while they were in jail. The ministers reported that Dr. Cunningham was "visibly affected" by the fact that his fellow ministers were in jail. The daily discussions and prayers with Dr. Cunningham impressed Rev. Skeete greatly. Rev. Skeete felt sorry for Dr. Cunningham and respected him even more, seeing clearly the pain that the Jackson minister was experiencing.[59]

With students returning home for the Christmas holiday, the Tougaloo activists suspended the church visit campaign until after the New Year. Counting the four arrests on December 15, Jackson police ended 1963 with a total of thirty-one arrests make in front of Jackson churches. Of the thirty-six ministers and laymen who made the trip to Jackson to participate in the witness in the last three months of 1963, eighteen were incarcerated. Yet the most telling statistic was that about half of the arrests were made after the Council of Bishops issued its strong from on November 13. Despite being told that their actions constituted an "outrage" on the part of Methodism, white Methodist laypeople in Jackson continued to call on police to enforce segregation in their churches. The bishops had asked laypersons to accede to the authority of their ministers, but the Methodist clergy in Jackson appeared unwilling to intervene to uphold the principles of their bishops. The example of Dr. W. J. Cunningham—a minister who opposed his church's closed-door policy, and who was becoming increasingly frustrated with the continuing arrests—demonstrated the tenuous position of dissenting pastors in Jackson. His lay leaders understood his position on race, but he reasoned that if he pressed too hard, as Dr. Selah and others had, he would separate himself from a congregation that he had led for only four months. For the time being at least, he chose to be their pastor, not a prophet.

"Jackson Has Become a Symbol of Our Common Sin"

WINTER 1964

By late 1963 and early 1964, Tougaloo students had various methods for combatting the persistence of racial discrimination in Mississippi's capital city. Many helped spread the word about another boycott of downtown businesses during the Christmas shopping season. They instead celebrated a "Black Christmas" on the Tougaloo campus to shift attention to the murders of Medgar Evers and President Kennedy. Some made repeated trips to the downtown public library, site of the city's first organized sit-in in 1961, or attended public events, such as the presentation of Handel's *Messiah*, in integrated groups on the campus of Millsaps. Others helped student Austin Moore convincing entertainers, like a few actors from *Bonanza* and Al Hirt, to cancel their performances in Jackson because of the city's segregation policies.[1] Yet the activity that many gravitated to was something they were accustomed to doing before they became involved in the movement. The church as an institution was a familiar space for them, but the exclusion policies of most of Jackson's churches illuminated the reality of racial discrimination and made that institution seem unrecognizable. The impulse to restore relevancy to the Christian faith drove these students and the dozens of ministers who vowed to join them in their weekly missions to Jackson's white churches.

Following a three-week-long hiatus during the Christmas and New Year holidays, the Jackson church visit campaign resumed on January 12, 1964. The day before, four chaplains from the State University of Iowa in Iowa City arrived in Jackson. All four were white, but for the first time in the campaign, the delegation of clergy included two women, as well as ministers of three denominations that had not yet participated in the witness: a Disciples of Christ minister, a Presbyterian, and an Episcopalian. Rev. Sally

Smith was an associate minister at First Christian Church, while Rev. Joan Bott was on staff at the Westminster Foundation at the university. Rev. John Kress served as an associate rector at Trinity Episcopal Church, and Rev. Bill Friday was on staff with the Wesley Foundation on campus. In keeping with the routine of previous weekends, the group sought to speak with as many local clergy as they could, securing meetings with a Presbyterian and an Episcopalian minister.[2]

On Sunday morning, January 12, integrated groups of ministers and students set out for St. Andrew's Episcopal, Central Presbyterian, and First Christian Church. Rev. Kress, Rev. Bill Friday, and two students entered St. Andrew's for the 9:30 a.m. Eucharist and sat down on their own, a change from other visits when an usher directed visitors to one of the rear pews. Though the church was open, the routine of seating black visitors in the rear fed the perception that church ushers were trying to segregate the seating. Rev. Friday informed Trumpauer that "there was no trouble," and that the integrated group was "well received." At Central Presbyterian, which students had not tried to attend since the second week of visits back in June, Rev. Bott and a few students tried to enter, but a policeman rushed over to them just as one of the female students put her hand on the church's doorknob. The group left the premises. At 11:00 a.m., Rev. Smith and Rev. Friday went with an integrated group to First Christian, whose ushers turned them away. This was the first return visit to First Christian since October 6, 1963, the morning of the first arrests at Capitol Street Methodist. First Christian had not yet found a replacement for Rev. Hulan, whom the church voted to remove in August. Despite being refused admittance, though, Rev. Smith, who was ordained in the Disciples of Christ, and Rev. Friday were able to converse with the ushers, including the chairman of the pulpit committee, for about twenty minutes before leaving. That night, Rev. Kress went back to St. Andrew's and met with high school and college-aged groups. He reported to Trumpauer that he got a good response. The other ministers and some white students went to the college group and evening services at Capitol Street Methodist. They told her that Rev. Granberry spotted them in the congregation and glared at them throughout the service.[3]

While ushers repeatedly turned away integrated groups outside most of the white churches in Jackson, out of state white ministers had some success entering churches as long as they acceded to certain conditions. A few days after the group of chaplains from Iowa departed, Rev. Robert A. Raines, a prominent Methodist minister who served as senior pastor of First Methodist Church in Germantown, Pennsylvania, arrived in Jackson and quickly became conscious of his freedom to speak without restraint. Though he was respected in his own right, local Methodists certainly knew of at least one of his family connections. He was the son of Bishop Richard C. Raines of Indiana, an outspoken advocate for integration in the denomination. Yet significantly, there is no evidence that most church people and segregationists in Jackson knew of the local civil rights activism of his two brothers. One brother, Rev. Richard Raines Jr., was part of the Detroit team that came down in November, while another brother, Rev. John Curtis Raines of New York, had been arrested in Jackson two years before as a Freedom Rider.[4]

Rev. Robert Raines came to Jackson to lead a devotional retreat for ministers in the Mississippi Conference, though he also became acquainted with various efforts of Jacksonians to steer the city toward moderation, and he came to grasp the determination of those working to thwart it. He led a retreat at Millsaps College for a group of ministers and then at Galloway for Methodists who were trying to start monthly Koinonia groups. As he later explained, these groups were meant to offer encouragement to likeminded Methodists and the "formation and strengthening of the liberal conviction of the Church." He also met with students and faculty at the college who were working to desegregate the school, and with a group of black ministers who apprised him of their efforts in the city. He later reported to his home congregation that he was filled with "admiration for their courage and their Christian devotion to non-violent methods," adding that they "live under a daily humiliation the like of which you and I could not bear without resort to violence."[5]

Additionally, Rev. Raines accepted an invitation from Dr. Cunningham to serve as guest preacher at Galloway on Sunday, January 19. Dr. Cunningham knew the danger of giving Rev. Raines such a platform, and specifically asked him to refrain from addressing the issue of race or open doors while he was in Jackson. In a letter written in advance of the trip, Dr. Cunningham explained that he was new to the congregation and "had had no time to build a good pastoral relationship that would stand the strain of some things I may later wish to say and do." Rev. Raines agreed to these limits and gave every indication to Dr. Cunningham that he intended to follow through with his promise. Yet after sticking to the script for most of the sermon that Sunday, he gave, in Dr. Cunningham's estimation, a "fiery peroration" castigating the church for its closed doors and for completely disregarding the Detroit declaration from the Council of Bishops, which their own bishop signed. As Dr. Cunningham later wrote, "The tension was so thick you could pick it up in your hands."[6]

Rev. Raines later admitted that breaking his word was not something he had intended to do. A few weeks later he apologized to Dr. Cunningham in a telegram, simply saying he felt compelled to take the stand that he did. While Dr. Cunningham got the impression that Rev. Raines was spontaneous in his actions that Sunday, there is at least one other indication that Rev. Raines knew exactly what he would say and had tipped off movement activists about his intentions. Tougaloo students and visiting ministers were conspicuously absent from Galloway premises before the service during which he preached. According to Trumpauer, they knew he would call from the pulpit for opening the church doors, and thus the other activists decided to relieve pressure at least for the morning.[7] In a letter to his congregation in Germantown, Pennsylvania, Rev. Raines explained his decision to speak out. He determined that the church community in Mississippi suffered from a lack of effective moral leadership, something that must have become more apparent with every day he spent in Jackson. He perceived that "the Church is a kept Church, controlled by the Citizens' Council," and he understood why so few white people spoke out publicly. He pointed to the intimidation and harassment of blacks and whites, even those expressing moderate positions. In addition to speaking out where others could not or would not, he chose to offer encouragement to moderates and activists in Jackson.

As Rev. Raines decamped to Pennsylvania, Dr. Cunningham struggled to deal with the fallout from the surprise sermon. Dr. Cunningham later wrote that his "desire to take the lead in reconciliation had been struck a smashing blow." Calls from incensed members began soon after the service ended, with many accusing Dr. Cunningham of inviting Rev. Raines for the sole purpose of speaking about the racial policy of Galloway. In conversations with outraged church members, Dr. Cunningham explained the understanding that he thought he had with Rev. Raines. Dr. Cunningham even telephoned Rev. Raines to verify their agreement and make clear that his actions "had created an embarrassing situation" for him. Rev. Raines later confirmed Dr. Cunningham's position in a telegram that Dr. Cunningham read at the next official board meeting.[8] While absolved from culpability in the matter, Dr. Cunningham felt that the damage was done and that the whole episode had only emboldened his detractors.

During the weekend of Rev. Raines's Koinonia retreat and his guest preaching at Galloway, another round of ministers descended upon Jackson to assist local activists in the church visit campaign. All four were from the Chicago area, and one of them, Rev. Martin Deppe, had helped organize the teams of ministers who participated in the witness effort over the previous three months. Rev. Deppe was pastor of Mandell Methodist Church in Chicago and active in the Interracial Council of Methodists and the newly created MCR. After Jackson police arrested the group of Chicago clergymen in October, Rev. Deppe had helped raise bail for them and for other incarcerated visitors through the Methodist-Evangelical United Brethren Freedom Fund. Two of the other four men who made the trip, Rolly Kidder and Darrell Reeck, were students at Naperville's Evangelical United Brethren Seminary. Reeck was a student intern at a EUB church, Chicago's Parish of the Holy Covenant, where the fourth member of the team, Hugh Stevens, was a leading layman. In advance of the planned merger between the Methodists and the EUBs, many in both denominations were becoming increasingly concerned about the persistent problem of racial discrimination within their church structures. Rev. Deppe wrote at the time that the Jackson church visit campaign was one key way to force both groups to confront the issue ahead of the union. He conceded that the Jackson witness "may be the wrong approach," but affirmed that it attempted "to expose a cancer in the Church to the Methodists in Jackson, to all Methodism, to the coming General Conference, to the E.U.B. Church, to ourselves in our own situations." For Rev. Deppe, Jackson was "just one situation" and the witness was "just one approach," but he felt confident that God called him to Mississippi's capital city because "Jackson has become a symbol of our common sin."[9]

The four men from Chicago arrived on the campus of Tougaloo the afternoon of Saturday, January 18, and, like other groups that preceded them, they set out to talk with as many local people as they could. Just a few hours after they pulled in, they talked with Rev. Raines and a group of black ministers in a meeting Rev. King arranged at the home of Rev. Alan Johnson, the pastor of Pratt Memorial Methodist Church, one of the larger black Methodist churches in Jackson. The Jackson men made a great impression on Rolly Kidder, who wrote home saying that it was especially informative to hear the local movement perspective. Rev. Johnson and the other Jackson ministers explained to the Chicago delegation and Rev. Raines that their greatest fear was inability to sustain their nonviolent campaign. The ministers pointed to lingering anger over the police brutality of the previous summer, and described the acquittal that the upcoming Byron de la Beckwith trial was likely to produce as a "fuse" that might set off violence.[10]

Saturday night, the visiting ministers had a rare opportunity to meet with white high school students, when two of the Chicago ministers attended a Jackson Youth for Christ (YFC) rally. The EUB seminarians were active in YFC in Chicago and accompanied a white Tougaloo student who had also been involved in the group back home. After the YFC assembly, Kidder and Reeck were able to speak briefly with the local director and to talk privately with several high school students. Kidder wrote that the white students "seemed more open and less acculturated than the adults," though he sensed that they still felt the subject of race to be taboo, that it could be "dangerous if they are caught talking about it." Later that night, the four Chicago men discussed their strategy for the next day's visits. Since they wanted to use Monday as a day to talk with white Methodist pastors and laypeople, something that would be impossible to do if they were incarcerated, the four decided to try to avoid arrest if they could. They planned to break into two teams, each accompanying a black student to a different Methodist.

One of the African American students who signed up this particular Sunday was Tom Armstrong, a veteran of the movement in Mississippi. As he later recalled, he joined the movement because of Medgar Evers. In 1956, Armstrong noticed that many African Americans—including his own relatives—were being removed from the voting rolls in Jefferson Davis County, his home. He attended an NAACP meeting and told Evers he wanted to help educate people on how to register to vote, something he then began and continued doing through the early 1960s. In 1961, he was one of the few native Mississippians who joined the Freedom Riders, and he was among the hundreds of group members arrested by Jackson police. When the church visit campaign began, he felt a personal connection with the tactic. As he later said, he grew up in the Holiness faith, and the reality of segregated churches "went against everything I knew and believed." He participated in many of the church visits in the fall 1963 and was eager to join in more the following semester.[11]

On January 19, integrated groups set out to try to attend morning worship services at St. Luke's Methodist and Capitol Street Methodist. Though they intended to avoid arrest, they were fully prepared for that possibility. Each of the four Chicago men gave a toothbrush and a pair of underwear to a Tougaloo student and dropped coins in their shoes so that they could purchase drinks and newspapers if they found themselves in jail. The ministers and students wrote Rev. King's home phone number on their wrists. Stevens and Reeck accompanied Jerry Ward, a black Tougaloo student, to St. Luke's. When they arrived, they noticed a squad car with policemen observing their movements from a parking lot across the street. The three approached

the front door of the church and immediately encountered a group of ushers. A brief exchange ensued, with the ushers made it clear that they would
not allow the three to enter. One of the ushers then motioned to the policemen across the street. When the police began approaching the church, the
three walked away and went instead to Pratt Memorial Methodist Church.[12]

Meanwhile, Rev. Deppe, Kidder, and Armstrong presented themselves at
Capitol Street Methodist. Kidder wrote at the time that the group felt "sort
of like commandos"—though he was beginning to have some doubt, silently wondering, "Why in the world I had to be in Mississippi." Walking toward
the church steps, they noticed a policeman trying to appear to direct traffic
move onto the sidewalk and speak into his radio. The three ascended the
front stairs, and three ushers ran down to intercept them. Rev. Deppe introduced his group to the head usher, who shook hands with the two white
men but declined to shake hands with Armstrong. The usher announced
that they needed to leave, that the official board declared the church to be a
"segregated church," adding "There will be no entrance here by force." Rev.
Deppe countered, "My understanding of the Methodist Church is that it is
open to all," adding, "Scripture says, 'Come unto me, ye who labor and are
heavy laden.'" The usher retorted that he did not want to argue and again
instructed them to leave, but Rev. Deppe persisted, "Who is Lord of the
Church?" The usher replied, "God is Lord of the Church, but these people
have built this church and they are responsible for it." Kidder then responded, "We are simply witnessing to the belief that in Christ there is neither
Greek nor Jew, male nor female, slave nor freeman." The usher's patience
was now at an end, and he barked at them while motioning to the policeman: "Don't preach to me. I've told you twice to leave and I'll tell you once
more." Wanting to avoid arrest, they shook the usher's hand and descended
the steps, though Kidder added, "I hope that you will be free some day."[13]

Though the three left the front of the building, outside the church they
encountered several members of Capitol Street and other visitors who talked with them for about twenty-five minutes. Two of the people who came
up to them were Rev. Edward McRae and his wife. Rev. McRae was one of
the twenty-eight ministers who signed the "born of conviction" declaration
and had been forced out of his Meridian church. He had transferred to the
Southern California—Arizona Conference later that summer, and he and
his wife were now back at their home church for the day. Rev. McRae told
the men how troubled he was with Capitol Street's intransigence and the
overall state of the Mississippi Conference. Kidder later wrote that these
exchanges outside Capitol Street were the most meaningful experiences he

had that weekend. He understood that "it took real courage for them to approach us," and that it was important to know that "within the Church all were not in agreement with the Church policies." Rev. Deppe, Kidder, and Armstrong then left Capitol Street and joined the others at Pratt Memorial, where Rev. Deppe reported they "were warmly greeted" and felt right at home.[14]

Wesley Memorial Methodist Church was celebrating its tenth anniversary that afternoon in a service that featured guest appearances by Bishop Marvin Franklin and District Superintendent Dr. J. Willard Leggett Jr. The Tougaloo activists and their Chicago guests decided to try to attend the commemoration as an integrated group, but as before they aimed to avoid arrest. They arrived as a large group of seven that included, in addition to the four Chicago men, Rev. King, Ida Hannah, and Dolores Dunlop. Rev. King usually avoided such overt participation in a visit, but he could not resist the opportunity to pressure the church while embarrassing Bishop Franklin and Dr. Leggett. Hannah and Dunlop were both actively involved in the local movement and the church visit campaign. Hannah had been arrested twice the previous October for trying to attend Capitol Street, while Dunlop had been arrested for trying to worship at Trinity Lutheran in late October.

When the integrated group presented at the doors of Wesley Memorial, it became apparent that their arrival took church officials by surprise. Policemen were nowhere in sight, and the ushers seemed astonished to see the group there on such an occasion. While one of the ushers announced himself as the chairman of the official board and began reading a statement explaining the church's closed-door policy, another usher ran inside, ostensibly to call the police. The chairman stopped after a few sentences, and said, "I can't go on," so another usher finished reading the statement. When he concluded, Rev. King pulled out and read the declaration on race affirmed by the Council of Bishops at their recent meeting in Detroit. When he finished, one of the ushers suggested that the bishops' declaration was only a recommendation. Rev. Deppe pointed out that yes, it was a recommendation, but it was something that Bishop Franklin had signed, and the church was thus defying their own bishop, who happened to be inside the sanctuary at the moment. The back-and-forth continued for a few more minutes. At one point, one of the ushers announced his disapproval of the church's closed-door policy, but reasoned that his view was not shared by the majority; the last time the policy came up for a vote before the official board, six wanted to open the church, while thirty-seven wanted it closed.

With the conversation coming an end, the chairman added, "We don't want to disrupt this service. Your visit will disrupt us and tear us apart. This is our church. We love it. Now please go. We don't want any trouble—we don't want an arrest here today." By this time, the police had arrived and were moving toward the group. Rev. King sensed that arrests were imminent, so he said, "Let us pray." He led a short prayer, followed by the Lord's Prayer, which the ushers reciting as well. Rev. Deppe wrote that some of the ushers "were visibly moved." The integrated team then left, noticing that a few ushers were talking with the police, presumably instructing them not to make any arrests.[15]

Later that day, an integrated group attempted to worship at Galloway Memorial Methodist and then attended St. Peter's Roman Catholic Cathedral. The four Chicago men accompanied Frank Crump, a black Tougaloo student, to Galloway, a church they intentionally avoided that morning because of Rev. Robert Raines's presence there. Though they were turned away, Nat Rogers, the chairman of the official board, agreed to meet with the Chicago men the next day. The group then proceeded to St. Peter's, where ushers welcomed them in, as they had welcomed all the previous groups of visitors. They heard Bishop Gerow speak about Vatican II, the recent ecumenical council in Rome, and visited with him afterwards. Bishop Gerow told the men he was in favor of the church visitation campaign, but acknowledged that with so few Catholics in the state he felt there was not much he could personally do. Like the black ministers the Chicago men talked with the night before, he seemed apprehensive about the future and the ability of local African Americans to withstand the temptation to resort to violence: "If I don't see a race riot involving 500,000 people in the near future, I will be surprised." Nevertheless, the evening at St. Peter's made a great impression on the Chicago visitors. Rev. Deppe found Bishop Gerow to be "a breath of fresh air," while Kidder could not help thinking that the open doors at St. Peter's were "quite a judgment upon the Protestant Church in Mississippi."[16]

On Monday, the four men from Chicago met with a variety of local Methodists, including Bishop Franklin, Rev. Granberry of Capitol Street, Rev. Dyess of Wesley Memorial, Rogers and another Galloway layman, and a Galloway youth director. The appointment with Rev. Dyess was rather one-sided, as he dominated the conversation and talked of his plan for "racial integration and sexual segregation of schools." Bishop Franklin and Rev. Granberry were together during the meeting with the Chicago team, an encounter Rev. Deppe described as thoroughly "depressing and exhausting." In what was becoming a leitmotif in their conversations with visiting ministers, Bishop Franklin and Rev. Granberry told the Northern ministers they were outsiders and intruders, comparing them to the carpetbaggers who invaded after the Civil War. The two felt that the Northern ministers were judging them, and that they should instead focus on problems in Chicago. Bishop Franklin and Rev. Granberry explained that they were pastors, not evangelists or prophets, so their role was to guide their congregations in difficult times. Asked why he would not assert his power more forcefully, Bishop Franklin said he had no such power, but that "the Church might be able to do something after school desegregation next Fall." Content to maintain the status quo, Bishop Franklin and Rev. Granberry balked at several suggestions from the Chicago men. They dismissed the proposal to accept one-year appointments of ministers from Chicago. They also refused to permit visiting teams to take part in a silent witness outside of Methodist churches in Jackson without police interference, though Bishop Franklin suggested that police refrained from making arrests the previous day because of his behind-the-scenes work with pastors in the preceding weeks. To Rev. Deppe, this attitude amounted to silence, which was "a loud vote for segregation."[17] The meeting with Rogers and Jim Campbell, an official board member at Galloway, was more cordial, though the two hoped to convince the Chicago group to help call off future visits. Rogers opposed the church's closed doors, but as he explained in an interview years later, he was given to compromise at the time. He tried to get the Chicago men to understand that the whole structure of society in Mississippi relied upon a strict separation of the races. The state's laws, politics, economy, and churches reinforced lines of demarcation that, until recently, Mississippians unconsciously accepted. Rev. Deppe recognized that church people feared any deviation from this way of life would "establish a crack in the dike," and could "burst the bubble of their illusion of Southern greatness and the myth of historical persecution."[18]

Before departing for Chicago, the group met with Tom Boone, the director of youth work at Galloway, who told the men about the growing frustration he experienced working within the church's closed-door policy. Boone arrived at Galloway several years before and, like the church's pastors, he had worked to steer church members toward racial toleration. For instance, he helped initiate discussion groups including college students at Galloway and students at Tougaloo. He recalled that most of these meetings had to be convened under the radar, usually at Riverside Park early on Saturday or Sunday mornings. When Dr. Selah resigned the previous June,

Boone wanted to quit as well, but Dr. Selah prevailed upon him, arguing that the church needed some continuity.[19] Boone felt that churches should take the lead on the issue, but he explained to the Chicago ministers that the church visits had made him confront the racial problem in a new way. As he approached the church on a recent Sunday evening, he noticed that an integrated group of young people was talking with a group of ushers. He walked toward them with the intention of trying to remove the students from the scene, but when he got close enough to hear the conversation between the ushers and the young people, what he heard deeply troubled him. As he walked away, one of the ushers approached him. Boone screamed at him, "You know we have no right to turn them away." He now recognized the reality of racial discrimination, something made visible by the rejection of African Americans before his own church doors. He went to the evening service, but was so anguished that he could not pray or sing; instead, he went to his office and wept, emerging "a different person." Though it remained unclear what he intended to do, it was important for the Chicago men and for the Tougaloo group that they had made another contact inside Galloway.[20]

While the Tougaloo activists may have gained an inside supporter at Galloway, the status of a key ally at Trinity Lutheran Church was becoming more doubtful. Rev. Koons had struggled to maintain his pastorate since activists began presenting themselves for worship at his church the previous summer. A January 19 congregational meeting would either open the doors to all races or face major repercussions from the denomination. Rev. Koons and Lutheran officials were unsure what the outcome would be, but they expected the worst. Dr. Franklin Clark Fry, president of the LCA, wrote Rev. Koons a letter a few days after Christmas, saying "No parish in the entire LCA is as constantly on my heart as yours and the same holds true for me personally."[21] Rev. Koons remained pessimistic about the future of Trinity and informed Lutheran leaders about Mississippi's church property bill, which allowed congregations operating under a trust to gain legal possession of their churches after a majority vote. Though he did not know for sure, Dr. Wood reasoned that the law might apply to Trinity. Around Christmas, Rev. Koons received a call from the Lutheran Board of American Missions asking him to enlist as a mission developer. He did not immediately accept the position, but he understood that he might have to take it if the church did not take the proper actions at the January 19 meeting. Two weeks before the annual meeting, he realized that it would not go well. On January 6, the church council decided not to put Dr. Wood's request on the agenda for the January 19 meeting, effectively ending any resolution of the matter that would meet the requirements of the denomination.[22]

The January 19 meeting began with elections to fill vacancies on the church council. Of the nine posts available, all went to segregationists; eight went to men who previously stood guard outside the church to prevent integrated teams from entering. Rev. Koons explained to Dr. Wood that church members even voted down racial conservatives who were not radical enough. One of his supporters, John Beales, then presented a motion to admit all visitors to worship services, thus reintroducing the key issue Dr. Wood asked the church to consider. Beales moved that the vote be taken by secret ballot in order to lessen the possibility of intimidation. As Rev. Koons wrote to Dr. Wood, this sent the segregationists into a "frenzy," and a majority voted to table the motion.

Afterward, Rev. Koons determined it was impossible for him to continue as pastor of Trinity, and he announced his resignation the following Sunday, January 26. While he explained that his decision came as a direct result of the church's decision the week before to disregard denominational policies and requests from Lutheran Church leaders, he ultimately determined that to continue at Trinity would constitute a violation of his ordinational vow. He read from part of the statement he gave at his ordination in 1935, when church leaders asked him if he would "preach and teach the pure Word of God in accordance with the Confession of the Evangelical Lutheran Church." He then quoted directly from the Confession, which stated, "The Church exists both as an inclusive fellowship and as local congregations gathered for worship and Christian service." Though not in the pulpit at Trinity Lutheran anymore, he encouraged the Tougaloo activists to continue visits to the church and to maintain pressure on the congregation as they considered Dr. Fry's directive.[23] Rev. Koons remained in Jackson for several more months, officially serving as a mission developer at a church in Forrest, Mississippi. He left the state for good in July 1964, receiving a call to a new pastorate at Holy Redeemer Church in Cedar Rapids, Iowa.

Rev. Koons now joined the ever-widening list of Jackson pastors who resigned or were forced to step down owing to moderate or liberal convictions on race, positions they articulated more vigorously because of the presence of African American visitors outside their church doors. Three men who became pastors of major downtown churches in 1953 and 1954—Dr. Clark of Capitol Street Methodist, Rev. Hulan of First Christian, and now Rev. Koons of Trinity Lutheran—were gone from their pulpits within a few months of each other. Moreover, of the white Protestant pastors who participated in the interracial ministers' meetings seven months before, only Dr. Moody McDill of Fondren Presbyterian remained at his post.

With segregationists controlling the direction of Trinity Lutheran Church, at least for now, many members who objected to its closed-door policy and the treatment of Rev. Koons left the church. The destination for most of them was a new mission in northeast Jackson, Ascension Lutheran. Two years before, denominational officials had set it up under the direction of Rev. F. W. Henkel, a field developer for the Board of American Missions. From the beginning, Rev. Henkel made it clear that the church would adhere to the standards of the synod, requiring the church to be open to all regardless of race. Over a dozen attended the first service on March 7, 1962, and the congregation grew slowly through 1963. Though the mission did not intend to be an alternative for Jackson Lutherans unhappy with the racial troubles at Trinity, Ascension clearly grew as a result of people leaving Trinity in late 1963. The denomination officially chartered the northeast mission as Ascension Lutheran Church on December 8, 1963, the same day Dr. Raymond Wood delivered the ultimatum to Trinity. By this time, Ascension had fifty-eight charter members and was set to call its first pastor, Rev. Henry M. McKay. Rev. McKay recalled later that, unlike the situation at Trinity, the bulk of the members at Ascension were not Mississippi Lutherans, but transplants from out of the state. Following the departure of Rev. Koons, dozens more promptly left Trinity, and many began attending Ascension Lutheran, including Fred Patton, the lay leader who had fought so vigorously for seven months to keep the church doors open to all. Another was Jack Moskowitz, who also objected to Trinity's treatment of black visitors and recognized that like-minded Lutherans were now going to Ascension. Though the exact number remained unclear, at least thirty people transferred from Trinity to Ascension in late 1963 and early 1964, with some promising to be part of a new mission in southwest Jackson then under development.[24]

With the students gone for a semester-end break the weekend of January 26, the church visit campaign resumed on February 2 with another delegation of white ministers and laypeople from out of state arriving in Jackson. Four of them were from the Pittsburgh area, and two were campus ministers. Rev. Randy Lunsford was head of the Wesley Foundation at Indiana State Teachers College in Indiana, Pennsylvania, and Rev. Fred Villinger served on staff with the United Campus Ministry at the University of Pittsburgh. Rev. Michael Kundrat worked with an urban ministry, Bethany House, while Myron W. Warman was an attorney and layman from

Uniontown. Myron Warman's brother, Dr. John B. Warman, was the district superintendent and lead delegate of the West Pennsylvania Conference to the upcoming general conference. The fifth visitor was Anne Carpenter, a white undergraduate at North Central College in Naperville, Illinois, a school affiliated with the EUB. The previous November, she had written Rev. King asking if she could participate in the Jackson witness, having been inspired by a presentation given by Rev. Richard Tholin and Rev. Sheldon Trapp, who were part of the October 27 witness. The two had talked about the need for money and supplies in Jackson, but for those students who were really interested, they suggested joining the campaign or even transferring to Tougaloo. Carpenter explained in her letter that she was particularly interested in church integration. She understood the danger in Mississippi and confessed to being scared, but was nonetheless determined to make the trip. She wrote that Christ "died for all of us and not just for middle class whites."[25]

On Sunday, February 2, integrated groups attempted to attend worship at Trinity Lutheran and Capitol Street Methodist, while two of the white ministers went to Galloway Memorial. Ushers at Trinity blocked the students, once again demonstrating their desire to ignore instructions from synod leaders. At Capitol Street, laymen turned away an integrated group that included Dr. Madabusi Savithri, a new Tougaloo professor and Fulbright scholar from India. The ushers said that they would admit Dr. Savithri, who was wearing her sari, but not the black student. The group did not press the ushers and instead left, though they later returned after the service to drop off copies of the Detroit statement from the Council of Bishops.[26]

Meanwhile, Professor Clarice Campbell accompanied Revs. Lunsford and Kundrat to Galloway. Earlier, the two ministers contacted Dr. Cunningham to obtain permission to distribute copies of the bishops' statement to church members after the service. He requested they not to do so, but assured them that the police would not intervene if they went ahead with their plans to visit. This assurance did not comfort at least one of them, who promptly threw up as he was in the midst of writing Rev. Ed King's phone number on his arm shortly before the group left. As expected, ushers admitted the group, but then one of the ushers, identifying himself as a member of the Pastoral Relations Committee, sat in the pew with them. Worried that the ministers might try to do something disruptive after the service concluded, he and another layman tried to keep the three penned in their pew as church members departed. The three eventually pushed their way out and reached the foyer area, where Revs. Lunsford and

Kundrat distributed copies of the bishops' statement to the few remaining church people. Professor Campbell observed from a distance and saw that the ministers were able to engage in lengthy conversations with several people, though one member threw the statement on the ground when he realized what it was.[27]

That night, the Pittsburgh team and others from Tougaloo returned to Galloway. Though ushers refused to admit the integrated group, they permitted the visitors to read quietly from the communion rites on the church steps. Across the street, the group noticed the police in conversation with a man Rev. King identified as Mayor Thompson. For Carpenter, the moment was especially poignant. She wrote, "As a Christian, it is painful to hear the meaningful songs of dedication, confession, and commitment coming from the communion service of a church and know that you or your friend cannot participate because he is of the 'wrong color.'" Though they were denied entry, the occasion did signal a possible new pattern in the eyes the Tougaloo activists. They recognized that this was the first time since October 1963 ushers and police allowed visitors to conduct their own service outside a church. Moreover, this marked the end of yet another Sunday without arrests and seemed to corroborate what they heard Bishop Marvin Franklin was doing behind the scenes. He was, apparently, somehow able to put a stop to arrests outside Methodist churches.[28]

The next day, four of the visitors secured meetings with Dr. Ashmore, editor of the *Mississippi Methodist Advocate*, and Bishop Franklin. Though they did not report anything substantive about either discussion, they found the meeting with Bishop Franklin to be "frank and honest." They also sat in on a few of the proceedings of Byron de la Beckwith's trial for the murder of Medgar Evers. At the trial, Chief Ray came up to the group and asked if they were from Pittsburgh. Rev. Lunsford asked him how he knew, and Chief Ray responded that he had known since Friday they were coming. The four men reasoned that a television station in Pittsburgh must have released the details of their trip too early.[29]

For the first time since October 6, the day of the first arrests outside a Jackson church, no out-of-state ministers were scheduled to accompany Tougaloo students on their rounds of visits on February 9. The activists therefore deliberately focused on only two churches, Fondren Presbyterian and St. Luke's Methodist. While St. Luke's remained a frequent target, the Tougaloo activists had eased their pressure on Fondren in the preceding weeks. Elders there had altered their racial policy in late October, instructing deacons to ask black visitors to attend elsewhere, but allowing them to

go to the balcony if they persisted. Rev. Bill Hutchinson, a white Tougaloo instructor and member of Fondren who had attempted to bring black
guests there before, received a letter from the session specifying the change.
For Rev. Hutchinson, this quasi-open-door policy was unacceptable, for "to
have conceded this 'compromise,' we would have been accepting a return
to the days of slavery, when blacks had to sit in the balcony." A few white
students met with Dr. McDill after a service over the Thanksgiving weekend, during which he elaborated on the divisions within the church, pointing out that the deacons had assigned a segregationist and a moderate to
the doors each Sunday. He added that several members of the church were
threatened by their employers with job loss if the church remained open.
After church elections and some new elders took office in late January, the
session had a lengthy discussion over the attendance policy and its effects
on the church, but the elders ultimately voted to reaffirm the status quo.[30]

The Tougaloo activists decided to apply pressure on Fondren for the
first time since elders there adopted the quasi-open- door policy. They also
wanted to make an impact on Race Relations Sunday, the occasion that
Fondren and other churches were recognizing,. Despite the official policy
to admit the activists if they insisted upon worshiping there, deacons at the
church doors barred the students this time. Joan Trumpauer reasoned that
a few men decided on their own to bar the students' entry. Meanwhile, ushers at St. Luke's Methodist also turned away an integrated group, just as they
had on previous Sundays. Yet, as with the attempted entrance into Fondren
on Race Relations Sunday, the visit to St. Luke's had additional significance,
because the church was also having a special service. A group of missionaries who were working in Panama was speaking during the service, and
one of the Tougaloo students seeking to worship there on this Sunday was
Panamanian. The student told the usher that she was from Panama, but he
remained unfazed. After the service, the Tougaloo activists were able to get
in touch with the missionaries and told them what happened, and the missionaries promised to "blast away" during a later appearance at the eleven
o'clock service.[31]

With the Lenten season beginning that week, the Tougaloo activists decided to intensify the campaign to include visits during weekday services.
On Ash Wednesday, February 12, another team of out-of-state ministers arrived to help. Rev. Law Hastings and Rev. Paul Schrading were colleagues
of the group from Pittsburgh that came to Jackson a week before, and
had agreed to make the trip to Jackson after receiving a call from someone with MCR.[32] Joining the two Pittsburgh ministers were two ministers

from Ames, Iowa, Rev. Wesley A. Anderson, an ordained Baptist, and Rev. James N. Carver, a Congregationalist.

The ministers from Pittsburgh and Ames attended Ash Wednesday services at Galloway and a Baptist church, and then accompanied students to communion services at Galloway on Thursday. Though the visit to a Baptist service did not involve an integrated group, it was the first time since the previous summer that participants in the church visit campaign tried to attend a white Baptist church. On the last occasion, ushers at First Baptist had turned away an integrated group. At the Thursday communion service at Galloway, the four ministers accompanied Memphis Norman, who had participated in many of the church visits, including an earlier February witness at Galloway where the ushers permitted the integrated group to hold a short service outside the church without interference from police standing nearby. Now, once again, ushers let the group stand on the church steps through the end of the service. Because church officials and police seemed to be providing a space for the students and their companions to witness at Galloway without interference, the students vowed to return to the church for communion services through the rest of Lent.[33]

The Tougaloo activists followed through and returned to Galloway during Lent, though they were without the company of out-of-state clergy for the next month. Leaders in the MCR and others seeking mandatory desegregation of all aspects of the Methodist Church planned to send teams to Jackson on Easter in order to highlight their cause in the run-up to the general conference in Pittsburgh in early May. They therefore decided to pull back direct participation in the weekly confrontations, but did so knowing that the students would continue the campaign as they had before MCR's involvement. One of the key adjustments that local activists had made since Rev. King invited non-Mississippians others to join in the weekly visits was to target Methodist churches more deliberately. Of the visits that had taken place since the first arrests in October, thirty out of a total of thirty-nine took place at Methodist churches. With the initial arrests occurring at a Methodist church, Methodist ministers and laymen who objected to closed church doors came to Jackson to witness to their convictions and to try to emphasize the need for an end to gradualism in the desegregation of the denomination. The Tougaloo activists recognized the strategic importance of targeting Methodist churches because it was a connectional denomination. As Trumpauer wrote at the time, "The Jackson thing seems to have the church moving."[34] While the focus on Methodist congregations underscored the reality of racial discrimination in those churches in the city, it had the effect of lifting pressure from other local churches and denominations, and it served to de-emphasize the ecumenical nature of the campaign prior to the arrival of out-of-state Methodist ministers and laymen. Before their involvement, only eight of the twenty-eight visits were to Methodist churches. With no Methodists arriving to accompany them, local activists now made more of an effort to visit churches of other denominations.

Significantly, even without outside help, Trumpauer reported that by mid-February more and more students wanted to participate in the church visit campaign, including students who had not been part of the Jackson movement at all.[35] Many students from Mississippi refrained from participating in overt demonstrations because they knew their parents would object, or they feared reprisals against their families back home. For some of them, therefore, trying to attend a white church seemed like a more defensible type of protest and was something that their parents would be more likely to understand. Doris Browne, for instance, participated in the church visit campaign even while avoiding other civil rights protests, because she knew that if police arrested her or if her parents somehow found out, she could simply explain that all she was trying to do was go to church. She reasoned that her parents, being particularly religious, would not be too shocked and would appreciate her rationale more than if she walked a picket line or engaged in sit-in at a restaurant.[36]

For the first weekend of Lent, the students targeted a variety of non-Methodist churches. On Friday, February 14, an integrated group attended the World Day of Prayer at St. Andrew's. Though the church was officially open, ushers at St. Andrew's usually tried to seat black visitors in the rear of the church, and the students had become accustomed to receiving a varied response from church members. On this day, there were no hostile looks or remarks. In fact, they reported that members came up to them and spoke in a "friendly fashion."[37] On Sunday, the Tougaloo activists attended Mass at Holy Family Church, though after the service, a man came up and told them to stay away from the church. On their way out, the students mentioned this threat to the priest, who assured them they were definitely welcome. He later told Bishop Richard Gerow that the man who had threatened them felt sorry for what he said to the students.[38]

Despite the students having attended Norwood Presbyterian and Fondren Presbyterian on previous occasions, this Sunday ushers at both churches prohibited the integrated groups from entering. Students tried to attend worship at Fondren at both morning services. During their first attempt, they encountered a man at the door they did not recognize. After he turned them away, someone in the Tougaloo group called Fondren's pastor, Dr. Moody McDill, to inform him of what happened. They knew he would object. The students tried again to attend the eleven o'clock service, even sending a decoy group ahead to distract the usher while the other team tried to enter through a side door. Yet church officials spotted both sets and forbade the African Americans in the groups from entering. One of the white students went in anyway and spoke with Dr. McDill, who simply said he was sorry.³⁹ This marked the second Sunday in a row that deacons barred integrated groups from Fondren, despite the church's quasi-open-door policy.

After ushers unexpectedly turned the integrated groups away from the two Presbyterian churches, the activists encountered something else that was new, though not entirely unforeseen. As three cars full of students were just about to reach the Tougaloo campus after the students had been re-jected from the two churches, they came upon a set of vehicles that began to threaten them. A pickup truck tried to force one car off the road and then proceeded to follow another one. Students in one of the cars reported that the truck's passengers cursed at them and tried to take pictures of the students. Then a Ford passed Rev. Hutchinson's car and pulled ahead of him. The Ford suddenly stopped at the turn-off leading to the Tougaloo campus, forcing him to put on the brakes as well. A red Volkswagen simul-taneously pulled up behind him, pinning his vehicle between the two cars. Rev. Hutchinson then saw a man jump out of the Volkswagen and head his way, so he quickly pulled onto the shoulder and, with just enough space to make it around the Ford, sped on to campus.⁴⁰

Days later, Bishop Gerow called together the first interracial ministers meeting in months. Bishop Gerow had attended several gatherings of a new white interfaith group, the purpose of which, he wrote, was to "exert influence in overcoming the spirit of racial prejudice." The first meeting was in November in the home of Beatrice Gotthelf, a Jewish laywoman, and in-cluded about a dozen other women and Rabbi Nussbaum, Rev. Thompson of First Unitarian, and Father Law. Gotthelf remembered these gatherings as consisting mostly of commiserating and trying to make contact with like-minded people.⁴¹ On February 17, Bishop Gerow hosted two black min-isters, Dr. Whitney and Rev. Brown, in his chancery office. He wrote that the purpose of their meeting was to propose suggestions that "might help in the quieting of the intense race hatred that has arisen."⁴² According to Bishop Gerow, Dr. Whitney talked at length about how "often things which may seem to others small bring pain to them," such as using courtesy titles only when addressing or discussing whites. Bishop Gerow added that the group did not make any formal resolutions, but resolved to continue the discussion later. After the meeting, someone pointed out that two policemen and a WLBT television truck were parked across the street to observe the men going in and out of the chancery office.[43]

During the next week, the Tougaloo activists returned to many of the same churches and once again barely escaped harm. At a Thursday Lenten communion service, Galloway ushers predictably turned an integrated group away. On Sunday, February 23, students attended Mass again at Holy Family Church, but this Sunday no one accosted them. Meanwhile, Rev. Hutchinson departed Tougaloo for Fondren with his wife and baby daughter riding in the front seat with him and Eli Hockstadler, a white student, riding in the back. A car began following them once they left the school gates. When they were about a mile from campus, five cars, including the red Volkswagen from the week before, suddenly surrounded his vehicle and forced him to stop. Rev. Hutchinson estimated that there were about twenty white men in the five cars. One of the men, wearing a stocking over his face and brandishing a lead pipe, made his way to the front of Rev. Hutchinson's car, while another man with a heavy mallet approached from behind. Just as the first man heaved the pipe towards the windshield—hitting the chrome above—Rev. Hutchinson hit the gas and headed on to Fondren. One of the trucks followed them into the lot, but the Hutchinsons and Hockstadler jumped out and went inside the church. They were able to find Dr. McDill and tell him what happened, and he directed them to the phone in the church office to call the authorities. Rev. Hutchinson called Dr. Beittell, president of Tougaloo College, who then called the Jackson police to see if they would escort the Hutchinsons and the student back to campus. The officer declined, saying they could not cross city lines. Ultimately, Dr. Beittell and a few other faculty members arrived to caravan them group back to the safety of campus.

Meanwhile, two white students from Tougaloo, Neil Hindman and Ray DeVogel, traveled to Rankin County to attend worship at Oakdale Baptist Church, a congregation about twenty miles away and between the cities of Brandon and Fannin. The two young men introduced themselves to the ushers standing outside and told them they were from Tougaloo. The ushers greeted them "warmly" and welcomed them inside.[44]

That afternoon, Jackson police and a few members of Fondren Presbyterian talked with the Hutchinsons about what happened to the drive to Tougaloo. Over the telephone, a sheriff told Professor Hutchinson that police would do anything to prevent lawlessness, but gave no assurances they would help in this particular situation. The county officer said the police would not protect church visitors, since city authorities saw the visitors' actions as a violation of the law. When Rev. Hutchinson asked the policeman if officers would provide support or escort for a car with all-white inhabitants, the officer said he would have to check. He called back later to say that no, police would not get involved in that way. A couple from Fondren came to the campus to talk with the Hutchinsons and expressed sincere concern over what occurred. With Rev. King, the couple came up with a plan to escort an all-white group from the campus to the church the following Sunday. Rev. King felt that because of the potential for violence, the Hutchinson family should not be involved again and that only white adults should go. He recruited Professor Campbell, an attendee at Galloway and a frequent driver on church visits, and a few others to attempt to go to Fondren on March 1. For their part, the Hutchinsons decided to stop trying to bring black visitors with them to Fondren.[45]

In addition to the physical confrontations on the streets of Jackson, Rev. King and Rev. Hutchinson began receiving menacing phone calls on an almost daily basis. The afternoon of the pipe-wielding incident, an unidentified male called Rev. King's house to say that he would kill him if he brought a baby with him again. The man obviously thought that it was Rev. King and his family in the car earlier in the day, unaware that Rev. King was not the only white church visitor who had a family at Tougaloo. Trumpauer wrote that some people just hung up calling, but most of the calls were "pretty filthy and threatening," and a few callers gave detailed descriptions of their intentions. One of the women's dorms at Tougaloo received several bomb threats, and students reported seeing the red Volkswagen and other suspicious-looking cars cruising on or around campus in the days that followed.[46]

With physical threats and confrontations on the rise, the Tougaloo activists received a very different kind of warning from state officials, one that put the very existence of the college in peril. In late February, Lieutenant Governor Carrol Gartin gave a speech at a civic club calling for an investigation to determine whether Tougaloo had violated its charter. He pointed out that the school was integrated, it included several Freedom Riders among its students, and it was overall a haven for "queers, quacks, quirks, political agitators and possibly some communists." The state, he suggested, should follow the lead of Tennessee, which recently closed the Highlander Folk School, a training ground for civil rights and labor organizers. A few state senators agreed and introduced a bill to revoke Tougaloo's charter. The legislation stalled in committee because senators were unsure whether or not the action was even constitutional, but their effort did seem to convince the Southern Association of Colleges and Secondary Schools to reexamine Tougaloo's accreditation, which the college had maintained since 1957.[47]

For the following Sunday, March 1, the Tougaloo activists decided to forego a visit to Fondren and instead sent a team to nearby St. James Episcopal. In the wake of the previous week's confrontations, several members of Fondren offered to accompany any visitors from Tougaloo. However, after conferring with them and other members of Fondren who impressed upon Rev. King the amount of pressure Dr. McDill was under, Rev. King called off any more visits to Fondren—at least this week. As Professor Campbell wrote, of the four white ministers the Jackson Citizens' Council had sought to run out of town, only Dr. McDill was left. The students planned to try to attend several other churches in Jackson on March 1, but ended up visiting only St. James Episcopal, and even then they arrived at the end of the service. Upon seeing what they believed to be a roadblock on their way to St. James, the car of black and white students turned around and took back roads to St. James. They finally arrived at the close of the service.[48] This was the second visit to St. James, the first being on October 13, the Sunday after the first arrests, when ushers admitted them.

In addition to the visit to St. James in Jackson, Neil Hindman and Ray DeVogel, two white Tougaloo students, returned to Oakdale Baptist Church in Rankin County, where church members had welcomed them the previous Sunday. As soon became evident, their honesty in informing the ushers the week before that they came from Tougaloo became a barrier to their efforts this Sunday. When they got out of the car, they saw a crowd of about twenty people out in front of the church, and then encountered three men who rushed over to where they were. One of the men told Hindman and DeVogel, "You all are from Tougaloo College and you're not welcome here." Hindman explained they were not planning to integrate the church, but merely wanted to attend worship and "bridge the communication gap." One of the laymen then said that if the pair did not leave, they would call in the police to arrest them. They left, and on their way back to Tougaloo, while still in Rankin County, a police officer in an unmarked car stopped them and spelled out more clearly how unwelcome the two young white men were. The policeman told them that they would not be allowed to return to any church in the county, and that he would consider it a personal threat if he saw them in the area again. Just to be sure they understood, he added, "I wish I weren't wearing this badge and I could do what I want!"[49] Blocked by church people and physically threatened by a police officer, Hindman and DeVogel abandoned their efforts to establish dialogue with white Baptists in Rankin County. The incident at Oakdale Baptist also highlighted segregationists' growing exasperation with the civil rights activities coming out of Tougaloo. While ushers at other churches turned away visitors because they arrived in integrated groups, until now no church had banned an all-white group solely on the basis of its association with the college.

The next week at the Thursday Lenten service, the Tougaloo activists continued with the pattern of being rejected by Galloway and then trying to attend non-Methodist churches on Sunday. On March 8, the students returned to Fondren Presbyterian after a week's hiatus and also went to First Christian, a church they last visited on January 12. In front of Fondren the integrated group encountered the same man out who had objected to their entry before, and the group left the premises. This was the third time in a row that a Fondren member turned away black students and laid bare the impediments Dr. McDill faced in trying to enforce the church's quasi-open-door policy. At First Christian, which still had not found a replacement for Rev. Hulan, an usher refused to let the integrated group enter. According to Trumpauer, the usher was at least cordial, even apologizing for mispronouncing "Tougaloo."[50]

The church visit campaign was now in its ninth month, and the racial policies of Jackson's churches remained relatively unchanged. With men at Fondren Presbyterian now turning away integrated groups and Trinity Lutheran intransigent in its closed-door policy, the Tougaloo activists could only count on open doors at the same places of worship as they had in June 1963: the city's Catholic and Episcopal churches and one lone Unitarian congregation. The Methodist churches continued to bar integrated groups despite the pressure tactics of Methodists from out of state. The arrests at four Methodist churches in late 1963 underscored the reality of racial segregation, and the Council of Bishops had responded with a strong statement advising local churches and their pastors to affirm equal rights in their various ministries. The Methodist churches in the city remained closed to black visitors, but significantly, Jackson policemen had thus far refrained from jailing any church door activists in 1964. Whether because Bishop Franklin or other Methodist leaders in the state asked Jackson police to hold back, or because activists eased up on targeting Methodist churches, the lack of arrests suggested Jackson officials had taken a new direction—or at least returned to the course of action they followed until October. Yet in the absence of police intervention, militant white segregationists were now taking matters into their own hands, urging the state to revoke the school's charter, and even phoning in threats to the Tougaloo activists as well as confronting them on the streets of Jackson.

Easter in Jackson

MARCH 1964

With the quadrennial General Conference of the Methodist Church convening in May 1964, Rev. King and the church visitors turned their focus once again on the Methodist churches in Mississippi's capital city. They aimed to apply more pressure to local congregations ahead of the conference, recognizing that the visits were succeeding in highlighting the reality of racial discrimination in the Methodist Church. Their effort had spurred the Council of Bishops in Detroit to issue a statement condemning the churches of Jackson. Still, in the four months since the resolution, Jackson's white Methodist churches remained closed. Attempts to worship at white Methodist churches on the part of local activists and their out-of-state supporters took on added significance because they sought to attend churches on the two holiest Sundays in the Christian calendar. If white churches were ever to admit African Americans to worship, surely they would do so on Palm Sunday or Easter—or so the activists thought. Instead, the Methodist churches once again barred the visitors' entry, and even blocked the admission of two Methodist bishops. Moreover, Jackson police ended their three-month-long non-intervention policy and stepped in to make more arrests. Following the Easter visits, Rev. King and the Tougaloo activists pulled back on future organized attempts, hoping for more forceful action by the general conference in mandating open doors in local congregations and turning their attention to the Mississippi Summer Project.

In the months preceding the general conference, Methodist leaders and laymen debated the problem of racial segregation in the denomination and the usefulness of the Jackson church visit campaign, with the conversation often spilling onto the pages of the *Christian Advocate*, the biweekly periodical of the Methodist Church. In early January, Bishop James K. Mathews defended the significance of the Detroit statement, writing that it marked "a new stage on the long road toward real brotherhood." To those who were journeying to Jackson or taking part in other protests in the South, he repeated that their primary responsibility was to work to improve race relations in the cities of their home ministries. He argued, "If we are not exercising our energies where we are, then we are in no position to insist on justice where we are not." Yet he also urged his readers not to fall into the trap of condemning the role of outsiders, for the "Christian's neighbor is in fact every man and his neighborhood is everywhere." Bishop Mathews pointed out that the Methodist Church was a connectional church, so the label of "outsider" had no place in the life of the denomination.[1]

In the following issue, a Methodist layman and ethics professor at the Divinity School of Vanderbilt University, Dr. James Sellers, aimed to provide readers with an insider's perspective on the white Southern mindset. He argued that Northerners needed to understand that white Southerners had very different conceptions of community and authority. When Northerners spoke connectionalism and the brotherhood of man, white Southerners proclaimed that true power resided on the local level by the will of the majority. This "compulsion to wall off the world" was nothing new, Dr. Sellers argued. He advised Northerners to learn to talk with Southerners within this framework, to put moral ideas in political language.[2]

In late February, Rev. Richard C. Raines Jr., a participant in one of the rounds of church visits in November, critiqued the Detroit resolution. He simply did not understand what the Detroit decision meant, "If the statement does not apply to bishops and their actions as well as to ministers and laity."[3] He contended that the failure to implement resolution made notions of "connectionalism" moot, for how connectional could a denomination be where no entity took responsibility for putting church teachings into practice?

In the weeks leading up to Easter Sunday, the Tougaloo activists continued their visits to churches on Sunday and to special Lenten observances during the weekdays. Though the students hoped that closed churches might finally admit African Americans during this key period on the Christian calendar, they encountered the same resistance as before. On Sunday, March 15, ushers at Capitol Street Methodist and Trinity Lutheran turned away groups of students, while another integrated group attended morning worship at St. James Episcopal.[4] With certain men at Fondren now regularly turning away black students, the activists could only count on the city's two large Episcopal churches, St. James and St. Andrew's, to admit integrated groups consistently.

With Holy Week approaching, Rev. King was beginning to lose patience with the lack of progress in tearing down racial barriers at the Methodist churches in Jackson. As he later wrote, he often wondered if he and the other activists were not pushing hard enough, wondering if perhaps he or other ministers should use their whiteness to their advantage and enter a church to actually disrupt a service. Law enforcement would arrest them on the same charges—trespassing and disturbing divine worship—anyway, and the tactic would potentially have a dramatic effect. At this point in the campaign, Rev. King wrote that he "wanted to shout, to preach to them," feeling that "these segregated churches had no right to celebrate Christian events as if they were not mocking Christianity by their segregation." He believed that white church people "received too much comfort from their white religion and that it should be disrupted."[5] Ultimately, he decided against an overt demonstration inside a church, though on Palm Sunday he and a few others did in fact enter two white churches. Efforts to remove the group provided Rev. King the opportunity to engage white churchgoers in the way he had envisioned.

On the morning of March 22, 1964, Palm Sunday, the Tougaloo activists returned to several of the churches they had attempted to attend in the preceding months.[6] That evening, a group that included two black students, the Kings, and Dr. Savithri, a native of India and a new faculty member at Tougaloo, tried to attend services at Galloway Memorial Methodist and St. Luke's Methodist. When they arrived at Galloway, they immediately noticed that there were no men guarding the church outside as on all the previous Sundays. Guessing that the ushers were just inside the front doors in the foyer area, the group decided to try to enter the church sanctuary through a side door. Rev. King noticed that on previous Sundays, church members used this door to avoid confronting the activists at the front doors. This time, however, the absence of ushers outside presented the activists with a unique opportunity to force white Christians to confront the exclusion policy of their church more directly. Rather than hearing about their ushers blocking African Americans, church members who tried to avoid the problem in the past would now see it firsthand. Rev. King wanted "the ministers and the congregation to see, to experience whatever would happen—our acceptance or our rejection." The service, which included the welcoming of boys and girls into church membership, was not yet underway, and Dr.

Cunningham had not entered the sanctuary. Rev. King opened the door and led the group inside, with Dr. Savithri following right behind him. Just after Dr. Savithri had taken a few steps inside, two men ran over to the group from the foyer area, and Jeanette King and the two black students back-pedaled out the door. With the eyes of the congregation fixed on Rev. King and Dr. Savithri, one of the men grabbed the latter's arm and began pushing her backwards toward the side door. In the next few seconds, Dr. Savithri shouted out in quick succession: "Take your hands off me"; "Don't touch me"; "I thought this was a Christian church"; "I am from India. If you want you can see my passport"; and "How would you feel if your women are treated like this by our men in India?" Rev. King tried to grab on to the door tightly in order to keep it open. Realizing that is group had the attention of the whole church, he started shouting as well: "Don't push that lady"; "Let her go"; "We just want to worship with you"; and "Please let my friends attend your service." Though it was unclear whether it was intentional or just part of the melee, one of the ushers kicked Rev. King in the shin and elbowed him in the stomach. Rev. King yelled out again: "Don't kick me, don't hit me. We'll leave."[7]

Having been forcibly ejected from Palm Sunday evening services at Galloway, Rev. King then suggested that they try to attend St. Luke's Methodist. As at Galloway, no men stood outside the church to block their entry, so the five walked undeterred through the front doors. They expected ushers to stop them once they got inside, but the one usher present just looked at them and did not intervene. With the service already underway, the group continued on and sat down in one of the pews. Then a few men came over and told the group that there had been a mistake and asked them to leave. The five stood up and began walking slowly toward the rear of the sanctuary. Rev. King and the others asked the same types of questions that activists asked on the church steps on previous Sundays: whether Christianity was for whites only, and what was so wrong with the group that they could not worship with the rest of the congregation? More men approached the five, apparently feeling that they were not exiting the church quickly enough. One man grabbed Dr. Savithri's arms. Rev. King explained to the men that she was a guest from India. She stopped walking and tried to reason with them as well, imploring them to "think of all the missionaries you send to India," and to "look straight into my eyes and tell me who ought to be ashamed." One of the men tried to come up with an apology, but Dr. Savithri continued on out the sanctuary. Rev. King looked around to see if he could locate the associate pastor of the church, Rev. Brooks Hudson, a former college roommate of his. He could not find him, and with the large assemblage of men now hovering around the group, Rev. King and the others left the church.[8]

The dramatic expulsion of the integrated group from two Methodist churches on Palm Sunday added a new dimension to the church visit campaign. The Tougaloo activists were now accustomed to being turned away outside of white churches, and knew that if they somehow eluded the ushers and were able to seat themselves, church officials would eventually ask them to leave—and might even use force to ensure compliance. Yet it was Dr. Savithri, not the two black students, who bore the brunt of the animosity. The local movement newsletter emphasized this peculiarity, pointing out that the two students "were virtually ignored." The day after the visits, the *New York Times* and the *Chicago Tribune* stressed the uniqueness of the incidents as well. The *Times* led with the headline, "Two Churches Eject an Indian Scholar in Mississippi City," while the *Tribune* ran with "Shove Hindu Woman Out of Two Churches." For readers of the two papers, which had often reported on the barring of African Americans from white churches in Jackson during the preceding ten months, the message was unmistakable. The churches started by posting guards and then police, who made dozens of arrests, but now white churches had physically expelled an Indian national from services. How far were Jackson's churches willing to go to preserve their racial purity, and how far were city authorities willing to push to enforce this social system? The two main Jackson newspapers, in contrast, declined to say anything about Dr. Savithri, instead highlighting the ejection of Rev. King, an activist familiar to local readers. According to articles appearing in each paper, someone alerted the police that Rev. King stood before the congregation at Galloway, asking that his friends be allowed to attend services before ushers threw him out.[9]

In a report that Dr. Savithri submitted to the Indian Embassy in Washington, DC, she summarized the evening and offered an explanation for the obstreperous response to her presence. She concluded that it was not so much her ethnicity or nationality that made her so objectionable, but rather her affiliation with Tougaloo. She described her encounters with white Jacksonians beyond the campus of Tougaloo, where "piercing looks and stares" predominated. She did not exactly know how the white residents of Jackson knew that she taught at Tougaloo, but many confronted her, making rude remarks such as, "What are you doing at Tougaloo with those niggers?" She surmised that people knew she taught there because her appointment to the college had been publicized.[10] Another possibility was that local

segregationists had already marked her as an agitator, as word spread of
her other efforts to undermine racial barriers in Jackson. Professor Campbell, for instance, recorded at least two instances that had occurred by mid-
March 1964, during which Dr. Savithri and others from Tougaloo had tried
to attend white movie theaters. Dr. Savithri saw the conduct of the ushers as a logical consequence of the larger problem: She had no freedom of
movement in Jackson. For her, the state's capital city was "a strange place—a
prison without walls."[11]

The forcible ejection of Dr. Savithri from Galloway marked a new low
for the church's pastor, Dr. Cunningham. He later explained that the incident left him with a "sinking feeling," though his thoughts mostly concentrated on its effect on the white youth who witnessed it. He questioned
how they could "now accept the church as a place where the teachings of
Jesus and mercy were taken seriously." In his memoir of his time at Galloway, Dr. Cunningham used the confrontation on Palm Sunday as an introduction to the sources of the church's closed-door policy. He reasoned
that his congregation did not act out of a "deliberate perversity and in-
nate willful meanness," but rather because of "the inability of many people,
even good and respectable people, to change their patterns of thought."
Dr. Cunningham recognized that people could not break away from what
they saw as their customs, but he went on to highlight the singular factor that Dr. Savithri underscored: The exclusion policy was the product
of attitudes about Tougaloo College and the people associated with it. The
fact that the church visit campaign originated with the school, and that
visiting ministers and movement activists found refuge there, only accentuated antagonistic feelings segregationists harbored about the perceived
leftist leanings of the school and the various activities on campus. For Dr.
Cunningham, the secretive and confrontational behavior of the Tougaloo
activists—what he called their "hit and run" Sunday tactics—not only ex-
acerbated the animosity toward the college, but also fed white Jacksonians'
feelings of "stranger hatred." While clearly sympathizing with this point of
view, Dr. Cunningham directed most of the blame at the Citizens' Council, which had succeeded in erecting "an almost impassable barrier" to between Tougaloo and the rest of the city.[12] Dr. Cunningham's reactions to Dr.
Savithri's removal succinctly summarized his own inner conflicts, which
one finds throughout his memoir. He simultaneously denounced the fundamental assumption of his flock, concluding that they clung tightly to the
status quo for fear of losing power over the familiar, but then identified
with the attitudes that gave the assumption expression, that those trying

to bring about change—the Tougaloo activists generally and Rev. King in particular—were misguided in their choice of tactics, which only served to invigorate hard core segregationists. Like others torn between the poles of conservative intransigency and liberal militancy, Dr. Cunningham accepted the inevitability of change, but he believed it should happen deliberately, diplomatically, and internally.

While still trying to process the dramatic evictions from two white churches on Palm Sunday, Rev. King and the Tougaloo activists turned their attention to Easter Sunday. It had now been over a month since ministers from the outside came to Jackson to join with the students in their church visit campaign. Earlier in the year, Rev. King received assurances from various sources that Methodist leaders were negotiating with the Mississippi Conference to try to make progress overturning the exclusion policies of local churches. He had been content to return the campaign to its local roots and discourage the help from visiting ministers while this process worked itself out, but by March, there were no signs that the negotiations or discussions with leaders in the conference were proving fruitful. He began to worry that easing the pressure on Methodist churches was actually having an effect opposite the intended one, that the Citizens' Council and other segregationist forces in the city now felt that victory was theirs, and that segregation was now assured in the city's Methodist churches. Rev. King also became concerned that the Citizens' Council was trying to overturn open-door policies at the Episcopal churches in the city, the only Protestant churches to consistently admit African American visitors since the beginning of the campaign.[13]

In early March, the Jackson Citizens' Council announced that laypeople in the city's Episcopal churches had recently formed a group to oppose admission policies in their churches. The group invited an outspoken Southern segregationist minister and board member of the national Citizens' Council, Rev. James P. Dees of Statesville, North Carolina, to speak in Jackson the Wednesday before Easter Sunday. A few months before, Rev. Dees formed and became the first bishop of the Anglican Orthodox Church, an Episcopal Church (USA) breakaway denomination. Though Rev. Dees formed the new church to restore aspects of the traditional liturgy, such as the use of the 1928 Book of Common Prayer, and to counter the liberal theological direction of the Episcopal Church, his views on race constituted a key facet of his message. He called integration an "amalgamation of the races" that he found to be "abhorrent to God." In his resignation statement on November 15, 1963, he cited the denomination's program of socialism, appeasement of communists, and "so-called civil rights" as reasons for his departure from the Episcopalian Church.[14]

With no discernable progress with the Methodist Church, and with the Citizens' Council now trying to close the doors of open churches, Rev. King once again welcomed help from beyond the state. During an MCR meeting in Cincinnati, Ohio, in early March, assembled clergy and laymen recognized that it would be impossible to send ministers to Jackson on Easter Sunday, since they needed to be at their own churches that day. So they decided that faculty members at seminaries could make the trip instead. Dr. Jeffrey Hopper, a native of New Jersey and an assistant professor of theology at Methodist Theological School (MTS) in Delaware, Ohio, stepped in to organize the Easter witness, contacting friends at Methodist seminaries throughout the country and asking them to send representatives to Jackson.[15]

With just a few weeks to prepare, Dr. Hopper enlisted three more colleagues on the faculty of MTS—native Southerners all—to join him: Dr. Vann Bogard Dunn, Dr. Paul M. Minus, and Dr. Charles Everett Tilson. Dr. Dunn was dean of the school and also officially a minister within the Memphis Annual Conference, which at the time was under the supervision of Bishop Marvin Franklin.[16] Dr. Dunn grew up in western Kentucky, but his real racial education came from his time serving as an army driver in Europe during the war, when the perspective from abroad caused him to re-evaluate the notion that the country was a model for democracy. After attending Duke Divinity School on the GI Bill, he pastored various churches in Kentucky and in Tennessee. Most recently he served at a church in Jackson, Tennessee, where he organized a set of unprecedented interracial meetings in the late 1950s. Dr. Minus, an assistant professor of church history at MTS since January, grew up in Columbia and Charleston, South Carolina. Like other ministers who participated in the Jackson witness, he credited the Methodist Student Movement with exposing him, in college and in graduate school, to a lot of the social ferment around him. Out of Yale Divinity School, he became a chaplain at Florida State University in the midst of that school's integration and took part in several local civil rights marches. Though set to affiliate with the West Ohio Conference, Dr. Minus was technically still a member of his home conference, the South Carolina Annual Conference.[17]

The fourth member of the team from MTS was the school's professor of Old Testament, Dr. C. Everett Tilson, a respected scholar and preacher throughout the denomination. Dr. Tilson was from Seven Mile Ford,

Virginia, in the southwestern part of the state. After receiving his graduate degrees at Vanderbilt University and setting up Belle Meade Methodist
Church in Nashville, he joined the faculty at Vanderbilt Divinity School.
While there, he organized several race relations conferences, including one
where he invited Dr. Martin Luther King Jr., to speak, and became involved
with several liberal-leaning organizations, such as the Highlander Folk
School in nearby Monteagle. He was well respected among his students,
who included Rev. Joe Way, the current associate at Capitol Street Methodist. In 1958, at the suggestion of Rev. Will Campbell and other friends,
Dr. Tilson wrote *Segregation and the Bible.* In the book, which he based
on lectures, Dr. Tilson directly confronted the alleged Christian defense
of segregation, rebutting with Scriptural passages arguments used by segregationists to defend racial barriers. He left Vanderbilt for MTS in 1960,
shortly before the Vanderbilt Divinity School expelled one of his students,
James Lawson, for allegedly acting as the ringleader for civil rights protests
in Nashville. According to Dr. Hopper and Dr. Minus, the decision to send
three Southerners was deliberate, for this move would seem to undermine
the dismissive label often affixed to visiting ministers, "outsiders."[18]

After solidifying the team from the MTS, Dr. Hopper and the others
enlisted faculty members from other seminaries, believing that the Easter
witness would be more meaningful if it included Methodist theological
professors from other parts of the country. With just nine days to go, they
placed calls and wrote letters to people they knew at Methodist and interde-
nominational seminaries, asking them to consider sending a delegation or
electing someone to come to Jackson on the seminary's behalf.[19] The faculty
at Drew Theological Seminary in Madison, New Jersey, met in official session to send a representative, and Dr. David James Randolph volunteered
to make the trip. As Dr. Randolph later recalled, the move was unusual on
the part of the seminary, for the faculty had never been involved in direct
action before. Yet all of them understood what was at stake: A positive resolution to the situation in Jackson could be a turning point for Methodism
and the civil rights struggle overall. For Dr. Randolph, the decision to step
forward was a natural product of the work he did locally and his conviction
that he had a moral obligation to answer the call for help. Though aware of
the burden of segregation since his childhood in Maryland, the defining
moment in his thinking about how his faith related to race was an experience he had while at Boston University School of Theology a few years
earlier. While he was serving a church in Lowell, Massachusetts, a fire swept
through a nearby tenement, and he was obliged to perform the funeral for

the tenants who died there, a mother and her children, all of whom were black. Inferior housing caused the fire, and Dr. Randolph immediately connected the dots between racism and housing policies. Moreover, he determined that "if the resurrection meant anything, it seemed to have to mean relating faith to the tragedy." He continued working on local housing issues while serving an inner city integrated parish in Wilmington, Delaware, before he accepted a position at Drew. He saw his decision to come to Jackson as a logical extension of what he was doing at home. Like the other ministers who made the journey, who were married and had young children, he remained committed to the idea that his witness would ultimately benefit his family and help realize an inclusive church and truly open society.[20]

Two more Methodist faculty members answered the call to participate in the Easter witness in Jackson. Dr. Henry B. Clark, an instructor in church and community at Union Theological Seminary in New York, agreed to join the effort as a representative of his school's faculty. Dr. Clark was a native of Reidsville, North Carolina, just north of Greensboro, and was officially "on trial" with the Western North Carolina Annual Conference. With Dr. Clark, five of the seven participating ministers had grown up in states below the Mason-Dixon line. Dr. Tyler Thompson, a renowned professor of the philosophy of religion at Garrett Theological Seminary in Evanston, Illinois, became the final member of the team. A few of his former students already took part in the church visit campaign, and Dr. Thompson accepted the invitation from another former student and cousin of his, Dr. Jeffrey Hopper. Unlike his colleagues in the Easter witness, Dr. Thompson knew firsthand the experience of being incarcerated. At the outset of World War II, Japanese troops captured him while he was doing missionary work in Singapore. Dr. Thompson ended up spending three years in a Japanese prisoner-of-war camp.[21]

The ministers arrived in Jackson separately on Good Friday and Saturday. As on previous weekends, they sought out meetings with local black and white church people before proceeding with attempted visits on Sunday. On Friday evening, Bishop Franklin met with Rev. King and Dr. Randolph. Later, Dr. Randolph reported to his colleagues only that the bishop and his wife entertained them graciously.[22] On Saturday morning, the seven visiting ministers met with Dr. Cunningham and a few Millsaps professors. Dr. Tilson later told an assembly at MTS that Dr. Cunningham was clearly a man in torment. Dr. Cunningham had considerable ability and a firm theological grounding, but he was "caught in conflict between a conscience that he cannot forget on one hand and a culture which he dares not oppose on the other." He recognized that something must be done to overturn his church's exclusion policy, but when the group asked him what he proposed to do, he admitted that if he did anything, his congregation would immediately expel him. Dr. Cunningham told the ministers that his only hope was for a change in leadership, a new bishop and a new district superintendent. The group also met with two Millsaps professors, who gave examples of harassment and intimidation they faced in their daily lives in Jackson. One professor explained how he had just signed a contract for the next year that included a clause permitting him to leave after that, while the other one described how he and his family had lived in Jackson for twelve years, but had concluded that it was "impossible to rear his children in the Christian tradition in this environment."[23]

The visiting ministers then secured a lengthy meeting with Dr. J. Willard Leggett Jr., the district superintendent of the Mississippi Conference. Dr. Leggett invited three other Jackson pastors, including Rev. Granberry of Capitol Street Methodist and Rev. Duke of Broadmeadow Methodist, one of the more outspoken segregationist ministers in the city, to reinforce his views in the discussion. Dr. Thompson later wrote the he and the others "were intent on a reconciling mission through a biblical and theological witness." Dr. Tilson recounted that he and his colleagues received a "liberal theological education" from Dr. Leggett and the others, for it was liberal "in the sense that we were exposed to ideas . . . which we'd never heard before." It was clear to Dr. Tilson "on any fair assessment of racism . . . [the four] are confirmed racists." The visiting ministers asked one of the Jackson ministers whether there was any incompatibility between the Gospel and segregation, and he resolutely said no. The Jackson minister went on to tell a story about how he regretted preaching once in a black church, coming away from the experience with the belief that blacks and whites maintained fundamentally distinct temperaments. Dr. Thompson recalled that the meeting reached a climax when Dr. Leggett assured the delegation that if anyone, including Bishop Franklin, came "to any of their churches with a 'nigra' he would be turned away—and if he persisted he would be arrested." Dr. Minus remembered that the discussion ended with Dr. Leggett leading the group in prayer, asking God to help them realize that they should not do what they planned to do the next morning.[24]

After discussions with various local white Methodist ministers, the seven visiting ministers met to decide whether or not to follow through with the visits the next day. They talked about what it meant to be ministers of reconciliation, with a passage from Second Corinthians—that God in Christ reconciled the world unto himself and entrusted Christians to proclaim the message of reconciliation—at the forefront of their minds. They hoped to advance this message of reconciliation and to instill their Jackson colleagues with the desire for an inclusive church in the state. Yet these discussions with local white pastors made it clear to the visitors that while there may in fact be men of good will in Mississippi Methodism, the Methodist leadership in the area was failing them. The ministers talked about what the resurrection meant to mankind if churches maintained closed-door policies, and they ultimately decided that Easter Sunday was the most appropriate day to testify to their belief in the Incarnation.[25]

Saturday evening, the visiting ministers concluded their discussions with local church people by meeting with a group of black ministers and laymen. Dr. Tilson reported that these men were "determined to take whatever steps [were] necessary to secure freedom for their fellow human beings." They described all the pressures that they and their families endured and said they remained anxious to receive all the outside help they could get. Dr. Tilson concluded that the black church in Jackson was a fitting example of a "transforming church," in distinct contrast to the "conforming church" of white Methodists in Mississippi. He saw that the black Methodists were "remarkably free," for they recognized that "the larger church was not the governor of Mississippi, not the bishop of white Methodism in Mississippi, but was Jesus Christ." For Dr. Tilson, Jackson's black churches were much like early Christian churches described in the New Testament, for they consisted of people who were in captivity who yet were not really captives because of the freedom they had in Christ.[26]

While the visiting ministers consulted with their Jackson colleagues, the Tougaloo activists learned the news that they had been hoping to hear since at least December: A few Methodist bishops were coming to Jackson to participate in the church visit campaign. Rev. King received word that Bishop James K. Mathews of the Boston area and Bishop Charles F. Golden of the Nashville-Birmingham area of the Central Jurisdiction decided to attempt to attend Galloway on Easter Sunday. Bishop Golden's jurisdiction included black Methodist churches throughout Mississippi. In the weeks after the November meeting of the Council of Bishops, the two bishops talked about coming to Jackson and intended to join in the December 8 witness, but they called the trip off when they were unable to convince other bishops to join them. Moreover, the two wanted to give the Jackson churches a few months to implement the anti-segregation statement made by the Council of Bishops. The Tougaloo activists understood that during the winter negotiations were taking place behind the scenes, including meetings between Bishop Franklin and Bishop Golden. Those discussions proved fruitless, and Bishop Golden suggested to Bishop Mathews that they attempt an Easter visit to Galloway, the state's largest Methodist church. Bishop Mathews later wrote, "I could do no other than agree." The two men had known each other since the late 1930s, when they attended Boston University together. They served together on the staff of the Board of Missions, and both became bishops in 1960.

They arrived in Jackson on Saturday and spent the evening formulating two statements, one that they would leave with Galloway and release to the press if ushers admitted them, and another they would release if the church turned them away. They deliberately made the decision not to alert the press beforehand, hoping for a quiet witness without fanfare.[27] Even though ushers at Galloway had barred all integrated groups since regular visits began in June 1963, the men held out hope that the circumstances of the day and the sight of two of the denomination's bishops—one of them African American—would make church officials more conscious of the immorality of their closed-door policy.

The Tougaloo activists, seven seminary professors, and two bishops awoke to a beautiful and sunny Easter Sunday. What they hoped to achieve in Jackson was being accomplished in a much grander spectacle two hundred miles away in Birmingham, where fifty thousand black and white Christians were assembling at Legion Field to hear Rev. Billy Graham. A committee of Birmingham church leaders and businessmen organized the ecumenical and interracial service. A year after the violent response of Birmingham law enforcement to civil rights demonstrators, and just six months after the bombing of a local church that left four girls dead, Rev. Graham declared to the integrated audience, "The problem of the world is that we are a planet in rebellion against God."[28]

At Galloway in Jackson, Bishops Mathews and Golden arrived shortly before the eleven o'clock worship service. The minutes of the official board noted that the attendance for the service was "a possible record" of 1,100.[29] The bishops ascended the front stairs and identified themselves to a group of ushers. They noticed stewards of the church guarding all of the other entrances and three policemen standing nearby. Nat Rogers, the chairman of the official board, spoke for the ushers and explained the policy of the church, which did not allow them to admit African Americans at this time. Bishop Mathews later said that Rogers seemed almost apologetic. The bishops then asked Rogers if they could see the pastor of Galloway. Rogers said they could not go inside, but told them he would try to locate Dr. Cunningham and bring him to them. Rogers found him and Rev. Clay Lee, the church's associate pastor, in a corridor near the sanctuary and told them there were two bishops outside asking for admittance. Dr. Cunningham later wrote that this was the first time Rogers or any usher alerted him to the presence of an integrated group seeking entrance into the church before a service. Dr. Cunningham told Rogers, "Let them in on my responsibility." According to Dr. Cunningham, Rogers predicted "dire consequences" if the ushers let the bishops inside and remained certain that they would not admit the bishops.

Meanwhile, Bishops Mathews and Golden remained outside talking with the ushers, who tried to explain that they just did not understand the problem, and that they should have given the church more notice of their visit. Bishop Mathews responded by saying they merely wanted to worship, so what would have been the point in giving advance warning? The bishops shook hands with a few church members who came up to them, saying how glad the two were to see them. Bishop Mathews later described the behavior of most of the members as courteous, but he did write that some onlookers were particularly hostile in their comments. When the visitors could hear the church service beginning, and it became clear that Dr. Cunningham was not coming outside, the bishops handed the ushers one of their two prepared written statements and left the church. Bishop Mathews later wrote that the outcome of the visit was truly a surprise, for despite the previous attempts, he felt "When the issue was sharply put, as we tried to do on behalf of all Methodism, they would respond in terms of faith rather than in terms of traditional social mores." Barred from a white Methodist church, the two bishops celebrated Easter at a black Methodist church nearby, Central Methodist Church.[30]

A statement, which the bishops released to the press and reprinted in full in the *Christian Century* a few weeks later, summarized their intentions that day. They opened by appealing to common sense: "A Christian's desire to participate in public worship—especially on Easter—should neither occasion surprise nor require explanation." The bishops acknowledged that they were well aware of Galloway's closed-door policy before ushers turned them away, but remained committed to common Methodist practice and principles and the conviction that as Methodist bishops, they were responsible "to the whole church for the whole church." They argued that Easter was a particularly appropriate day to proclaim these beliefs, for the day offered "not only victory over death but infinite possibility for renewal of

individuals and of churches and of society." They were now "deeply concerned for the witness of the whole church before the world," and prayed
that all would come to "fully know Christ and the power of His resurrection
and the fellowship of His suffering."[31]

As ushers at Galloway turned two Methodist bishops away from Easter
services, the seven seminary professors left the Tougaloo campus to pick up
two African American men, Robert Talbert of McComb and David Walker
of Jackson, on their way to Capitol Street Methodist. Talbert was a twenty-
two-year-old activist who had been arrested by McComb police in 1961,
when he and two others tried to sit in the white section of a waiting room
at the Greyhound bus station. The ministers went over the strategy for their
visit. Dr. Dunn would act as spokesman and would speak softly. They discussed how they needed to remain dignified and polite throughout the witness; they could not do anything that others could interpret as constituting
a disturbance. They decided that if an officer from the church asked them
to leave the premises, they would decline to do so. Dr. Thompson wrote a
few weeks later that they reasoned at the time they "had to say No to the
church's assertion of the right to turn us away." The church had the power to
do so, but the group felt, "We would have to deny that it had the right" and
"would take the consequences."

Before they left the Tougaloo campus, Rev. King warned the ministers
that they might encounter a Citizens' Council roadblock on the way downtown. Two cars did, in fact, stop them, but evidently because their own car
carried no black passengers, the Tougaloo group was allowed them to proceed. The professors stopped by the offices of the COFO to pick up Walker
and Talbert, and Rev. Ed King led the group in a meditation, reading from
Psalm 123. Exiting the COFO offices, Rev. King pointed out Chief Ray, who
was across the street in a police car. Then about five police cruisers passed
by, one of them with a police dog in back. Dr. Dunn saw this as "a deliberate
attempt of course to intimidate the Negroes and of course to intimidate us."[32]

The integrated group of nine arrived at Capitol Street Methodist about
fifteen minutes before the eleven o'clock service. Around the church they
noticed as many as a dozen police officers, who began to converge behind
the ushers when they sighted the group. As the team approached the front
steps of the church, a set of ushers hastily ran down, and one of them told
the group to stop and not come any further. The ushers then formed a line
across the stairs, and Robert Talbert, David Walker, and the seven ministers reciprocated by spreading out along the sidewalk and the grass. After
a member of the team appeared to try to walk around the line of ushers,

James Cox, spokesman for the ushers, barked, "No end runs!" Dr. Dunn then announced, "We are Methodist Christians who would like to worship the Risen Lord with you in this church today." Cox responded, "You aren't going to integrate this church. The policy of the official board of this church is to deny admission to all Negroes. You can stand here all day, but you aren't coming in this church." Recognizing an opening, Dr. Dunn asked, "Do you mean we can stand here?" The usher clarified, saying, no, they must move on. When Dr. Dunn asked why they could not just stand there, Cox explained, "No questions and no answers. If you don't move on at once, I will ask the police to put you under arrest." Dr. Dunn restated the desire of the group to worship at the church. Cox then turned to one of the policemen behind him and gave him unambiguous instructions: "Officer, take them away." The officer walked up to Dr. Dunn and asked him if he understood what the usher was asking, and Dr. Dunn said yes. The policeman then announced to the group, "If you don't move on, I will place you under arrest." Dr. Dunn replied, "I guess you'll have to arrest us," and the officer declared them all under arrest. As the nine waited for a patrol wagon, Dr. Dunn asked the officer if he would have arrested them without being requested to do so by the usher. The policeman answered no, he would not have arrested them unless the usher called for his intervention.[33]

The arrest of the seven seminary professors and the two black laymen on Easter Sunday were the first made in front of Jackson churches since mid-December, and brought the total number of arrests made since early October to forty. When they arrived at Jackson's city jail, officers told the arrestees the city was charging them with disturbing divine worship and trespassing (authorities later dropped the trespassing charge). Officers then interviewed them and asked each if he had ever spent any time in jail. Dr. Tyler Thompson's response added some poignancy to the moment; he said yes, that he spent three years in a Japanese internment camp. The men spent the next two nights incarcerated segregated in separate sections of the jail. The professors later stressed that overall the officers treated them quite well, though they heard comments by jailors that suggested to them that black prisoners did not fare as well. Dr. Tilson told a reporter from the New York Times that he and the other professors received better treatment from the police than from leaders of the Methodist Church in Mississippi. They passed the time sharing stories—particularly about Dr. Thompson's experience, which most of them knew little about. The professors received dozens of telegrams from family and supporters and welcomed a few visitors, including Dr. Lee Reiff, a professor at Millsaps and a member of Capitol Street

Methodist, and two Catholic priests. One of the priests attended a seminary near MTS. The other was Father Bernard Law, who told Dr. Everett Tilson that he read his book, *Segregation and the Bible*, several years before.[34]

On Monday, March 30, the nine appeared before Municipal Court Judge James L. Spencer, who heard arguments and testimony for about two hours. The professors and their lawyer, R. Jess Brown, tried to establish that they did not disturb public worship, for they never raised their voices or made threatening gestures. They pointed out that no one came near them during their attempted visit. Moreover, they could see no possibility that people inside the church could have heard them or known what was occurring outside. In fact, the arresting officer testified that he saw no evidence of a disturbance of the peace.

For Judge Spencer, however, the issue was not whether there was a physical or vocal disturbance. Instead, the central question as he saw it was whether or not a congregation had the right to worship in their chosen manner. He explained, "This country has not reached the station where a group of persons who seek to worship in the way they want to, have to be told by someone else to do it this way or that way." He concluded simply, "A congregation has the right to worship in the way it desires without someone coming from Illinois or from any other place to tell a congregation to do it any other way." Judge Spencer looked at the nine and told them they knew what the attendance policy of the church was before they tried to worship there, and that the police had arrested others on earlier attempts. He added, "Just as you gentlemen feel equally strong about certain issues, so too this congregation and other persons have strong feelings." He declared them guilty of disturbing divine worship, sentenced each to six months in jail, and ordered each to pay a $500 fine.[35] Echoing the argument employed since the first trial in October, the city attorneys stated—and Judge Spencer reaffirmed—that disturbance of public worship could arise a result of the mere presence of African Americans seeking to worship at an all-white church. The race of individuals, not their actions or words, constituted the disturbance.

While the seminary professors and two laymen remained in jail, Dr. Cunningham grappled with the realization that his church had barred two of his denomination's bishops from worshiping on Easter Sunday. A few hours after the incident, he went to the home of one of his lay leaders and let his emotions pour out. When he regained his composure, he explained that the stress had become unbearable and told the church official he intended to step down. He spoke of the "double tragedy" of the situation at

Galloway, which comprised "a minister not near retirement age and without an appointment, and a large and potentially great church unable to find a suitable pastor because of its racial discord." The lay leader persuaded Dr. Cunningham not to resign, but a meeting the next morning only discouraged him further. Bishop Franklin came to his office and told him how outraged he was that Dr. Cunningham allowed ushers to turn away two of his colleagues from worship. He told Dr. Cunningham, "If they had been admitted, he would have stood by [him]." As Dr. Cunningham later wrote, this was the first time Bishop Franklin ever mentioned Galloway's admission policy, and certainly the first time the bishop ever intimated publicly or privately that the official board should open the church doors.[36]

Later in the week, Dr. Cunningham wrote Bishop Golden to tell him how distressed he was, and to clarify that he specifically requested that the ushers admit both bishops. Dr. Cunningham described his dilemma, stating that since arriving at Galloway in September that he had tried to work with a few laymen he trusted to arrive at an effective strategy. He said he was choosing to remain at the post because "there is need, need that we all come into conformity with Methodist principle and law and, above all, the spirit of Christ." He urged Bishop Golden to "not lose faith in us" and to keep the church in his prayers. Dr. Cunningham concluded by inviting Bishop Golden to meet with him and a few laymen during his next trip to Jackson. Bishop Golden wrote back, saying that he and Bishop Mathews were not trying to make Dr. Cunningham's task more difficult. Bishop Golden explained, though, that the two had "a higher commitment to make our own witness on the basis of our own convictions." He affirmed, "The action of your official board is completely out of line with Methodist policy and practice and has usurped authority which belongs to the pastor of a local church in our Methodist system." He accepted Dr. Cunningham's request to meet at a later time, but hoped that Galloway would change its admission policy before next month's general conference.[37]

Bishop Golden received other letters from Mississippi Methodists expressing astonishment at what occurred on Easter Sunday in Jackson. J. P. Stafford, the lay leader of the Mississippi Conference since 1948 and an early defender of the "born of conviction" statement, explained that it seemed to him the incidents resulted from the conference's "weak leadership and cowardly vacillation when a firm decision would have changed the picture." Without naming individuals, he pointed to the "unholy alliance of leading church officials with the Citizens' Council." The real tragedy of the situation with the Mississippi Conference was that he and other lay people "have been forced to stand against the ministerial leadership we had hoped to follow." Bishop Golden wrote back, saying that Stafford's letter was "one of the most meaningful among the many [he] received." Rev. Jim Waits, pastor of Epworth Methodist Church in Biloxi, forwarded Bishop Golden a copy of a letter he wrote to Bishop Franklin. Over a year after helping to author the "born of conviction" manifesto, Rev. Waits was clearly exasperated with the state of the conference in the wake of the incidents on Easter Sunday. He called on Bishop Franklin to exercise leadership to address what he deemed to be heresy on the part of Galloway and Capitol Street Methodist. For Rev. Waits, the turning away of two bishops and the arrest of Methodist seminary professors jeopardized the connectional system of the denomination and made a mockery of the teaching of Scripture. Bishop Golden wrote back, thanking Rev. Waits for his witness and expressing hope that the general conference would take action allowing pastors to follow Methodist teachings without fear of reprisal from their congregations.[38]

Echoing a sentiment that his colleagues expressed privately Dr. Sam Ashmore, editor of the *Mississippi Methodist Advocate*, publicized his frustration in an editorial that appeared soon after the Easter incidents. He understood the feelings of those who resented their churches becoming battlegrounds for the racial conflict within the denomination, but pronounced the actions against the church visitors during the past six months were beyond comprehension. He found it unbelievable that Methodists trying to attend a Methodist church in Jackson could be arrested for trespassing and sentenced to excessive fines and six months in jail. He catalogued the upsetting incidents of the Easter season, from the Panamanian who wanted to hear a missionary from her home country, to the Palm Sunday incident when ushers physically evicted Dr. Savithri from two churches. The turning away of two Methodist bishops from a Methodist church on Easter "makes us wonder if the [closed-door] policy is consistent with Christ's teaching that 'whosoever will may come.'"[39] Dr. Ashmore called for prayer but did not map out an exit strategy for the conference. Instead, he simply aimed to offer assurance to like-minded Methodists that they were not alone in feeling embarrassed and disturbed by recent events.

If the seminary professors and bishops came to Jackson to gain a first-hand understanding of the situation and to help clarify the predicament facing the Methodist Church, they left the state's capital city with the feeling that the central question before May's general conference was clear. In reports to their colleagues at theology schools and in an essay Dr. Thompson published in the *Christian Century*, the professors reiterated the crucial

decision now before their fellow Methodists. Delegates needed to reconcile the stated belief of the church, that the House of God was open to all,
with the reality of racial discrimination in local congregations. Methodist
churches in Jackson not only forbade African Americans to attend worship, at least one church continued to seek the arrest of people trying to
worship in integrated groups.[40] Though the exclusion policies of individual
congregations were symptoms of the overriding problem of segregation
throughout the structures of the church, the continued recalcitrance of
Jackson Methodist laypeople and local authorities to align with Methodist principles—even after pleas from the Council of Bishops—highlighted
the need for conference delegates to take a definitive and binding position
on desegregation of the denomination. The ten-month-long campaign and
the recent shocking incidents at churches in Jackson—particularly the barring of two of the church's bishops from a worship service on the holiest of
days—underscored the fallacy of gradualism. Some churches, left to their
own schedules and procedures, remained uninterested in responding to
appeals from their fellow Methodists, regardless of status. If anything, lay
leaders at Galloway and Capitol Street Methodist demonstrated even more
intractability on Easter Sunday than at any point during the campaign.
The bishops and seminary professors, their colleagues who participated in
previous efforts, and their supporters throughout the denomination recognized that the time for volunteerism had passed. God, they decided, chose
Jackson to manifest the cancer within the church, and it was now time to
extirpate it once and for all.

"The Nation Needs Our Witness Now"

APRIL 1964

A s Rev. Ed King and other local activists made plans for the general conference, they saw signs of progress in the white church community of Jackson. A new conference-wide group took shape to rally support for the Methodist Church in Mississippi ahead of the general conference, and to counter the efforts of the segregationist MAMML. Several new congregations formed, signaling that the campaign was making an impact, forcing white church people to take a stand on race. Meanwhile, Southern Presbyterians voted to mandate open-door practices in their churches, indicating a potential resolution to the standoff at Fondren, and heightening expectations that delegates to the general conference would take similar action. When the Jackson church visit campaign began, Rev. King and the students did not intend to shine a spotlight on the shortcomings of one denomination, but the initial arrests in October and the subsequent involvement of out-of-state ministers brought the focus of their effort to the Methodist Church. Students continued to visit non-Methodist white churches in April as the school year wound down, but the Tougaloo activists and their allies now turned their attention to achieving a fundamental shift at the quadrennial assembly in the racial practices of the denomination.

For Rev. King, the ten-month-long church visit campaign had run its course. He and the other local activists felt they had given the white church people of Jackson a chance to recognize the immorality of segregation and to bring about change internally. Sensing that the campaign had trained enough attention on the reality of racial discrimination in the Methodist Church, they now hoped that change would come from the outside, that the general conference would mandate immediate desegregation of all the structures in the denomination. To underscore the problem of segregation at the assembly, the Tougaloo activists and MCR planned a prayer pilgrimage and an all-night vigil in Pittsburgh during the decisive votes on the future of the church. The result fell short of their goals, but after nearly a year of trying to establish dialogue and demonstrate the possibilities of true brotherhood among the city's Christians, they turned their attention to the Mississippi Summer Project.

In early March, a new Methodist group, the Fellowship of Loyal Churchmen (FLC), emerged to organize support for and allegiance to the denomination. In a lengthy statement published in the *Mississippi Methodist Advocate*, FLC admitted that its members were not of one opinion as to the solution to the problems facing the Methodist Church. But all agreed they would remain faithful to the denomination regardless of the decisions that came out of the general conference. Recognizing the continuing exodus of ministers from the conference, the statement insisted that ministers must be allowed to work in an environment where church people respected differing views and recognized their pastor's freedom of expression. In contrast to the current milieu, they hoped that Mississippi Methodists would express their divergent opinions "in a climate of Christian love that will promote a deeper and richer fellowship among ministers and laity." Leaders of the group included Francis Stevens and Rev. Clay Lee, the associate minister at Galloway.[1] Though FLC did not identify MAMML by name, and did not take an explicit stand on the issue of segregation, the positions of the FLC clearly distinguished them from the segregationist group, which had threatened secession from the denomination and had disputed the principle of freedom of the pulpit. Rev. King later wrote that he was disappointed and amazed that such a long statement could ignore the church arrests, but he appreciated the group's sincerity and recognized that the members of FLC were not in a position to give voice to anything stronger. Nevertheless, he felt that FLC developed too late to deal with the crisis facing the conference and Mississippi in general. If it had surfaced a decade before, when MAMML appeared, then FLC "might have given significant leadership to the silent people who would have welcomed liberal ideas and moderate leadership."[2]

Direct quarrels between FLC and MAMML burst into the open following the Easter Sunday incidents. FLC announced its support for the editors of the *Mississippi Methodist Advocate*, which engendered some enmity after likening the barring of the two Methodist bishops from Galloway on Easter to witnessing the crucifixion of Christ.[3] Two days later, MAMML responded by charging that FLC and the *Mississippi Methodist Advocate* were being

misleading, that Mississippi Methodists would not accept the forced integration of its churches. MAMML argued that the reunion of the denomination a few decades before was only achieved because of assurances that
African Americans would worship in separate churches. They proclaimed
that Methodists in the state would not accept any outcome from the general
conference that would integrate local Methodist churches, since no white
Methodist churches in the state admitted blacks, and most official boards
in the state had adopted policies against "mixing."[4] As in their response to
the "born of conviction" statement a year before, MAMML cut through
the calls for moderation to what they felt was the fundamental question,
whether or not Methodist churches in the state should integrate. For them,
FLC's pledge of loyalty to any outcome from the general conference was
just a veiled way of saying that FLC would tolerate desegregation of the
denomination's structures, including its individual congregations.

While moderate and liberal Methodists in Jackson fought to maintain
a united front in advance of a national conference, many of their Lutheran counterparts gravitated toward to new missions in Jackson. After Rev.
Koons resigned from Trinity in January 1964, many of his supporters hoped
he would become pastor of one of the two missions. Yet LCA officials felt
that Ascension and the southwest mission needed men who were less controversial and instead settled upon two recent seminary graduates, Rev.
Henry M. McKay, who accepted a call to Ascension Lutheran, and Rev. Jack
Zipperer, who arrived in June to lead the southwest mission.[5] Rev. McKay
grew up in Macon and Savannah, Georgia, and was set to graduate from
Lutheran Southern Seminary in Columbia, South Carolina. In mid April,
just three weeks after he accepted the post, an integrated group of black students and white students from Tougaloo attended worship services at Ascension. A church member recorded in the "historical events" ledger, "The
congregation is to be praised and thanks given to Almighty God for the fine
Christian spirit and welcome shown our visitors."[6] Even though Rev. Henkel prepared the church for this possibility, Rev. McKay found that open
doors still bothered some members, especially those who were Mississippi
natives. A few voiced their disagreement, citing the students' sincerity in
wanting to worship, and decided to leave Ascension. The students returned
the following week and again on three Sundays in May before the school
year ended. Rev. McKay later recalled that he tried to greet them as warmly
as he could, and many other members did as well.[7]

Just a few days after African Americans attended Ascension Lutheran
Church for the first time, the regional synod voted to clarify the mandate

that congregations must remove racial restrictions, and Trinity Lutheran Church in Jackson announced that that they would submit to the new directive. Meeting in Augusta, Georgia, a convention of the Southeastern Synod of the LCA affirmed that "church councils and congregations be requested to rescind actions that have been taken by them concerning racial discrimination contrary to the policy of the church." A member of the executive board announced that Trinity had "already taken steps to remove references to prior action setting up racial barriers." The synod then decided it would ask Trinity to host the next convention. Trinity's vice-president, Fritz Schluetter, who spearheaded the effort to ban African American visitors from Trinity and even enlisted the aid of the Mississippi State Sovereignty Commission to support his efforts the preceding year, announced on April 16 that Trinity accepted the invitation to hold the 1965 synodical meeting in Jackson.[8] Trinity's decision to abide by the denomination's racial policies was certainly a precondition for the church to host the next convention, but as Dr. Raymond Wood, president of LCA, and other leaders had asserted for months, it was a decision that the members of Trinity also had to make in order to call a new pastor and remain in good standing with the denomination. The Tougaloo activists read the news of the reversal of the admission policy at Trinity and vowed to test it. On April 19, just as Ascension Lutheran welcomed black students to morning worship for the second consecutive Sunday, ushers at Trinity once again turned away an integrated group of students from morning worship.[9] Days after Jackson newspapers publicized the church's decision to take steps to remove racial barriers, the action by Trinity ushers indicated the church still had more steps to ascend to comply with LCA dictates.

Meanwhile, racial conservatives in Jackson's Episcopal parishes moved to establish an independent and whites only congregation. This decision came on the heels of a late-March visit by Rev. James P. Dees, a Citizens' Council board member from North Carolina and the recent founder of a breakaway denomination, the Anglican Orthodox Church. The Jackson Citizens' Council urged its members to attend Dees's talk, citing the open-door practices of local Episcopal parishes and the role that Bishop John Allin played the year before as the "spokesman for the Negro agitators." The organizing committee of the new congregation, Holy Trinity Church, planned to affiliate with the new denomination and reiterated Rev. Dees's rationale for exiting the Episcopal Church, pointing to its liberal theological drift and support of NCC, the ecumenical group that, among other things, was then lobbying for passage of the Civil Rights Act. In a short invitational letter published in mid- April, the committee elaborated, writing that it could no longer support a church making contributions to NCC, when those monies were then used to lobby Congress and to pay "bail bonds for agitators who come into our State for the avowed purpose of causing trouble."

In late April, Holy Trinity Church filed its charter of incorporation and publicly invited "all interested white Christians" to meet in fellowship services each Sunday at the King Edward Hotel. The church's leaders promised to "return the mission of the Church back to its mission of Christ and Him crucified." With a dozen charter members, Holy Trinity boasted sixty attendees from various denominational backgrounds by late May. Later in the year, Holy Trinity Church found a new home at the site of the old Westminster Presbyterian Church on West Capitol Street, and the church received its first rector, Rev. Carl B. Wiener, a former minister from the Mississippi Methodist Conference. A newspaper advertisement from Holy Trinity directed interested people to the "white church" on the south side of the street, a not-so-subtle reminder of its raison d'être.[10]

Just as delegates to the general conference of The Methodist Church arrived in Pittsburgh for a two-week session, the general assembly of the Presbyterian Church in the US (Southern) voted on a series of measures to desegregate their churches and presbyteries. The denomination added a new statement to its directory of worship: "No one shall be excluded from participation in public worship in the Lord's House on the grounds of race, color or class." After voting down a measure that would request but not mandate full integration of the presbyteries, the assembly approved an official recommendation to integrate the denomination's forty-three black churches into their respective geographical presbyteries. Dr. John Reed Miller, pastor of First Presbyterian in Jackson, condemned the move: "This is the type of coercion that will put our churches in the area in a tailspin." He pointed out, "It's been constitutional to have segregated Presbyteries for all these years . . . why the push now?" To cap off these moves, the assembly voted to increase its financial support for NCC. Once again, Dr. Miller led the chorus of dissent, denouncing NCC's recent proposal to recruit youth for civil rights work in the Delta region as "an invasion . . . without invitation from responsible Protestant churches of the Delta."[11]

Delegates were no doubt spurred to act so decisively by segregationist intransigence, but Jackson was not the only or even the most high-profile bulwark of racial conservatism in the denomination. The assembly was also moved to act because it was due to hold its next meeting at Second Presbyterian Church in Memphis, the largest church in the denomination that was barring integrated groups from morning worship services. With the presbyteries still needing to approve the new mandate concerning admission policies of individual congregations, the Southern Presbyterians took the added step of voting to hold future assemblies only in churches that maintained open-door policies. They elected to delay implementation of the rule for three years because the denomination was already under contract with Second Presbyterian. Yet, delegates did vote to ask the Memphis church to drop its racial barriers ahead of the 1965 meeting.[12]

Rev. King and the Tougaloo activists hoped the general conference of the Methodist Church would follow the Southern Presbyterians' lead in mandating an end to segregation in the various structures of the denomination. The Methodist Church did not sanction the segregationist policies that the white Jackson churches practiced, but the absence of any measure that would ensure compliance with Methodist beliefs or punish wayward congregations would provide individual churches the space they needed to maintain their exclusionary policies. On one level, therefore, they wanted the delegates to amend the Methodist *Discipline* to make clear that Methodist churches and programs were open to all, regardless of race. Yet the related but larger issue for most liberal Methodists was speeding up the termination of the Central Jurisdiction. The denomination created it as a temporary administrative body to appease white Southern church people during the 1939 union, but on the twenty-fifth anniversary of its inception, leaders of the Central Jurisdiction saw it as an anachronistic and embarrassing stain on the church. As one writer in the *Christian Century* pointed out, the enduring segregated structure of the denomination was an "impediment to the kinds of contacts which could, ultimately, help to dissolve the patterns of racial exclusiveness within the local church."[13] Who could blame the white church people of Jackson for their feelings of exclusiveness, when the very structure of the church inhibited opportunities for interracial contact?

The previous two general conferences began to move toward dismantling the Central Jurisdiction, but a principle of volunteerism had prevailed. In 1956, delegates set up the procedure for churches and annual conferences to transfer out of the Central Jurisdiction into their appropriate geographical jurisdiction. With only a few churches following this course, the 1960 general conference commissioned a committee of thirty-six to study the issue and provide the 1964 assembly with a plan of action for eliminating the Central Jurisdiction. One of the thirty-six members was John Satterfield, the arch-segregationist Mississippi layman and advisor to Governor Ross

Barnett. Anxious to see the 1964 general conference abolish the all-black conference, the 1960 Central Jurisdiction annual conference established its own commission to study the issue, the Committee of Five. As expected, the Committee of Thirty-Six announced ahead of the 1964 general conference that it would recommend a reaffirmation of the principle of volunteerism, while the Committee of Five vowed to present a series of memorials (petitions) that would eliminate all racial barriers and vestiges of racial discrimination in the church.[14]

In the weeks leading up to the general conference, the students and the ministers in MCR took steps to focus the delegates' attention on resolving the problem of racial discrimination in the church. They mailed all the delegates a copy of a recent issue of *Behold*, the newsletter of the Inner City Methodist Ministers' Fellowship in Chicago, which contained a series of essays by people connected to the Jackson church visits. It included an update on the litigation efforts, a summary of the campaign, and a word of caution that a spirit of compassion and open dialogue should guide the church integration cause. Another essay provided a theological grounding for the cause. In it, the authors argued that racial segregation in the denomination and the culture to which the Methodist Church was capitulating were manifestations of one central problem: Methodists were rejecting God's command for the church to be one. For the authors, God merely chose Jackson to dramatize "that part of Christ's body known as Methodism its sinful brokenness."[15]

Additionally, the Tougaloo activists and MCR made plans for a pilgrimage to Pittsburgh that would gather together the Jackson church visitors, their supporters, and others seeking decisive action for one final witness. They organized plane rides and buses for Methodist students and laypeople from various points in the East, including one from Jackson, and planned to picket and hand out leaflets outside of the Civic Arena. Their presence would culminate with a six-hour-long "Living Memorial for Freedom," consisting of singing and rallying.[16]

Eager to tell their side of the story regarding the incidents at Jackson churches, racially conservative Methodist leaders in the city compiled a fifteen-page response to the *Behold* issue with the intention of putting a copy in each delegate's mailbox at the general conference. Entitled *His Name in Vain*, the booklet sought to reframe the debate. Instead of focusing on whether or not it was Christian to exclude someone from worship on account of race, the writers questioned the methods and underlying purposes of the activists, arguing that the integrated groups were simply not sincere in wanting to worship in the white churches of Jackson. One writer catalogued examples of when the groups allegedly disturbed worship services, highlighting the Palm Sunday incidents when the group shouted inside churches; the few Sundays where white ministers kneeled at their pew throughout the worship service; and the short services that some activists held on the church steps. Another argued that the campaign was really an act of reprisal on the part of Rev. King, and that it was driving even more of a wedge between local whites and blacks. Avoiding any discussion of the Christian response to racial segregation, the writers affirmed the right of a governing board of an individual congregation to adopt its own set of rules concerning whom to admit or exclude from worship services, regardless of that church's connection to a national body.[17]

Rev. King led the group from Tougaloo, and some arrived in Pittsburgh in time for the opening session. Ida Hannah, Bette Poole, and Julie Zaugg joined Rev. Donald Walden and Rev. Gerald Forshey in attending First Methodist Church in Pittsburgh, worshipping together finally as a group five months after being barred and arrested outside of Capitol Street Methodist. Rev. Forshey explained that it was important to bring the three students up to Pittsburgh, as the "girls did a service to the whole church by exposing themselves to this kind of affront." Other Tougaloo students involved in the Jackson witness and movement activities arrived by bus later in the week, including Eli Hockstadler, Austin Moore, and Joan Trumpauer, a veteran activist and behind-the-scenes coordinator of the church visits. When their bus left Jackson, it travelled on the Natchez Trace, which was federal property, all the way to Nashville to avoid any local police interference. They brought with them a charred cross that white supremacists had burned on the school campus a week earlier. Tougaloo physics professor and Galloway member John Garner was on the bus, as were two members of Capitol Street, Dr. Lee Reiff, professor of religion at Millsaps College, and Martie Turnipseed, a Millsaps student and frequent guest at Tougaloo meetings.[18]

While the general conference met in session, beginning on April 26, members of MCR, young people from the Methodist Student Movement, and civil rights activists maintained a picket and handed out leaflets in front of the Civic Arena. One of the handouts contrasted the "claim" with the "practice" at Capitol Street Methodist Church in Jackson. Shown under the heading "claim" was a copy of a visitor's registration card from the church, which stated that Capitol Street "has extended a warm and friendly welcome to all who have sought to worship and serve God here." On the right, under "practice," appeared a photocopy of the *New York Times* article from a month earlier detailing the arrest of the seven seminary professors and laymen at the church. Another handout, entitled "Why We Witness," explained that people of MCR were carrying out daily demonstrations out of the same love for the church and witness to their faith as any other delegate to the general conference. The inside pages alerted readers to the recent news that Southern Presbyterians had taken steps to mandate an end to the denomination's segregated administrative structures and enforce open-door policies in its churches. The leaflet pointedly asked, "Southern Presbyterians Vote Against Voluntarism, *Why Can't We*?"[19]

The day before the activists' "Living Memorial," general conference delegates voted overwhelmingly to prolong the policy of voluntarism regarding the elimination of the Central Jurisdiction for another four years.[20] With the adoption of the Committee of Thirty-Six's recommendations, the *Jackson Daily News* assured its readers that the plan was something the white Southern delegates "could live with." An editor at the *Christian Century* later spelled matters out more clearly: "It is no secret . . . that Southeastern Jurisdiction delegates, resentful of what they consider unbrotherly, even hypocritical urgings by northern churchmen, had arrived with drafts for withdrawal if the principle of voluntarism had been dispensed with."[21]

Hours after delegates defeated measures to speed up desegregation of the structure of the church, over a thousand Methodist ministers, students, and other laypeople gathered nearby for the planned "Living Memorial for Freedom." At midnight Saturday morning, May 2, the program commenced at the Smithfield Street Methodist Church, with an overflow crowd gathering at Smithfield Street Congregational Church. Attendees included many non-delegates who had participated in the Jackson witness, such as Rev. John A. Collins, Rev. Paul Minus, Rev. Fitts Herbert Skeete, Rev. Richard Teller, Rev. Al Tomer, and their wives. At both churches, the "Southern-style freedom rally" began with the singing of hymns and freedom songs, led by Bernice Reagan of SNCC.[22] Attendees heard speeches by Rev. James Lawson and several students active in the movement in the South. Dr. Reiff and Professor Garner gave testimonials on life in the churches and community of Jackson. Rev. King later recalled that the most powerful address was from Martie Turnipseed, a white Millsaps student and Capitol Street Methodist attendee. Struggling to contain her tears, she implored the delegates to take strong action against segregation. To those moderates and others arguing that this type of action might trigger a mass withdrawal of white Southern churches, she explained that many did not realize that many white

Southern church people knew segregation was wrong, and that they and black Methodists would feel abandoned if delegates acceded to the wishes of Southeastern Jurisdiction representatives.[23]

When it was his turn to speak, Rev. King, too, let his frustrations pour out. He admitted he had "a feeling of desperation," recognizing that the moderate delegates to whom he and others were directing their appeal were probably not even present at the rally. As he later wrote, he was trying to inspire and even shock white Mississippians, fearing for his own life and fearing the violence he anticipated would accompany the Mississippi Summer Project, set to start in a few weeks, and the beginning of public school desegregation in the fall. Overall, he aimed to confront the idea propounded by Southeastern Jurisdiction delegates, who claimed that the South won by the vote on Friday, emphasizing instead that the South had really lost in the decision. He argued that all of the church people who took stands against segregation, mainly because they felt they had the backing of the denomination, were now deserted. Rev. King pointed to the burned cross that the Tougaloo students brought with them, now at the church altar surrounded by Easter lilies, and said that this was "the symbol of what Mississippi means by voluntarism." The *Jackson Daily News*, in a front-page article entitled "Mississippi Lambasted by Tougaloo Chaplain," provided an inventory of this and other strident quotes from his speech. The newspaper reported that Rev. King singled out Dr. Miller of First Presbyterian as "a sort of chaplain of the white Citizens' Council of Mississippi." Yet Rev. King reserved his most provocative language for delegate John Satterfield, whom he called "the chief functioner of the Nazi operation that operates the state of Mississippi," adding that Satterfield received $20,000 a year to lobby against the civil rights legislation currently before Congress. Though aware of how inflammatory his language was—a woman who knew Satterfield even confronted him afterwards—Rev. King refused to back down from his characterization of Satterfield. He later wrote, "I did—and do still—consider that this man already had his hands covered with blood."[24]

The "Bishops' Hour" and Holy Communion follow the freedom rally. Church people heard from seventeen Methodist bishops, denominational officials, and theology professors, many of whom were directly involved in the Jackson church visit campaign. Three of the speakers, Bishops Golden and Mathews, and Dr. Tilson, participated in the Jackson witness on Easter Sunday, while two of them, Dr. Grover Bagby of the Board of Christian Social Concerns and Thelma Stevens of the Women's Division, worked behind the scenes to secure bail and legal funds for those arrested in Jackson in the preceding months. During the sacrament of Holy Communion, when the program aimed to emphasize the "broken body," the featured speaker was Aaron Henry, the president of the Mississippi NAACP.[25]

At eight a.m., around a thousand assembled activists and church members marched from the two congregations to the Civic Arena. Each wore an armband that depicted a cross breaking the links of a chain, the symbol of the MCR. Austin Moore, holding the charred cross recently burned at Tougaloo, led the procession. Some carried placards bearing direct pleas to the general conference delegates, such as "Love Is Central, Not Jurisdictional" and "Methodism + Segregation ≠ Christian Witness." Other posters spoke more generally to the movement: "In Christ There Is No East Or West" and "Bigot or Brother?"[26] When the demonstrators reached the arena, some knelt along the ramps leading to the main entrance, while others marched in single file as a picket, strategically positioning themselves so that each delegate would have to pass through them to enter the complex. At some points, they knelt or walked in silent protest, while at other times they joined in singing familiar freedom songs and hymns like "The Church's One Foundation Is Jesus Christ Our Lord."[27]

Though the conference had already voted to continue with voluntary abolition of the Central Jurisdiction over the next four years, activists held out hope that their allies inside could devise other ways to hasten its elimination. One of the key issues before the conference was the proposed merger of the seven hundred thousand-member EUB with the ten million-member Methodist Church, a move complicated by the existence of the Central Jurisdiction. Many EUB ministers, including several Chicago-based pastors who participated in the Jackson witness, were determined not to permit the union until the Methodist Church desegregated all of its structures. Dr. William Astor Kirk, one of the members of the Central Jurisdiction's Committee of Five, led the passage—on a close vote—of an amendment to the unification proposal, specifying that the merger of the two churches would not include the all-black jurisdiction, which would effectively mandate that the Methodist Church desegregate before unification. Since it still needed the approval of the regional conferences of both churches, and the unification meetings were not slated to start until 1966, the earliest the merger— and thus the elimination of the Central Jurisdiction— would occur was 1968, the same target date as before. Yet Dr. Kirk's amendment was a clear directive challenging the principle of gradualism. As the *Jackson Daily News* alarmingly reported to its readers, the new vote was significant in that "it is the first mandatory legislative action taken by the Methodist Church to desegregate."[28]

The Tougaloo activists and others trying to steer the denomination away from its segregationist practices then turned their attention to the other key issue that brought them from Jackson: enactment of an unambiguous new law mandating the immediate end to exclusionary attendance policies. Delegates had already approved a report from the Committee on Christian Social Concerns that called upon all pastors and church boards to admit visitors without reference to race, though the report did not have the force of law. A different report by the Committee on Membership and Evangelism would change the Methodist *Discipline*, in effect church law. Without any floor debate, the general conference quickly approved by a show of hands the new Methodist Church law, which read:

> The Methodist Church is a part of the church universal. Therefore, all persons, without regard to race, color, national origin, or economic condition, shall be *eligible* to attend its worship services, to participate in its programs, and to be admitted into its membership anywhere in the connection.[29] (emphasis added)

Liberal Methodists at first thought that they had won. Rev. Forshey wrote a few weeks later that open church doors was now the law of the church, while Rev. King also felt that this change meant that Jackson churches could no longer close their doors to black visitors. He reasoned at the time that segregationists in the denomination seemed content now to focus their efforts on sustaining the Central Jurisdiction.[30]

Yet it soon became clear to Rev. King and others clamoring for a truly open church that the wording of the new law left plenty of wiggle room for lay boards and ministers to keep their churches closed to black visitors. Almost immediately after the delegates passed the measure, debate began over its interpretation, centering upon the word "eligible." Bishop John O. Smith of Atlanta pointed out the ambiguity of the term, reading it to mean that a white church was not obliged admit someone of another race. He explained, "Eligible means that they are free to go and should be admitted," but added that he did not know "if that makes it binding on them to be let in." Bishop Mathews countered that Methodist churches were under a "compulsion of faith to abide by the intent of the law and thus are obligated to throw open their doors to everyone." He maintained that the pastor of a church was responsible for fulfilling the intent of the law and, ultimately, the bishop of the area was the last line of enforcement.[31]

Rev. Granberry and Satterfield returned to Jackson proclaiming a victory for the status quo. Rev. Granberry assured a men's group at his church that even with the new policies, he did not feel "there would be immediate drastic changes," and that it was unlikely a vote for the elimination of the Central Jurisdiction would pass by the requisite two-thirds of the jurisdictions.[32] John Satterfield, addressing the Mississippi Annual Conference of the Methodist Church in late May, felt so satisfied with the outcome of the general conference that his central message was that there was no need for conservative Methodists to withdraw from the denomination, as some were urging. He argued that the country was just going through a period of hysteria. When this passed, he was confident that most Americans, and Methodists, would realize, "What is best for both races [would be to] maintain our own separate churches, our own separate denominations," and "work as brothers together in the same church under segregation, in a Christian, brotherly, proper spirit."[33] Satterfield tried to allay the fears of those worried about other changes, particularly regarding admission policies. He explained that the word "eligible" was in effect their escape clause. Referring to a section in another report specifying that a Christian should follow his or her conscience, he concluded, "By the same rule we have a pattern to follow in Mississippi and the Southeastern Jurisdiction," and "if it is a matter of conscience with us we have the right by church action to be disobedient to this provision."[34] Deeming segregation to be a "pattern" and one's commitment to segregation "a matter of conscience," Satterfield aimed to provide breathing space for his fellow conservatives to continue the battle to preserve their social system within the Methodist Church.

Bishop Franklin offered his first assessment in an address to the North Mississippi Annual Methodist Conference meeting in Jackson, which included a few guest ministers from the Central Jurisdiction, a small but symbolically momentous step. He developed upon the observations he shared with the Council of Bishops, affirming that it was wrong to deny anyone the opportunity to worship in a church: "I can't imagine Jesus turning the back of his hand and saying, no you can't worship here." Yet even this declaration required a set of qualifiers, for he told Methodist ministers and laypeople that the racial problems facing the state would be best solved by local people. Alluding to the students and others set to pour into the state for civil rights work that summer, he said, "The resident forces are the redemptive forces in any society."[35] These words were a fitting coda for a man at the end of his tenure. He finally conceded the very argument that Tougaloo activists repeatedly articulated on the steps of Methodist churches in Jackson, that it was against Christ's teachings to reject someone from His house on the basis of race—but then backtracked to assert that the white people of Mississippi knew best how and when to act on this principle. He seemed resigned to letting someone else provide the leadership he was so unwilling to offer during the final year of his tenure. Because of age restrictions, Bishop Franklin retired in July 1964, after heading the North Mississippi and Mississippi Methodist Conferences for sixteen years.

As the Tougaloo activists and their allies began to reflect upon the Methodist general conference in succeeding weeks, their assessments aligned with those of their adversaries. Rev. King wrote simply, "The Methodist Church failed to move against the segregated structures of the church in any significant fashion."[36] Rev. Forshey also emphasized that the conference yielded little change. He pointed out that MCR had a key role in clarifying the issues before the conference and making clear to the world that "the Methodist position of voluntarism is not the only Methodist position." Yet the Methodist Church "lost its chance to obey the will of God radically," and "in four years, the world will little care whether or not there is a Central Jurisdiction." As to the crucial question of why the delegates failed to abolish the Central Jurisdiction immediately and adopt other strong measures, he concluded—after examining the vote totals by jurisdiction—that those seeking change lost "because of Northern abandonment of the Negro position."[37]

Despite their disappointment, many of the activists came out of the general conference with a renewed sense of camaraderie and purpose. For Rev. King, participating in the vigil and fellowshipping with like-minded Methodists whose support sustained him in the previous year gave him new strength to go back to Mississippi. He felt afraid but ready for the summer ahead.[38] Rev. Forshey wrote to the Tougaloo activists that the greatest moment for him at the conference was kneeling at the alter at the communion service during the Living Memorial, and receiving the sacraments from black hands, feeling for at least a moment "that I truly belonged to the family of God." He then turned to the future, sharing his own misgivings about the activists' commitment to nonviolence. He thanked the activists for showing him the "tremendous moral force" of nonviolence and allowing him to participate in the campaign and lead the rally, all "stepping stones to my own freedom." He was grateful as well for another gift, the burned cross which the Tougaloo activists presented to him before departing Pittsburgh.

He wrote that it was "the gift of the Christ of shame, broken and deserted and abandoned by his people and celebrated by those who also have participated in this brokenness."[39]

Rev. King and the Tougaloo activists returned to Jackson feeling strangely content. While they had not yet succeeded in unlocking most of the white church doors in the city, they could see signs of progress, which they highlighted in correspondence with their supporters throughout the country. Trumpauer wrote several people that, owing to changes made at the denominational conferences, the movement expected most of the churches in Jackson to open by the end of the summer. She emphasized that black students were now welcome at several churches, had joined the Unitarian church, and were thinking of joining Ascension Lutheran. She pointed to the formation of FLC as a positive sign that white Methodists in the state were organizing to combat the segregationist forces.[40] Rev. King also perceived that change was imminent. He later wrote that he had "satisfaction in knowing that the question of any possible significant action by the white moderates was settled." The Tougaloo activists gave white people a chance to change by employing what they felt was a reasonable tactic, trying to attend church. Failure to permit even this activity demonstrated to Rev. King that white moderates had forfeited their moral responsibility, and now the activists could move ahead with the more radical action of the Mississippi Summer Project. Rev. King was pleased knowing that he and the others gave all they had. For nearly a year, they tried to present the moral argument for ending racial discrimination as unambiguously and sensibly as they could.[41]

"The Church Needs a Scapegoat"
1964–73

Feeling they had given white church people in the state's capital city an opportunity to moderate their racial beliefs and practices, in June 1964 the Tougaloo activists turned their attention to organizing for the Mississippi Summer Project. As Rev. Ed King later wrote, "It was good that the effort had been made" to confront white Christians with the immorality of segregation, but now "we waited for the burning crosses and bombs that we knew would come."

In hindsight, the connections between violence and attempts to open church doors were clear enough to Rev. King. In early 1964, Rita and Michael Schwerner spent time in Jackson with Rev. King and the Tougaloo activists, and learned the details of the church visit campaign. As the Schwerners set up a community center in Meridian, Michael went around to local clergy to inform them of their intentions and to try to enlist help. Rebuffed by religious leaders in Meridian, the Schwerners still recognized the sway that ministers and white churches held in the community, and they decided church visits would be a logical, measured way to begin testing access to public accommodations in the city. Their first attempt to attend a white church with a black friend failed in February, but then a white minister at another church in Meridian invited them to attend as an integrated group in March. Though harassing phone calls and surveillance were common before they attended worship services at the white church, the successful visit intensified threats against the Schwerners. The *Meridian Star* denounced church integration in an editorial, and, a few days later, the Meridian police briefly detained Michael for no apparent reason. In June 1964, a year after the killing of Medgar Evers, Michael Schwerner and two other civil rights volunteers, James Chaney and Andrew Goodman, went missing in Phila-delphia, Mississippi, and were later found murdered.[1]

As the church visit campaign drew to a close, many of the participants set out to resolve their legal situations following their arrests. Their Jack-son attorneys and leaders in the Methodist Church and NCC labored to convince city attorneys to dismiss the charges against them, something they were unable to accomplish until late 1966. Jackson officials dropped the cases at least in part because two of the churches involved in the ar-rests, Galloway Memorial Methodist and Capitol Street Methodist, reversed their closed-door policies in early 1966 when the congregations experi-enced another round of visits. The opening of Galloway came at a cost, though, as Dr. W. J. Cunningham stepped down as senior pastor only three years into his tenure. Meanwhile, after bearing the brunt of physical threats made against his family owing to his racial convictions, Dr. J. Moody Mc-Dill stepped down at Fondren Presbyterian in early 1966. He was the last of the remaining long-serving white Protestant ministers in Jackson who preached racial toleration in the crucial years before civil rights legislation and court decrees. While some churches belatedly opened their doors in the mid-1960s, First Baptist did not officially renounce its exclusion policy until 1973. Rather than leading the cause for racial justice, these white churches deferred opening their doors until federally mandated desegregation of public facilities, including the city's public schools, was well underway.[2]

Until those who had been arrested were able to strike a deal with Jack-son officials, the thirty-seven students, ministers, and laymen lived with the possibility that, if the city decided to prosecute them, they could face fur-ther incarceration. Since the initial arrests on October 6, 1963, attorneys for the students and ministers—William Kunstler and Arthur Kinoy of New York, John Pratt of the NCC, and R. Jess Brown of Jackson—had employed a two-pronged strategy. To delay and try to prevent the city from prosecut-ing the defendants in state court, the attorneys succeeded in removing the cases to federal court using an 1866 civil rights statute. Though Judge Har-old Cox remanded the cases back to state court, the defendants' maneuver prevented the city from swiftly prosecuting them as city attorneys did the first detainees.[3] Secondly, following the first arrests, Kunstler and the other attorneys initiated what they termed "legal direct action," filing a federal lawsuit asking for injunctive relief against the state. In *Poole v. Barnett*, the plaintiffs requested a restraining order to prevent further arrests and pros-ecutions for church visitation activities, maintaining that the city of Jackson was denying the constitutional rights of the students and ministers. The plaintiffs alleged that the police intervened to advance a state policy of segregated worship independent of the desires of local church ministers and lay people.

On January 9, 1964, Judge Cox denied the plaintiffs' motion for injunctive relief, indicating that the Jackson police stepped in to make arrests because of the segregationist policies of the congregations, not the segregation policy of the state. Kunstler immediately filed an appeal with the United States Court of Appeals for the Fifth Circuit. The city attorneys seized on Cox's ruling and immediately set out to jumpstart trial proceedings for those who had been arrested at the churches up to that point. Beginning on January 15, the city planned to prosecute all of the students, ministers, and laymen arrested since October 6 over five days. The move by city attorneys caught many of the defendants off guard, with some receiving little warning they were due in court in a matter of days. Rev. Skeete and the others from New York, for instance, learned that they needed to appear in Jackson the day before their trial started. As they arrived in Jackson, the attorneys for the ministers asked the court of appeals to stay these prosecutions and any others until the court had an opportunity to consider the appeal of Cox's ruling. On January 16, city attorneys agreed to delay the church visit trials until after the court of appeals ruled. Sensing urgency from all parties, the appellate court set an emergency hearing for February 13 in Jacksonville, Florida.[4]

At the hearing in February and in motions and briefs filed in succeeding months, the appellants argued that when Jackson police made the arrests, the state of Mississippi interfered with the constitutional rights of the church visitors. Relying on testimony given by Mayor Thompson, policemen, church officials, and the arrested students before Judge Cox in late October 1963, Kunstler and the other attorneys sought to show how no Jackson minister or lay person asked the police officers to intervene. The "underlying arrests were engineered *solely* by the State without a single request for them by any member, officer, trustee or pastor" of the three churches involved.[5] (emphasis original) Not only did the testimony prove that the mayor and police officers received no orders from churches to make the arrests, it showed that the ministers of two of the churches involved were opposed to their congregations' racial segregation. The appellants argued that the state of Mississippi, through its agents—the city of Jackson and its mayor—was using police measures and trespass statutes to try to enforce a policy of racial segregation, a clear violation of equal protection clause of the Fourteenth Amendment and various court decisions since *Brown v.*

Board of Education. During oral argument, the judges seemed most troubled by this aspect of the case. They remained skeptical that the police were in fact acting independently of the churches, believing instead that church members must have requested the arrests in some overt or covert manner. In a separate line of argument, Kunstler held that the state was trying to impose a requirement forbidding integrated worship, a clear violation of the free exercise of religion clause of the First Amendment. The appellants' attorneys pointed out that the city could not produce any evidence demonstrating that the visitors were in fact disturbing divine worship or engaging in disorderly activities that constituted a breach of peace. The police officers admitted that they could not prove that a worship service was even underway when they stepped in to make arrests.

In mid-March, Kunstler filed a new motion with the court of appeals asking that Judge Cox's ruling be reversed, citing evidence demonstrating Cox's prejudice against African Americans, which rendered him "incapable of administering fair and impartial justice to these appellants and the class of Negro citizens." Attached to the motion was a copy of a March 9 news article from the *New York Times* about a lawsuit before Cox's court. At the hearing, John Doar of the Department of Justice argued a suit trying to speed up the voter registration process in Canton. Cox had repeatedly referred to black voter applicants as "a bunch of niggers" and, at one point, said that a large group of black applicants who appeared before the registrar in Canton was "acting like a bunch of chimpanzees." For Kunstler, the federal judge's conduct laid bare Cox's bigotry and demonstrated that appellants could not receive due process in his court.[6]

While Kunstler sought to prove how government authorities in Mississippi were denying the church visitors their constitutional rights, John Pratt filed an amicus curiae brief with the court of appeals, aiming to establish that the segregation practices of the Methodist and Lutheran churches in Jackson were contrary to the stated beliefs and policies of their respective denominations. With Cox asserting that local authorities intervened to provide police support for church policies, Pratt intended to point out that the churches were violating their own rules. Pratt originally hoped for each of the denominations to present its own brief, but because of the timing of the emergency hearing and the speed with which the court was considering the appeal, he presented the amicus brief solely on behalf of the CRR and the general board of NCC. This was the first brief ever filed by the commission. To elucidate the official policy of the Methodist Church, Pratt cited various statements in the Methodist *Discipline*, as well as declarations by the Council of Bishops dating from 1948 on that elucidated the church's condemnation of racial discrimination and belief that there was no place in the denomination for enforced segregation. He explained that the LCA was a young denomination and had yet to hold its first national convention, though leaders in the church went to great lengths in the preceding year to spell out the necessity for congregations to maintain open-door policies. Pratt included a 1963 pastoral letter from the president of LCA and resolutions by the executive council and Southeastern Synod of LCA affirming the requirement for Lutheran church doors to remain open to all. Pratt concluded that even if the individual congregations maintained their own policies regarding segregated worship, these practices would not validate the actions of the Jackson police. Those closed-door policies were in clear violation of the policies of the denominations.[7]

In briefs filed by Thomas Watkins and the city attorney, E. W. Stennett, who represented Mayor Thompson and other officials named as appellees in the suit, the city maintained that police arrested church visitors because the latter refused to recognize the right of a church to forbid their entry. Watkins, a long-time member of Galloway, began by stating that no state statute or city ordinance prohibited integrated worship services. He pointed out that several predominantly white churches in Jackson routinely admitted African Americans to their services. Watkins explained that in the view of the mayor and city officials, a church—a "private institution" beyond the reach of the Fourteenth Amendment—maintained the right to include or exclude whomever they wished. At a church with a clear closed-door policy, visitors who insisted upon entering were in violation of two Mississippi statutes dating from 1942 and governing trespass and disturbances of persons assembled for religious worship. Countering appellants' assertion that the disturbing worship violation was dubious at best, Watkins cited several other case histories to show that in order to be charged with these offenses, one did not need to enter a church building; disturbing a single member of a congregation could result in such a charge. According to the city, law enforcement officers were merely exercising their normal and necessary police powers to protect private church from disturbances and trespassing.[8]

On September 18, 1964, the US Court of Appeals for the Fifth Circuit affirmed Judge Cox's ruling. In denying the appeal, the judges explained that they had deferred a final decision until after the Supreme Court issued a ruling on a group of civil rights cases involving similar trespass statutes. In the five cases decided in June, the high court sidestepped one of the principle constitutional questions at issue, whether or not a police officer

enforcing the segregation policy of a property owner constituted state action prohibited by the Fourteenth Amendment. Given the Supreme Court
decision, the circuit judges held that Cox did not err in denying the activists' request for an injunction. The judges added that they saw many unresolved factual issues in *Poole v. Barnett*, which they felt could best be settled
by a full hearing of the case before the trial court in Jackson.[9]

Attorneys for the appellants decided not to appeal the decision in *Poole
v. Barnett* to the Supreme Court, concluding that success at that level was
unlikely. At the time Pratt said, "We are better off going to trial on the mer-
its than trying to play around with injunctive procedures." He understood
the main fallacy of their case. As the appellate judges pointed out, it seemed
unclear that the police truly acted on their own initiative in making the
arrests. Pratt determined that this issue would best be resolved "by a full
evidential presentation" where "the state has the burden . . . on any ancillary
procedures."[10]

Beginning in late 1964, Pratt and other attorneys and Methodist officials
worked with the city attorneys to try to have the charges against the thirty-
seven dismissed. For their part, the city was in no hurry to bring the defendants to trial. Grover Bagby surmised that the city and the new bishop in
Mississippi, Edward Pendergrass, felt that the continuing threat of prosecutions was curtailing church visits. Moreover, he deduced that city and local church leaders wanted to avoid further embarrassment by prosecuting
the defendants. Privately, Rev. King, Pratt, and others debated techniques to
resolve the legal situation. With the major facts of the cases nearly identical, the attorneys tried to find a way to consolidate them. To induce the
city to drop the charges against all of those charged, Rev. King proposed
to threaten a restart of the church visit campaign—this time sending integrated groups en masse to Galloway and Capital Street.

Another factor complicating speedy resolution of the cases— and a logical explanation for why the city was so reluctant to make any definitive
move toward dismissal or prosecution—was a suit filed by one of the defendants, John Garner, against the Jackson police. On October 20, 1963, Jackson
police arrested Garner, a member of Galloway, in the church's education
building, along with three of his guests, including one of his black students.
A year to the day later, Garner filed a false arrest suit in the US District
Court for the Southern District of Mississippi against the two arresting officers, Chief J. L. Ray and Officer J. R. Griffith. Attorneys for Garner seized
upon the issue raised by the plaintiffs in *Poole v. Barnett* about the applicability of trespass and disturbing divine worship statutes, given how the

attempted visits actually transpired. In Garner's case, though, the actions of the police were even more problematic. Not only was he a member of the church and a habitual attendee at the Sunday school class he intended to attend that morning (facts that rendered the trespass charge moot), the entire incident occurred in the education building of the church, far from the sanctuary where worship was due to commence in an hour. Moreover, even if one took literally the closed-door policy enacted by Galloway's official board, Garner explained, the policy said nothing about barring black guests from Sunday school. Furthermore, the actions of the police deprived Garner and his guests of an opportunity to summon the church's pastor to seek his views. The Methodist Church *Discipline* clearly spelled out that everyone had a right to seek admission, a right with which the police interfered by stepping in before the minister had a chance to clarify policy. Garner noted that black guests had routinely participated in many non-worship activities at the church in the past.[11] The defendants countered that they had reasonable cause to believe that the plaintiff and his fellows were trespassing and disturbing worship. Defendants were careful not to mention exactly how they knew when to step in—whether because of some overt signal or a nonverbal understanding between the police officer and the church official—other than to say that the police made the arrests after Garner denied a request by an officer of Galloway to leave the premises.[12]

The city and the attorneys for the thirty-seven church visitors were unable to resolve the cases until November 1966. Garner's legal action and the possibility of other false arrest suits clearly played a role in prolonging the negotiations. Pratt, Bagby, and Bishop Pendergrass remained in contact with city attorneys through 1965, feeling that they could secure a dismissal of the cases. In a November 1965 letter to Dr. Paul Minus, Bagby and Pratt cited changes in the atmosphere in Jackson and within the Methodist church and its leadership in Mississippi as reasons for optimism. During Thanksgiving week of 1965, city attorneys met in Jackson with Pratt, Francis Stevens, and Bishop Pendergrass. Jackson officials revealed that they were willing drop the charges against all the church visitors if the defendants agreed to sign a release freeing the state, the city, and the churches from claims of unlawful arrest. City attorneys indicated that they would only dismiss the cases after receiving releases from all thirty-seven defendants. In letters to his clients, Pratt reminded the defendants that, in consenting to the releases, they would forfeit a substantial right. Yet, he added that he and other attorneys involved agreed that a false arrest suit would have little chance of success.

In 1965, Al Bronstein, an attorney in the Jackson office of the Lawyers Constitutional Defense Committee, stepped forward to help resolve the cases. With most of the defendants signing releases—John Garner held out with his suit still pending—Bronstein secured a dismissal for all of the cases except Garner's in late November 1966. The city agreed to drop all charges, to pay court costs, to return the bail bonds, and to free defendants from any further financial liability arising from their arrests.[13]

The decision by city attorneys to drop the charges against the church visitors stemmed in part from major developments within the Mississippi Conference and at Galloway and Capitol Street in 1965. Early that year, A. Dudley Ward, chairman of the Secretarial Council of the Interboard Commission on the Local Church, filed a petition with the Judicial Council of the Methodist Church asking that body to determine whether the racial segregation policies of the Jackson churches were against church law. With the arrests occurring before changes were made to the *Discipline* in the 1964, Ward argued that the Jackson churches exceeded their authority in refusing to admit those police later arrested based on the laws in the 1960 *Discipline*. Ward pointed out that the real purpose of the petition was to help clarify the church's rules for the defendants with cases pending before the courts. On April 28, 1965, the judicial council ruled it did not have jurisdiction to decide on a petition from the secretarial council. Nevertheless, the judicial council did rule, based on their reading of the 1964 *Discipline*, that they found "no ambiguity in the position of the Methodist Church on the right of all persons to attend its worship services or, after appropriate vows, to be admitted to membership in any local church in the connection." The judicial council ruling was an attempt to remove any uncertainty about the legality of closed-door policies in white congregations of the denomination. If Methodist churches in Jackson thought they could continue to bar African Americans from worship as they had before the 1964 general conference, then the ruling should have settled the issue. Even the *Jackson Daily News* recognized the significance of the decision, headlining its report on the front page, "Methodists Told to Let Negroes In."[14]

Enforcement of the council decision fell upon Methodist officials in Mississippi, especially Bishop Pendergrass. At the Mississippi Methodist Conference that met at Galloway in early June 1965, he spelled out his first substantive position on race as bishop. Jackson newspapers noted that his statements came in response to a petition from members of MAMML, who wanted the bishop to make clear his position on the racial agenda of NCC and integration of local congregations. For their part, MAMML leaders saw

NCC and its role in the Mississippi Summer Project and the ongoing Delta Ministry as "part of the communist plans to create hatred and violence in the State of Mississippi."[15] The bishop sidestepped a direct confrontation with those efforts, saying instead that Mississippi Methodists should become more active in the organization to help steer it in the direction they desired. On the matter of integration, he declared that Methodist policy was clear: "Any member of any Methodist church is entitled to worship at any other Methodist church," a decidedly more narrow interpretation of Methodist law than the recent judicial council ruling. Bishop Pendergrass added that the problem of desegregated worship "cannot be solved by legislation" and must "ultimately be solved in the hearts and minds of the individual members of our local churches." While avoiding any language demanding that white Methodists open their churches, he did try to convince them that it was in their best interests to end their exclusionary policies: "It should be apparent to any thinking churchman that no congregation can deepen the spiritual lives of its members and make an effective witness to Jesus Christ by placing special ushers at the doors of the church to select who will and will not be allowed to participate in the worship services."[16] He believed that color bars were harming laypeople and churches, but he remained content to allow both to affirm these beliefs at their own pace and on their own terms.

A few weeks after Bishop Pendergrass's statement, members of MAMML met in Jackson and decided to formally secede, forming a breakaway denomination, the Association of Independent Methodists. The announcement surprised no one, for many in MAMML had been threatening withdrawing from the Methodist Church well before the 1964 general conference. Yet the decision resulted from a failure to achieve the massive withdrawal originally envisioned by MAMML leaders. In John Satterfield's report to MAMML members following his return from the general conference in May 1964, he highlighted the "unanimity of opinion among the representatives of the Southeastern Jurisdiction." He argued that if the time came for withdrawal, "It should be taken by the Southeastern Jurisdiction as a whole, or, should this be impossible, by a large segment thereof." Satterfield felt that it would be disastrous "to have churches withdraw one by one, here and there."[17]

Yet such a large-scale and region-wide exit never materialized. Affirming the action taken at the general conference in Pittsburgh, delegates to the all-white Southeastern Jurisdictional Conference voted overwhelmingly in July 1964 to begin the process of merging with eight all-black Central Jurisdiction conferences. Satterfield had pledged to continue the fight from within and appeal the decision to the judicial council. With a majority of jurisdictional representatives endorsing moves made at the general conference, MAMML downgraded its goals. Its board of directors adopted a resolution calling for withdrawal of the Mississippi and North Mississippi Annual Conferences from the Methodist Church, with the hope of joining them with a new Methodist church in the South. In succeeding months, MAMML gathered a petition of grievances for Bishop Pendergrass and circulated questionnaires gauging the support for withdrawal in the state. The bishop's response at the Mississippi Conference in early June 1965, which he gave on behalf of his cabinet of district superintendents, made clear his position on race, while establishing that no support for withdrawal existed within the leadership of the two conferences.

With their visions for a massive pullout severely diminished, MAMML leaders called a meeting for June 1965, inviting all of those "who believe that separations of the races is necessary, and who reject the 'social gospel,' and who want no part of the NCC." [18] Close to one thousand Mississippi Methodists assembled at the Jackson meeting, voting to dissolve MAMML and to reorganize as the Association of Independent Methodists. Officers of the group, most of whom served in the leadership of MAMML, distributed material on how to organize a congregation, including how to file suit to gain control of a local Methodist church property following the guidelines set forth in the 1960 statute. Rev. B. K. Hardin, who had resigned his post at Boling Street Methodist Church in Jackson, gave the keynote address as the association's new executive director, launching an attack on the racial positions of the Methodist Church and the denomination's ties to NCC. A few days after the meeting, leaders of the association announced the formation of two new churches in Jackson, which would meet together at the Robert E. Lee Hotel with Rev. Hardin officiating. Jack Pepper, the association's president, said that about fifty members from Galloway Memorial Methodist, sixty members from Boling Street, and an unspecified number from St. Luke's and Wells Memorial would constitute the new churches. A month later, the Jackson churches reorganized as First Independent Methodist Church and Riverside Independent Methodist Church. Though Pepper was quick to point out that the possibility of integrated worship was not the only reason for the withdrawal, those on the outside understood the meaning and timing of the decision. As Dr. Cunningham later wrote, if "Galloway, Capitol Street, and St. Luke's Methodist Churches could have remained permanently segregated as a Methodist principle, the Independent Methodists would have had no reason for being." [19]

Though the visitation campaign ceased as a formal, organized activity after the 1964 general conference, Galloway members and their African American guests continued to challenge the church's closed-door policy. In late May 1964, for instance, ushers turned away Professor Garner and two of his black students from worship services. Garner aimed to see if the church was going to shift its practices in light of the changes made to the *Discipline* at the 1964 general conference.[20] On Easter Sunday 1965, one year after Galloway ushers turned away two Methodist bishops, over a dozen men and two policemen prevented Professor Campbell and two of her black students from worshipping at the church. With this backdrop of sporadic visits, and at Dr. Cunningham's invitation, Bishop Pendergrass held several informal talks with the officers of Galloway before and after his announcement at the Mississippi Annual Conference in 1965. Dr. Cunningham recalled that Bishop Pendergrass never pressed the lay leaders to end the closed-door policy at Galloway, with laymen prevailing upon the bishop to accept their belief the church risked losing too many more members if the church opened the doors. In fact, Dr. Cunningham maintained that Bishop Pendergrass never articulated the same rationale for desegregating the churches that he had given at the conference. At no time did Bishop Pendergrass instruct the laymen to change the church admission policy. For his part, Dr. Cunningham told him that over a hundred members were intent on joining the Independent Methodists, and that the estimated loss to the church budget for the remainder of 1965 would be about $7,600. Dr. Cunningham maintained that the church could sustain the loss because others committed to the church had stepped forward with increased giving. Bishop Pendergrass, however, reasoned that the best way forward would be to change the pastorate of the church. At various time during the summer of 1965, he proposed to Dr. Cunningham that he step down as senior pastor, even though he was less than two years into his tenure. On one occasion, Bishop Pendergrass told him, "The church needs a scapegoat."[21]

Through the fall of 1965 and early 1966, Dr. Cunningham and leaders on Galloway's Commission on Christian Social Concerns made a series of critical decisions that finally unlocked the doors of the church to African Americans. Dr. Cunningham initiated the process when he invited Bishop Gerald Kennedy of Los Angeles to lead a four-day preaching revival at Galloway in mid-October 1965. Dr. Cunningham later wrote that he proposed the idea to the official board as a way of turning "our minds away from the almost-consuming psychic illness of race." The revival, however, had the opposite effect. Bishop Kennedy was a recognized leader on inclusiveness in the denomination, having given a resounding episcopal address to open the 1964 general conference and welcoming to his jurisdiction some Mississippi ministers displaced for their civil rights stands, including Rev. Jerry Furr, a former associate pastor at Galloway. In anticipation of the revival, Dr. Cunningham and Bishop Kennedy sought to clarify whom exactly the church would admit to services. According to Dr. Cunningham, Bishop Kennedy insisted only that Galloway welcome black pastors and their wives, saying that the church did not necessarily need to dispense with the closed-door policy entirely and admit all African Americans.[22] Bishop Kennedy, on the other hand, maintained that he told Dr. Cunningham he would not preach unless the church were open to all who came. Dr. Cunningham deliberated with lay leaders, and then he and Bishop Kennedy came to an understanding that ushers would admit all who came peacefully and in a good spirit. Earlier, Bishop Kennedy received a letter from a Millsaps student inquiring whether he could bring some black guests with him to the revival services.[23]

Two weeks before Bishop Kennedy's visit to Jackson, the official board of Galloway held an emergency meeting to consider repealing the closed-door policy from 1961. Eleven out of the thirteen members of the Commission on Christian Social Concerns of Galloway presented the board with their recommendation to rescind the policy. Robert Ezelle, chairman of the commission, explained that their proposal was not due only to Bishop Kennedy's impending arrival. He described how, over the preceding year, commission members sent out questionnaires to other large downtown churches in other cities inquiring about their policies, and researched the racial history of Galloway and the old Southern Methodist Church. The surveys from other churches indicated that those who admitted African Americans suffered "less troubles" than those who refused to open their doors. Ezelle told the board, "All indicators point to the fact that we took a wrong turn in 1961, a turn that has since split and torn us apart." He reminded board members that he and others proposed a repeal both formally and informally a number of times in the previous years, only to hear rebuttals that yes, the policy was morally wrong, but the time to correct it had not arrived. Ezelle argued, "We are already late; let's delay no longer."

A minority responded that a repeal would only "open old wounds" that were in the process of healing. After the presentation of arguments, the official board voted sixty to forty-one to table the commission's motion.[24] Though a majority of the board defeated the move to repeal the closed-door policy, this "trial balloon," as Dr. Cunningham called it, signified that the church was a step closer than it had been to aligning itself with Methodist policy.[25]

Though the official board declined to permanently change the admission policy, church officials were content to fulfill the wish of Bishop Kennedy and Dr. Cunningham to relax the closed-door policy for the duration of the revival. The two men had different understandings of the mandate to admit black visitors, confusion that trickled down to the ushers at the church doors. During each of the sessions over the four-day period, African Americans presented themselves and, during some of the services, Galloway ushers admitted and seated them. For the first time in at least five years, black and white Jacksonians worshipped together in Galloway. Justifying the admission of African Americans during the revival services but not to any service in previous years, one usher explained to the *Clarion-Ledger* that since none of the visitors to the revival breached the peace, they could be seated, and the ushers would still remain within the boundaries of the 1961 policy.[26] The usher may have been unaware of the deal struck between Bishop Kennedy and Dr. Cunningham, or he meant to signal a new and more literal interpretation of the original closed-door policy. Either way, his rationale was specious for anyone vaguely familiar with the circumstances surrounding the previous visits and arrests at Galloway.

As with visits to Trinity Lutheran Church during the summer and fall of 1963, the admission of African Americans into Galloway during revival week depended upon which ushers, if any, were at the door. On one night, an integrated group of students and adults from Tougaloo sat in a pew in front of Mayor Thompson and his family. The *Clarion-Ledger* reported that the mayor ignored the visitors, though he pledged to continue attending the church despite its apparent desegregation. Yet the next day, ushers turned away Claire Collins Harvey, an active Methodist laywoman who had served on the national board of Christian social concerns for the previous decade. For the past four years, she led one of the Jackson movement's key groups, Womanpower Unlimited. The usher told her she could not enter because of the group that "crashed" the church the night before. Galloway's minister of evangelism, Rev. John E. Sutphin, apologized to her later that day, and Bishop Kennedy called her, urging her to try again. Harvey returned with her pastor and his wife, her district superintendent and his wife, and her mother. Ushers admitted the group, and she reported that being "graciously received by many in the congregation."[27] On another night, an usher turned away Clarice Campbell, enrolled at the University of Mississippi in the graduate program in history, and two of her guests, Zenobia Coleman

and Julie Bender, both of whom were librarians at Tougaloo. When an usher grabbed Campbell and one of the two black women and tried to shove
them out the door, Campbell swung around him and into the sanctuary to
try to find one of the pastors of the church. She located Rev. Sutphin, who
confronted the usher and explained that the revival was a special meeting
in which the doors of the church were open to all. Rev. Sutphin then tried to
convince the two black women, who by this point had retreated to their car,
to return, but they responded that they were not interested in going where
they were not wanted.[28]

With Galloway ushers admitting a few groups of African Americans to
the revival services, some clearly expected the doors of the church to remain open. When Bishop Kennedy returned to California, he reported he
sensed "a sigh of relief among that Galloway Memorial congregation that at
last they had turned the corner and come through." Lawyers for the thirty-
seven arrestees and denominational leaders pointed to the opening of Galloway as one reason they thought they could now secure a dismissal of the
church arrest cases. Yet the Sunday following Bishop Kennedy's preaching
services, the ushers at Galloway made clear that their admission of some
African Americans during the revival was an anomaly. On October 17, ushers turned away six Tougaloo students, telling them to go to their own place
of worship.[29]

To keep up the pressure on Galloway after Bishop Kennedy's visit, Tougaloo students, Professor Garner, and Howard Spencer, a white layman from
Vicksburg and member of the National Council of the Methodist Student
Movement, presented themselves for worship at the church on most Sundays through the end of the year. In addition, integrated groups returned
to St. Luke's and Capitol Street Methodist churches, where ushers continued to turn them away. As Spencer explained, the national media, including
Christian Century, seemed to be under the impression that Galloway was
integrated when, in fact, the church was "just as segregated as ever." Each
time they appeared, the groups tried to remind the ushers of the policies
and statements in the Methodist *Discipline*. The only Sunday an integrated
group succeeded in entering was when they arrived at Galloway before ushers assumed their posts outside. On some Sundays, the ushers lost their patience when the visitors tried to remain on church property. On December
12, the visitors found the side doors locked and, when they tried to ascend
the steps to the front doors, a group of ushers pushed them down. The next
Sunday, an even larger group of ushers drove the students down when they

began singing Christmas carols on the church steps. Spencer wrote that an usher kicked him in the stomach when he refused to leave the steps.[30]

With a renewed visitation campaign underway, lay leaders at the church formally proposed to Dr. Cunningham that he voluntarily step down as senior pastor. A few weeks after Bishop Kennedy's visit, Nat Rogers and others on the Pastoral Relations Committee met with Dr. Cunningham and announced that he would not be invited back after next year's annual conference. Rogers explained that he had received about twenty phone calls from church members calling for Dr. Cunningham's removal since the revival. These members felt that admission of African Americans to services during that week proved that Dr. Cunningham had been working to integrate the church all along. Rogers did not agree with these sentiments but said, "The fact remained that they were there, true or false, and the atmosphere of the church was so charged with emotion that these ideas could not be dispelled by any appeal to logic or to reason." Though Dr. Cunningham had resisted the advice of Bishop Pendergrass to resign in the preceding months, he now recognized he did not have the confidence of his own Pastoral Relations Committee. He told the group that he "would not attempt to impose myself upon the congregation." Days later, he and a few of the committee members met with Bishop Pendergrass, who said upfront that he wanted the men to leave him out of any decision regarding Dr. Cunningham's status. Without support from his bishop, Dr. Cunningham submitted a formal letter of resignation to Nat Rogers on December 13, 1965.[31]

With Dr. Cunningham soon to be out of the picture, segregationists within Galloway renewed their push to ensure that the church remained an all-white congregation. During regular official board meetings in November and December 1965, one member presented resolutions calling on "the congregation, the pulpit, the Sunday school, and the church office [to] remain an unintegrated white church." Board members defeated the resolution by secret ballot at the latter meeting, where Rogers announced Dr. Cunningham's resignation.[32] Though it remained unclear what specifically swayed the vote, the realization that the church needed to call a new pastor certainly guided the thoughts of board members. Professor Garner, who attended the meetings, wrote that several board members suggested that Galloway could not secure the type of minister it wanted unless the church rescinded the closed-door policy.[33] Moreover, the renewal of weekly visits by integrated groups made it clear that the problem of segregation was not going away. Just months after defeating a motion to rescind the closed-door policy, the recent vote—an outcome attributed in part to the impending vacancy of the pulpit—demonstrated that a full reversal was now possible.

On January 10, 1966, Galloway's official board voted sixty-five to forty to repeal the 1961 closed-door policy. Specifically, the board voted "to open the doors of our church, without regard to color, to all who wish to enter our services of worship." Before the vote, Rogers presented the recommendation of all but one of the members of the Pastoral Relations Committee, calling for the church to open its doors. He singled out the need to do so in order to recruit "a man of the reputation and leadership which we hoped we should get." Though the desire to fill the pulpit with a capable minister directed the thinking of many members—Dr. Cunningham called this impulse a "sinister influence"—several other catalysts contributed to reversing the policy. Dr. Cunningham pointed to the "patience of a devoted minority who never lost faith in the possibility of the open door" and the various preachers who spoke before the church, beginning with Dr. Selah, and planted the seeds of change. The racial climate itself was transforming owing to the passage of civil rights legislation and the announcement by the Jackson Chamber of Commerce that businesses should comply. He acknowledged the positive influence of those churches in Jackson that consistently admitted African Americans for worship. Finally, without citing the specific role of the church visit campaign, Dr. Cunningham concluded that "conscience was at work" in the minds of the ushers and others responsible for enforcing the color bar. He mentioned that one of the chief ushers told him, "I don't want to turn anyone away any more," though to the end Dr. Cunningham maintained that the church visit campaign was a mistake and was not responsible for opening the doors of the church.[34]

Following the repeal of Galloway's exclusion policy, African Americans began routinely walking through the open doors of the historic church. Some, like Ola M. Tatum, were members of black Methodist churches in Jackson and went to Galloway to share in the momentous occasion. Others came as guests of church members. John and Margrit Garner frequently brought Tougaloo students with them. The students attended the college-age Sunday school class and then joined the Garners during the worship service. The opening of worship services led to other interracial opportunities. In the spring, the first integrated commencement of the University of Mississippi School of Medicine took place in Galloway's sanctuary. In their occasional letter to friends eleven months after the church reversed its policy, the Garners indicated other areas of progress as well. The church hosted an interracial and ecumenical panel of women, during which which each panelist described discrimination she experienced. Sunday school classes promoted more fruitful dialogue about race, with at least two inviting leaders of the Delta Ministry to talk to them. The Garners concluded that Dr. Cunningham "was able to take much of the hatred of the congregation with him."

In a report written a month after the opening of the church doors, Dr. Cunningham estimated that an additional fifteen members left after the January vote. In total, about three hundred members had left in the preceding months, most of them going to one of the Independent Methodist churches. Yet Galloway's financial losses were not sizable; he calculated it to be about $12,000. Contemplating his own future, Dr. Cunningham asked Bishop Pendergrass for an appointment within Mississippi, pointing out that he would like to fill a vacancy in the Meridian District. Bishop Pendergrass declined, insisting that Dr. Cunningham would arrive with too much baggage. Instead, Bishop Pendergrass steered him out of state. Dr. Cunningham gave his final sermon at Galloway on June 12, 1966, and accepted a call to Central Methodist Church in Decatur, Alabama. With the color bar of the church lifted, Dr. W. B. Selah returned to Galloway to preach the month of August 1966, three years after he stepped down.[35]

As Galloway reversed its exclusion policy and began to move forward, some Tougaloo students and faculty turned their attention to Capitol Street Methodist. Integrated groups recommenced their visits to the church following Bishop Kennedy's revival and, in the wake of the opening of Galloway in January, they became much more forceful in seeking to open downtown Jackson's other large white Methodist church. Over three weekends in February and early March 1966, Howard Spencer and Tougaloo students and faculty confronted the ushers of Capitol Street, who responded with a degree of hostility and violence that was fortunately absent for much of the earlier church visit campaign. Spencer and Garner detailed the events in a letter they mailed to all the bishops of the Methodist Church. On one Sundays, an usher told a student, "You young jackass, I am going to kill you." Students heard other church members say, "We ought to go out to Tougaloo and blow up the whole place." When the groups did not move or leave church property, the ushers shoved them back. One student suffered a sprained ankle. Another student had a bruise on her mouth where an usher hit her. Spencer's shin was bruised from where an usher kicked him. During each of the confrontations, police stood nearby observing, never intervening.[36]

In early March 1966, the official board of Capital Street followed Galloway's lead by rescinding the closed-door policy of the church. According to Professor Garner, the deciding vote on the issue occurred at an official board meeting that actually began with a vote to reaffirm the exclusion policy. Following this initial decision to maintain the status quo, a moderate member—wanting to make sure that others fully understood the ramifications of continuing to flaunt Methodist policy—made a motion to create a special guard unit to bar visitors so the church would not be financially liable in any suits resulting from enforcing segregation. The motion passed, but only two members stepped forward to serve on this guard detail. Recognizing that members had lost the will to sustain the closed-door policy, the official board proffered a new vote, which resulted in a reversal. Capitol Street Methodist officially opened its doors to black visitors. Spencer and Garner wrote a new letter to the bishops explaining that on March 13, integrated groups attended the church without incident.[37]

As Galloway Memorial Methodist and Capitol Street Methodist churches brought their policies of forced segregation to an end, the first months of 1966 also saw the conclusion of the ministry of the last of the white Protestant pastors who had consistently spoken out in favor of racial equality in the years before and during the Jackson church visit campaign. Dr. J. Moody McDill resigned from Fondren Presbyterian Church effective March 1, 1966, after twenty-three years as the pastor of the congregation. He had fought to keep the church open to all, but since African Americans began visiting the church in the preceding three years, he and his family became targets of violence and physical threats. On several occasions, a sniper shot at Dr. McDill as he returned home at night from the church. To avoid the light, he crawled on his hands and belly to get into the house. He later determined that the gunman was the same man who shot Medgar Evers and Rev. Donald A. Thompson, the minister of First Unitarian Church who survived a murder attempt in 1965 and then fled the state.[38] On another occasion, Dr. McDill returned home to find a car tearing out of his driveway. A passenger in the car threw a chain out the window at him. Dr. McDill described it as a choker chain used to keep dogs at bay. After the family went through a series of mailboxes that were destroyed by cherry bombs, he installed a new mailbox in front of the house. The "terrifying environment" that surrounded his family's last years in Jackson became too much to bear. He felt he could deal with the threats, but he "could not stand the threats being made against my wife and daughters." He accepted a position as associate secretary of the Department of Christian Family Education with the Board of Christian Education of the Southern Presbyterians in Richmond, Virginia.[39]

Dr. McDill joined the other exiled white Protestant pastors who tried to guide their Jackson congregations toward racial toleration in the years after the *Brown* decision. The circumstances were more brutal for Dr. McDill than for the other long-tenured ministers—Dr. W.B. Selah of Galloway, Dr. Roy C. Clark of Capitol Street Methodist, Rev. Roy S. Hulan of First Christian, and Rev. Wade Koons of Trinity Lutheran Church—men who resigned or were forced out because of their convictions. Dr. McDill outlasted the others by two years, benefiting from a church that was somewhat receptive to his leadership. Yet his insistence on open doors and inclusiveness brought out the extreme elements within the closed society of Jackson and forced him to take refuge elsewhere.

While some of the congregations that maintained segregation policies during the height of the church visit campaign opened their doors within a few years, a least one church did not change its policy for a decade. First Baptist was an early target for the church visitors because of its size and its strategic location across from the capitol building, and because some of the state's most notable segregationists—the Hederman family and Gov. Ross Barnett—were members. Shortly after the initial visits to First Baptist on June 9, 1963, the church formally adopted a closed-door policy. With individual Baptist congregations controlling their own policies, the Tougaloo activists gave up trying to attend worship at white Baptist congregations in the city after July 1963, turning their attention to churches whose national bodies could provide leverage for change on the local level. By the early 1970s, First Baptist had a new senior pastor, Dr. Larry G. Rohrman, who expanded the church, making it the largest congregation of any denomination in the state. In January 1973, the thirty-four- year-old pastor received an award as one of "America's Top Ten Outstanding Men" from the US Junior Chamber of Commerce for his efforts spearheading relief work after Hurricane Camille. Yet some civil rights leaders in the state denounced his selection, pointing out the all-white practices of First Baptist. Charles Evers called the honor "the biggest mockery yet." At a press conference in Jackson, journalists questioned Dr. Rohrman about the racial practices at his church. Dr. Rohrman seemed unclear on the admission policy, saying, "It remains to be seen whether or not the church would admit black visitors."[40]

On January 28, 1973, the Sunday after Dr. Rorhman made these comments, First Baptist ushers turned away an integrated group of three from morning services and five black youths from evening services. The chairman of the greeting committee explained to reporters that Dr. Rohrman knew full well the long-standing policy against interracial worship, though

he pointed out that "the pastor has nothing to do with the thinking" behind the policy.[41] According to the official history of First Baptist, a group
of church leaders met with Dr. Rohrman that week and, after a four-hour
discussion, agreed to present the deacons with a resolution amending the
admission policy of the church. Though the maneuvering behind the scenes
remained unclear, several of Dr. Rohrman's assistant pastors stepped forward to advocate opening of the doors. One was Dr. Joe McKeever, who
recalled that he was unaware of the closed-door policy until the ushers
blocked integrated groups in late January. He preached racial equality and
remained open about his views on integration during his previous call as
pastor of a church in Greenville, Mississippi, in the late 1960s. During one
of the meetings with Dr. Rohrman the week after the integration attempt, a
deacon announced a rumor that students from Mississippi College, a Baptist institution in nearby Clinton, planned to picket the church the following Sunday. The deacon wanted Dr. McKeever and another minister to go
to the school and "put a stop to it." Both ministers declined, saying they
actually agreed with the students. Though the deacon reported that black
and white students from the college planned to come to First Baptist en
masse, a student wrote in the school's newspaper that he only wanted to
bring one classmate with him to worship. The student then received a call
from Dr. Rohrman, who tried to dissuade him from making the integration attempt, questioning the student's intentions and saying that the time
was not yet right for such a move. The student responded by pointing out
that if he really wanted to be disruptive or seek publicity, then he would
have indicated that he planned to bring dozens of African Americans with
him and informed the news media of the visit. Instead, he maintained that
several black classmates had asked if they could go with him to worship at
First Baptist in the past and, knowing "the attitude First Baptist had toward
people who happen to be black," he decided to take only one. After the call
from Dr. Rohrman, however, he decided against trying at all.[42]

On Saturday, February 3, deacons voted 140 to 19 "to continue to receive
into its regular services all persons who sincerely desire to worship and further resolves that it will not admit any persons or organized groups who
come for the purpose of demonstrating, who seek to disrupt, or who seek
publicity." Though the wording of the policy still gave ushers free reign to
forbid certain visitors—the phrase "to continue to receive" was a particularly misleading articulation of their practices in the preceding decade—the
new resolution overturned the previous policy, which clearly stated that the
church intended to "confine its assemblies and fellowship to those other

than the Negro race."[43] On Sunday, February 4, the congregation formally adopted the new policy. Si Brantley, a seventeen-year-old member of the church at the time, recalled that Dr. Rohrman spoke out convincingly for the change, saying, "a church is for all believers." Few members rose up in opposition to the new policy. Brantley remembered only one elderly member saying he would never return to the church if they permitted black visitors. Two weeks after the vote, two black Baptist ministers from Jackson, Rev. Emmett C. Burns and Rev. R. L. T. Smith, reported that they attended worship at First Baptist and "were received very warmly by the pastor, officers, and members of the church."[44]

In the early 1960s, segregationists worried that integration would enter Mississippi "through the front door of churches." They enacted new legislation to ensure that congregations that wanted to remain segregated could do so by breaking away from national bodies and taking their property with them. When civil rights activists and supporters tried to underscore the immorality of racial discrimination by attempting to worship in white churches, segregationists mostly succeeded in blocking the attempts. The stubborn refusal of the visitors to cease their campaign in the face of continual rejection at the doors of churches triggered state government intervention and thirty-seven arrests. The visits and the arrests in Jackson highlighted the reality of racial discrimination within regional and national denominations, helping to convince bodies in each to clearly spell out that forced racial segregation was against the will of God. In 1965, when it became clear that segregationists in the Mississippi Methodist Conference could no longer maintain the racial purity of their congregations, they formed a new independent denomination. Within a matter of months, those members who remained at Galloway and Capitol Street voted to admit black visitors, though these decisions had little to do with a sudden realization that their exclusion policies were un-Christian. Changes in admission practices came after the initial phases of desegregation in Jackson's public schools, and after the enactment of federal civil rights and voting rights legislation and an announcement by the Jackson Chamber of Commerce urging compliance. Integration did not come to Mississippi through the doors of churches because of the fierce determination of segregationists to protect their last sanctuary.

Afterword

"Doing a Little Something to Pave the Way for Others"

The tactic of church visitation was just one of many forms of direct action employed by civil rights activists to test access to public spaces during the 1960s, but the approach held special meaning for the Tougaloo students, the laypeople, and the dozens of ministers who traveled to Jackson in 1963 and 1964. They meant to testify to their Christian convictions when they sought admission to all-white church services. Though participants came to the campaign with distinct experiences that framed their understanding of racial issues, they shared a sense of the potential usefulness of trying to engage white Christians in dialogue and attempting to demonstrate the oneness of mankind through integrated worship. Many who recalled their involvement in the campaign forty-five years later saw it as a decisive moment in their lives and a turning point in civil rights activism and other social issues.

Though many of the Tougaloo activists who joined in the church visit campaign participated in concert with other local efforts to break down the barriers of racial discrimination, the uniqueness of the tactic—trying to attend whites only churches in small groups—provided the students a direct and unambiguous means through which to apply religious convictions. One of the prevailing themes the students emphasized was that they visited white churches simply because the notion of segregated worship was so foreign to their understanding of Christianity. Thomas Armstrong, who participated frequently and was arrested during a January witness, recalled that because he grew up in the Holiness Church, he had a very personal reason for participating in the visits. He held that the "segregated church just went against everything I knew and believed," and being turned away from white churches totally confused him. Though church visitation was just one aspect of what the local movement was doing, Armstrong maintained, "The idea of it was great." He felt that "the religious element of segregated society should be the one to change," and that one "would think that it would be the first to have good people speaking up."[1] Bette Poole's father, who was a Baptist preacher, taught her that no one was better than she. Poole, whom police arrested twice for attempting to worship at white churches, remembered always suffering from cognitive dissonance when in a segregated environment and feeling called to be an agent of change. She joined the church visit effort because it was a clear way to expose the immorality of segregation. Poole saw that by turning her and other activists away, the white churches were essentially saying that they would only admit church members into their services, which seemed a backward mission for a congregation proclaiming Christ. Together with other movement activities in which she participated during that period—she worked to register voters in the Delta the summer of 1964—she regarded the experience as one of empowerment. She recollected not feeling weak anymore. She felt that an individual could affect change.[2]

Ida Hannah, another two-time church arrestee, also grew up in the Baptist church, where her parents and others taught her that all are God's children. She recalled that in one sense, she wanted to attend a white church out of inquisitiveness. She saw how whites treated blacks outside of church, and she aimed to see if matters were different inside the church. Yet she also wanted to worship in a white church because she believed that if people from two races could worship together, then they would understand each other. Whites would understand that "we are all seeking salvation together." She participated in other movement activities, such as canvassing for voters, but for her, nothing demonstrated the goal of interracial brotherhood as clearly as the church visit campaign. Though her religious motive was at the forefront, she desired to change her home state overall, particularly so that her younger siblings and future children could "enjoy all the freedom they could." During one of her arrests, a police detective, recognizing that she was the only one in the group from Mississippi, asked her if she planned on remaining and rearing her children in the state. She replied, "Of course, but first I've got to help clean Mississippi before I bring a child into this state." Like many of the activists, Hannah worried about how her family would react if they ever found out about her involvement in the movement, so she kept quiet about it as long as she could. Her parents learned of her activism when most others did, seeing a television news broadcast highlighting her arrest at Capitol Street Methodist Church. Hannah's parents expressed shock, reminding her that she should have thought differently about doing such a thing because of where she lived, in Leake County. One of her neighbors told her bluntly she was not reared to behave like that. Fortunately, her parents never received any threats, something she credits to the respect and independence they enjoyed in the community. Though she admitted being a private person—she never publicly mentioned her involvement in the church visits or the movement in her thirty-five years as a teacher— she talked about her activism with her children. More recently, some of her grandchildren wrote in school essays that she was their hero. Hannah felt uncomfortable with such a tribute, believing instead that she was merely "doing a little something to pave the way for others."[3]

While many of the Tougaloo students saw their participation in the church visits as an extension of other movement activities and protests in which they engaged, for some, enlisting in the campaign was the extent of their activism. These students emphasized that the tactic of trying to go to church seemed more acceptable than other direct action methods, especially in the eyes of their parents. Joan Trumpauer, who helped coordinate the visits, recalled trying to underscore this point when she stood before the school during chapel, and at various meetings trying to recruit others to the campaign. One of the students who wanted to take part in the movement and decided upon church visitation as the means was Doris Browne. She did not aim to tell her parents about her involvement at the time—and did not do so until years later—but she felt that if police arrested her at a church, her actions would meet the approval of her parents in Biloxi, for they were particularly religious. Browne sensed that her family would understand that she was doing more than just demonstrating. Like her parents, she believed in one God and was really just trying to worship. Another student who became involved in the campaign but eschewed other protest activities was Camille Wilburn. She wanted to participate more in the movement, but feared repercussions on her parents who were educators in Okolona. She answered the call to go on visits to St. Andrew's Episcopal Church because she was the only Episcopalian and knew that the Episcopal churches in Jackson were more accepting than others. Yet the negative reactions from some of the members of St. Andrew's surprised her and triggered a re-evaluation of the Episcopal church, though she ultimately reasoned that the members' behavior was more indicative of their status as Mississippians than as Episcopalians.[4] For Browne and Wilburn, the church visit campaign was an entryway into the movement. Though being arrested would have changed how their parents and home communities viewed them, at the time, visiting churches was a comfortable way to be involved while remaining true to their convictions.

The church visit campaign gave many students an opportunity to affirm their Christian beliefs, but the effort steered at least one non-religious student, Austin Moore, toward the faith. Moore's involvement in the campaign was more peripheral, driving students to churches on a few Sundays. He mostly busied himself with spearheading the effort to discourage artists from performing before segregated audiences in Jackson. His role as a local movement leader brought him to the general conference in Pittsburgh, an event that changed everything for him. His father, like other newspaper readers throughout the country, saw a picture of him carrying the charred cross during the living memorial. Moore's father immediately ordered his son to leave Mississippi and move to California, where Moore has lived ever since. Participating in such a public way in the prayer pilgrimage and having to explain it to his father caused him to reevaluate his own spirituality. In addition to other pursuits, he became an ordained minister.[5]

Like most of the Tougaloo activists, the ministers who traveled to Jackson to participate in the church visit campaign and joined the students in Pittsburgh for the living memorial saw their efforts as a Christian "witness," a word they used repeatedly in discourse with each other at the time and when they recalled the events forty-five years later. They meant to testify to Christ's teachings and the principles of the Methodist Church: that all men are brothers; that Christ offered Himself for the sins of the whole world; and that the House of God was open to the whole family of God. They believed, as Rev. Al Bamsey recalled, that the church needed to move more decisively toward equality. Church visitation constituted one part of an overall effort to change the institution, but the campaign was essential because it tried to move the church from the bottom up. By witnessing in Jackson, the ministers aimed to elucidate and highlight the crucial issues ahead of the general conference, beginning with the recognition by all that racial discrimination was a reality in local churches.

For Rev. David James Randolph, this was one of the main accomplishments of the church visit campaign. The actions of the white Methodist churches in Jackson demonstrated that if one intended to worship interracially, one would have to go to jail. The Methodist Church had to choose sides: Either affirm the beliefs of the Methodist Church, or the practices of the white Mississippi Methodist churches. As Rev. Ed Hiestand and Rev. Paul Minus remembered, the church visits helped Methodists face the problem, that sickness existed in the church. Because of national press coverage of the campaign, the white delegates from the Southeastern Jurisdiction could no longer claim that their churches were open. For Rev. Paul Lowley, the disease of racial discrimination festered because local churches felt they had the liberty to form their own policies. The visits therefore helped expose a structural problem in the church that the denomination needed to correct. Rev. Lowley felt, "If the local church is made to feel that they have control over polity, they will think that they have control over their theology."[6] The campaign ultimately asked church members to consider to what extent they truly wanted to be a connectional church.

After travelling to Jackson, conversing with local people, and trying to attend churches in integrated groups, visiting ministers returned home to find new opportunities to discuss the issue of race. Several of the groups, such as the teams from Chicago and the seminary professors from the Methodist Theological School in Ohio, discussed their witness during special assemblies held soon after their return. Many of them talked about their experience from the pulpit, trying to defuse misunderstanding about their motivations for going, and using the visit as a chance to focus parishioners on racial problems in their own cities. Rev. Al Bamsey of St. Claire Shores, Michigan, wrote to the Tougaloo activists that he and others from the Detroit area were "carrying on the fight" in their own segregated communities. He said that on Race Relations Sunday, he and others leveled with the congregations again. Rev. Bamsey reported that more parishioners were willing to get involved in the struggle, and that opposition in the churches was not as entrenched as it had been. When Rev. A.W. Martin came back to his church outside of Nashville, Tennessee, he preached more on race to his congregation, though he recalled "not trying to slap them in the face with it." He used the visit as a springboard to focus more on Race Relations Sundays, inviting Rev. Joseph Lowery to his church just two months after his trip to Jackson. Like Rev. Martin, Rev. Richard Teller tried not to overwhelm his congregation with sermons on race, feeling that some ministers closed the doors of communication with the church if they talked exclusively about the matter. Yet he remembered preaching about his trip the first Sunday after he returned home and, as news filtered through the mostly Republican suburb of Tipp City, Ohio, he sensed that his involvement made the issue of racial discrimination more visible. Rev. Ed Hiestand remembered that he tried to emphasize to his congregation outside of Chicago that he and the other ministers were trying to help the church face the problem of racism. Jackson was just a symbol; "The church was trying to deny the very nature of the church." Rev. Randy Lunsford wrote to the

Tougaloo activists about the wide range of reactions that people in Indiana, Pennsylvania, were having to his visit. He reported that one tangible outcome was the creation of a new local Christian-based group to combat racial prejudice, and said that the organization planned to lead the effort to desegregate the town's swimming pool. Rev. Sally Smith wrote that her group's visit received extensive local news coverage in Iowa City and Cedar Rapids, Iowa, and they appeared as guests on radio programs and were set to speak to several local groups about the situation in Jackson. Moreover, she said that all of the churches in Iowa City would be emphasizing human relations in programs the following Sunday, with members of the group preaching at most churches.[7]

The ministers and laymen from Ohio who participated in the Jackson witness were also eager to talk about their involvement back home. In the days following Rev. Al Tomer's arrival back in Kenton, he recognized that many people throughout the small town were discussing his role in the Jackson witness. To dispel any more gossip, he contacted the local newspaper, the *Kenton Times*, and convinced editors there to allow him to write a series of articles about what he experienced in Jackson. Rev. John Wagner returned to Ohio to find strong interest in his trip and estimated that he spoke to fifteen church groups and clubs in the succeeding weeks. He felt that most people were simply eager to hear an accurate description of what was occurring in Jackson, regardless of whether they approved of his role. Robert Meeks, a layman, wrote Rev. King after his arrest, explaining that the campaign gave him a unique opportunity to witness at home. In January 1964, he was helping a young Arab friend apply for American citizenship, and a federal officer, who was black, asked Meeks if he had ever been arrested. He said yes, that in fact he had been arrested two months earlier in Mississippi for trying to go to church with a black minister. The officer smiled, and the two made arrangements to attend Meeks's Methodist church together in Lakewood, Ohio. Meeks also remained in touch with Rev. Frank Dement, the pastor of St. Luke's Methodist in Jackson, the church where Meeks, Rev. Donald E. Hall, and Rev. Woodie White were arrested. Meeks passed along the sentiments of Rev. Dement, who wrote explaining that members of his official board were suggesting an end to the church's closed-door policy. Ed Craun, another layman, wrote to the Tougaloo activists that the involvement of the group from Ohio produced discussions in a number of churches in the Cleveland district, and that he and others received dozens of phone calls and letters from people inquiring about the witness. Craun said, "One result of this trip in my life has been a very great internal pressure to speak forth at every opportunity on the power of prayer and the Holy Spirit." Yet, at least one minister found that many adults reacted like their counterparts in Jackson, denying that there was a problem. Dr. Jeffrey Hopper, a seminary professor at the MTS, found that his church's youth group was the only one that wanted to hear from him.[8]

The ministers welcomed opportunities to talk about the problem of race in their communities and within their denominations, but the discussions with parishioners for at least a few of the minsters centered upon defending their involvement in the witness. When Rev. Elmer Dickson returned to Westchester, Illinois, after being released from jail in Jackson, church members called a special board meeting. His lay leaders then asked him to promise the church not to engage in that type of activism again. Rev. Dickson replied that he had no plans for a similar witness, but insisted that he could not make such a promise. He told them he "would be guided by what God's Spirit called me to do at a time when America was in the midst of significant change." He and several of his cellmates from Chicago decided that their own churches needed to experience a visitation exchange, so a team of black Methodists came to Rev. Dickson's church. He later recalled that the visit did not cause any significant problems.[9] Rev. Richard Raines returned to his church on the outskirts of Detroit, Michigan, to find that members had called a special meeting in his absence to decide whether or not to ask for his removal. Though his trip to Jackson triggered the emergency meeting, many were already upset over his earlier move to put a poster in front of the sanctuary welcoming people of all races to worship services. The church recently relocated out of downtown Detroit after trying to avoid interaction with the growing black community in their old neighborhood. Rev. Raines learned later that he survived the vote from this meeting because one of the church's most respected members, an elderly woman, spoke convincingly in support of him. Though the incidents resulted in more conversations about race and with African Americans in the church, Rev. Raines remained skeptical that his participation in the witness impacted any members greatly.[10]

When the four seminary professors from the Methodist Theological School in Ohio returned, some on the school's board of trustees called for the dismissal of one returnee, the school's dean, Dr. Van Bogard Dunn, though support for the professors was more widespread among the student body and other faculty. One trustee, Ed Crouch, recalled that he was one of those wanting Dr. Dunn fired. A native Southerner, Crouch felt that the professors were unnecessarily intruding in a local problem that would best be solved by local people. He saw Dr. Dunn as the ringleader, someone who

needed to take responsibility for the group's actions. Dr. Dunn later emphasized that the controversy with the trustees stemmed from his decision before the trip to avoid seeking the approval of the president of the seminary,
Dr. Walter Dickhaut. Though years later he admitted he was insensitive in
not consulting his superior, Dr. Dunn remembered that he simply assumed
taking part in the witness was the right thing to do. It never occurred to
him to ask the president or anyone else whether the group should go. Another one of the four, Dr. Arthur Jeffrey Hopper, recalled that Dr. Dickhaut
was a bit upset about their involvement, but the president bore the brunt
of the attacks on the professors and ultimately resisted calls for rebukes
or for anyone's dismissal. Dr. Dickhaut later presided over an assembly at
the school's library, where each of the four shared different aspects of their
witness in Jackson. Dr. Dickhaut said, "We are grateful and we are proud,"
that "these men have walked right into the middle of trouble and suffering
which will involve every single one of us before this chapter is concluded."[11]

While the involvement of the four professors from MTS in Ohio offend-
ed some of the school's trustees, their witness inspired at least a few students
and opened up opportunities for others to get involved in the Southern
movement. Walter Dickhaut, a nephew of the school's president, recalled
being rather indifferent to the issue of civil rights during his early time as
a student. He remembered hearing Dr. Everett Tilson constantly preach on
the issue of race during chapel services and, at one point, he thought that
if he heard Dr. Tilson give another sermon on civil rights, he would quit.
He gradually came to understand the relevance of the Christian faith to
civil rights, and saw that what the professors did in Jackson was merely the
natural product of what the professors were trying to get students to understand in class. Months later, Dickhaut helped organize a busload of students
to take part in the protests in Selma, Alabama.[12] Another student, Joseph
Sprague, was already heavily involved in various movement activities, and
joined Dr. Dunn on a return trip to Jackson just a few weeks after the conclusion of the general conference in Pittsburgh. A group of a half dozen
students and professors from MTS came to Jackson at the invitation of local
black leaders, who wanted help maintaining integration at public facilities
that activists succeeded in opening earlier. Sprague recalled that they were
in Jackson for nearly two weeks, attending nightly rallies and interacting
with the black community. One of the other professors on the trip was a
Hebrew scholar and, in several visits with black clergy, he used his expertise
to debunk many of the biblical myths, such as the curse of Ham, that white
supremacists often pointed to in defending racist ideologies. Yet years later,

what Bishop Sprague remembered most was the truly interracial aspect of the whole experience. He sensed that many of these activities, such as playing basketball with young people, involved interactions that constituted the first time the black youngsters intermingled this way with white people. He remembered with awe the determination of the black community, especially those members who opened their homes to groups in grave physical danger, and the courage of men like Rev. Ed King, who possessed a deep theological understanding that he put into everyday action.[13]

Though most of the visiting ministers were already actively involved in trying to steer their own churches and communities toward greater inclusiveness before they travelled to Jackson—and many considered themselves to be movement activists—some saw their experience as a turning point in their own ministries and their concern for race issues at home. Rev. Al Tomer called his participation in the Jackson witness a "trigger event" for confronting local racial discrimination. Shortly after his return to Kenton, Ohio, he and a Presbyterian laymen—the two constituted the social action committee for the town's council of churches—tried to convince the eight barbers in the town to cut the hair of black men, who otherwise had to travel thirty miles to get their hair cut. Rev. Tomer found that this incident provoked more controversy than his trip to Jackson. All of the barbers, including three who were members of Rev. Tomer's church, refused. The district superintendent was eager to move him out of the church, so he was placed at an inner-city church in Toledo, where Rev. Tomer became active in open housing legislation. Like other ministers involved in the Jackson witness, Rev. Tomer worked to encourage cross-racial appointments in Methodist churches. In the early 1980s, he became the first district superintendent in his conference to appoint an African American to a white church. Rev. John Wagner, who travelled to Jackson with Rev. Tomer, recalled that the Jackson witness was a defining moment for his ministry, for he had not been involved in social justice issues in the conference before the trip. He remembered that he joined the effort because he felt called to do so, not because he was trying to help desegregate the denomination. Yet his outlook changed significantly upon his return, for the witness gave him a chance to be in the midst of a social justice campaign. He felt that it was now part of his heritage. He participated in several sit-ins at federal courthouses and, as an elected delegate to jurisdictional conferences, labored to put together interracial slates of clergy and laity. Rev. Bill Wells, who admitted being reluctant to participate in the church visit campaign, returned to North Carolina feeling "more committed than ever to doing something to integrate our lives."

As the state director for campus ministries, he worked to ensure the desegregation of all state conferences and activities and drove some students to marches and voter registration drives in Montgomery, Alabama.[14]

Participation in the Jackson witness, and the notoriety that came with it, catapulted some to positions of leadership on civil rights issues in their communities and within the Methodist Church. Rev. John A. Collins, who was chair of the social action committee while in seminary and was organizing a mostly black East Harlem church, returned to New York to find that his involvement and arrest made him even more of a leader on social justice issues in his conference. He regarded his participation as a watershed event, firming up his own commitment to racial issues while he served in the congregation for another five years, and when he became program director for social concerns in the conference in the succeeding years. Rev. Ed Hiestand recalled that the witness experience gave him credibility as a civil rights leader in his town, especially within the black community. He believed that the Jackson witness helped him feel the vulnerability of blacks so he could better minister to African Americans. Rev. Richard Raines echoed his sentiments, remembering how the witness educated him about how much he did not know about racism. Until he saw racial discrimination first hand and experienced it in the company of a black man, he felt that he did not truly know the world or understand the feelings of African Americans. The experience taught him to seek out all of the other unfinished justice questions in the country, a lesson he continues to try to apply. Rev. Woodie White, a black minister who served a mostly white congregation in Detroit, saw his role in the church visit campaign as a defining moment in his life. Up to that point, he worked vigorously to combat Northern-style racism and welcomed the invitation from his friend from seminary, Rev. King, to come to Mississippi. The experience broadened his perspective and gave him insight into linking the struggle between North and South. When the denomination finally moved decisively to end segregation in the church in 1968, he became head of a new Methodist agency, civil rights. Though he was already recognized as a civil rights leader within the denomination by that time, he believed that Methodists elected him to this position because of his participation in the Jackson witness. Significantly, both he and Rev. Fitts Herbert Skeete later became bishops of the Methodist Church.[15]

While other movement activities questioned whether or not segregation was ethical or constitutional, the Jackson church visit campaign pushed ministers and church people to consider whether segregation was Christian. Throughout the effort, ushers and others seeking to block African

Americans from worship services at white churches tried their best to avoid the question, choosing instead to reframe the witness as just another political protest or demonstration. Recognizing that they could not defend their practice with Scripture, laymen raised their own concerns, doubting the sincerity and motivations of the visitors. They told those seeking admission—many of whom they recognized as activists in the sit-in and picketing phase of the Jackson movement—that if they really wanted to worship God, they could go to their own churches. Ushers told the white and black ministers and laymen who accompanied the students that they were outsiders meddling in the internal affairs of Mississippi churches. Informed by the discourse of the time objecting to federal civil rights legislation, laymen insisted their churches were private property, and they could exclude whomever they wanted. The ten- month-long campaign seemed to segregationists like any other civil rights protest or demonstration.

Yet this analysis demonstrates that the students and the laymen and ministers who joined them tried to attend white churches because their Christian beliefs directed them to testify to the oneness of mankind. The evidence—from the surviving records from the 1960s, to the dozens of interviews conducted forty-five years later—points to an overall impression of sincerity of Christian faith and principles. Participants saw one another as equal in the eyes of God; the pejorative term "outsider" meant nothing to them. Though they came from different denominational backgrounds, they saw churches as unifying spaces in which to proclaim the unity of God's children. The notion of segregated worship contradicted basic teachings of Christ, the writings of St. Paul, and the fundamental doctrines of the denominations to which the churches belonged. Unlike the men blocking their entry, the visitors had the backing of Scripture and denominational beliefs. Because the activity itself was so intertwined with the beliefs of the participants, it became futile to try to separate the two. Visiting white churches repeatedly was indeed a form of protest, for they went to the churches expecting ushers to dispute their convictions and turn them away. The church visit was a type of demonstration—a Christian witness, as the ministers called it. All of the participants surely had supplementary motives. Yet the ushers and others enforcing the color bar failed to recognize that the dichotomy they created between a protest activity and a worship activity never existed in the minds of the church visitors.

Moreover, the Tougaloo activists deliberately avoided doing anything that resembled most other civil rights protest activities. On all but the first round of visits, the Tougaloo activists never deliberately alerted the local press to their intentions. In the months before ministers joined them, the groups presenting themselves for worship never included more than four people. After the first arrests others went with the students, but four remained the typical team size, and the total never reached more than nine—nothing that could qualify as a mass demonstration. They arrived in Sunday dress, often with Bibles in hand, just like any other guest or member. Students presented themselves to the ushers politely and, when conversations resulted, there is no evidence that voices were raised. Other than visits in November and December 1963, when the teams realized that police would arrest them regardless of the circumstances, the groups routinely departed the churches after an official insisted that they leave. Though the press and others commonly referred to the church visit activity as a kneel-in—trying to link it with other forms of passive resistance like the sit-in—the church visitors only dropped down on their knees on a few Sundays. The only evidence of an actual disturbance, on Palm Sunday in 1963, was when a group succeeded in entering a church, and ushers instigated a fracas by forcibly removing them.

Some white pastors in Jackson tried to prepare their parishioners for the end of legalized segregation—with some working harder and with more consistency than others to smooth this process—but the presence of black visitors outside the churches presented a new test for their ministries and congregations. Dr. Roy Clark, Rev. Roy Hulan, Rev. Wade Koons, Dr. Moody McDill, and Dr. W. B. Selah all had at least nine years at the helm of their respective churches in Jackson before the first visits, serving during a period that included the announcement of the *Brown* decision and the heightened climate that followed it. They worked hard to build goodwill and earn respect from their laypeople. Some, like Dr. Selah, were moderates at heart but conservatives in process. By the early 1960s, Dr. Selah preached that segregation was morally wrong, but he felt that forced integration of public schools and accommodations was a mistake. With the Jackson movement focused on trying to knock the white business community off balance prior to June 1963, the shift to church visitation compelled white ministers to take an unambiguous stand on forced segregation one way or the other. None of the ministers specifically invited the church visitors to worship services, and some resented the tactic itself, feeling that it upset the work they and their allies were trying to accomplish inside the churches to moderate the beliefs and practices of church members. In one important respect, they were right, for the church visits directly and indirectly tore many of these congregations apart. Well-respected and long-tenured pastors left their pulpits, depriving their congregations and the Jackson church community of valuable leadership at a time when the city needed it most. Though some members resolved to reform from within, many families who called their particular church home for generations left as well, deciding they could only worship in a sanctuary open to all. Their departures deprived churches of moderating voices. Some churches began a decline in membership that took decades to reverse, while others, like Capitol Street and First Christian, never recovered. Yet, by exposing the reality of a color bar on the doors of the House of God, the church visit campaign shook white Christians from their comfortable but unstable moorings and brought to light the crisis that was already simmering below the surface. White church people may have felt content in their beliefs and practices before African Americans began presenting themselves for worship at their churches, but racial discrimination contradicted the basic teachings of their faith and the policies of their denominations. The church visitors merely uncovered a fundamental problem within the congregations themselves.

Segregationists labored to create and preserve the racial purity of their congregations in order to maintain a consistency with other facets of their social system, but because they were losing the fight elsewhere they fought particularly hard to thwart the church visitors. The stakes were apparent at the time, and they became even more so as the decade went on. In the summer of 1966, Medford Evans, a national Citizens' Council leader and member of the newly created Riverside Independent Methodist Church in Jackson, declared to the board of directors of the Jackson Citizens' Council that the battle for public school integration was lost, but the war was not over. He told them that he talked nearly every day to the deacons of Riverside, who constantly assured him that the church would not integrate. He wanted to believe his lay leaders, but reasoned, "If their children go to integrated schools, they will integrate the First Baptist Church, the Riverside Independent Methodist Church, and everything else in Jackson."[16] Evans and other segregationists regarded their churches as their only remaining sanctuaries on which to practice their whites only way of life.

The Tougaloo activists failed to open most of the church doors during the course of their campaign, but the church visits made segregation visible in an aspect of people's lives that had otherwise gone unchallenged as a sanctuary of racial purity. The visits forced churchgoers to confront the morality of segregation; one could no longer ignore weekly reminders that the boundaries of racial exclusion extended right through the church doors. For Gov. William Winter, who attended Fondren Presbyterian when

Dr. McDill took a stand for open doors, the church visits made Christian beliefs in the Southern church relevant once again. By testing "the one institution that should have stepped up," the church visits "pricked at the heart of Christianity—the heart of southern religion."[17] For those like Gov. Winter, the campaign was part of a painful but necessary effort to banish white supremacy from the church.

Though Sunday morning worship is still the most segregated hour, some of the churches that were targeted by the integrated groups in 1963 and 1964 have come a long way. In early 1991, Bishop Woodie White preached at St. Luke's Methodist, the very church where police arrested him in December 1963 because of his race. He chose not to make a spectacle of the occasion—he was randomly assigned to preach there during a Council of Bishops meeting in the city—though the moment served as a private reminder that his participation in the campaign was not in vain. In 1991 and again in 2005, Bishop James Mathews preached at Galloway Memorial Methodist, the church that barred him on Easter Sunday, 1964, because he accompanied a black bishop, Charles Golden, to the church. On the later occasion, I observed over a dozen African Americans in the audience and in the choir. The headline across the bulletin read "Open Hearts, Open Minds, Open Doors," the new motto of the Methodist Church. Bishop Mathews made references to the church's past, emphasizing to the members of Galloway that they could not change history, but they could change the meaning of history. I saw John and Margrit Garner, who, though no longer members of the church, now felt welcome at the place they tried hard to change from within in the 1960s. Also there was Rev. Ed King, who teaches Sunday school and administers the healing and wholeness Eucharist services every Wednesday at Galloway. He is now an active member of the very church that repeatedly barred his entry because of his insistence that segregated worship was contrary to Christianity.

Acknowledgments

This book has been a decade in the making and has involved the collective labor of many folks. The project benefitted from the keen insight of friends and mentors at the University of Mississippi, including Ted Ownby, Charles Wilson, Charles Ross, and Curtis Wilkie. Joseph Ward and others in the history department encouraged my work and helped with research and travel grants for my many trips to Jackson and beyond. Others outside of the Oxford orbit were helpful as I completed additional research and refined this project into book form, especially Joseph Reiff, Milton Winter, Michael O'Brien, and Stephen Haynes and the Memphis congregational racial reconciliation group that he organized.

I want to thank the many librarians and archivists whose assistance proved invaluable. Those who helped especially with my many queries and extended visits to their collections are Clarence Hunter at the Mississippi Department of Archives and History, Debra Macintosh at the J. B. Cain Archives in Mississippi Methodism at Millsaps College, Frances Lyons-Bristol at the General Commission of Archives and History at Drew University, Mary Woodward of the Diocese of Jackson, Joel Thoreson of the Archives of the Evangelical Lutheran Church in America, and McGarvey Ice at the Disciples of Christ Historical Society.

If the documents form the backbone of this book, the interviews I conducted with people about all angles of this story certainly form the heart. Those often painful conversations with former Tougaloo students, ministers, and church people, some now passed, continue to have the most meaning for me. I am particularly indebted to Susan Dunn, Richard H. Hulan, Margaret McDill Pitts, and Lee Tilson for their generosity in sharing with me their fathers' personal documents. Two activists in particular, Joan Trumpauer Mulholland and Ed King, opened other doors for me and were vital to telling the story of the church visit campaign from the inside.

Many thanks are due to the kind folks at the University Press of Mississippi and my editor, Craig Gill, who championed this project in its early stages and patiently shepherded it to its present form. The readers he located offered valuable suggestions and ideas for revision; this book is vastly improved because of their efforts.

I am especially fortunate to teach and serve as history chair at St. Mary's Episcopal School in Memphis, a place that supports scholarship from its faculty and nurtures scholarly habits in its students. The St. Mary's community is a truly unique one, and it is a blessing to be a part of it.

Most importantly, I would like to thank my extended family for their encouragement and embrace of this project. My parents, Richard and Kathryn Lyon of Lexington, Kentucky, urged me to get a graduate degree in history and supported me throughout the process. My wife, Sally, is my best friend and the best editor one could have.

Abbreviations

AME	African Methodist Episcopal Church
COFO	Council of Federated Organizations
CORE	Congress of Racial Equality
CRR	Commission on Religion and Race of the National Council of Churches
EUB	Evangelical United Brethren Church
FBI	Federal Bureau of Investigation
FLC	Fellowship of Loyal Churchmen
GBCSC	General Board of Christian Social Concerns of the Methodist Church
GCAH	Council of Bishops, General Commission on Archives and History
ICM	Interracial Council of Methodists of Metropolitan (or Greater) Chicago
LCA	Lutheran Church of America
MAMML	Mississippi Association of Methodist Ministers and Laymen
MCR	Methodists for Church Renewal
MTS	Methodist Theological School, Delaware, Ohio
NAACP	National Association for the Advancement of Colored People
NCC	National Council of Churches
PHS	Presbyterian Historical Society
SCEF	Southern Conference Educational Fund
SCLC	Southern Christian Leadership Conference
SNCC	Student Nonviolent Coordinating Committee
WSCS	Women's Society of Christian Service of the Methodist Church
YFC	Youth for Christ

Notes

CHAPTER 1
Introduction

1. Anne Moody, *Coming in Age of Mississippi* (New York: Delta Trade Paperbacks, 2004), 311–12.

2. Because of the subjectivity of the monikers "conservative," "moderate," and "liberal," the use of these words has been avoided as much as possible. However, in my own mind—and in the minds of many readers, I am sure—I have found these designations helpful in clarifying distinctions along a spectrum of beliefs. Here and henceforth, moderates and liberals will often be mentioned together because they agreed that racial segregation was discrimination; that it was thus a moral and Christian concern; and that change must come. Yet they differed in tone, tactics, and timetables. Moderates in this analysis offered a mild or implicit rebuke of segregation and charted a gradual, temperate course of change that eschewed the overt pressure and manipulation exemplified by protestors' direct action techniques. Moderates disapproved of the closed-door policies of the churches, yet found the church visitors' tactics to be too radical and often counterproductive to the work they were doing to steer their churches toward inclusiveness. Liberals, on the other hand, were much more explicit and unequivocal about the immorality of segregation and demanded bold, immediate change through the use of nonviolent passive resistance techniques and pressure tactics like church visits and kneel-ins. Conservatives avoided or rebutted the argument that racial segregation was discrimination and aimed to create and preserve closed church doors.

CHAPTER 2
"When Integration Comes to Mississippi, It Will Enter through the Front Doors of Churches"
1954–60

1. "Say State Presbyterians Would Secede If Proposed Union Goes into Effect," *Jackson Daily News*, June 1, 1954, 1. Also found in Randy J. Sparks, *Religion in Mississippi* (Jackson, MS: University Press of Mississippi for the Mississippi Historical Society, 2001), 228.

2. "Mississippi Enacts Church Racial Law," *New York Times*, April 1, 1960, 33.

3. Ernest Q. Campbell and Thomas F. Pettigrew, *Christians in Racial Crisis: A Study of Little Rock's Ministry* (Washington, DC: Public Affairs Press, 1959), 156–61. Professors Campbell and Pettigrew analyze the effectiveness of local ministers dealing with the desegregation crisis in Little Rock, Arkansas, in 1957, and they have a thorough and helpful compilation of all the denominational responses to *Brown* in the appendix of the book.

4. "Local Church Balks at Integration Edict," *Clarion-Ledger*, June 11, 1954, 1–2; "Alexander Predicts Union of Presbyterian Churches Will Fail to Get Approval," *Jackson Daily News*, June 3, 1954, 4. Additionally, the general assembly approved a resolution to unite with the Presbyterian Church in the USA and the United Presbyterian Church (pending a vote by the presbyteries), thus voting to end the schism that preceded the Civil War. According to these press accounts, the issue of race was clearly intertwined with the issue of union. The pastor of First Presbyterian Church in Jackson, Dr. John Reed Miller, led the effort against the proposed union at the general assembly. See "Say State Presbyterians Would Secede If Proposed Union Goes Into Effect," "Southern Presbyterians Vote in Favor of Union with Northern Branches," *Jackson Daily News*, June 1, 1954, 1. In November, the Presbyterian Synod of Mississippi voted sixty to forty-eight to refuse to comply with the recommendations of the general assembly regarding desegregation. See "Presbyterians Back Segregation, Giving Okay to Sharp Report by Dr. Gillespie," *Jackson Daily News*, November 5, 1954, 7.

5. Campbell and Pettigrew, *Christians in Racial Crisis*, 137–8; "Southern Baptists Defend Segregation Ruling of Court," *Jackson Daily News*, June 5, 1954, 1.

6. Charles Marsh, *God's Long Summer: Stories of Faith and Civil Rights* (Princeton: Princeton University Press, 1997), 99–100; "Non-Segregation Action by Baptists Convention Is Not Binding Here, Leaders Say," *Jackson Daily News*, June 6, 1954, 1.

7. "Non-Segregation Action By Baptists Convention Is Not Binding Here, Leaders Say," *Jackson Daily News*, June 6, 1954, 1, 4; "A Deplorable Action," *Jackson Daily News*, June 6, 1954, 8.

8. The deacons discussed a racial policy on several occasions in the succeeding decade, but never formally voted to close the doors of First Baptist until June 9, 1963, the same day that church ushers turned away Tougaloo students from worship services there. See Richard and Nannie McLemore, *History of the First Baptist Church* (Jackson, MS: Hederman Brothers, 1976), 262.

9. Campbell and Pettigrew, *Christians in Racial Crisis*, 154; Edwin L. Brock, "Methodism's Growing Cleavage," *Christian Century*, August 24, 1955, 971.

10. Stevens, Thelma, and A. Dudley Ward, *The Methodist Church and Race: A Guide to Understanding the Central Jurisdiction and Race Relations* (Washington, DC: Division of Human Relations and Economic Affairs, 1962), 5–6. For a complete history of the Central Jurisdiction, see James S. Thomas, *Methodism's Racial Dilemma: The Story of the Central Jurisdiction* (Nashville, TN: Abingdon Press, 1992).

11. "Franklin Asserts Council Not a Legislative Body," *Mississippi Methodist Advocate*, 3.

12. Though MAMML was officially chartered in 1955, it emerged out of several efforts fighting integration in the Methodist Church in the preceding years. MAMML leaders themselves traced the group to 1951 or to the "Voluntary Committee of Christian Laymen" created by John Satterfield and others in 1950. See John Satterfield, "A Plea For Unity," *Mississippi Methodist Advocate*, February 10, 1965, 3; Francis Stevens, "A Sign of Change in Mississippi

Methodism," *Concern*, September 1, 1965, 8–9. Randy Sparks writes that MAMML began
through the sponsorship of the Circuit Riders, Inc. See Sparks, *Religion in Mississippi*, 234.
Mississippi was not the only state to see the rise of pro-segregationist lay groups during this
initial period of massive resistance. See Numan Bartley, *The Rise of Massive Resistance: Race
and Politics in the South During the 1950s* (Baton Rouge: Louisiana State University Press,
1969), 299–302.

13. "Methodists Firmly Favor Segregation," *Jackson Daily News*, March 31, 1955, 1; "Methodists Battle Integration Ideas," *Clarion-Ledger*, April 1, 1955, 10.

14. The group was first called the "Jackson States' Rights Association," though news articles were quick to point out that it was part of the Mississippi Association of Citizens' Councils. "'States' Rights' Group Here Set to Oppose Integration," *Clarion-Ledger*, March 25, 1955, 12;
"States Rights Group Is Formed Here to Preserve Segregation in States," *Jackson Daily News*,
March 25, 1955, 12.

15. Will D. Campbell, *Race and the Renewal of the Church* (Philadelphia: Westminster
Press, 1962), 18–19.

16. Branch, *Born of Conviction*, 48; "MSCS Reaffirms Charter OK; Whitsett Hits White
Councils," *Clarion-Ledger*, April 27, 1955, 1, 10; Reiff, "Born of Conviction: White Methodists
and Mississippi's Closed Society," 60.

17. Branch, *Born of Conviction*, 55–60; Stevens and Ward, *The Methodist Church and Race:
A Guide to Understanding the Central Jurisdiction and Race Relations*, 6; Thomas, *Methodism's
Racial Dilemma*, 84–92, 99–104.

18. Branch, *Born of Conviction*, 59–60; Stevens and Ward, *The Methodist Church and Race:
A Guide to Understanding the Central Jurisdiction and Race Relations*, 6. Branch notes another
interesting reaction to Amendment IX. The Methodist Student Movement, meeting in North
Carolina, voted seventeen hundred to thirty-five to immediately abolish the Central Jurisdiction. The student who presented this resolution was Paul Cotton of McComb, a student at
Mississippi Southern College and president of the Mississippi Methodist Student Movement.

19. "Church Tax Bill Is Aimed at Integration," *Jackson Daily News*, March 24, 1956, 1;
"Churches Allowing Integration Would Lose Tax Integration," *Jackson Daily News*, March 25,
1956, 5.

20. News articles and the roll call in the state senate proceedings identify her only by her
married name of Mrs. John Farese of Ashland, the Senate's only woman. See "Church Tax Bill
Called Dangerous," *Jackson Daily News*, March 27, 1956, 1.

21. "Church Tax Bill Called Dangerous," *Jackson Daily News*, March 27, 1956, 1.

22. Ibid.

23. "That Church Tax," *Jackson Daily News*, March 27, 1956, 6.

24. Branch, *Born of Conviction*, 78; "Mississippi Enacts Church Racial Law," *New York
Times*, April 1, 1960, 33. One of the other authors of the bill was Sen. George Yarbrough, one of
the authors of the 1956 church tax bill.

25. "Information Bulletin Number 17, Mississippi Association of Methodist Ministers and
Laymen," February 1960, 2, Mississippi Association of Methodist Ministers and Laymen, Holloman (Garland) Papers, Mississippi State University Special Collections; "Information Bulletin Number 18, Mississippi Association of Methodist Ministers and Laymen," March 1960,

1–3, Ibid. The "Information Bulletin" was published from 1958 to 1965. There is no complete repository for these newsletters, though the following collections contain multiple copies: Civil Rights and Methodism (Jackson, MS) Collection, Mississippi Department of Archives and History; Holloman (Garland) Papers, Special Collections, Mississippi State University; John C. Satterfield Collection, Archives and Special Collections, University of Mississippi; John David Humphrey Sr. Papers, Special Collections, Mississippi State University; Robert Bergmark Papers, Millsaps College Archives.

26. "Church Bill Dispute Flares as Opposition Speaks Out," *Clarion-Ledger*, February 17, 1960, 1, 12. The *Clarion-Ledger* printed an itemized list of those within the Mississippi Conference who opposed the measure, including dozens of churches and conference boards and groups such as the Mississippi Methodist Student Movement and the *Mississippi Methodist Advocate*. Bishop Joseph Brunini of the Catholic Church and Joe T. Odle, editor of the *Baptist Record*, also came out against legislation. See Branch, *Born of Conviction*, 79–80; Joe T. Odle, "Church and State," *Baptist Record*, February 4, 1960, 4; Joe T. Odle, "A Dangerous First Step," *Baptist Record*, February 25, 1960, 4; "Legislative Action," *Southern School News*, March 1960, 7. The *New York Times* reported that Presbyterian leaders in Mississippi denounced the legislation as well, but did not say who the leaders were. See "Mississippi Seeks New Curb," *New York Times*, March 6, 1960, 50; "Secession Laws Upset Methodists," *New York Times*, March 17, 1960, 57.

27. *Journal of the House of the State of Mississippi, At A Regular Session Thereof in the City of Jackson, Commencing Tuesday, January 5, 1960, Ending Wednesday, May 11, 1960* (Jackson, MS: Hederman Brothers, 1960), 361; *Journal of the Senate of the State of Mississippi, At A Regular Session Thereof in the City of Jackson, Commencing Tuesday, January 5, 1960, Ending Wednesday, May 11, 1960* (Jackson, MS: Hederman Brothers, 1960), 256; "Second Church Bill Is Offered in House," *Clarion-Ledger*, February 17, 1960, 1, 12; "Mississippi Enacts Church Racial Law," *New York Times*, April 1, 1960, 33. The senate approved the measure twenty-nine to sixteen, while the house voted eighty-seven to thirty-seven in favor.

28. "Oral History Memoir of Reverend Roy C. Clark, St. John's Methodist Church, Memphis, Tennessee, August 2, 1965," 39, Roy C. Clark Private Papers.

29. Branch, *Born of Conviction*, 85–87; William Astor Kirk, "Committee of Five" (Church Desegregation and the Jackson, MS, Witness, First Methodist Church, Chicago, Illinois, October 4, 2008); "Methodists Commend Behavior in Sit-Ins," *Clarion-Ledger*, May 8, 1960; Stevens and Ward, *The Methodist Church and Race: A Guide to Understanding the Central Jurisdiction and Race Relations*, 6–7; Thomas, *Methodism's Racial Dilemma*, 104–9. Dr. Kirk was a political scientist (having desegregated the graduate school at the University of Texas at Austin) and was on staff with the General Board of Church and Society of the Methodist Church. Bishop James S. Thomas, the author of *Methodism's Racial Dilemma*, was another of the five members of the Central Jurisdiction's Committee of Five.

30. Leon T. Moore and J. Wesley Hole, *Journal of the 1964 General Conference of the Methodist Church, Volume II* (Nashville, TN: Methodist Publishing House, 1964), 1268–69. Moore and Hole quote from the 1960 *Discipline*.

31. Stevens and Ward, *The Methodist Church and Race*, 15–16.

32. Clayborne Carson, ed., *The Student Voice, 1960–1965: Periodical of the Student Nonviolent Coordinating Committee* (Westport, CT: Meckler, 1990), 7.

33. "Kneel-Ins Held Integration Key; Episcopal Group Supporting Racial Unity Opens First Annual Talks in South," *New York Times*, January 9, 1961, 28. For a more comprehensive account of kneel-ins throughout the South in 1960, see Stephen Haynes, *The Last Segregated Hour: The Memphis Kneel-Ins and the Campaign for Southern Church Desegregation* (Oxford: Oxford University Press, 2012), 11–29.

34. Cynthia Griggs Fleming, *Soon We Will Not Cry: The Liberation of Ruby Doris Smith Robinson* (Lanham, MD: Rowman & Littlefield, 1998), 56.

35. Joan Trumpauer Mulholland, interview with the author; "Kneel-Ins Held in Four Churches," *Washington Post*, August 29, 1960; Alex Poinsett, "Reverse Integration in Mississippi," *Ebony*, January 1963, 25. For a compilation of news clippings about the Alexandria kneel-ins, see Joan Trumpauer Mulholland Papers, Reel 5. For more on Trumpauer, see Mike O'Brien's *We Shall Not Be Moved* (Jackson: University Press of Mississippi, 2013), 32–41.

CHAPTER 3

Jackson Ministers Proclaiming their Convictions

1961–63

1. W. B. Selah, "The Freedom Riders," undated sermon, 1, Box 2, Folder 9, Selah Scrapbook, Mississippi Department of Archives and History. This was the sermon that Dr. Selah wrote in case any Freedom Riders attempted to worship at the church. He mentions that after the Atlanta kneel-ins the preceding August, the official board adopted a policy that if black activists presented themselves for worship, "the Chairman of the Board would meet them . . . and advise them that their attendance would result in the preacher reading a statement concerning their presence." Though it is unclear, the statement suggests that the activists would be admitted.

2. Though people at the time referred to the closed-door policies as "segregation" policies, I find it more precise to use the term "exclusion" to distinguish it from segregation policies that seated African Americans in the balcony or other designated areas in churches and seated areas.

3. Roy Hulan, "A Local Minister's Experience in Revolution 1963," 1–3, Roy S. Hulan Subject File, Disciples of Christ Historical Society.

4. "Dr. Gillespie Tells Citizen Council Appeal Integration Ruling to People," *Jackson Daily News*, January 26, 1956, 10. Though Dr. Selah gave the invocation, it is significant to note that he may have felt uneasy about his participation in the meeting. The newspaper was quick to point out that Dr. Selah left the meeting shortly after he delivered the prayer. Paul Harvey located an address by Dr. Selah called "The Doctrine of Separate But Equal Opportunities for All Races." Though it remains unclear to whom this speech or report was directed, Dr. Selah clearly affirms separate but equal as a social control on the sexual amalgamation of the races. See Paul Harvey, *Freedom's Coming: Religious Culture and the Shaping of the South from the Civil War through the Civil Rights Era* (Chapel Hill: University of North Carolina Press, 2005), 230.

5. "The Climate of Freedom, A Sermon by Dr. W. B. Selah, Delivered at Galloway Memorial Methodist Church, Jackson, Mississippi, Sunday, March 23, 1958," 2, Pat and Phin Stevens Private Papers, personal collection. Because Dr. Selah was not vocal enough in defending

integration and the rule of law, Pat and Phin Stevens had left Galloway by 1961. Phin Stevens had chaired the board of stewards in the 1950s and had been a member of Galloway for forty years. In contrast to my analysis, historian Joseph Crespino sees little contradiction between Selah's racial position in the 1950s and his position in the 1960s. See Joseph Crespino, "The Christian Conscience of Jim Crow: White Protestant Ministers and the Mississippi Citizens' Councils, 1954–1964," *Mississippi Folklife*, Fall 1998, 41–42.

6. Ray E. Stevens, *Galloway Church History: Book I* (Jackson, MS: Ray E. Stevens, 1996), 86–89. Stevens's book is a collection of official board minutes and other documents from Galloway.

7. Ibid., 92. The minutes indicate that the resolution was submitted by Hugh Smith.

8. Selah, "The Freedom Riders," undated sermon, 1–2, Selah Scrapbook, Box 2, Folder 9, MDAH.

9. Ibid., 93–95; Minutes of the meeting of the official board of Galloway Memorial Methodist Church, June 12 1961, Folder 4, W. J. Cunningham / Galloway Church Collection, Archives and Special Collections, J. D. Williams Library, University of Mississippi; W. J. Cunningham, *Agony at Galloway: One Church's Struggle with Social Change* (Jackson, MS: University Press of Mississippi, 1980), 5. The minutes indicate that Robert Ezelle spoke out in opposition to the closed-door resolution, while five members, including John R. Wright, a MAMML and Citizens' Council leader, rose to support it.

10. Dr. W. B. Selah, "Galloway and the Race Issue," manuscript, Box 1, Folder 2, Selah Papers, J. B. Cain Archives of Mississippi Methodism, Millsaps College.

11. "Brotherhood, A Sermon By Dr. W. B. Selah, Minister, November 19, 1961," 4–5, manuscript, Box 1, Folder 4.2, Selah Papers, J. B. Cain Archives of Mississippi Methodism, Millsaps College.

12. Rev. Jerry Furr to Professor James W. Silver, 28 January 1963, James Silver Collection, Archives and Special Collections, University of Mississippi.

13. "Born of Conviction," *Mississippi Methodist Advocate*, January 2, 1963, 2. The most thorough analysis of the statement, the twenty-eight men, and the context of the Mississippi Conference can be found in Joseph T. Reiff's *Born of Conviction: White Methodists and Mississippi's Closed Society* (New York: Oxford University Press, 2016). The statement was also reprinted in Jackson, Mississippi's two major newspapers, the *Clarion-Ledger* and the *Jackson Daily News*. See "Twenty-Eight Ministers Urge No Discrimination," *Clarion-Ledger*, January 3, 1963, 12; "Methodists Urge 'Freedom of the Pulpit,'" *Jackson Daily News*, January 3, 1963, D3. For an in-depth comparison and analysis of public statements given by Southern ministers and groups during the movement era, see Reiff, *Born of Conviction*, 72–82. An interesting comparison in both content and chronology is the statement from white religious leaders in Birmingham responding to Governor George Wallace's "segregation forever" inaugural address, which they published just weeks after "Born of Conviction." See S. Jonathan Bass, *Blessed Are the Peacemakers* (Baton Rouge: Louisiana State University Press, 2001), 18–23.

14. "Oral History Memoir of Reverend Roy C. Clark, St. John's Methodist Church, Memphis, Tennessee, August 2, 1965," 8–9, Roy C. Clark Private Papers; "Bishop Says Church Forbids Forced Mix," *Clarion-Ledger*, January 15, 1963, 1; "Methodists Declare Mixing Voluntary," *Jackson Daily News*, January 15, 1963, 1, 7; "A Statement from the Bishop and Cabinet of the

Mississippi Methodist Conference," *Mississippi Methodist Advocate*, January 16, 1963, 2; "Pastor Wins Backing of Church Board on Position against Bias," *Mississippi Free Press*, January 19, 1963, 1, 4. "Lay Activities," *Mississippi Methodist Advocate*, January 9, 1963, 11; "Endorses Statement of Ministers," *Mississippi Methodist Advocate*, January 9, 1963, 11; "28 Ministers Supported on Racial Stand," *Clarion-Ledger*, January 4, 1963, 14. In the same issue in which the *Jackson Daily News* printed Bishop Franklin's statement, the newspaper reprinted a 1954 editorial by Bishop Warren A Candler of the Methodist Church in Georgia in which he argued, "Racial lines are ordained by God." See "Methodist Bishop Airs Views on Segregation," *Jackson Daily News*, January 15, 1963, 6.

15. "Mississippi," *Southern School News*, May 4, 1955, 8. The precise origin of MAMML is a matter of dispute. MAMML leaders themselves traced the organization to 1951 or to the "Voluntary Committee of Christian Laymen" created by John Satterfield and others in 1950. See John Satterfield, "A Plea For Unity," *Mississippi Methodist Advocate*, February 10, 1965, 3; Francis Stevens, "A Sign of Change in Mississippi Methodism," *Concern*, September 1, 1965, 8–9.

16. "Methodist Group 'for' Segregation," *Clarion-Ledger*, January 11, 1963, 1. The statement was also reprinted in the *Citizen*, the official journal of the Citizens' Council of America. See *Citizen*, January 1963, 10–13.

17. Ibid., 7.

18. Ibid., 7; "Open Schools Asked; Pastors' Statement Opposed by Board," *Southern School News*, February 1963, 17.

19. "Selah States Stand on Race Integration," *Clarion-Ledger*, January 7, 1963, 1, 3. Erle Johnston, who became director of the Mississippi State Sovereignty Commission later in the year, remembered Dr. Selah's response as "the strongest statement on moderation made in Mississippi" at the time. See Erle Johnston, *Mississippi's Defiant Years, 1953–1973: An Interpretive Documentary with Personal Experiences* (Forest, MS: Lake Harbor Publishers, 1990), 188. At the time, Rev. Furr was the only Jackson-based minister to sign the statement, though another signer, Rev. Joe Way, would become an associate at Capitol Street Methodist in June 1963. For more on Rev. Furr and Rev. Way, see Reiff's *Born of Conviction*.

20. John and Margrit Garner to "Dear Friends," March 1963, Box 1, Folder 2, Garner Letters, Mississippi Department of Archives and History.

21. "Congregation, Pastors Disagree," *Commercial Appeal*, January 16, 1963, 14; "Galloway Board Issues Statement on Ministers," *Clarion-Ledger*, January 15, 1963, 1, 6; "A Statement of the Official Board of Galloway Memorial Methodist Church, January 14, 1963," Box 1, Folder 19, Bishops' Papers, J. B. Cain Archives in Mississippi Methodism, Millsaps College.

22. Ray E. Stevens, *Galloway Church History, Book 1* (Jackson, MS: Roy E. Stevens, 1996), 104.

23. John and Margrit Garner to "Dear Friends," March 1963, Box 1, Folder 2, Garner Letters, Mississippi Department of Archives and History.

24. Ibid.

25. Stevens, *Galloway Church History, Book I*, 105–7.

26. By the end of the year, half of the twenty-eight will have transferred out of the state. While this unenthusiastic reaction to the manifesto and the ministers who signed it dominated the press coverage at the time and continued to frame much of the discourse since, religious scholar Joseph T. Reiff has found that eight of the twenty-eight signers remained in

the Mississippi Conference for the rest of their careers. For Reiff, the negative memory of the event obscures the success that over one quarter of the signers had in sustaining their prophetic ministries in the state. See Joseph T. Reiff, *Born of Conviction*, xvi–xxi; Reiff, "Conflicting Convictions in White Mississippi Methodism: The 1963 'Born of Conviction' Controversy," *Methodist History* 49:3 (April 2011), 168–69. For more on the twenty-eight and how the statement impacted individual congregations, see Nicholson, James B., "A Trail Through the Wilderness," *New South*, March 1963, 5; McMillan, George, "Silent White Ministers of the South," *New York Times Magazine*, April 5, 1964, 114; "Membership May Be Given Chance To Vote on Pastor," *Jackson Daily News*, January 14, 1963, 3; "Pastor Wins Backing of Church Board on Position against Bias," *Mississippi Free Press*, January 19, 1963, 1, 4; Official Board of the Oakland Heights Methodist Church to Bishop Marvin Franklin, 11 February 1963, Box 1, Folder 19, Bishops' Papers, J. B. Cain Archives in Mississippi Methodism, Millsaps College; "Transfers Out of Mississippi Conference," manuscript, Box 1, Folder 20, Bishops' Papers, J. B. Cain Archives in Mississippi Methodism, Millsaps College; "Statement of the Position of the Official Board of Carthage Methodist Church, January 6, 1963," manuscript, Box 1, Folder 19, Bishops' Papers, J. B. Cain Archives in Mississippi Methodism, Millsaps College; "3 Pastors Ousted by Mississippians," *New York Times*, January 19, 1963, 4; "Ministers' Statement Stirs Public Reaction," *Clarion-Ledger*, January 8, 1963, 1, 10; "Journal, 1963 Session, Mississippi Conference, the Methodist Church, Southeast Jurisdiction," 95, J. B. Cain Archives in Mississippi Methodism, Millsaps College.

27. Dr. Roy Clark, interview with the author; "Oral History Memoir of Reverend Roy C. Clark, St. John's Methodist Church, Memphis, Tennessee, August 2, 1965," 30–32, Roy C. Clark Private Papers.

28. "Oral History Memoir of Reverend Roy C. Clark, St. John's Methodist Church, Memphis, Tennessee, August 2, 1965," 47–52.

29. Ibid.

30. "Oral History Memoir of Reverend Roy C. Clark, St. John's Methodist Church, Memphis, Tennessee, August 2, 1965," 28, Roy C. Clark Private Papers.

31. "Coming to Grips with the Real Issue, A Sermon Preached at Capitol Street Methodist Church by Dr. Roy C. Clark, January 13, 1963, Text Acts 5:29," Box 7, Folder 344, Ed King Collection, Mississippi Department of Archives and History (hereafter, MDAH); "Rev. Roy Clark Says Pulpit Freedom Is Main Issue," *Jackson Daily News*, January 14, 1963, 7.

32. "Resolutions Voted by Congregations of Dekalb Circuit," Box 1, Folder 19, Bishops' Papers, Box 1, J. B. Cain Archives in Mississippi Methodism, Millsaps College.

33. "Methodist Bishop Airs Views on Segregation," *Jackson Daily News*, January 15, 1963, 6.

34. "Church Groups Urge Militant Mixing," *Jackson Daily News*, January 15, 1963, 22; "Church Mix Drive Pleasing to King," *Jackson Daily News*, January 16, 1963, 24.

35. "Some Actions Southeastern Jurisdictional Council," *Mississippi Methodist Advocate*, March 20, 1963, 2.

36. "Ministers to Discuss Segregation, Church," *Jackson Daily News*, March 18, 1963, 8; Stevens, *Galloway Church History, Book I*, 92; "Race Mixing Called 'Crime Against God,'" *Clarion-Ledger*, March 22, 1963, A15.

37. "Where Has the Methodist Church Drifted? Remarks by Medford Evans before the Mississippi Association of Methodist Ministers and Laymen in Conference, King Edward Hotel, Jackson, Mississippi, March 21, 1963," "Church," Box 2, Bill Minor Papers, Special Collections, Mississippi State University; "Methodists Demand Segregated Churches," *Jackson Daily News*, March 22, 1963, 4; "Race Mixing Called 'Crime Against God,'" *Clarion-Ledger*, March 22, 1963, A1.

38. "Minutes of the Council of Bishops of the Methodist Church, San Francisco, California, April 16–18," 756–57, 2313-4-2, folder 24, Council of Bishops, General Commission on Archives and History (GCAH).

39. Ibid., 759; "Bishops Speak on Race Relation," *Mississippi Methodist Advocate*, May 1, 1963, 1.

CHAPTER 4

"There Can Be No Color Bar in the House of God"

Spring 1963

1. Ed King, "Jackson Movement, Spring 1963," manuscript, 59–62, Edwin King Private Papers.

2. Ed King, interview with the author; King, "Jackson Movement, Spring 1963," 63.

3. "Negro Worshipers Accepted at First, Birmingham," *Baptist Record*, April 18, 1963, 1; King, "White Church, Part I," 10. The *Baptist Record* article does not list the three churches that refused to admit black visitors. Interestingly, the two Birmingham churches that admitted black visitors on Easter were pastored by two of the eight men to whom Dr. King directed his "Letter from a Birmingham Jail." Dr. King's "Letter" responded to a plea for moderation from eight white religious leaders, which local newspapers published the previous Saturday. See Bass, *Blessed Are the Peacemakers*, 1–27.

4. Myrlie B. Evers and William Peters, *For Us, the Living* (Garden City, NY: Doubleday, 1967) 265; John R. Salter Jr., *Jackson, Mississippi: An American Chronicle of Struggle and Schism* (Hicksville, NY: Exposition Press, 1979), 101, 107, 111.

5. Evers and Peters, *For Us, the Living*, 265; "Officials, Negroes to Confer," *Clarion-Ledger*, May 16, 1963, 1; Salter, *Jackson, Mississippi*, 108–10; "Contacting Informants in an Attempt to Ascertain if Negro Agitators Plan to Come to Jackson, Mississippi, in the Near Future for the Purpose of Demonstrating as They Are Presently Doing in Birmingham, Alabama," May 16, 1963, Investigation by Mississippi Sovereignty Commission, SCR ID# 3-74-1-17-4-1-1, Sovereignty Commission Online.

6. Ed King, interview with the author. According to Salter, the Mississippi NAACP mailed copies of the resolution on May 13 to Governor Barnett, Mayor Thompson, the Jackson City Commission, the Jackson Chamber of Commerce, the Jackson Junior Chamber of Commerce, the Downtown Jackson Association, the Bankers Association, and the Mississippi Economic Council. See Salter, 106. "Need Plan; Proposes Churches Be Ready," *Clarion-Ledger*, May 19, 1963, A9; Hensley, J. Clark, *By the Grace of God: A Delightful Journey* (Jackson, MS: Dallas Printing Company, 1992), 189; Dick Barnes, interview with the author; George and Jan Purvis, interview with the author; Richard and Nannie McLemore, *The History of the First*

Baptist Church (Jackson, MS: Hederman Brothers, 1976), 262, 286. Efforts to obtain deacons' minutes directly from Calvary Baptist Church, Woodland Hills Baptist Church, and First Baptist Church were unsuccessful.

7. Evers and Peters, *For Us, the Living*, 266–67; Myrlie Evers-Williams and Manning Marable, *The Autobiography of Medgar Evers* (New York: Basic Civitas Books, 2005), 280–83; Salter, *Jackson, Mississippi: An American Chronicle of Struggle and Schism*, 120–21. For a thorough analysis of the television speech by Medgar Evers and its larger meaning, see Michael Williams, *Medgar Evers: Mississippi Martyr* (Fayetteville: University of Arkansas Press, 2011), 240–48.

8. In addition to Rabbi Nussbaum, this network of like-minded clergy included Bishop Richard Gerow of the Natchez-Jackson Diocese of the Roman Catholic Church, Rev. Edward Harrison of St. Andrew's Episcopal Church, Rev. Roy Hulan of First Christian Church, Dr. W. B. Selah of Galloway Memorial Methodist Church, Dr. Roy C. Clark of Capitol Street Methodist Church, Rev. Wade Koons of Trinity Lutheran Church, and Dr. Moody McDill of Fondren Presbyterian.

9. "Oral History Memoir of Rabbi Perry Nussbaum, Temple Beth Israel, Jackson, Mississippi, August 5, 1965," 37–45, Oral History of Contemporary Mississippi Life and Viewpoint, Millsaps College Archives. For a thorough analysis of how another group of religious leaders in a major Southern city responded to the racial crisis, see S. Jonathan Bass, *Blessed Are the Peacemakers* (Baton Rouge: Louisiana State University Press, 2001).

10. "Oral History Memoir of Reverend Roy C. Clark, St. John's Methodist Church, Memphis, Tennessee, August 2, 1965," 35–36, Roy C. Clark Private Papers.

11. The attendees were Bishop Richard O. Gerow, Bishop Duncan Gray Sr., Bishop John Allin, and Bishop Marvin Franklin.

12. "Diary of Bishop Gerow, Volume VI, 1960–1966," 1616–19, Richard O. Gerow Collection, Archives of the Diocese of Jackson.

13. R. O. Gerow to "Dear Father," 23 May 1951, 2, R. O. Gerow to "Dear Father," 25 June 1951, 1–2, Correspondence of Bishop Richard O. Gerow, Richard O. Gerow Collection, Archives of the Diocese of Jackson. Bishop Gerow dealt with at least six different incidents on behalf of open doors in the years immediately following the 1954 *Brown* decision. See correspondence of Bishop Richard O. Gerow, Richard O. Gerow Collection.

14. Ibid. I was unable to find Father Gasper's first name.

15. Attending this meeting were the white Catholic and Protestant bishops Rev. Roy Hulan, Dr. Moody McDill, Dr. Roy Clark, and Rev. Wade Koons, and Rabbi Perry Nussbaum. Bishop Allin invited Rev. Douglass Hudgins of First Baptist Church, but, as Bishop Gerow wrote, Rev. Hudgins "was able to find an excuse to absent himself." Ibid., 1618–19.

16. Ibid., 1618–20; King, "Jackson Movement, Spring 1963," 65–67; Salter, *Jackson, Mississippi*, 127.

17. Ibid., 128.

18. Ibid., 128.

19. "Mayor's Stand Supported by Jackson C of C," *Clarion-Ledger*, May 23, 1963, 1.

20. "Diary of Bishop Gerow, Volume VI, 1960–1966," 1620–21, Richard O. Gerow Collection; "Oral History Memoir of Reverend Roy C. Clark, St. John's Methodist Church, Memphis,

Tennessee, August 2, 1965," 53–54, Roy C. Clark Private Papers; Salter, *Jackson, Mississippi*, 130; "Negro Leaders Refuse to Talk Over Demands; Reject Mayor's Plea, Quit Racial Meeting," *Clarion-Ledger*, May 28, 1963, 17; King, "Jackson Movement, Spring 1963," 68.

21. The mayor's meeting (with movement and non-movement individuals) included E. W. Banks of People Funeral Home, Rev. G. R. Haughton of Pearl Street AME Church, Rev. S. Leon Whitney of Farish Street Baptist Church, Professor I. S. Sanders formerly the principal of Lanier High School, Rev. R. L. T. Smith, Rev. L. L. Williams, Rev. G. W. Williams, Rev. F. L. Barnes, Rev. T. B. Brown, Rev. Charles Jones, Rev. C. P. Payne, Mrs. Elizabeth Moman, Rev. E. A. Mayes, Professor James C. Gooden, Joseph F. Albright, Sidney R. Tharp, and Percy Greene. See "Violence Flares as NAACP Backed Sit-Ins Start Here," *Jackson Advocate*, June 1, 1963, 1, 2; King, "Jackson Movement, Spring 1963," 69; "Negro Leaders Refuse to Talk Over Demands; Reject Mayor's Plea, Quit Racial Meeting," *Clarion-Ledger*, May 28, 1963, 1, 17.

22. Salter, *Jackson, Mississippi*, 130–31.

23. Among the white leaders were Bishops Joseph B. Brunini and Richard O. Gerow of the Diocese of Natchez-Jackson, Bishops John M. Allin and Duncan M. Gray of the Episcopal Diocese of Mississippi, Bishop Marvin Franklin of the Mississippi Methodist Church, Dr. Chester A. Quarles and Dr. William P. Davis of the Mississippi Baptist Convention, and Rabbi Perry Nussbaum of Temple Beth Israel. Rev. Roy C. Clark of Capitol Street Methodist joined the group, while Dr. Douglas Hudgins of First Baptist Church again declined an invitation to attend. "Ministers Are Urging Race-Communications," *Clarion-Ledger*, May 29, 1963, 12; "Religious Leaders Confer on Jackson Race Problem," *Mississippi Register*, June 7, 1963, 1; "Statement by the Rev. Edwin King, Chaplain of Tougaloo Southern Christian College to Broadway Congregation Church, New York City, June 9, 1963," Box 8, Folder 377, Ed King Collection, MDAH.

24. King, "Jackson Movement, Spring 1963," 70–73; "Oral History Memoir of Reverend Roy C. Clark, St. John's Methodist Church, Memphis, Tennessee, August 2, 1965," 60–62, Roy C. Clark Private Papers.

25. Hulan, Roy S., "A Local Minister's Experience in Revolution 1963," 2, Roy S. Hulan Papers, Disciples of Christ Historical Society; "Oral History Memoir of Reverend Roy C. Clark, St. John's Methodist Church, Memphis, Tennessee, August 2, 1965," 54, 63, Roy C. Clark Private Papers.

26. "Oral History Memoir of Reverend Roy C. Clark, St. John's Methodist Church, Memphis, Tennessee, August 2, 1965," 73; "Religious Leaders Confer on Jackson Race Problem," *Mississippi Register*, June 7, 1963, 1.

27. Ed King, "Bacchanal at Woolworth's," in *Freedom Is a Constant Struggle: An Anthology of the Mississippi Civil Rights Movement* (Montgomery, AL: Black Belt Press, 1999), 29.

28. John Dittmer, *Local People: The Struggle for Civil Rights in Mississippi* (Urbana: University of Illinois Press, 1994), 161–62; Anne Moody, *Coming of Age in Mississippi* (New York: Delta Trade Paperbacks, 2004), 290–92; "The Revolution," *Time*, June 7, 1963, 17; "Terribly Dangerous: The Battle of Jackson," *Newsweek*, June 10, 1963, 27–28; Williams, *Medgar Evers*, 253. *Newsweek* showed time-lapse photos of the assault on Memphis Norman. Bennie Oliver was later sentenced to thirty days in jail and fined $100. Applying Mississippi's new anti-demonstration statutes, the judge sentenced Norman to six months in jail and a $500 fine.

Ed King, "Bacchanal at Woolworth's," 31–32; "Negroes' Claim Refuted in Violence Wake Here; Lunch Counter Shut in Walgreen Store," *Clarion-Ledger*, May 29, 1963, 1, 19; "The Revolution," *Time*, June 7, 1963, 17; "Terribly Dangerous: The Battle of Jackson," *Newsweek*, June 10, 1963, 28–29. *Newsweek* declared the "first shot in the battle of Jackson" to be "a jet of mustard, fired by a bouffant blonde." Salter, *Jackson, Mississippi*, 136. The most thorough account of the Woolworth sit-in, including information about most of those at the scene, can be found in Michael O'Brien's *We Shall Not Be Moved* (Jackson: University Press of Mississippi, 2013).

29. "Negroes' Claim Refuted in Violence Wake Here; Lunch Counter Shut in Walgreen Store," *Clarion-Ledger*, May 29, 1963, 1, 19; Williams, *Medgar Evers*, 253–54.

30. Salter, *Jackson, Mississippi*, 137–39.

31. Chamberlain, Daphne Rochelle, "'And a Child Shall Lead the Way': Children's Participation in the Jackson, Mississippi, Black Freedom Struggle, 1946–1970," Thesis (PhD), University of Mississippi, 2009, 141–42; Evers and Peters, *For Us, the Living*, 273–77; "19 Persons Are Jailed in City Demonstrations; 3 Negro Youths Held After Rock-Throwings," *Clarion-Ledger*, May 30, 1963, 12; Bill Hutchinson, "Memorial Day Memories of Mississippi," *Your Smithfield Magazine*, May 2008, 13; "Agitators Seek Troops, Mayor Thompson Says; Operation at Columbus Is Rumored in Jackson," *Clarion Ledger*, May 31, 1963, 10A; "Police Jail Over 600," *Mississippi Free Press*, June 8, 1963; Salter, 139, 145–48.

32. Affidavit by Rev. King, May 30, 1963, Box 8, Folder 366, Ed King Collection, MDAH; Salter, *Jackson, Mississippi*, 150.

33. Dittmer, *Local People*, 165; Williams, *Medgar Evers*, 261–62.

34. "Police Detain Wilkins and Other Agitators Saturday," *Clarion-Ledger*, June 2, 1963, 1, 12.

35. Evers and Peters, *For Us, the Living*, 281–82; King, "Injunctions in Jackson," manuscript, 1–5, Ed King Private Papers; "Racial Focus in Jackson Moves into Local Courts," *Clarion-Ledger*, June 7, 1963, 1; Salter, *Jackson, Mississippi*, 174–75; Williams, *Medgar Evers*, 262–65.

36. King, "Injunctions in Jackson," manuscript, 1–5, Ed King Private Papers; "Racial Focus in Jackson Moves into Local Courts," *Clarion-Ledger*, June 7, 1963, 1; Salter, *Jackson, Mississippi*, 174–75; "Racial Focus in Jackson Moves into Local Courts; Chancery Injunction Is Object of Study Here," *Clarion-Ledger*, June 7, 1963, A10.

37. "Investigation of Agitators in Hinds and Madison Counties and Patrolling Tougaloo College," June 4, 1963, Mississippi Sovereignty Commission Investigation, SCR ID# 3–74-1-19-1-1-1, 3-74-1-19-2-1-1, 3-74-1-19-3-1-1, 3-74-1-19-4-1-1, 3-74-1-19-5-1-1.

38. "Methodists Select Conservative List," *Clarion-Ledger*, May 29, 1963, 1.

39. "Stafford Is Omitted on Methodist List," *Clarion-Ledger*, May 30, 1963, A12.

40. "Methodists Sever King Connections," *Clarion-Ledger*, June 1, 1963, 1, 16.

41. Handwritten notes by King at Mississippi Conference of the Methodist Church, May 30–31, 1963, Box 8, Folder 368, Ed King Collection, MDAH; "Journal, 1963 Session, Mississippi Conference, the Methodist Church, Southeast Jurisdiction," 93, J. B. Cain Archives in Mississippi Methodism, Millsaps College; Rev. King was officially accepted into the Central Jurisdiction in July 1964, becoming the first white minister in the church to affiliate with the all-black jurisdiction. See "King Accepted as Minister in Negro Conference," *Jackson Daily News*, July 16, 1964, 8.

42. "Bigotry Recrucifies Christ, Selah Says," *Atlanta Journal*, June 5, 1963.

43. Dr. Roy Clark, interview with the author.

44. Typewritten, undated manuscript, Box 2, Folder 9, Selah (William Bryan) Scrapbooks.

45. "Diary of Bishop Gerow, Volume VI, 1960–1966," 1621–22, Richard O. Gerow Collection.

46. "Church Unit Firm against Racial Bias," *Los Angeles Times*, June 8, 1963.

47. "National Council of Churches of Christ in the U.S.A, A Report of the President's Temporary Committee of Six on Race, Approved by the General Board on June 7, 1963," Reel 43, Frames 994–95, Student Non-Violent Coordinating Committee Papers; "Report of the Executive Director to the Commission on Religion and Race of the National Council of Churches, July 26, 1963," 5, Commission on Religion and Race, 1963–65, Box 1, John David Humphrey Sr. Papers.

48. Though no organized church visits occurred in Jackson before June, there were some examples of spontaneous visits. On one Sunday before the May demonstrations, two Tougaloo students—one white and one black—asked Professor Hutchinson to drive them to a white Baptist church. They wanted to try to attend the evening prayer services, and Professor Hutchinson agreed to accompany them. When they pulled into the church parking lot and got out of the car, three men rushed from the church and told them, "You cannot come into this church. This is a private house of God." The three returned to their car and left for campus. Bill Hutchinson, interview with the author; Bill Hutchinson, "Memorial Day Memories of Mississippi," *Your Smithfield Magazine*, May 2008, 12–13.

49. "The Prophet and the Preacher," manuscript, 161–62, Ed King Private Papers.

50. "Pastors Ask Reassignment as Churches Bar Negroes," *Commercial Appeal*, June 10, 1963, 1.

51. Dick Barnes, interview with the author. Barnes remembers that this painful moment of being forced to turn African American visitors away was a major factor in steering his family out of the church. He had been a member for forty years.

52. George and Jan Purvis, interview with the author. Efforts to obtain deacons' minutes directly from Calvary Baptist and Woodland Hills Baptist were unsuccessful.

53. Thomas B. Morgan, "Five Days in Mississippi," *Look*, 90, Box 2, Accretion (Oversize), Ed King Collection, Archives and Special Collections, J. D. Williams Library, University of Mississippi; "Negroes Attempt to Visit Six Jackson Churches," *Baptist Record*, June 13, 1963, 1, 2; "Six Churches Turn Away Negroes," *Clarion-Ledger*, June 10, 1963, 1, 10.

54. Ibid.; King, "Prophet and the Preacher," 162–63; Salter, *Jackson, Mississippi: An American Chronicle of Struggle and Schism*, 180; Selah, "Galloway and the Race Issue," 1; Stevens, "Galloway Church History, Part I, 113"; Typewritten, undated manuscript, Box 2, Folder 9, Selah (William Bryan) Scrapbooks.

55. McLemore, *The History of the First Baptist Church*, 262. Efforts to obtain deacons' minutes directly from First Baptist were unsuccessful. The selective minutes of the deacons' meeting available on microfilm at the Mississippi Department of Archives and History make no mention of the resolution. At the regular deacon's meeting on June 11, 1963, the minutes show that "J. H. Wells wished to thank the Chairman of the Deacons for the manner in which

these times of strife had been handled." Moreover, Dr. Hudgins "spoke briefly of our church's problems and asked for the Board's continuing prayers." See "First Baptist Church, Minutes of Deacon's Meeting," Roll # 36107, MDAH.

56. Ibid., 262, 286.

57. "Oral History Memoir of Reverend Roy C. Clark, St. John's Methodist Church, Memphis, Tennessee, August 2, 1965," 42, Roy C. Clark Private Papers.

58. Ibid., 43–45; Rev. Seth Granberry, "A Pastor Speaks," *His Name in Vain* (Jackson, MS: sponsored by a voluntary committee of Jackson, Mississippi Methodists, 1964), 9. Capitol Street Methodist Church shut down thirty years later, and its surviving records are available at the J. B. Cain Archives of Mississippi Methodism at Millsaps College. No official board minutes or resolutions from this period could be found in this collection; neither does the church's official history mention the closed-door policy or the church visits. See Effie P. Johnson, *Capitol Street United Methodist Church History, Volume II, 1950–1996* (Jackson, MS: History Committee of Capitol Street United Methodist Church, 1996), available at MDAH.

59. "Oral History Memoir of Reverend Roy C. Clark, St. John's Methodist Church, Memphis, Tennessee, August 2, 1965," 46, Roy C. Clark Private Papers.

60. Roy Clark, interview with the author.

61. David Ruff Grant, *To God Be the Glory: An Autobiography* (Jackson, MS: Dallas Printing Company, 1993), 110. Efforts to obtain deacons' minutes or any documents directly from Broadmoor Baptist were unsuccessful. While Rev. Grant never allowed the church to officially vote on a closed-door policy, he writes in his autobiography that he never mentioned his position on black visitors in a sermon until after the murder of James Chaney, Michael Schwerner, and Andrew Goodman in June 1964. Paraphrasing himself, he remembers saying, "No person has a right to disrupt a worship service to prove a point and that it ought not be allowed. I also stated that I believed all people of all races should be welcomed to our services any time they came for the purpose of worship." See pages 109–10.

62. King, "Final Conversation with Medgar Evers," 16, manuscript, Ed King Private Papers. For more on the final days of the life of Medgar Evers, see Williams, *Medgar Evers*, 268–69, 278–84.

63. King, "Final Conversation with Medgar Evers," 16–17.

CHAPTER 5
"I Began to Have a Little Hope"
June 1963

1. Evers and Peters, *For Us, the Living*, 308–10; Salter, *Jackson, Mississippi*, 188, 192, 195–205; "An End and a Beginning," *Newsweek*, June 24, 1963, 32–34. This article included a picture of the clubbing of John Salter (see page 32).

2. "Thompson Says Courts Are Place for Disputes," *Clarion-Ledger*, June 14, 1963, 1, 5.

3. "Agitators Are Warned of U.S. Court Decision; High Federal Tribunal Backs Hinds Injunction," *Clarion-Ledger*, June 15, 1963, 1, 8.

4. James F. Findlay Jr., *Church People in the Struggle: The National Council of Churches and the Black Freedom Movement, 1950–1970* (New York: Oxford University Press, 1993), 79.

Rev. T. M. Taylor, the secretary of the general council of the General Assembly of the United Presbyterian Church, led the delegation.

5. "Funeral March Finishes in White-Led Agitation," *Clarion-Ledger*, June 16, 1963, 14; King, "Funeral of Medgar Evers," manuscript, 2–5, Ed King Private Papers; Salter, *Jackson, Mississippi*, 209–10; Evers and Peters, *For Us, the Living*, 316. For more on the funeral of Medgar Evers, see Williams, *Medgar Evers*, 289–92.

6. King, "Funeral of Medgar Evers," 10–25; Moody, *Coming of Age in Mississippi*, 308–9; Evers and Peters, *For Us, the Living*, 319–22; "Funeral March Finishes in White-Led Agitation," *Clarion-Ledger*, June 16, 1963, 1, 14, 16; "Negroes Attend Jackson Church," *Commercial Appeal*, June 17, 1963, 1; "Demonstration Quelled at Slain Negro's Rites: Two White Men Lead Crowd," *Los Angeles Times*, June 16, 1963, 1, 8, 16; "Funeral March Finishes in White-Led Agitation," *Clarion-Ledger*, June 16, 1963, 1; Salter, *Jackson, Mississippi: An American Chronicle of Struggle and Schism*, 213–16.

7. "Diary of Bishop Gerow, Volume VI, 1960–1966," 1623–27, Richard O. Gerow Collection; Hazel LeBlanc Whitney, interview with the author. For Bishop Gerow's full statement reacting to the assassination of Medgar Evers, see "Bishop Gerow Comments on Racial Developments," *Clarion-Ledger*, June 15, 1963, 5. Bishop Gerow, Father Law, and Bill Minor drafted the statement. Bishop Gerow also met with Myrlie Evers at the funeral home on June 14. Though neither Medgar nor Myrlie Evers was Catholic, their children attended a Catholic school.

8. Hazel LeBlanc Whitney, interview with the author.

9. Ibid., 1627–30.

10. Ibid., 1630–31; "JFK, Church Leaders Talk Racial Committee Proposal," *Clarion-Ledger*, June 18, 1963, 1, 8. The *Clarion-Ledger* reported that Bishop Marvin Franklin and Dr. Chester Quarles were also at the White House conference, but were not necessarily in the smaller meeting with the president. Bishop Gerow did not list the two as being part of the meeting with the president. The article states, "Kennedy's telephone call to Thompson may have followed a private conversation here with one or more of five Jackson religious leaders." See "Council's Talks Moving toward Racial Solution," *Clarion-Ledger*, June 19, 1963, 1, 14. Hazel LeBlanc Whitney recalled that her husband saw a distinction between the attitude of the president and that of the attorney general. Though they were operating under different pressures, President John Kennedy thought the Jackson movement was trying to push things too fast, while Attorney General Robert Kennedy got angry about the situation in Jackson and specifically told Rev. Whitney to "give them hell."

11. Kennedy, John F., *Papers of John F. Kennedy, Presidential Papers, President's Office Files: Presidential Recordings, Logs, and Transcripts: Civil Rights, 1963* (Boston: John F. Kennedy Library, 1984), 22A.4, 6–10; 22B.1, 1–3.

12. "Council's Talks Moving toward Racial Solution," *Clarion-Ledger*, June 19, 1963, 1, 14.

13. "City Continues Work for Racial Situation," *Clarion-Ledger*, June 20, 1963, 1, 14; "No Compromise, Mayor Declares," *Clarion-Ledger*, June 22, 1963, 1.

14. The *Clarion-Ledger* identified the drivers of the other cars involved. The driver of the car that hit King and Salter was Edna Robinson. She swerved into their lane after hitting or being hit by eighteen-year-old Prat Pyle. See "CR Leaders Injured in Car Wreck," *Clarion-Ledger*, June 19, 1963, 7. Salter does not identify Pyle by name, but does identify him as the

son of "a former public official ... one of Jackson's most prominent Citizens' Council members." See Salter, *Jackson, Mississippi: An American Chronicle of Struggle and Schism*, 231–33. John Salter left Tougaloo in September, 1963, to work at the Southern Conference Educational Fund (SCEF), joining Ella Baker, Carl and Anne Braden, Rev. Fred Shuttlesworth, and Dr. Jim Dombrowski. The *Clarion-Ledger* announced his send-off, reminding readers, "Salter led demonstrators in the initial disturbances in Jackson, Miss., this summer." See "Salter Joins Pro-Mix SCEF," *Clarion-Ledger*, September 26, 1963, 2.

15. Diary of Bishop Gerow, Volume VI, 1960–1966, 1627, Richard O. Gerow Collection;

16. King, "Funeral of Medgar Evers," 35; "On Our Knees: The Story of the Jackson Church Visits," November 18, 1963, manuscript, Ed King Collection, MDAH.

17. Mark K. Bauman and Berkley Kalin, eds., *The Quiet Voices: Southern Rabbis and Black Civil Rights, 1880s to 1990s* (Tuscaloosa: University of Alabama Press, 1997), 244–51; "Oral History Memoir of Rabbi Perry Nussbaum, Temple Beth Israel, Jackson, Mississippi, August 5, 1965," 26, Oral History of Contemporary Mississippi Life and Viewpoint; Perry E. Nussbaum, "And Then There Was One in the Capital City of Mississippi," *Central Conference of American Rabbis Journal*, October 1963, 15–19; Perry E. Nussbaum, "Memoirs," Part I, 21–26, Part II, 4–14, Box 4, Folder 5, Perry E. Nussbaum Papers, 1947–72, American Jewish Archives.

18. "Oral History Memoir of Rabbi Perry Nussbaum, Temple Beth Israel, Jackson, Mississippi, August 5, 1965," 38–40, Oral History of Contemporary Mississippi Life and Viewpoint, Millsaps College Archives; Clive Webb, *Fight Against Fear: Southern Jews and Black Civil Rights* (Athens: University of Georgia Press, 2001), 206. Much to Rabbi Nussbaum's dismay, no black students visited Temple Beth Israel until May 1965. See "Oral History Memoir of Rabbi Perry Nussbaum, Beth Israel, Jackson, Mississippi, August 5, 1965," 39.

19. "Eighteen Negroes Try More Churches," *Clarion-Ledger*, June 17, 1963.

20. "Militancy Grows in Jackson Drive," *New York Times*, June 17, 1963, 12; Moody, Anne, *Coming of Age in Mississippi* (New York: Delta Trade Paperbacks, 2004), 311. The exchange between the young women and the members of First Christian is taken from the *New York Times* article. Moody's recounting of the white woman's retort to the ushers was this: "Who are we to decide such a thing? This is a house of God, and God is to make all of the decisions. He is the judge of us all."

21. King, "White Church, Part III," 76, manuscript, Ed King private papers; Hulan, Dr. Richard H., interview with the author; Hulan, Roy S., "A Local Minister's Experience in Revolution 1963," 3, Roy S. Hulan Papers, Disciples of Christ Historical Society; Hulan, Roy S., "When Men Are At Odds," *Christian*, September 22, 1963, 4–5. Rev. Hulan's sermon on June 16, 1963, is reprinted in this issue of the *Christian*. Dr. Richard Hulan, Rev. Hulan's son, explains that because of the architecture of the church (solid double doors between the nave and the narthex), his father could not see what was happening outside the sanctuary, and thus would not have known about what his ushers did until afterward. Moreover, the *New York Times* specified that the ushers were waiting on the church lawn for Moody and Lopsky.

22. "Eighteen Negroes Try More Churches," *Clarion-Ledger*, June 17, 1963, 1; "Four Jackson Negroes Attend White Church," *Los Angeles Times*, June 17, 1963, 16; "June 10, 1963, page 22, Session Minutes, 1963–67, Central Presbyterian Church (Jackson, MS)," C. Benton Kline Jr.

Special Collections and Archives, John Bulow Campbell Library, Columbia Theological Seminary. The motion approved at the session meeting read,

> That under the circumstances three Elders . . . be appointed to be available to meet any person presenting himself or herself for admission to any activity of the church, whose presence in their judgment, is likely to disturb the tranquility, peace, unity, or dignity of worship, or otherwise interfere with the orderly conduct of any church activity, and to attempt to persuade such person or person to leave. Should person or persons persist in an effort to enter, said Elder or Elders shall take such action as seems reasonable and necessary.

23. Ibid.; McLemore, *The History of the First Baptist Church*, 262.

24. Salter, *Jackson, Mississippi: An American Chronicle of Struggle and Schism*, 174–75.

25. Sherwood Willing Wise, *The Cathedral Church of St. Andrew: A Sesquicentennial History, 1839–1989* (Jackson, MS: Cathedral Church of St. Andrew, 1989), 157.

26. John Anderson, interview with the author; "Investigation of Integrated Meeting at the St. Andrew's Episcopal Church, Jackson, Mississippi, Night of March 28, 1961;" Mississippi State Sovereignty Commission Investigation, SCR ID#: 2–55–2–55–1–1–1, 2–55–2–55–2–1–1, Sovereignty Commission Online; "Local Negroes Propose Ride to Washington," *Jackson Daily News*, June 26, 1961, 1, 12; Wise, 144. Dr. Roy C. Clark and Rev. Wade Koons also visited the riders on at least one occasion, but did so beyond the eyes of the media (likely by entering the jail through a back door). "Mississippi Rector Under Attack For Joining In Biracial Meeting," *New York Times*, April 14, 1961; "A Troublesome Tape," *Living Church*, April 23, 1961; "Council Doubts Telegram Is Sent by Rector," *Jackson Daily News*, June 1, 1962; *The Episcopal Church in Mississippi, 1763–1992* (Jackson, MS: Episcopal Diocese of Mississippi, 1992) 117–19; "Telegram Touches Off Charges at Meet Here," *Jackson Daily News*, May 18, 1962, 12; Wise, *The Cathedral Church at St. Andrew*, 138–54.

27. John Fontaine, interview with the author; Caroline Keller-Winter, interview with the author; Wise, *The Cathedral of St. Andrew*, 158.

28. "Bar Vigorously Raps Civil Rights," *Clarion Ledger*, June 23, 1963, 1, 3; Senate Committee on the Judiciary, Literacy Tests and Voter Requirements in Federal and State Elections, 87th Cong., 2nd Sess., 1962, 245–59; "Bar Vigorously Raps Civil Rights," *Clarion Ledger*, June 23, 1963, 1, 3; Wise, Sherwood Willing, *The Way I See It: Then and Now* (Jackson, MS: n.p., 1996), 79–85.

29. Caroline Keller-Winter, interview with the author.

30. Ibid., John Fontaine, interview with the author.

31. "Four Jackson Negroes Attend White Church," *Los Angeles Times*, June 17, 1963, 16.

32. John Anderson, interview with the author; Wise, *The Way I See It*, 84.

33. John Fontaine, interview with the author; "Four Jackson Negroes Attend White Church," *Los Angeles Times*, June 17, 1963, 1, 16; "Negroes Attend Jackson Church," *Commercial Appeal*, June 17, 1963, 1; "Militancy Grows in Jackson Drive," *New York Times*, June 17, 1963, 1, 12;

34. "Eighteen Negroes Try More Churches," *Clarion-Ledger*, June 17, 1963, 10; Moody, *Coming of Age in Mississippi*, 311–12; Wise, *The Way I See It*, 85.

35. John Anderson, interview with the author; Moody, *Coming of Age in Mississippi*, 312; Wise, *The Cathedral Church of St. Andrew*, 160; Wise, *The Way I See It*, 85.

36. King, "White Church, Part I," manuscript, 8, Ed King private papers.

CHAPTER 6

"The Christian Church Is Down the Road"

Summer 1963

1. For more on Jackson movement activities during the summer of 1963, including other sit-ins, see Chamberlain, "'And a Child Shall Lead the Way,'" 161–62.

2. Pharis Harvey, interview with the author; John, Margrit, and Stephen Garner to "Dear Friends," 17 November 1963, 3, Garner Letters; Pharis J. Harvey, director, ecumenical work camp, Tougaloo Southern Christian College, undated, SCR ID #: 3–74–1–27–2–1–1, Sovereignty Commission online; "Ecumenical Volunteer Service Project, Tougaloo Southern Christian College, July 5–August 5, 1963, Leaders' Report by Pharis J. Harvey," manuscript, 4, Box 2, Folder 71, Ed King Collection; "Ecumenical Volunteer Service Project, Tougaloo Southern Christian College, July 5–August 5, 1963, Leaders' Report by Pharis J. Harvey," manuscript, 1, Box 2, Folder 71, Ed King Collection; Clarice T. Campbell and Oscar Allan Rogers Jr. *Mississippi: The View from Tougaloo* (Jackson: University Press of Mississippi, 1979), 205.

3. Pharis Harvey, interview with the author.

4. Lisa Anderson Todd, interview with the author.

5. Ivory Phillips, interview with the author. Just a few weeks before the work camp, Thelma Sadberry prompted an investigation by the Sovereignty Commission when she walked into a whites only ladies room after she applied for a job as a social worker trainee at the Mississippi welfare department. See Sovereignty Commission investigation, "Integrating Toilet Facilities in the Woolfolk Office Building", SCR ID #: 2–55–11–8–1–1, Sovereignty Commission Online.

6. Pharis Harvey, interview with the author; Ivory Phillips, interview with the author.

7. Lisa Anderson Todd, interview with the author.

8. "Ecumenical Volunteer Service Project, Tougaloo Southern Christian College, July 5–August 5, 1963, Leaders' Report by Pharis J. Harvey," manuscript, 4, Box 2, Folder 71, Ed King Collection, MDAH; Lisa Anderson Todd, interview with the author.

9. "Church Mix Groups Fail in Attempts," *Clarion-Ledger*, July 22, 1963.

10. "Negro Is Rejected by Houston Church, *New York Times*, June 12, 1963, 21; "Negro Seeks To Join First, Houston," *Baptist Record*, June 6, 1963, 1, 2; "Negroes Picket Houston Church," *Baptist Record*, August 1, 1963, 1; "Negro Denied Membership at Houston Church," *Baptist Record*, June 20, 1963, 1, 2;

11. George and Jan Purvis, interview with the author.

12. Mary Hendrick, interview with the author.

13. "On the Religious Front," *Christian Century*, July 24, 1963, 925–26; "Selah Going to Missouri," *Clarion-Ledger*, June 15, 1963, 8; Stevens, *Galloway Church History: Book I*, 131; "Transfers Out of Mississippi Conference," manuscript, Box 1, Folder 20, Bishops' Papers, J. B. Cain Archives of Mississippi Methodism.

14. Verna R. Wood to Dr. W.B. Selah, 11 June 1963, Box 1, Folder 1, Selah (William Bryan) Scrapbooks, Mississippi Department of Archives and History; Carroll Brinson to Dr. W. B. Selah, 11 June 1963, Box 1, Folder 1, Selah (William Bryan) Scrapbooks, Mississippi Department of Archives and History; Francis Stuart Harmon to Dr. W. B. Selah, 11 June 1963, Box 1, Folder 1, Selah (William Bryan) Scrapbooks, Mississippi Department of Archives and History; Francis Harmon, Letters to the Editor, *Clarion-Ledger*, June 15, 1963; Francis Stuart Harmon, Letters to the Editor, *Clarion-Ledger*, 10 June 1963, Box 48, Folder 1, National Council of Churches in the United States of America, Division of Christian Life and Mission Records, 1945–1973, Presbyterian Historical Society (PHS); Ann Hewitt to Dr. W. B. Selah, 19 June 1963, Box 1, Folder 2, Selah (William Bryan) Scrapbooks, Mississippi Department of Archives and History.

15. Stevens, *Galloway Church History, Book I*, 131. Includes copy of letter from Dr. Selah to William Neely, August 2, 1963.

16. Ibid., 130. Includes copy of letter from Rev. Furr to William Neely, July 31, 1963. For more on the fallout at Galloway stemming from the June 9 visits and the fates of Dr. Selah and Rev. Furr, see Reiff, *Born of Conviction*, 161–63.

17. John, Margrit, and Stephen Garner to "Dear friends," 30 June 1963, 2, Box 1, Folder 2, Garner (John and Margrit) Letters, Mississippi Department of Archives and History; Stevens, *Galloway Church History, Book I*, 113.

18. Dr. Roy C. Clark, interview with the author.

19. Cunningham, *Agony at Galloway*, 8; "Born of Conviction," *Mississippi Methodist Advocate*, January 2, 1963, 2. Like many of the other signers of "born of conviction," Rev. Jerry Trigg left the state within the next year. Rev. Jerry Trigg's transfer to the Indiana Conference was effective May 29, 1964. See "Transfers Out of Mississippi Conference," manuscript, Box 1, Folder 20, Bishops' Papers, J. B. Cain Archives in Mississippi Methodism, Millsaps College.

20. Cunningham, *Agony at Galloway*, 9.

21. *Journal, 1964 Session, Mississippi Conference, the Methodist Church, Southeast Jurisdiction*, 152nd Annual, Held in First Methodist Church, Gulfport, Mississippi, May 26–29, 1964, J. B. Cain Archives in Mississippi Methodism, Millsaps College; Hugh O. Smith to "Dear Bill (W. B. Selah)," undated, Selah (William Bryan) Scrapbooks, Mississippi Department of Archives and History; Stevens, *Galloway Church History Book I*, 129.

22. Cunningham, *Agony at Galloway*, 9–10; "Galloway Methodist Preacher Is Chosen; Clark Transferring," *Clarion-Ledger*, August 12, 1963, A1; "Eighteen Negroes Try More Churches," *Clarion-Ledger*, June 17, 1963, 1, 10; John, Margrit, and Stephen Garner to "Dear friends," 30 June 1963, 3, Box 1, Folder 2, Garner (John and Margrit) Letters, Mississippi Department of Archives and History.

23. John, Margrit, and Stephen Garner to "Dear friends," 17 November 1963, Box 2, Folder 6, Robert Bergmark Papers, Millsaps College Archives.

24. "Kneel-Ins Active Here Sunday," *Jackson Advocate*, July 27, 1963, 5.

25. Pharis Harvey, interview with the author.

26. "Church Mix Groups Fail In Attempts," *Clarion-Ledger*, July 22, 1963, A1.

27. Dr. Roy C. Clark, interview with the author. Like church lay boards in Jackson and other parts of the South, the official board at St. John's debated whether or not to seat African

Americans. This debate occurred soon after Dr. Clark arrived. After concluding that issuing a statement or initiating a closed-door policy would only invite black activists to come, the church board decided to leave the issue alone and quietly seat any activists who came. Dr. Clark reasoned that it was better to avoid a conversation about racial inclusiveness until the issue arose. It never did, as black activists did not attempt to worship at St. John's during this time.

28. "Church Session Withholding Funds for Council Support; Presbyterian Group Hits Pro-Integration Report," *Jackson Daily News*, June 6, 1957, 4; "Pro-Integration Fought By State Presbyterians," *Jackson Daily News*, April 29, 1958

29. "Free Elector Plans Given Huge Sendoff," *Clarion-Ledger*, June 18, 1963, 1, 15; William J. Simmons, interview with the author.

30. "Church Mix Groups Fail In Attempts," *Clarion-Ledger*, July 22, 1963, A1. Pharis Harvey, interview with the author; Ivory Phillips, interview with the author.

31. "Ecumenical Volunteer Service Project, Tougaloo Southern Christian College, July 5—August 5, 1963, Leaders' Report by Pharis J. Harvey," 4.

32. Pharis Harvey, interview with the author.

33. Evelyn A. Cairns (Prairie City, OR) to "Mr. King," 17 October 1963, Box 9, Folder 446, Ed King Collection, MDAH.

34. Ivory Phillips, interview with the author.

35. Lisa Anderson Todd, interview with the author.

36. Charles W. Koons, interview with the author; Wade Koons, "The Jackson, Mississippi Problem," 1, undated, Fry—Southeastern Synod 1963–64, Re Trinity Jackson, Mississippi, Evangelical Lutheran Church Archives; Wade H. Koons, Pastor File, Wartburg Theological Seminary.

37. Fred W. Patton to "All Members of Trinity Lutheran Church," 24 July 1963, SCR ID # 3–79–0–1–2–1–1, Sovereignty Commission Online; Wade Koons, "The Jackson, Mississippi Problem," 1, undated, Fry—Southeastern Synod 1963–64, Re Trinity Jackson, Mississippi, Evangelical Lutheran Church Archives. Koons identifies the church member involved as L. P. Roberts Jr.

38. Wade Koons, "The Jackson, Mississippi Problem," 1, undated, Fry—Southeastern Synod 1963–64, Re Trinity Jackson, Mississippi, Evangelical Lutheran Church Archives.

39. "Jacksonian Attends Lutheran Meeting," *Jackson Daily News*, May 6, 1963, 14; "Southeastern Synod of the Lutheran Church in America, Minutes, Second Annual Convention, April 30, May 1, 2, 1963," 103.

40. Raymond D. Wood to Fred Patton, 17 July 1963, SCR ID # 3–79–0–2–1–1–1, Sovereignty Commission Online.

41. Fred W. Patton to "the Members of Trinity Lutheran Church," 26 July 1963, SCR ID # 3–79–0–1–1–1–1, Sovereignty Commission Online.

42. Wade Koons, "The Jackson, Mississippi Problem," 1, undated, Fry—Southeastern Synod 1963–64, Re Trinity Jackson, Mississippi, Evangelical Lutheran Church Archives.

43. "Ecumenical Volunteer Service Project, Tougaloo Southern Christian College, July 5–August 5, 1963, Leaders' Report by Pharis J. Harvey," 4–5; Wade Koons, "The Jackson, Mississippi Problem," 1, undated, Fry—Southeastern Synod 1963–64, Re Trinity Jackson, Mississippi,

Evangelical Lutheran Church Archives; Ivory Phillips, interview with the author; Lisa Anderson Todd, interview with the author.

44. Memo from Virgil Downing to Erle Johnston, July 30, 1963, SCR ID # 3–79–0–3–1-1-1, 3–79–0–3–2-1-1, Sovereignty Commission Online.

45. Erle Johnston Jr. to O. F. Schluetter, 19 August 1963, SCR ID # 3–79–0–4-1-1-1, 3–79–0–4-2-1-1, Sovereignty Commission Online.

46. Activity Report for Month of July, 1963, Virgil Downing, Investigator, SCR ID #7–4–0–104–4-1-1, Sovereignty Commission Online.

47. D. L. "Dock" Luckey, August 22, 1963, memo, Fry—Negro Question 1963–64, Re Trinity Jackson, Mississippi, Evangelical Lutheran Church Archives; "Conflicts Over Segregation Arise in Mississippi's Churches," New York Times, January 5, 1964, L71; King, "White Church, Part I," 78–80; Kunstler, Deep in My Heart, 249. Rev. Wade Koons told Rev. Jack Zipperer, who arrived in June 1964 to lead a Lutheran mission in Southwest Jackson, about a novel tactic that Commissioner Luckey utilized to keep out unwanted visitors. Rev. Koons told him that Commissioner Luckey printed membership cards for all official members of Trinity Lutheran that they had to present upon entering the sanctuary. Those without cards, namely black guests, were not allowed to enter.

48. Wade Koons, "The Jackson, Mississippi Problem," 1–2, undated, Fry—Southeastern Synod 1963–64, Re Trinity Jackson, Mississippi, Evangelical Lutheran Church Archives; Wade Koons to Rev. Dr. Franklin Clark Fry, 11 September 1963, 1–2, Fry—Negro Question 1963–64, Re Trinity Jackson, Mississippi, Evangelical Lutheran Church Archives.

49. Memo from Erle Johnston Jr. to file, August 29, 1963, SCR ID # 3–79–0–5-1-1-1, Sovereignty Commission Online; Neil R. McMillen, The Citizens' Council: Organized Resistance to the Second Reconstruction, 1954–1964 (Urbana: University of Illinois Press, 1971), 336–38.

50. "Meeting with Committee of Citizens' Council, Plaza Building, Jackson, Mississippi, November 9, 1962," Sovereignty Commission Investigative Report, SCR ID # 1–3-0–11-1-1-1, 1–3-0–11-2-1-1, Sovereignty Commission Online; "White Students From Millsaps College Reported to Be Visiting Frequently at Tougaloo Christian College," Sovereignty Commission Investigate Report, SCR ID# 2–55–10–54–1-1-1, Sovereignty Commission Online; Erle Johnston, Mississippi's Defiant Years, 1953–1973: An Interpretive Documentary with Personal Experiences (Forest, MS: Lake Harbor Publishers, 1990), 230.

51. Some Methodists participated in the March on Washington specifically to protest the color line in their denomination. See Rev. Harry Kiely, "Where Were Methodists at the March," Concern, October 15, 1963.

CHAPTER 7
"Saving the Churches from Integration"
August–October 1963

1. Carl and Martha Brannan, interview with the author.

2. Roy S. Hulan, "A Local Minister's Experience in Revolution 1963," 3, Roy S. Hulan Papers, Disciples of Christ Historical Society.

3. Ibid.

4. Ibid, 1–2; Roy Hulan to "Dear Fambly," 13 August 1963, Richard H. Hulan private collection.

5. Roy S. Hulan, "A Local Minister's Experience in Revolution 1963," 4, Roy S. Hulan Papers, Disciples of Christ Historical Society.

6. "A Statement From Roy S. Hulan to the Members of First Christian Church, Jackson, August 20, 1963," 1–2, Richard H. Hulan private collection.

7. "Four Freedoms of Our Faith, Read Luke 4:14–30, A Sermon preached by Roy S. Hulan at First Christian Church, Jackson, Mississippi, on August 25, 1963," Richard H. Hulan private collection.

8. Roy S. Hulan, "A Local Minister's Experience in Revolution 1961," 4; Dr. Richard Hulan, interview with the author.

9. "Dr. Cunningham to Occupy Local Pulpit Sunday," *Clarion-Ledger*, September 7, 1963, 5; Reiff, *Born of Conviction*, 188–92. Rev. Granberry's arrival was not without its own degree of controversy, as lay leaders at Capitol Street objected to being excluded from the process of determining Dr. Clark's successor. See Reiff, *Born of Conviction*, 190.

10. "Church Group Raps Racial Segregation," *Clarion-Ledger*, September 1, 1963, 6.

11. "Civil Rights Act Would Give JFK 'Dictator' Power," *Clarion-Ledger*, September 8, 1963, A17; "Civil Rights Act Would Give JFK 'Dictator' Power," *Clarion-Ledger*, September 15, 1963, B4. The identical headlines are not a mistake.

12. Clarice T. Campbell, *Civil Rights Chronicle: Letters from the South* (Jackson, MS: University Press of Mississippi, 1997), 176

13. Ibid. 176; King, "White Church, Part IV," 94; "White Clergyman Shot in Jackson," *Southern Courier*, August 28, 1965. Rev. Thompson was shot in the back in 1965 for his efforts on behalf of the civil rights in Mississippi. He survived, but after another attempt on his life, he left the state for good. Campbell does not mention the name of the Presbyterian church.

14. Ed King Manuscript, Introduction, 1, Folder 10, Ed King Collection, Archives and Special Collections, J. D. Williams Library, University of Mississippi; King, "Funeral of Medgar Evers," manuscript, 35, Ed King Private Papers.

15. "Four Children Dead in Church Bombing," *Clarion-Ledger*, September 16, 1963, 1, 8.

16. "Four Little Girls," *Mississippi Methodist Advocate*, September 25, 1963, 3.

17. "Tougaloo Opens 95th Session," *Clarion-Ledger*, September 19, 1963, A3; King, "White Church, Part I," 10–12.

18. Ann Washburn McWilliams, interview by Edwina Robinson, April 28, 1981, 3, Mississippi Baptist Historical Commission, Oral History Program, Mississippi College; Satterfield, "The NAACP, CORE, the Methodist Church and the SNCC—To Worship or Demonstrate?" *His Name in Vain*, 7. Local and national newspaper reporters were present during many of the church visits, but the only evidence of news cameras was during the June visits. In an interview years later, an editor of the *Baptist Record* said that the visitors were turned away "because the newspapers and TV cameras would meet them there and the people of the churches thought they were trying to attend church to get publicity, rather than for real worship." Satterfield also wrote that when students attempted to worship at Galloway on the day of the first church visits, June 9, they "were greeted by the cameramen and reporters" and

"correctly spaced for good photography, they slowly ascended the steps and stated in tones proper for effective recording that they had come to worship."

19. Thomas B. Morgan, "Five Days in Mississippi," *Look*, 90, Box 2, Accretion (Oversize), Ed King Collection, Archives and Special Collections, J. D. Williams Library, University of Mississippi; "Church Bill On Calendar for House," *Clarion-Ledger*, March 1, 1960, 1; "Withdrawal Groundwork Mapped Out," *Clarion-Ledger*, June 21, 1965, 6; James W. Silver, *Mississippi: The Closed Society* (New York: Harcourt, Brace and World, 1963), 53. See Chapter 1 for a more thorough analysis of the church property law.

20. Erle Johnston Jr. to O. F. Schluetter, 19 August 1963, SCR ID # 3–79–0–4–1–1–1, 3–79–0–4–2–1–1, Sovereignty Commission Online.

21. Marsh, *God's Long Summer*, 133–34; Satterfield, "The NAACP, CORE, the Methodist Church and the SNCC—To Worship or Demonstrate?," *His Name in Vain*, 7–8; "Six Churches Turn Away Negroes," *Clarion-Ledger*, June 10, 1963, A1.

22. Cunningham, *Agony at Galloway*, 14.

23. "Aspect, A Project of the Information and Education Committee, Jackson Citizens' Council," August Bulletin, 1963, Vol. 1, No. 1, 1, Archives and Special Collections, J. D. Williams Library, University of Mississippi.

24. John Dittmer quotes Myrlie Evers who wrote that the "change of tide in Mississippi" began with the "Tougaloo Nine" sit-in. See John Dittmer, *Local People*, 89; "Aspect, A Project of the Information and Education Committee, Jackson Citizens' Council," August, 1963, 1.

25. Ibid., 1–2. This newsletter does not identify the church by name, but the description clearly fits the events that transpired at Trinity Lutheran Church in July and August, 1963.

26. Ibid., 2. Another notable development in the integration of Jackson occurred in mid-September, when two black men sat on juries in Hinds County Circuit Court. The trials were appeals to convictions of demonstrators from the June protests. The *Clarion-Ledger* quoted the clerk as saying, "It was probably the first time Negroes had served on trial juries in Mississippi." See "Negroes Are on Juries Hearing Demo Appealers," *Clarion-Ledger*, September 18, 1963, 2; "More Negroes Draw Duty on Hinds Juries," *Clarion-Ledger*, September 19, 1963, 7.

27. W. J. Simmons, interview with the author. Simmons attended First Baptist at the time. While Simmons cannot remember with certainty, he did not dispute the perception held by Rev. King and others that the routine placement of guards "standing watch" over Jackson churches was done under the auspices of the Jackson Citizens' Council; Dick Barnes, interview with the author; Mary Hendrick, interview with the author; George and Jan Purvis, interview with the author; Cunningham, *Agony at Galloway*, 15–16.

28. "On Our Knees: The Story of the Jackson Church Visits," November 18, 1963, 2, Box 9, Folder 434, Ed King Collection, MDAH; also reprinted in Ed King, "White Church, Part 1," 26.

29. W. J. Simmons, interview with the author. The major historical analysis of the first decade of the Citizens' Council does not mention or address the council's reaction to the Jackson church visit campaign. For more on the Citizen's Council during this era, see Neil R. McMillen, *The Citizens' Council: Organized Resistance to the Second Reconstruction, 1954–1964* (Urbana: University of Illinois Press, 1971). For a good example of the use of Christianity to defend segregation in Jackson, see Dr. Medford Evans, "A Methodist Declaration of Conscience on Racial Segregation," *Citizen*, Vol. 7, No. 4, January 1963. When I asked Mr. Simmons

about the thinking behind the response of the Jackson Citizens' Council to the church visit campaign, he began by pointing out the historical resentment of Tougaloo among many in the Jackson community because Tougaloo harbored proponents of the social gospel

30. King, "White Church, Part I," 16.

31. Although the exact date is unknown, some time in mid- to late September, after the church bombing, Rev. King and a black student, Marvin Palmore, successfully entered Galloway's chapel. There were no guards at the door, and they took Communion at the altar from Dr. Cunningham with everyone else. This was the first successful entrance into Galloway, but it was an accident that the guards soon corrected. See Cunningham, *Agony at Galloway*, 19–20; King, "White Church, Part I," 14.

32. "Aspect, A Project of the Information and Education Committee, Jackson Citizens' Council," September, 1963, 2; "Council Plans Fight against Church Mixing," *Clarion-Ledger*, September 22, 1963, A16. W. J. Simmons, interviewed February 8, 2006, could not recall the specific reasoning behind the timing of this announcement. Asked if the Citizens' Council felt that Jackson churches were in danger of opening their doors because of the church bombing, and the fact that several churches had recently admitted blacks, Simmons said, "That seems like a logical conclusion."

33. "The Role of the Lord's People: Evangelization, Not Equalization, Said to be Task of the Church," *Clarion-Ledger*, September 23, 1963, 1, 2; See Dittmer, *Local People*, 64–65, for a discussion of the Hederman brothers.

34. King, "White Church, Part I," 16; Hazel Brannon Smith, "The Gospel According to Citizens' Council," *Northside Reporter*, October 3, 1963, 2. Hazel Brannon Smith received a Pulitzer Prize in 1964. For more on Smith, see Mark Newman, "Journalist Under Siege," in *Mississippi Women: Their Histories, Their Lives* (Athens: University of Georgia Press, 2003), 220–34.

35. Joan Trumpauer Mulholland, interview with the author.

36. Wade Koons, "The Jackson, Mississippi Problem," 2, undated, Fry—Southeastern Synod 1963–1964, Re Trinity Jackson, Mississippi, Evangelical Lutheran Church Archives.

37. "Rev. Wade Koons, Pastor, Lutheran Church, Jackson, Mississippi, Mississippi Bureau of Identification Case Report," September 24, 1963, SCR ID # 3–79–0-6-1-1-1, Sovereignty Commission Online; Erle Johnston Jr. to Kirby Walker, superintendent of schools, 30 September 1963, SCR ID # 3–79–0-7-1-1-1, Sovereignty Commission Online.

38. O. Fritz Schluetter to Rev. Wade H. Koons, 24 September 1963, SCR ID # 3–79–0-8-1-1-1, Sovereignty Commission Online; Wade Koons, "The Jackson, Mississippi Problem," 3, undated, Fry—Southeastern Synod 1963–64, Re Trinity Jackson, Mississippi, Evangelical Lutheran Church Archives.

39. King, "White Church, Part I," 28–29; Seth W. Granberry, "A Pastor Speaks," *His Name in Vain*, 9–10. In fact, Rev. Granberry later publicly defended the right of an official board to take such an action. See page 10.

40. King, "White Church, Part IV," 34–35; Seth Granberry Jr., interview with the author.

41. "World-Wide Communion Sunday," *Mississippi Methodist Advocate*, September 11, 1963, 2; King, "White Church, Part I," 31A; Rev. Seth W. Granberry, "A Pastor Speaks," *His Name in Vain*, 9.

42. Lenora Marquis, interview with the author; Gov. William Winter, interview with the author.

43. Bill Hutchinson, interview with the author; Bill Hutchinson, "Memorial Day Memories of Mississippi," *Your Smithfield Magazine*, May 2008, 12–13.

44. "Minutes of the Called Meeting of the Fondren Presbyterian Church Held in the John Campbell Officers' Room on May, 26, 1963 at 9:45 a.m."; "Minutes of the Called Meeting of the Fondren Presbyterian Church Held in the John Campbell Officers' Room on September 8, 1963 at 4:00 p.m."; "Minutes of the Called Meeting of the Fondren Presbyterian Church Held in the John Campbell Officers' Room on September 22, 1963 at 10:40 a.m."; "Minutes of the Called Meeting of the Fondren Presbyterian Church Held in the John Campbell Officers' Room on September 29, 1963 at 7:00 p.m."; "Minutes of the Called Meeting of the Fondren Presbyterian Church Held in the John Campbell Officers' Room on October 6, 1963 at 9:45 a.m.," *Fondren Presbyterian Church, Volume 10*, Fondren Presbyterian Church Archives; Bill Hutchinson, interview with the author; Bill Hutchinson, "Memorial Day Memories of Mississippi," *Your Smithfield Magazine*, May 2008, 13, 77; William Winter, interview with the author. One of the key, peculiar features of the Fondren Presbyterian Church property (that set it apart from many of the other churches visited this Sunday) was that one could drive into the parking lot and approach the church without having to go on any sidewalks or other city property.

45. King, "White Church, Part IV," 47.

46. Ida Hanna Sanders, interview with the author.

47. Bette Anne Poole Marsh, interview with the author; Bette Anne Poole Marsh, "Panel #1: Jackson Witness—Students," (Church Desegregation and the Jackson, MS, Witness, Chicago, IL, October 4, 2008).

48. "Capitol Street Methodist Church Messenger, Vol. 1.4, No. 30, October 6, 1963," Bulletins, Box 8.8, Capitol Street United Methodist Church Papers, J. B. Cain Archives in Mississippi Methodism, Millsaps College

49. Report on Arrest of Three Students in Jackson, Mississippi, October 9, 1963, 2, Box 2597-7-7-2, Folder 1, Bail Bond Money, Jackson, Mississippi, 1963–67, Woman's Division of Christian of Christian Service, GCAH; Affidavit in Bette Poole, et al., Against Ross Barnett, et al., in the United States District Court for the Southern District of Mississippi, Jackson Division, Sworn to before me this 12th day of October, 1963, Box 1, Folder 17, Tougaloo Nine Sit-In Collection, Mississippi Department of Archives and History; An Appeal from the United States District Court for the Southern District, Brief for the Appellants, No. 21196, 2, Box 50, Folder 15, National Council of Church of Christ in the United States of America-Division of Christian Life and Mission Records, 1945–73, PHS; Ida Hannah Sanders, interview with the author; Rev. Seth Granberry, "A Pastor Speaks," 9; William Kunster, *Deep in My Heart* (New York: Morrow, 1966), 245–46; Summary Report on Arrests at Methodist Church in Jackson, Mississippi, Oct. 6, 1963 (based on oral statements of Bette Poole, Julie Auzgg, Ida Catherine Hannah told to Rev. Edwin King), Box 9, Folder 432, Ed King Collection, MDAH.

50. "What Kind of Christians?," *Mississippi Free Press*, October 12, 1963, 2.

51. King, "White Church, Part I," 61, 49.

52. Florence Little (treasurer of the Woman's Division of Christian Service of the Board of Missions of the Methodist Church) to Ed King, 8 October 1963, Box 9, Folder 438, Ed King Collection, MDAH; "Memo, 10.8.63 telephone conversation, Mrs. Porter Brown and Mr. King, re: 3 girls in jail in Jackson, Mississippi," Box 2597-7-2, Folder 1, Bail Bond Money, Jackson, Mississippi, 1963–1967, Woman's Division of Christian Service, GCAH; "Memo, 10.9.63 conversation between Rev. Ed King and Anna Thielz, administrative assistant to Mrs. Porter Brown," Box 2597-7-2, Folder 1, Bail Bond Money, Jackson, Mississippi, 1963–67, Woman's Division of Christian Service, GCAH; Report on Arrest of Three Students in Jackson, Mississippi, October 9, 1963, 1, Box 2597-7-7-2, Folder 1, Bail Bond Money, Jackson, Mississippi, 1963–1967, Woman's Division of Christian of Christian Service, GCAH; Campbell, *Civil Rights Chronicle: Letters from the South*, 184–85.

53. Clarice T. Bagby, "Kneel-Ins," *Concern*, November 1, 1963, 12–13.

54. "Memo, 10.8.63 second telephone conversation, Mrs. Porter Brown and Dudley Ward, re: 3 girls in jail in Jackson, Mississippi," Box 2597-7-2, Folder 1, Bail Bond Money, Jackson, Mississippi, 1963–67, Woman's Division of Christian Service, GCAH.

55. "Three Tougaloo Women Students Still in Jail," *Clarion-Ledger*, October 8, 1963, 13; "A Tragedy of Errors," *Mississippi Methodist Advocate*, October 16, 1963, 7; Ida Hannah Sanders, interview with the author; "Negroes Arrested at a White Church," *New York Times*, October 7, 1963, 36; "They Went to Church—So Two Chicago Co-eds Get Year in Dixie Jail," *Chicago Daily News*, October 8, 1963, 1.

56. Ida Hannah Sanders, interview with the author.

57. William Doyle, *An American Insurrection: James Meredith and the Battle of Oxford, Mississippi, 1962* (New York: Anchor Books, 2001), 34.

58. Findlay, *Church People in the Struggle*, 76; Robert Spike (executive director of CRR) to John D. Humphrey (Interboard Council of Grenada), 2 October 1963, National Council of Churches Correspondence, Box 1, John David Humphrey Sr., Papers; John M. Pratt, Report on the Release of 57 Prisoners in Mississippi, August 23, 1963, 1–8, Box 47, Folder 31, National Council of Churches of Christ in the United States of America, Division of Christian Life and Mission Records, 1945–73, PHS. The Clarksdale delegation included several Methodist leaders, including Bishop Charles Golden of the Central Jurisdiction and Dr. A Dudley Ward and Dr. Grover Bagby of the Board of Church and Society.

59. Press release, Commission on Religion and Race, National Council of Churches, New York City, October 11, 1963, Box 1, Folder 17, Tougaloo Nine Library Sit-In Collection, Mississippi Department of Archives and History (also found in SNCC Microfilm, Reel 7, Frames 383–84).

60. King, "White Church, Part I," 51–52.

61. "Jackson Aides Sued on Church Arrests," *New York Times*, June 13, 1963, 77; Kunstler, *Deep in My Heart*, 246; Kunstler, "The Jackson, Mississippi Right—To Worship Litigation," *Behold*, December, 1963, 3–5; plaintiff complaint of Bette Poole, et al. Against Ross Barnett, et al. in the US District Court for the Southern District of Mississippi, Jackson Division, 3–4, Box 1, Folder 17, Tougaloo Nine Library Sit-In Collection, Mississippi Department of Archives and History; "Suit Filed to Erase Mix Law," *Clarion-Ledger*, October 13, 1963, A12.

62. "They Went to Chicago," *Chicago Daily News*, October 8, 1963.

63. Francis B. Stevens to Dorothy Chapman, 24 October 1963, Box 2597-7-7-2, Folder 1, Bail Bond Money, Jackson, Mississippi, 1963–1967, Woman's Division of Christian Service, GCAH; Francis B. Stevens "To Whom It May Concern," 9 November 1964, 3, Methodism in Mississippi, Box 1, John David Humphrey Sr., Papers. Bishop Marvin Franklin's successor, Bishop Edward J. Pendergrass, felt confident enough in Stevens's investigation to quote it verbatim in a 1964 essay concerning the problems facing the Methodist Church in Jackson. See "An Evaluation of Methodism in the Jackson Area, By Edward J. Pendergrass," 3, Methodism in Mississippi, Box 1, John David Humphrey Sr., Papers; More Data on Jackson, Mississippi, 1444-2-6, folder 11, Jackson, Mississippi, Administrative Records of the Division of World Peace of the General Board of Church and Society, GCAH; Ed King to William (Bill) Kunstler, 9 October 1963, Box 9, Folder 438, Ed King Collection, MDAH; William J. Simmons, interview with the author.

64. "National Affairs," *Newsweek*, January 28, 1963, 32. The brief news account does not mention whether the black visitors insisted upon remaining on the church property after ushers barred their entry. The church visits in Albany were part of a city-wide desegregation effort; "Minister Held as 2 Sit-Ins Fail at First Baptist Church," *Atlanta Constitution*, July 1, 1963, 8; "Court Continues Case of Sit-In Minister," *Atlanta Constitution*, July 2, 1963, 19; "Sixty-Seven Year Old Minister Held in Atlanta Jail," *Student Voice*, November 18, 1963, 2; "Virginia Negroes Seized at Church," *New York Times*, July 29, 1963, 10. As far as I can tell, the Virginia arrests were the first mass arrests of church visitors.

CHAPTER 8
"We Knew Strength and We Knew Peace"
October 1963

1. Report on Visit to Jackson, Mississippi, by Rodney Shaw on the Weekend of October 12–14, 1963, 1–2, Box 1444-2-6, Folder 11, Jackson, Mississippi, Administrative Records of the Division of World Peace of the General Board of Church and Society, GCAH.

2. Jack Woodward, interview with the author.

3. King, "White Church, Part I," 56–61. For more on Rev. Joseph Way, see Reiff, *Born of Conviction*, 188–92.

4. Donald E. Collins, *When the Church Bell Rang Racist: The Methodist Church and the Civil Rights Movement in Alabama* (Macon, GA: Mercer University Press, 1998), 40–45, 62, 76. Birmingham-Southern readmitted Marti Turnipseed in the fall of 1964. King, "White Church, Part I," 56–61; Harold E. Zaugg, "Black and White Together, Lake Bluff, Illinois, October 1963," 1, Box 9, Folder 434, Ed King Collection, MDAH.

5. Woodie White, interview with the author.

6. King, "White Church, Part I," 68.

7. Ibid., 69–70.

8. "Chicago Clergyman and Three Co-eds Turned Away by Mississippi Church," *Chicago Daily News*, October 14, 1963; Confrontation on the Steps of the Capitol Street Methodist Church, Sunday Morning, October 6 [*sic*], 1963, 1–2, Box 1444-2-6, Folder 11, Jackson, Mississippi, Administrative Records of the Division of World Peace of the General Board of Church

and Society, GCAH; King, "White Church: Part I," 70–71; "Negro Girls Turned Away From Church," *Clarion-Ledger*, October 14, 1963, 8.

9. Confrontation on the Steps of the Capitol Street Methodist Church, Sunday Morning, October 6 [*sic*], 1963, 2–4, Box 1444-2-6, Folder 11, Jackson, Mississippi, Administrative Records of the Division of World Peace of the General Board of Church and Society, GCAH.

10. King, "White Church, Part I," 70–71.

11. Visits with Church Leaders in Jackson, Mississippi, by Rodney Shaw on Weekend of October 12–14, 1963, Box 1444-2-6, Folder 11, Jackson, Mississippi, Administrative Records of the Division of World Peace of the General Board of Church and Society, GCAH.

12. "Negro Girls Turned Away From Church," *Clarion-Ledger*, October 14, 1963, 8; Campbell, *Civil Rights Chronicle: Letters from the South*, 185. The *Clarion-Ledger* article does not mention the church visit to Our Redeemer Lutheran on October 13. While Campbell does not identify the church by name, it was most likely Our Redeemer Lutheran Church. Campbell describes the church turning the students away the week before. Given what we know about Trinity Lutheran at this time, and the newspaper accounts that identify the churches visited the week before, it was most likely Our Redeemer.

13. Campbell, *Civil Rights Chronicle: Letters from the South*, 185.

14. King, "White Church, Part I," 71–72.

15. "Chicago Clergyman and Three Co-eds Turned Away by Mississippi Church," *Chicago Daily News*, October 14, 1963.

16. "Co-eds' Conviction in Church Incident Tragic: Brashares," *Chicago Sun-Times*, October 15, 1963, 16; "Two Co-eds Again Turned Away by White Church in Mississippi," *Chicago Daily News*, October 15, 1963.

17. Martin Deppe, A Memory of Lee Rayson, Civil Rights Attorney, Gerald Forshey Project.

18. Gerald E. Forshey, "God Has Chosen the Racial Issue to Purify the Church," *Behold*, October 1963, 2–4; Robert Lovin, "New Theology—Forshey," (Church Desegregation and the Jackson, MS, Witness, Chicago, Illinois, October 4, 2008); Florence Forshey, "Panel #2: Witness—Clergy Teams" (Church Desegregation and the Jackson, MS, Witness, Chicago, Illinois, October 4, 2008). Rev. Gerald Forshey and Rev. Ed King were likely the only two white Methodist ministers assigned in the Central Jurisdiction at the time.

19. Elmer A. Dickson, Civil Rights Memories by Rev. Elmer A. Dickson, 1, Gerald Forshey Project; Rev. Elmer A. Dickson, "Panel #2: Witness—Clergy Teams" (Church Desegregation and the Jackson, MS, Witness, Chicago, Illinois, October 4, 2008).

20. Don Walden, Jackson Report—Relations and Communications with Methodist Clergy of Jackson, 1, Gerald Forshey Project.

21. "Stafford Is Omitted on Methodist List," *Clarion-Ledger*, May 30, 1963, 1A, 12A; John, Margrit, and Stephen Garner to "Dear Friends," 17 November 1963, 2; Nicholas Von Hoffman, "Church Integration Efforts in Mississippi: Pro and Con," *Chicago Daily News*, October 26, 1963, 28; Don Walden, Jackson Report—Relations and Communications with Methodist Clergy of Jackson, 4, Gerald Forshey Project.

22. Ibid., 2–3; John, Margrit, and Stephen Garner to "Dear Friends," 17 November 1963, 2.

23. Ed McKusker, "Deputy Police Chief Sought to Keep Peace," *Clarion-Ledger*, October 26, 1963, 3.

24. Thomas H. Watkins, "Pending Litigation Against the City of Jackson and the State of Mississippi," *His Name in Vain* (Jackson, MS: sponsored by a voluntary committee of Jackson, Mississippi Methodists, 1964), 11–12.

25. Don Walden, Jackson Report—Relations and Communications with Methodist Clergy of Jackson, 1, Gerald Forshey Project.

26. "Integrationists' Case in Federal Court," *Christian Advocate*, November 7, 1963, 24.

27. King, "White Church, Part I," 74; Elmer Dickson, Civil Rights Memories by Rev. Elmer A. Dickson, 2; Joan Trumpauer Mulholland, interview with the author.

28. John Garner, interview by John Dittmer and John Jones, February 13, 1981, transcript, 14, Mississippi Department of Archives and History.

29. Ibid., 6–33.

30. Margrit Garner, interview with the author.

31. Schedule of Church Visits for October 20, Box 9, Folder 432, Ed King Collection, MDAH.

32. "Minutes of the Called Meeting of the Fondren Presbyterian Church Held in the John Campbell Officers' Room on September 29, 1963 at 7:00 p.m.," "Minutes of the Called Meeting of the Fondren Presbyterian Church Held in the John Campbell Officers' Room on October 6, 1963 at 9:45 a.m.," "Minutes of the Called Meeting of the Fondren Presbyterian Church Held in the John Campbell Officers' Room on October 6, 1963 at 7:30 p.m.," *Fondren Presbyterian Church, Volume 10*, Fondren Presbyterian Church Archives.

33. Lenora Marquis, interview with the author; Margaret McDill Pitts, interview with the author; William Winter, interview with the author.

34. "Twelve Arrested at Churches Here Sunday," *Clarion-Ledger*, October 21, 1963, 5.

35. An Appeal from the United States District Court for the Southern District, Brief for the Appellants, No. 21196, 29, Box 50, Folder 15, National Council of Church of Christ in the United States of America, Division of Christian Life and Mission Records, 1945–73, PHS.

36. An Appeal from the United States District Court for the Southern District, Brief for the Appellants, No. 21196, 4, Box 50, Folder 15, National Council of Church of Christ in the United States of America, Division of Christian Life and Mission Records, 1945–73, PHS; King, "White Church, Part I," 80; Wade Koons, "The Jackson, Mississippi Problem," 2, undated, Fry—Southeastern Synod 1963–64, Re Trinity Jackson, Mississippi, Evangelical Lutheran Church Archives. Deputy Police Chief John Lee Ray was a familiar presence during the Freedom Rides in Jackson and continued to be one during the Jackson church visit campaign. For more on Ray, see M. J. O'Brien's *We Shall Not Be Moved*, 71–72.

37. Elmer A. Dickson, Civil Rights Memories by Rev. Elmer A. Dickson, 2; "Twelve Jailed in Mississippi for Appearance at Church and Sunday School," *Concern*, November 1, 1963, 15. *Concern* was a semi-monthly magazine published by the General Board of Christian Social Concerns of the Methodist Church.

38. John, Margrit, and Stephen Garner to "Dear Friends," 17 November 1963, 3, Garner Letters; W. J. Cunningham, *Agony at Galloway: One Church's Struggle with Social Change* (Jackson, MS: University Press of Mississippi, 1980), 15; and King, "White Church, Part I," 77–78.

39. Ibid., 75.

40. Nicholas Von Hoffman, "Six Ask U.S. Take Over Dixie Case; Arrested Chicago Ministers, Co-eds File Petitions," *Chicago Daily News*, October 21, 1963, 1, 7.

41. Thomas H. Watkins, "Pending Litigation Against the City of Jackson and the State of Mississippi," *His Name in Vain* (Jackson, MS: sponsored by a voluntary committee of Jackson, Mississippi Methodists, 1964), 12.

42. Seth W. Granberry, "A Pastor Speaks," *His Name in Vain* (Jackson, MS: sponsored by a voluntary committee of Jackson, Mississippi Methodists, 1964), 10.

43. An Appeal from the United States District Court for the Southern District, Brief for the Appellants, No. 21196, 3, Box 50, Folder 15, National Council of Church of Christ in the United States of America, Division of Christian Life and Mission Records, 1945–73, PHS; Ed McCusker, "Deputy Police Chief Sought to Keep Peace," *Clarion-Ledger*, October 26, 1963, 3.

44. Clarice Campbell, *Civil Rights Chronicle: Letters from the South* (Jackson, MS: University Press of Mississippi, 1997), 186; Bill Hutchinson, interview with the author; Bill Hutchinson, "Memorial Day Memories of Mississippi," *Your Smithfield Magazine*, May 2008, 77; Schedule of church visits for October 20, 1963, Box 9, Folder 432, Ed King Collection, MDAH.

45. "Twelve Arrested at Churches Here Sunday," *Clarion-Ledger*, October 21, 1963, 5.

46. Elmer A. Dickson, Civil Rights Memories by Rev. Elmer A. Dickson, 3; John, Margrit, and Stephen Garner to "Dear Friends," 17 November 17, 1963, 3; King, "White Church, Part I," 78; Cunningham, *Agony at Galloway*, 15. A discrepancy exists over the phone calls regarding the arrests. Rev. King wrote that Dr. Cunningham "was called by Margrit almost as soon as he finished his sermon" (see King, "White Church, Part I," 78), while Dr. Cunningham wrote, "After church when I heard of the incident, I immediately phoned the instructor's wife to comfort her and went posthaste to the city jail to do what I could to effect the release of the two young men"(see Cunningham, *Agony at Galloway*, 15). For what it is worth, in Dr. Cunningham's account, published seventeen years after the incident, he mistakenly wrote that police arrested only "a young white instructor at Tougaloo College" and "a Negro youth."

47. Gerald Forshey and Bishop Brashares, Box 9, Folder 432, Ed King Collection, MDAH. The note also informed Bishop Brashares, "Seth Granberry assured us that if you and Bishop Golden [Bishop Charles Golden of the all-black Central Jurisdiction of the Methodist Church] were to present yourselves at the door of the Capitol Street Methodist Church next Sunday you would be arrested."

48. Hoffman, "Church Integration Effort in Mississippi: Pro and Con," *Chicago Daily News*, October 26, 1963, 28.

49. Elmer A. Dickson, Civil Rights Memories by Rev. Elmer A. Dickson, 3.

50. King, "White Church, Part IV," 18–19.

CHAPTER 9
"Betraying Jackson"
Late October—Early November, 1963

1. James Reed, Information Helpful to Those Involved in the Jackson, Miss. Project, 1–2, Gerald Forshey Project.

2. Criticisms Received Regarding Bail Provided for Three Girls in Jackson, Mississippi, 1–7, Box 2597-7-2, Folder 1, Bail Bond Money, Jackson, MS, 1963–67, Woman's Division of

Christian Service, GCAH; Esther G. Palmer to Dorothy Chapman, 22 October 1963, Box 2597-7-7-2, Folder 1, Bail Bond Money, Jackson, Mississippi, 1963-67, Woman's Division of Christian Service, GCAH; Babs Strauss to Dorothy Chapman, 22 October 1963; Francis B. Stevens to Dorothy Chapman, 24 October 1963, Box 2597-7-7-2, Folder 1, Bail Bond Money, Jackson, MS, 1963-67, Woman's Division of Christian Service, GCAH.

3. Mrs. J. Fount Tillman to "Dear Mississippi Friends," 21 October 1963, Box 2597-7-7-2, Folder 1, Bail Bond Money, Jackson, MS, 1963-67, Woman's Division of Christian Service, GCAH.

4. "Denies Rights to Go to Church," *Christian Century*, October 30, 1963, 1324-25.

5. Bernard Law, "Cause for Concern," *Mississippi Register*, November 1, 1963, 4; "Arrests at Church Suggest a Police State," *Northside Reporter*, November 7, 1963, 2. Hazel Brannon Smith's denunciation of the police state—while declining to denounce the right of churches to bar black visitors—fits well with the findings of historian Mark Newman. According to Newman, Smith was undergoing her own transformation on race at this time. The violence and intimidation against black citizens in Mississippi convinced her of the need for outside intervention. By 1964, she was urging passage of federal civil rights legislation and welcoming volunteers from the Mississippi Summer Project into Holmes County. See Mark Newman, "Journalist Under Siege," in *Mississippi Women: Their Histories, Their Lives* (Athens: University of Georgia Press, 2003), 228-29.

6. William Kunstler, *Deep in My Heart* (New York: Morrow, 1966), 246; Plaintiff complaint of Bette Poole, et al. against Ross Barnett, et al. in the United States District Court for the Southern District of Mississippi, Jackson Division, 3-4, Box 1, Folder 17, Tougaloo Nine Library Sit-In Collection, Mississippi Department of Archives and History; "Suit Filed to Erase Mix Law," *Clarion-Ledger*, October 13, 1963, A12.

7. William M. Kunstler, "The Jackson, Mississippi Right-to-Worship Litigation," *Behold*, December 1963, 3-4.

8. King, "White Church, Part IV," 4.

9. "In U.S. Court: 'Pray-In' Group Given Hearing," *Jackson Daily News*, October 21, 1963, 1, 4.

10. An Appeal from the United States District Court for the Southern District, Brief for the Appellants, No. 21196, 2, Box 50, Folder 15, National Council of Church of Christ in the United States of America, Division of Christian Life and Mission Records, 1945-73, PHS; Ed McCusker, "Deputy Police Chief Sought to Keep Peace," *Clarion-Ledger*, October 26, 1963, 3.

11. King, "White Church, Part IV," 12.

12. Thomas H. Watkins, "Pending Litigation Against the City of Jackson and the State of Mississippi," 11.

13. King, "White Church, Part IV," 7; Kunstler, *Deep in My Heart*, 248; Cunningham, *Agony at Galloway*, 15. Dr. Cunningham did not realize it at the time, but later wrote that his "naïveté was showing," for "how absurd was the very idea of actual collusion between our church officials and police officers regarding the arrest of anyone at church!"

14. Affidavit reprinted in part in Ed McCusker, "Deputy Police Chief Sought to Keep Peace," *Clarion-Ledger*, October 26, 1963, 3, and Thomas Watkins, "Pending Litigation Against the City of Jackson and the State of Mississippi," 11.

15. King, "White Church, Part IV," 10.

16. "Methodists Request Move On Agitators," *Clarion-Ledger*, October 19, 1963, 1. In 1965, Rev. Hardin is listed as a member of the board of directors of the Jackson Citizens' Council, the only minister on the board. I could not, however, locate any evidence that Rev. Hardin was active in the Jackson Citizens' Council in 1963. See *ASPECT: A Project of the Information and Education Committee, Jackson Citizens Council, May 1965 Bulletin, Vol. II, No. 10*, 2, Box 2, Folder 8, Robert Bergmark Papers, Millsaps College Archives.

17. King, "White Church, Part IV," 11; Ed McCusker, "Deputy Police Chief Sought to Keep Peace," 3.

18. Kunstler, *Deep in My Heart*, 247.

19. Ibid., 249–50; Dudley Lehew, "Federal Judge Denies Change of Authority," *Clarion-Ledger*, October 22, 1963, 8.

20. "In U.S. Court: 'Pray-In' Group Given Hearing," *Jackson Daily News*, October 21, 1963, 1, 4; Dudley Lehew, "Federal Judge Denies Change of Authority," *Clarion-Ledger*, October 22, 1963, 8; "Judge Cox Denies Change in Authority," *Jackson Daily News*, October 22, 1963, 2.

21. Kunstler, *Deep in My Heart*, 250; Ed McCusker, "Deputy Police Chief Sought to Keep Peace," *Clarion-Ledger*, October 25, 1963, 3; "Take Custody of Agitators," *Clarion-Ledger*, October 25, 1963, 1.

22. John, Margrit, and Stephen Garner to "Dear Friends," 17 November 1963, 4, Garner Letters; King, "White Church, Part IV," 12; Kunstler, *Deep in My Heart*, 250; Ed McCusker, "Deputy Police Chief Sought to Keep Peace," *Clarion-Ledger*, October 25, 1963, 3.

23. "Minutes of the Called Meeting of the Fondren Presbyterian Church Held in the John Campbell Officers' Room on October 23, 1963, at 7:30 p.m.," *Fondren Presbyterian Church, Volume 10*, Fondren Presbyterian Church Archives; Richard and Nannie McLemore, *The History of the First Baptist Church* (Jackson, MS: Hederman Brothers, 1976), 262; Minutes of the meeting of the Official Board of Galloway Memorial Methodist Church, June 12, 1961, Folder 4, W. J. Cunningham / Galloway Church Collection, Archives and Special Collections, J. D. Williams Library, University of Mississippi; and "A Statement of the Official Board of Galloway Memorial Methodist Church, January 14, 1963," Box 1, Folder 19, Bishops' Papers, J. B. Cain Archives in Mississippi Methodism, Millsaps College.

24. Kunstler, *Deep in My Heart*, 251; King, "White Church, Part IV," 22, 26.

25. Richard Tholin, "Panel #2: Witness—Clergy Teams" (Church Desegregation and the Jackson, MS, witness, First Methodist Church, Chicago, Illinois, October 4, 2008); Richard Tholin, "Why We Were There," *Telescope-Messenger*, December 21, 1963, 16–18; Nicholas Von Hoffman, "Four Chicago Area Ministers in Dixie Integration Effort," *Chicago Daily News*, October 25, 1963.

26. Richard Tholin, "Panel #2: Witness—Clergy Teams" (Church Desegregation and the Jackson, MS, Witness, First Methodist Church, Chicago, Illinois, October 4, 2008).

27. Richard Tholin, "Why We Were There," *Telescope-Messenger*, December 21, 1963, 16.

28. Letter from Dick (Richard) Tholin to "Dear Ed," November 15, 1963, 1–2, Box 9, Folder 446, Ed King Collection, MDAH.

29. Clarice Campbell, *Civil Rights Chronicle*, 187.

30. "Police Arrest Two Ministers Here Sunday," *Clarion Ledger*, October 28, 1963, 5. Contrast this to his statements in court. See Ed McCusker, "Deputy Police Chief Sought to Keep Peace," *Clarion-Ledger*, October 26, 1963, 3.

31. Richard Tholin, "Why We Were There," *Telescope-Messenger*, December 21, 1963, 17.

32. "Jackson Police Seize Clergy After 'Kneel-In,'" *Los Angeles Times*, October 28, 1963, 15; "Police Arrest Two Ministers Here Sunday," *Clarion-Ledger*, October 28, 1963, 5; "Two Ministers Arrested Here," *Jackson Daily News*, October 28, 1963, 7.

33. "Statement by Eli Hockstadler," Box 9, Folder 432, Ed King Collection, MDAH.

34. Richard Tholin, "Why We Were There," *Telescope-Messenger*, December 21, 1963, 17.

35. "EUB Ministers Protest," *Christian Advocate*, November 7, 1963, 24; Gerald Forshey, "Divided Flocks in Jackson," *Christian Century*, November 27, 1963, 1470.

36. Edgar Hiestand Jr., interview with the author.

37. Arthur North, interview with the author; Barry Shaw, interview with the author; "To the Council of Bishops of the Methodist Church, From Two Ministers Who Visited Jackson, Mississippi, on the Weekend of November 3, 1963," 3, Folder: Methodism in Mississippi, Box 1, John David Humphrey Sr., Papers.

38. Ibid.; Edgar Hiestand Jr., interview with the author.

39. Ibid., Campbell, *Civil Rights Chronicle: Letters from the South*, 189–90.

40. Ibid.

41. "To the Council of Bishops of the Methodist Church, From Two Ministers Who Visited Jackson, Mississippi, on the Weekend of November 3, 1963," 1–3, Folder: Methodism in Mississippi, Box 1, John David Humphrey Sr. Papers. Over forty years later, Rev. North's views on his involvement in church visit campaign remained unchanged, while Rev. Shaw's views have shifted somewhat. He now admits that they probably should have pressed the issue more to try to get arrested. He acknowledges that the actions of the two bishops on Easter Sunday 1964 (when they were turned away from Galloway) reaffirmed his belief that the campaign was worthwhile.

42. John Dittmer, *Local People*, 205.

43. Al Bamsey Subject File, 3, Collection of the Detroit Conference Archives; Paul Lowley Subject File, 3, Collection of the Detroit Conference Archives; Archie Rich Subject File, 5, Collection of the Detroit Conference Archives; and Charles Sutton Subject File, 2, Collection of the Detroit Conference Archives. This group included Rev. Al Bamsey, the associate pastor of Grosse Point Methodist Church, Rev. Paul Lowley, pastor of St. Mark's Methodist Church, Rev. Richard C. Raines Jr., pastor of Whitfield Methodist Church, Rev. Archie Rich of River Rouge Methodist Church, and Rev. Charles Sutton, an associate pastor at Central Methodist Church.

44. Al Bamsey, interview with the author; Paul Lowley, interview with the author; Richard Raines, interview with the author.

45. Ibid.

46. Richard C. Raines, "Dear Brother Pastor," *Behold*, October 1963, 4.

47. Richard Raines, interview with the author.

48. Al Bamsey, interview with the author; Richard Raines, interview with the author. Rev. Bamsey remembers rather humorously that he kept wishing for the service to end because his knees were getting tired.

49. Paul Lowley, interview with the author; Letter from Al Bamsey to "Dear Joan," March 4, 1964, Box 9, Folder 446, Ed King Collection, MDAH.

50. Ray Stevens, *Galloway Church History, Book I*, 138–41.

CHAPTER 10
Behind the "Magnolia Curtain"
November–December 1963

1. "Bishops Denounce Racial Segregation," *Christian Advocate*, December 5, 1963, 20–21; Ralph Lord Roy, "Methodists: Crisis of Conscience," *Nation*, March 16, 1964, 264–65.

2. Arthur North, interview with the author.

3. "Bishops Denounce Racial Segregation," *Christian Advocate*, December 5, 1963, 20–21; Ralph Lord Roy, "Methodists: Crisis of Conscience," *Nation*, March 16, 1964, 264–65; Marvin Franklin, "The Bishop's Column," *Mississippi Methodist Advocate*, November 20, 1963, 2; "Bishops Denounce Racial Segregation," *Christian Advocate*, December 5, 1963, 21. As part of the first set of kneel-ins in Atlanta in 1960 that targeted a variety of churches and denominations, activists showed up at the church where Bishop John Owen Smith gave his inaugural sermon as bishop of Georgia. An usher at St. Mark Methodist in Atlanta told them they could not enter, but another church official stepped forward and told them they had every right to worship there. They were seated and talked with Bishop Smith after the service. See "Negro Students Attend Six White Churches Here," *Atlanta Constitution*, August 8, 1960, 6. The following Sunday, black students were turned away from two other Methodist churches in Atlanta, Grace Methodist Church and Druid Hills Methodist. See "Negro Worshipers Push New Kneel-In," *Atlanta Constitution*, August 15, 1960, 10. In August 1963, ushers at First Methodist Church in Athens admitted a group of black students. See "Negro Youths Attend Athens White Churches," *Atlanta Constitution*, August 26, 1963, 7.

4. Letter from Harry Denman to Bishop Roy H. Short, undated, "Minutes of the Council of Bishops of the Methodist Church, Detroit, Michigan, November 12–14, 1963," 1078–1079, Box 2313-4-2, Folder 25, Council of Bishops, GCAH.

5. Letter from Rev. James D. Nixon to Bishop Roy H. Short, November 6, 1963, "Minutes of the Council of Bishops of the Methodist Church, Detroit, Michigan, November 12–14, 1963," 1087, Box 2323-4-2, Folder 25, Council of Bishops, GCAH; "An Anguished Appeal to the Council of Bishops on Freedom to Worship," "Minutes of the Council of Bishops of the Methodist Church, Detroit, Michigan, November 12–14, 1963," 1088, Box 2323-4-2, Folder 25, Council of Bishops, GCAH.

6. "Statement of the Council of Bishops of the Methodist Church, Adopted November 13, 1963, Detroit, Michigan," Box 1, Folder 2, Selah Papers; "Text of Bishops' Message," *Christian Advocate*, December 5, 1963, 20.

7. "Bishops Denounce Racial Segregation," *Christian Advocate*, December 5, 1963, 20–21; King, "White Church, Part IV," 56; Ralph Lord Roy, "Methodists: Crisis of Conscience," *Nation*, March 16, 1964, 264–65.

8. "To the Council of Bishops," *Behold*, December 1963, 13–14.

9. Martin Deppe, "Panel #3: Methodists for Church Renewal and the Pilgrimage to Pittsburgh" (Church Desegregation and the Jackson, MS, Witness, First Methodist Church, Chicago, Illinois, October 4, 2008).

10. Ibid.; Arthur Jeffrey Hopper, interview with the author; "Methodists for Church Renewal, Volume 1, December 1963," Box 9, Folder 437, Ed King Collection, MDAH; Ralph Lord

Roy, "Methodists: Crisis of Conscience," *Nation*, March 16, 1964, 265. Also on the steering committee were two seminary professors at Methodist Theological School in Delaware, Ohio, Rev. Arthur Jeffrey Hopper and Dr. C. Everett Tilson, who would be part of the Jackson witness on Easter Sunday.

11. Ladner, Joyce, Austin Moore, and Julie Zaugg, "Statement of the Council of Bishops of the Methodist Church," *Voice of the Movement*, November 15, 1963, 1–3, Box 2, Folder 80, Ed King Collection, MDAH.

12. The contingent from the Detroit area included Rev. Woodie White of East Grand Boulevard Methodist Church, Rev. Donald E. Hall of Campbell Avenue Methodist Church, Rev. Robert E. Willoughby of Mount Olivet Methodist Church in Dearborn, Rev. Stanley Bailey of Madison Heights Methodist Church, Rev. James Nixon of Grosse Pointe Methodist Church, and Dr. Charles Morton of Metropolitan Baptist Church. Rev. Nixon's associate at Grosse Pointe, Rev. Al Bamsey, participated in the witness the previous weekend. The contingent from Cleveland, Ohio, included two ministers, Rev. John M. Badertscher of Oedlhoff Methodist Church and Rev. Kenneth Lee Houghland of Trinity Methodist Church, and two Methodist laymen, Ed Craun and Robert Meeks.

13. Charles Morton, interview with the author.

14. Woodie White Subject File, 4, Collection of the Detroit Conference Archives.

15. Woodie White, interview with the author.

16. John Badertscher, Tuesday, November 19, 1963, Hinds County Jail, Jackson, Mississippi, 1–2, Forshey Project; John R. Freshwater to "Mr. King," 18 November 1963, Box 9, Folder 446, Ed King Collection, MDAH; Robert H. Courtney to John Pratt, 10 December 1965, Box 50, Folder 8, National Council of Churches of Christ in the United States of America, Division of Christian Life and Mission Records, 1945–73, PHS.

17. Ibid., 3.

18. Robert L. Meeks to Grover Bagby, undated, Box 1433–6-7, Folder 2, Jackson Arrest Cases Folder 2, 1963–67, Administrative Records of the Division of Human Relations and Economic Affairs of the General Board of Church and Society, GCAH; Woodie White, interview with the author.

19. "Five Ministers Jailed in Jackson Racial Drive," *Los Angeles Times*, November 18, 1963; "Ten Arrested at Churches Here Sunday," *Clarion-Ledger*, November 18, 1963, 7.

20. Ibid.; Charles Morton, interview with the author; Robert E. Willoughby to "Dear Joan," 4 May 1964, Box 9, Folder 446, Ed King Collection, MDAH; John M. Pratt, "The Revolution of 1963, An Address to the 13th Annual Alumni Ministers' Conference, Union Theological Seminary, New York City, January 7, 1964," SNCC Files, Reel 8, Frame 262–63; "Statement by Charles Morton and James Nixon," Box 9, Folder 432, Ed King Collection, MDAH; Rev. Robert Willoughby, undated memo, Box 9, Folder 447, Ed King Collection, MDAH.

21. This was the first and last documented attempt at Broadmeadow. In Rev. Duke's January 20, 1965, sermon, he further explained his views on race: "I know Christianity works when given a chance and I also know that integration has not worked on any level or in any area where it has been tried . . . . All attempts at forced integration is unchristian since it inevitably results in abnormal conditions in which both races suffer or become less than their best." See "Sermon, January 20, 1965, Broadmeadow Methodist Church, Charles Duke, Pastor, Born of the Spirit, Scripture: John 3: 1–8," 1–2, Box 7, Folder 344, Ed King Collection, MDAH.

22. John Badertscher, Tuesday, November 19, 1963, Hinds County Jail, Jackson, Mississippi, 3, Gerald Forshey Project; "Ten Arrested at Churches Here Sunday," *Clarion-Ledger*, November 18, 1963, 7.

23. Statement of Arrest at St. Luke's Methodist Church, Jackson, Mississippi, Box 9, Folder 432, Ed King Collection, MDAH; Woodie White, interview with the author.

24. John Badertscher, Tuesday, November 19, 1963, Hinds County Jail, Jackson, Mississippi, 3, Gerald Forshey Project; Robert Courtney to John Pratt, December 10, 1965, Box 50, Folder 8, National Council of Churches of Christ in the United States of America, Division of Christian Life and Mission Records, 1945–74, PHS; Charles Morton, interview with the author; Woodie White, interview with the author.

25. Francis B. Stevens, "To Whom It May Concern, November 9, 1964," 3, Methodism in Mississippi, Box 1, John David Humphrey Sr. Papers. During the first official board meeting following the arrests at Broadmeadow, Francis Stevens stated his objection to the arrests and tried to lobby for change in the church's closed-door policy. Though he was unsuccessful, he continued to be a voice of moderation in his church and in the Mississippi Conference.

26. Bruce Russell, "The Way of the Cross," *Los Angeles Times*, November 19, 1963, 4.

27. Albert E. Tomer to "Mr. King," 30 October 1963, Box 9, Folder 446, Ed King Collection, MDAH; Richard Teller, interview with the author; Albert Tomer, interview with the author; John Wagner, interview with the author.

28. Ibid.

29. King, "White Church, Part IV," 42–43; John Wagner to "Dear Joan," undated, Box 9, Folder 446, Ed King Collection, MDAH; Joan to "Dear," 12 December 1963, 1, Reel 5, Joan Trumpauer Mulholland Papers; John Wagner, interview with the author; Albert Tomer, "Two Worlds Behind a Magnolia Curtain, Part II, The Plight of the Moderate," *Kenton Times*, December 5, 1963, 1.

30. Richard Teller, interview with the author.

31. Albert Tomer, interview with the author; Albert Tomer, "Two Wolds Behind a Magnolia Curtain, Part I, The Curtain Makers," *Kenton Times*, December 4, 1963, 1, 5.

32. John Wagner, interview with the author.

33. King, "White Church, Part IV," 43–44; Albert Tomer, "Two Worlds Behind a Magnolia Curtain, Part II, The Plight of the Moderate," *Kenton Times*, December 5, 1963, 1. John Wagner, interview with the author. The student beaten at the lunch counter that the ministers refer to fits the description of Memphis Norman, who suffered the most at the Woolworth's sit-in in May 1963.

34. Richard Teller, interview with the author; Albert Tomer, "Two Worlds Behind a Magnolia Curtain, Part III: The Events of Sunday and Conclusions," *Kenton Times*, December 7, 1963, 1; Joan Trumpauer to "Dear," 12 December 1963, 1–2, Reel 5, Joan Trumpauer Mullholland Papers.

35. John Wagner to "Dear Joan," undated, Box 9, Folder 446, Ed King Collection, MDAH; John Wagner, interview with the author.

36. King, "White Church, Part IV," 44–45; Albert Tomer, "Two Worlds Behind a Magnolia Curtain: Part III, The Events of Sunday and Conclusions," *Kenton Times*, December 7, 1963, 1.

37. Joan to "Dear," 12 December 1963, 2. Reel 5, Joan Trumpauer Mulholland Papers; Camille Wilburn McKey, interview with the author.

38. John Wagner to "Mr. and Mrs. King," 30 November 1963, Box 9, Folder 446, Ed King Collection, MDAH; John Wagner, interview with the author.

39. Joan Trumpauer to "Dear," 12 December 1963, 1, Reel 5, Joan Trumpauer Mulholland Papers; Joan Trumpauer to "Reverend Wagner," 16 December 1963, Box 9, Folder 446, Ed King Collection, MDAH.

40. "A Call to the Churches for Action to Meet the Crisis in Race Relations, Resolution Adopted by the General Assembly, December 6, 1963," 1–2, Box 48, Folder 1, National Council of Churches of Christ in the United States of America, Division of Christian Life and Mission Records, 1945–1973, PHS; Report of the Executive Director, Commission Meeting, New York City, January 16, 1964, 1–2, Box 47, Folder 31, National Council of Churches of Christ in the United States of America, Division of Christian Life and Mission Records, 1945–73, PHS.

41. A. W. Martin, interview with the author; A. W. Martin, "The Lawson Affair, the Sit-Ins, and Beyond," 1–5, A. W. Martin private papers.

42. William Wells, interview with the author.

43. John Dittmer, *Local People*, 90; James M. Lawson, interview by Dallas A. Blanchard, October 24, 1983, Interview F-0029, transcript, Southern Oral History Program Collection, University Library, University of North Carolina at Chapel Hill.

44. Joan Trumpauer to "Dear," 12 December 1963, 2–3, Reel 5, Joan Trumpauer Mulholland Papers; A. W. Martin Jr. to "Dear Joan," 12 March 1964, Box 9, Folder 446, Ed King Collection, MDAH.

45. Ibid; A. W. Martin, interview with the author; William Wells, interview with the author.

46. Joan Trumpauer to "Dear," 12 December 1963, 3, Reel 5, Joan Trumpauer Mulholland Papers.

47. "Methodist Clergy to Test Church Ban in the South," *New York Times*, December 14, 1963, 16; "New York Clerics Seized in Jackson," *New York Times*, December 16, 1963, 16; James K. Mathews, *A Global Odyssey: The Autobiography of James K. Mathews* (Nashville: Abingdon Press, 2000), 274.

48. Charles Koons, interview with the author; Wade Koons, "The Jackson, Mississippi Problem," 2, undated, Fry–Southeastern Synod 1963–64, Re Trinity Jackson, Mississippi, Evangelical Lutheran Church Archives; Raymond A. Petrea to Franklin Clark Fry, 2 October 1963, 1–2, Fry—Responses to Pastoral Letter 1963, Trinity Jackson, Mississippi, Evangelical Lutheran Church Archives; Franklin Clark Fry to Raymond A. Petrea, 7 October 1963, Fry—Responses to Pastoral Letter 1963, Trinity Jackson, Mississippi, Evangelical Lutheran Church Archives.

49. "Synod President's Message to Trinity Lutheran Church, Jackson, Mississippi, December 8, 1963," 1–3, Fry–Southeastern Synod 1963–64, Re Trinity Jackson, Mississippi, Evangelical Lutheran Church Archives; Wade Koons to Franklin Clark Fry, 12 December 1963, 1–2, Fry–Southeastern Synod 1963–64, Re Trinity Jackson, Mississippi, Evangelical Lutheran Church Archives; Raymond D. Wood to Franklin Clark Fry, 13 December 1963, Fry–Southeastern Synod 1963–64, Re Trinity Jackson, Mississippi, Evangelical Lutheran Church Archives.

50. Rev. John A. Collins of Manhattan should not be confused with Rev. John Collins of Cincinnati, who took part in the witness on November 24 with other ministers from Ohio.

51. Clarice Campbell, *Civil Rights Chronicle*, 194; W. J. Cunningham, *Agony at Galloway*, 30; F. Herbert Skeete, interview with the author; David B. Ver Nooy, interview with the author.

Dr. Cunningham quotes in full from a report that the four men gave to their board of Christian social concerns.

52. John A. Collins, interview with the author; F. Herbert Skeete, interview with the author; David P. Ver Nooy, interview with the author.

53. John A. Collins, interview with the author; David P. Ver Nooy, interview with the author; Cunningham, *Agony at Galloway*, 31–32; F. Herbert Skeete, interview with the author; Campbell, *Civil Rights Chronicle*, 194; Joan Trumpauer, "Greetings," 11 January 1963, 1, Joan Trumpauer Mullholland Papers.

54. David P. Ver Nooy, interview with the author

55. Ibid.; John A. Collins, interview with the author; Cunningham, *Agony at Galloway*, 31–34. As an amusing side-note, informants for the Mississippi State Sovereignty Commission must have thought that either Bishop Golden or one of the New York ministers was Dr. Martin Luther King Jr. Erle Johnston Jr., the director of the Mississippi State Sovereignty Commission, authored a memo on December 16 saying, "We have been informed that Rev. Martin Luther King was in Jackson, Saturday night, December 14, and held a meeting with a mixed group of students about plans to stage new sit-ins at Jackson churches. We are informed that Rev. King now has a house available to him on the Tougaloo College Campus at which future meetings will be held nearly every week." See SCR ID #: 3-74-1-51-1-1-1, Sovereignty Commission Online.

56. Cunningham, *Agony at Galloway*, 31–34; David P. Ver Nooy, interview with the author.

57. Campbell, *Civil Rights Chronicle*, 193–94; John A. Collins, interview with the author; Cunningham, *Agony at Galloway*, 33–34; "Four Arrested at Churches," *Clarion-Ledger*, December 16, 1963; Joan Trumpauer to "Greetings," 11 January 1963, 2, Reel 5, Joan Trumpauer Mulholland Papers; "New York Clerics Seized in Jackson," *New York Times*, December 16, 1963, 16; F. Herbert Skeete, interview with the author; David P. Ver Nooy, interview with the author.

58. Ibid.; F. Herbert Skeete, interview with the author; David P. Ver Nooy, interview with the author.

59. John A. Collins, interview with the author; Cunningham, *Agony at Galloway*, 34; F. Herbert Skeete, interview with the author; David P. Ver Nooy, interview with the author.

CHAPTER 11
"Jackson Has Become a Symbol of Our Common Sin"
Winter 1964

1. For more on Jackson movement activities during the winter and spring of 1964, see Chamberlain, "'And a Child Shall Lead the Way,'" 170–73.

2. Joan Trumpauer to "Greetings," 27 January 1964, 1, Reel 5, Joan Trumpauer Mulholland Papers; Mail List, Ministers Who Have Come, 2, Box 9, Folder 442, Ed King Collection, MDAH. The names of Presbyterian and Episcopalian clergy in Jackson who met with the Iowa group are unknown, though, given their previous record of meeting with other groups, they were most likely Dr. Moody McDill of Fondren Presbyterian and Rev. Christoph Keller of St. Andrew's Episcopal

3. Bill Friday to "Dear Joan," 4 March 1964, Box 9, Folder 444, Ed King Collection, MDAH; Joan Trumpauer to "Greetings," 27 January 1964, 1, Reel 5, Joan Trumpauer Mulholland Papers.

4. Clarice Campbell knew of the connection, but others outside the movement, such as Dr. W. J. Cunningham, did not. See Campbell, *Civil Rights Chronicle*, 196–97.

5. "Koinonia," *Mississippi Methodist Advocate*, January 15, 1964, 1; Cunningham, *Agony at Galloway*, 21; "Aspect, A Project of the Information and Education Committee, Jackson Citizens' Council," February Bulletin, 1964, Vol. 1, No. 7, 2, Archives and Special Collections, J. D. Williams Library, University of Mississippi. As explained in the *Mississippi Methodist Advocate* article, Koinoia is a Greek word that "expresses the bond which binds Christians to one another, to Christ, and to God." The Jackson Citizens' Council reprinted a copy of a recent MAMML information bulletin, which itself was a mimeographed copy of a letter that Rev. Robert Raines wrote, and that he originally included in a bulletin of his church.

6. Cunningham, *Agony at Galloway*, 21; "Aspect, A Project of the Information and Education Committee, Jackson Citizens' Council," February Bulletin, 1964, Vol. 1, No. 7, 2, Archives and Special Collections, J. D. Williams Library, University of Mississippi; Stevens, *Galloway Church History: Book I*, 149.

7. Joan Trumpauer to "Greetings," 27 January 1964, 2, Reel 5, Joan Trumpauer Mulholland Papers.

8. Cunningham, *Agony at Galloway*, 22; Stevens, *Galloway Church History*, 146–49. Stevens includes a copy of the telegram from Rev. Raines as well as several letters Dr. Cunningham received about the situation.

9. Martin Deppe, Mississippi Journal: A Report of a Church Visitation to Jackson, Mississippi, January 18–20, 1964, February 2, 1964, 1–2, Martin Deppe Private Papers; Joan Trumpauer to "Greetings," 27 January 1964, 2, Reel 5, Joan Trumpauer Mulholland Papers.

10. Rolly Kidder, Letter Home by Rolly Kidder, January 1964 Weekend, 1, Gerald Forshey Project; Darrell Reeck to "Dear Agitators," 12 March 1964, Box 9, Folder 446, Ed King Collection, MDAH.

11. Thomas Armstrong, interview with the author; Thomas Armstrong, "Panel #1: Jackson Witness—Students," (Church Desegregation and the Jackson, MS, Witness, Chicago, IL, October 4, 2008).

12. Rolly Kidder, Letter Home by Rolly Kidder, January 1964 Weekend, 1, Gerald Forshey Project; Darrell Reeck to "Dear Agitators," 12 March 1964, Box 9, Folder 446, Ed King Collection, MDAH.

13. Martin Deppe, Mississippi Journal: A Report of a Church Visitation to Jackson, Mississippi, January 18–20, 1964, February 2, 1964, 1–2, Martin Deppe Private Papers; Rolly Kidder, Letter Home by Rolly Kidder, January 1964 Weekend, 1–2, Gerald Forshey Project.

14. Martin Deppe, "Panel #2: Witness—Clergy Teams," (Church Desegregation and the Jackson, MS, Witness, Chicago, IL, October 4, 2008); Martin Deppe, Mississippi Journal: A Report of a Church Visitation to Jackson, Mississippi, January 18–20, 1964, February 2, 1964, 2–5, Martin Deppe Private Papers; Rolly Kidder, Letter Home by Rolly Kidder, January 1964 Weekend, 2, Gerald Forshey Project.

15. Ibid.

16. Ibid.

17. Martin Deppe, Mississippi Journal: A Report of a Church Visitation to Jackson, Mississippi, January 18–20, 1964, February 2, 1964, 5, Martin Deppe private papers. The idea of segregating students by sex as a response to racial integration orders was a popular one. With

three school districts in the state under orders to begin phasing in desegregation one grade at a time, beginning in the fall of 1964, Governor Paul Johnson announced his support for sexual segregation. See "Paul Proposes Pupil Segregation by Sex," *Jackson Daily News*, July 8, 1964, 1.

18. Ibid., 4; Darrell Reeck to "Dear Agitators," 12 March 1964, Box 9, Folder 446, Ed King Collection, MDAH; Nat Rogers, interview with the author.

19. Tom Boone, interview with the author.

20. Martin Deppe, Mississippi Journal: A Report of a Church Visitation to Jackson, Mississippi, January 18–20, 1964, February 2, 1964, 7, Martin Deppe Private Papers; Joan Trumpauer to "Greetings," 27 January 1964, 2, Reel 5, Joan Trumpauer Mulholland Papers. Tom Boone did not recall this particular conversation.

21. Franklin Clark Fry to Wade H. Koons, 27 December 1963, Fry Correspondence K 1963–64, Evangelical Lutheran Church Archives.

22. Raymond D. Wood to Franklin Clark Fry, 8 January 1964, Fry-Southeastern Synod 1963–64, Re Trinity Jackson, Mississippi, Evangelical Lutheran Church Archives; Report of the Rev. Wade H. Koons, Pastor, Annual Congregational Meeting, January 19, 1964, 4, Fry-Southeastern Synod 1963–64, Re Trinity Jackson, Mississippi, Evangelical Lutheran Church Archives.

23. Charles W. Koons, interview with the author; "Koons Resigns as Pastor of Jackson Church," *Jackson Daily News*, January 27, 1964, 7; Wade Koons to Raymond Wood, 20 January 1964, 1–2, Fry-Southeastern Synod 1963–64, Re Trinity Jackson, Mississippi; Wade Koons to Franklin Clark Fry, 27 January 1964, 1–2, Fry Correspondence K 1963–64, Evangelical Lutheran Church Archives; Report of the Rev. Wade H. Koons, Pastor, Annual Congregational Meeting, January 19, 1964, 4–6, Fry-Southeastern Synod 1963–64, Re Trinity Jackson, Mississippi, Evangelical Lutheran Church Archives; Joan Trumpauer to "Dear," 12 December 1963, 3, Reel 5, Joan Trumpauer Mulholland Papers; Joan Trumpauer to "Greetings," 18 February 1964, 4, Reel 5, Joan Trumpauer Mulholland Papers.

24. "Historical Events," 1–2, Ascension Lutheran Church Archives; "Membership Installation," Ascension Lutheran Church Archives; Jean Kidd, interview with the author; Henry M. McKay, interview with the author; Jack Moskowitz, interview with the author. "Historical Events" indicates that of the thirty-two people who left Trinity Lutheran, it was understood that those living in southwest Jackson would form the nucleus for a new mission church. The southwest Jackson mission, which became Resurrection Lutheran Church, called its first pastor, Rev. Jack Zipperer, in June 1964.

25. Anne Carpenter to Rev. Ed King, 13 November 1963, Box 9, Folder 446, Ed King Collection, MDAH; "Ministers and Other Mailings," 2–3, Box 9, Folder 448, Ed King Collection, MDAH. Like the visiting teams before them, this group planned for the possibility of arrests and the need to post bail. The Pittsburgh-area men wrote down the name of the individual Rev. Ed King was supposed to contact if they were jailed, while Anne Carpenter wrote, "Don't call my parents!" Instead, she wrote that Rev. King should call the chaplain at North Central College, seminarian Rolly Kidder, or Rev. Richard Tholin. See Ministers and Other Mailings, 2–3, Box 9, Folder 448, Ed King Collection, MDAH.

26. Anne Carpenter, Anne Carpenter Explains Civil Rights Experience, Box 9, Folder 444, Ed King Collection, MDAH; Joan Trumpauer to "Greetings," 18 February 1964, 4, Reel 5,

Joan Trumpauer Mulholland Papers; Fred Villinger to Joan Trumpauer, 11 March 1964, Box 9, Folder 444, Ed King Collection, MDAH.

27. Ibid.; Clarice Campbell, *Civil Rights Chronicle*, 200; Randy Lunsford to Joan Trumpauer, 6 March 1964, Box 9, Folder 444, Ed King Collection, MDAH; Michael Kundrat to Joan Trumpauer, 6 March 1964, Box 9, Folder 444, Ed King Collection, MDAH.

28. Anne Carpenter, Anne Carpenter Explains Civil Rights Experience, Box 9, Folder 444, Ed King Collection, MDAH; Ed King to Robert Raines, 10 February 1964, Box 9, Folder 446; Randy Lunsford to Joan Trumpauer, 6 March 1964, Box 9, Folder 444, Ed King Collection, MDAH; Michael Kundrat to Joan Trumpauer, 6 March 1964, Box 9, Folder 444, Ed King Collection, MDAH; Joan Trumpauer to "Greetings," 18 February 1964, 4, Reel 5, Joan Trumpauer Mulholland Collection; Fred Villinger to Joan Trumpauer, 11 March 1964, Box 9, Folder 444, Ed King Collection, MDAH. The group at the evening service at Galloway included Rev. Ed King and Memphis Norman.

29. Michael Kundrat to Joan Trumpauer, 6 March 1963, Box 9, Folder 444, Ed King Collection, MDAH; Randy Lunsford to Marvin Franklin, 15 March 1963, Box 9, Folder 444, Ed King Collection, MDAH; Randy Lunsford to Joan Trumpauer, 6 March 1963, Box 9, Folder 444, Ed King Collection, MDAH.

30. Bill Hutchinson, interview with the author; Bill Hutchinson, "Memorial Day Memories of Mississippi," *Your Smithfield Magazine*, May 2008, 77; Joan Trumpauer to "Dear," 12 December 1963, 2, Reel 5, Joan Trumpauer Mulholland Papers; "Minutes of the Called Meeting of the Fondren Presbyterian Church Held in the John Campbell Officers' Room on January 26, 1964, at 4:30 p.m.," *Fondren Presbyterian Church*, Volume 10, Fondren Presbyterian Church Archives.

31. Joan Trumpauer to "Greetings," 18 February 1964, 4, Reel 5, Joan Trumpauer Mulholland Papers.

32. Fred Villinger to Ed King, 9 February 1964, Box 9, Folder 446, Ed King Collection, MDAH. Rev. Schrading was Rev. Fred Villinger's supervisor at the United Campus Ministry at the University of Pittsburgh

33. Joan Trumpauer to "Greetings," 18 February 1964, 4–5, Reel 5, Joan Trumpauer Mulholland Papers. The name of the Baptist church is unknown.

34. Ibid., 5.

35. Ibid., 5.

36. Doris Browne, interview with the author.

37. Joan Trumpauer to "Greetings," 18 February 1964, 5, Reel 5, Joan Trumpauer Mulholland Papers.

38. "Diary of Bishop Gerow, Volume VI, 1960–66," 1662, Richard O. Gerow Collection, Archives of the Diocese of Jackson. The church visits to Catholic churches in Jackson coincided with calls to integrate Catholic schools. In his entry the same day he describes the visit to Holy Family Church, Bishop Gerow offers his own views. He concludes, "The Negroes are welcome in our churches, but to attempt to integrate our schools at this time of strong tensions would be disastrous."

39. Joan Trumpauer to "Greetings," 18 February 1964, 5, Reel 5, Joan Trumpauer Mulholland Papers. Joan Trumpauer noted that this was the second visit to Norwood Presbyterian Church, and that ushers there admitted an integrated group to worship on a previous occasion.

40. Campbell, *Civil Rights Chronicle*, 201; "Danger on the Road," *Voice of the Movement*, February 27, 1964, 3, Box 2, Folder 80, Ed King Collection, MDAH.

41. Beatrice Gotthelf, interview with the author; "Diary of Bishop Gerow, Volume VI, 1960–66," 1652, Richard O. Gerow Collection, Archives of the Diocese of Jackson.

42. The other white ministers who attended were Bishop Joseph Brunini, Bishops John Allin and Duncan Gray Sr., of the Episcopal Church, Bishop Marvin Franklin of the Methodist Church, Rabbi Perry Nussbaum, Rev. Moody McDill of Fondren Presbyterian, Rev. Seth Granberry of Capitol Street Methodist, Rev. W. J. Cunningham of Galloway Memorial Methodist, and Rev. Robert Lawrence of Covenant Presbyterian.

43. "Diary of Bishop Gerow, Volume VI, 1960–66," 1660–1661, Richard O. Gerow Collection, Archives of the Diocese of Jackson.

44. Ibid., 1662; Campbell, *Civil Rights Chronicle*, 204; "Danger on the Road," *Voice of the Movement*, February 27, 1964, 3, Box 2, Folder 80, Ed King Collection, MDAH; Bill Hutchinson, interview with the author; Bill Hutchinson, "Memorial Day Memories of Mississippi," *Your Smithfield Magazine*, May 2008, 79; Joan Trumpauer to "Greetings," 11 March 1964, 3–4, Reel 5, Joan Trumpauer Mulholland Papers; "School Is Center of Race Protests," *New York Times*, March 15, 1964, 48; Statement, March 5, 1964, Box 9, Folder 431, Ed King Collection, MDAH.

45. Campbell, *Civil Rights Chronicle*, 205; Pat Hutchinson to "Dear Family and Friends," 9 March 1964, Box 1, Folder 3, Garner (John and Margrit) Letters, MDAH.

46. "Danger on the Road," *Voice of the Movement*, February 27, 1964, 3, Box 2, Folder 80, Ed King Collection, MDAH; Joan Trumpauer to "Greetings," 11 March 1964, 4–5, Reel 5, Joan Trumpauer Mulholland Papers.

47. "Tougaloo Measure Is Introduced," *Clarion-Ledger*, February 21, 1964; "School Is Center of Race Protests," *New York Times*, March 15, 1964, 48.

48. Joan Trumpauer to "Greetings," 11 March 1964, 4–5, Reel 5, Joan Trumpauer Mulholland Papers.

49. "Statement, March 5, 1964," Box 9, Folder 431, Ed King Collection, MDAH.

50. Joan Trumpauer to "Greetings," 11 March 1964, 3–4, Reel 5, Joan Trumpauer Mulholland Papers.

CHAPTER 12
Easter in Jackson
March 1964

1. James K. Mathews, "The Bishops Speak on Race," *Christian Advocate*, January 2, 1964, 7–8.

2. James Sellers, "Church and Race: An Overview," *Christian Advocate*, January 16, 1964, 8–9.

3. Richard C. Raines Jr., "On Bishop Mathews and Race," *Christian Advocate*, February 27, 1964, 13.

4. Joan Trumpauer to "Greetings," 29 April 1964, 3, Reel 5, Joan Trumpauer Mulholland Papers.

5. King, "White Church, Part IV," 107.

6. Local press accounts mention that ushers turned away integrated groups at Capitol Street Methodist Church, Galloway Memorial Methodist Church, and St. Luke's Methodist Church on Palm Sunday, though it remained unclear whether those were morning visits or referred to events that evening. See "Usher Minister from Church as Negro Plea Made," *Jackson Daily News*, March 23, 1964, 16; Joan Trumpauer wrote that she was not exactly sure, but thought that Briarwood Methodist, St. Luke's Methodist, and Fondren Presbyterian were all visited that morning. See Joan Trumpauer to "Greetings," 29 April 1964, 3, Reel 5, Joan Trumpauer Mulholland Papers.

7. Cunningham, *Agony at Galloway*, 50; King, "White Church, Part IV," 105–7; Statement by Dr. Madabusi Sevithri, March 23, 1964, 1–3, Series 1, Civil Rights and Methodism (Jackson, MS) Collection, Mississippi Department of Archives and History. Dr. Savithri's statement is also reprinted in full in *Agony at Galloway*. See pp. 47–50.

8. King, "White Church, Part IV," 103–5; Statement by Dr. Madabusi Savithri, March 23, 1964, 1–3, Series 1, Civil Rights and Methodism (Jackson, MS) Collection, Mississippi Department of Archives and History.

9. "Violence in the Churches," *Voice of the Movement*, March 27, 1964, 6, Box 9, Folder 450, Ed King Collection, MDAH; "Shove Hindu Woman Out of Two Churches," *Chicago Tribune*, March 23, 1964, B14; "Two Churches Eject an Indian Scholar in Mississippi City," *New York Times*, March 23, 1964, 19; "King Ushered From Services; Mixers Barred," *Clarion-Ledger*, March 24, 1964, 11; "Usher Minister from Church as Negro Plea Made," *Jackson Daily News*, March 23, 1964, 16.

10. "Statement by Dr. Madabusi Sevithri, March 23, 1964," 3.

11. Campbell, *Civil Rights Chronicle*, 199, 204; "Statement by Dr. Madabusi Sevithri," March 23, 1964, 3.

12. Cunningham, *Agony at Galloway*, 50–54. The chapter in which Dr. Cunningham reprints Dr. Savithri's statement to her embassy and gives his response is appropriately—if hyperbolically—titled, "A Possible Diplomatic Incident."

13. Jeffrey Hopper, interview with the author; Van Bogard Dunn, Jeffrey Hopper, Paul M. Minus, and Everett Tilson, Report on Trip to Jackson, Mississippi, Easter 1964, transcript, 1964, Methodist Theological School in Ohio Library.

14. "Integration in Our Churches," *Aspect, A Project of the Information and Education Committee, Jackson Citizens' Council*, March Bulletin, 1964, Vol. 1, No. 8, 1, Archives and Special Collections, J. D. Williams Library, University of Mississippi; Shattuck, *Episcopalians and Race*, 118; James P. Dees, Statement of the Most Rev. James P. Dees, Presiding Bishop of the Anglican Orthodox Church, Made When He Resigned as Priest from the Protestant Episcopal Church on November 15, 1963, 2, North Carolina Collection, Wilson Library, The University of North Carolina at Chapel Hill. Theological differences were at the forefront of Rev. Dees's mind in deciding to resign and lead a breakaway denomination. He pointed first to a recent statement by the Archbishop of Canterbury, claiming that heaven would be a place for many non-Christians, including atheists, but Dees's statement also laid bare his views on race. Like many other racial conservatives rallying in opposition to the Civil Rights Act, then before Congress, Rev. Dees framed the civil rights program and the legislation forced intrusions

into the rights of individuals. He denounced the Episcopal Church's involvement with the National Council of Churches, which, among other beliefs and platforms, stood for "forced racial integration."(5) In a separate section, he wrote that he was gravely concerned for his country, whose constitution was based "on the basic economic factor of private property and on concern for the preservation of our national sovereignty and individual freedom,"(6) a clear reference to the legislation pending before Congress. Finally, he expressed dismay that the Episcopal Church was "actively working to destroy race, peace, and American culture by advocating the use of force by the Federal Government."(7)

15. Jeffrey Hopper, interview with the author. The official name of the school is Methodist Theological School in Ohio.

16. At the time, Bishop Franklin oversaw Western Tennessee, in addition to the two white Mississippi conferences. Dr. Dunn's participation would therefore be the first witness directly involving a minister from within Bishop Franklin's jurisdiction.

17. Van Bogard Dunn Interview, Methodist Theological School in Ohio, Oral History Conducted by Rev. Dr. Paul Grass in Winter 1994, from the private library of Rev. William H. Casto Jr., PhD, professor emeritus, Methodist Theological School in Ohio; Gerry H. Dunn, interview with the author; Susan Dunn, interview with the author; Paul Minus, interview with the author.

18. Oral History of Everett Tilson, Recorded June 3, 2003, Interviewed by K. G. Bennett, Nashville Room, Nashville Public Library, Everett Tilson Papers; Jeffrey Hopper, interview with the author; Paul Minus, interview with the author; Reiff, *Born of Conviction*, 191. For more on the Nashville sit-ins and James Lawson's expulsion from Vanderbilt, see James M. Lawson, interview with Dallas A. Blanchard, October 24, 1983, Interview F-0029, transcript, Southern Oral History Program Collection, the university library, University of North Carolina at Chapel Hill.

19. Ted Weber to Jeffrey Hopper, 23 March 1964, Correspondence 1960–91, Box 8, Folder 48, Theodore R. Weber Papers, Pitts Theology Library Archives, Emory University.

20. David James Randolph, interview with the author.

21. "Evanston Prof Arrested at Church Door," *Chicago Tribune*, March 30, 1964, 10.

22. David James Randolph, "A Report to the Dean and the Faculty of the Theological School of Drew University," April 2, 1964, 1, Everett Tilson Papers.

23. Van Bogard Dunn, Jeffrey Hopper, Paul M. Minus, and Everett Tilson, "Report on Trip to Jackson, Mississippi, Easter 1964," transcript, 1964, Methodist Theological School in Ohio Library.

24. Ibid.; Paul Minus, interview with the author; Tyler Thompson, "Another Pilgrimage to Jackson," *Christian Century*, April 22, 1964, 511–12.

25. David James Randolph, interview with the author; David James Randolph, A Report to the Dean and the Faculty of the Theological School of Drew University, April 2, 1964, 1, Everett Tilson Papers.

26. Van Bogard Dunn, Jeffrey Hopper, Paul M. Minus, and Everett Tilson, Report on Trip to Jackson, Mississippi, Easter 1964, transcript, 1964, Methodist Theological School in Ohio Library.

27. "Bishops Seek to Bolster Council Stand on Race," *Christian Advocate*, April 23, 1964, 21; James K. Mathews, *A Global Odyssey: The Autobiography of James K. Mathews* (Nashville, TN: Abingdon Press, 2000), 273–74; James Mathews, "A Communication: Easter in Jackson," *Christian Century*, April 15, 1964, 479.

28. "Graham Speaks at Birmingham Rally," *Baptist Record*, April 2, 1964, 2.

29. Stevens, *Galloway Church History, Book I*, 153.

30. Cunningham, *Agony at Galloway*, 55–56; Mathews, *A Global Odyssey*, 273–74; James Mathews, "A Communication: Easter in Jackson," *Christian Century*, April 15, 1964, 479; "Church Mixing Blocked," *Clarion-Ledger*, March 20, 1964, 1; "Church Mixing Group Arrested Here Sunday," *Jackson Daily News*, March 30, 1964, 6; "Easter in Jackson," *Concern*, April 15, 1964, 15; Nat Rogers, interview with the author; "News Release, March 31, 1964, Commission on Public Relations and Methodist Information, the General News Service of the Methodist Church, J. E. Lowery," Box 144-2-6, Folder 11, Jackson, Mississippi, Administrative Records of the Division of World Peace of the General Board of Church and Society, GCAH; "News Release, the Nashville-Birmingham Area of the Methodist Church, Charles F. Golden, Resident Bishop," Box 9, Folder 429, Ed King Collection, MDAH; "Seven Ministers Held in Jackson," *New York Times*, March 30, 1964, 14. Nat Rogers confirmed that he was the one who turned the bishops away, but he did not recall the conversation with Dr. Cunningham.

31. Mathews, "A Communication: Easter in Jackson," *Christian Century*, April 15, 1964, 479–80.

32. Dittmer, *Local People*, 107; Thompson, "A Communication: Another Pilgrimage to Jackson," *Christian Century*, April 22, 1964, 512; Van Bogard Dunn, Jeffrey Hopper, Paul M. Minus, and Everett Tilson, Report on Trip to Jackson, Mississippi, Easter 1964, transcript, 1964, Methodist Theological School in Ohio Library.

33. Ibid.; David James Randolph, A Report to the Dean and the Faculty of the Theological School of Drew University, April 2, 1964, 2, Everett Tilson Papers; A Statement Prepared by Van Bogard Dunn, A. Jeffrey Hopper, Paul M. Minus Jr., and Everett Tilson, Jackson, Mississippi, Box 1444-2-6, Folder 11, Administrative Records of the Division of World Peace of the General Board of Church and Society, GCAH; Tyler Thompson, "Another Pilgrimage to Jackson," *Christian Century*, April 22, 1964, 512.

34. Ibid.; "Seven Methodist Clerics Assail Their Church After Trial in South," *New York Times*, April 1, 1964, 26.

35. Ibid.; "Church Mixers Convicted, Plan to Appeal," *Jackson Daily News*, March 31, 1964, 15; "Judge Chides Nine in Church Mix Try," *Clarion-Ledger*, March 31, 1964, 4.

36. Cunningham, *Agony at Galloway*, 56–57.

37. W. J. Cunningham to Charles F. Golden, 7 April 1964, Box 1553-6-4, Folder 3, Correspondence 1960–64, Peter Murray Collection, GCAH; Charles F. Golden to W. J. Cunningham, 15 April 1964, Box 1553-6-4, Folder 3, Correspondence 1960–64, Peter Murray Collection, GCAH.

38. J. P. Stafford to Charles F. Golden, 30 March 1964, Box 1553-6-4, Folder 3, Correspondence 1960–64, Peter Murray Collection, GCAH; Charles F. Golden to J. P. Stafford, 15 April 1964, Box 1553-6-4, Folder 3, Correspondence 1960–64, Peter Murray Collection, GCAH; Jim L. Waits to Marvin A. Franklin, 3 April 1964, Box 1553-6-4, Folder 3, Correspondence

1960–64, Peter Murray Collection, GCAH; Charles F. Golden to Jim L. Waits, 16 April 1964, Box 1553-6-4, Folder 3, Correspondence 1960–64, Peter Murray Collection, GCAH.

39. "The Travail of Mississippi Methodism," *Mississippi Methodist Advocate*, April 8, 1964, 3.

40. Randolph, interview with the author; Randolph, A Report to the Dean and the Faculty of the Theological School of Drew University, April 2, 1964, 2, Everett Tilson Papers; A Statement Prepared by Van Bogard Dunn, A. Jeffrey Hopper, Paul M. Minus Jr., and Everett Tilson, 1, Jackson, Mississippi, Box 1444-2-6, Folder 11, Administrative Records of the Division of World Peace of the General Board of Church and Society, GCAH; Tyler Thompson, "Another Pilgrimage to Jackson," *Christian Century*, April 22, 1964, 512.

CHAPTER 13
"The Nation Needs Our Witness Now"
April 1964

1. "Report of Fellowship of Loyal Churchmen, A Movement for Loyalty to United Methodism," *Mississippi Methodist Advocate*, March 5, 1964, 2.

2. King, "White Church, Part IV," 129–31.

3. "Methodist Group Endorses Advocate Editorial Stand," *Jackson Daily News*, April 14, 1964, 4.

4. "Methodist Segregation Group Raps 'Fellowship,'" *Clarion-Ledger*, April 16, 1964, 4.

5. "Historical Events," 1–2, Ascension Lutheran Church Archives; Henry M. McKay, interview with the author; Charles Koons, interview with the author; Jack Zipperer, interview with the author.

6. "Historical Events," 2, Ascension Lutheran Church Archives.

7. Ibid.; Henry M. McKay, interview with the author. One of the black students, John Henry Brown, became a member of Ascension Lutheran Church in November 1965 and, in 1967, he received a commission as a Lutheran missionary to Tanzania. Dr. McKay later recalled that his pastoral relationship with Brown was important to his ministry. He said he cried with "affirmation and joy" when Brown told him he had been called to Tanzania. The news came at a time when Dr. McKay feared for his life, as he had just gotten off the phone with Dr. Moody McDill of Fondren Presbyterian, who told him he had found a shoebox full of explosives in his mailbox.

8. "Lutherans Say Removal [*sic*] Racial References," *Jackson Daily News*, April 17, 1964, 14; "Synod Meet Coming Here," *Clarion-Ledger*, April 17, 1964, 8.

9. Joan Trumpauer to "Greetings," 29 April 1964, 3, Reel 5, Joan Trumpauer Mulholland Papers.

10. "Aspect, A Project of the Information and Education Committee, Jackson Citizens' Council," March Bulletin, 1964, Vol. 1, No. 8, 1, Archives and Special Collections, J. D. Williams Library, University of Mississippi; "A Resolution," April 10, 1964, 1–2, SCR ID#: 6–38–0-1–2-1–1, 6–38–0-1–3-1–1, Sovereignty Commission Online; "The Organizing Committee, Holy Trinity Church" to "Dear Fellow Churchmen," 16 April 1964, 1, SCR ID#: 6–38–0-1–1-1–1, Sovereignty Commission Online; "Conservative Anglican Church Formed Here," *Jackson Daily News*, April 28, 1964, 12; "May 21, 1964, Holy Trinity Church (Anglican)," SCR ID#: 6–38–0-3–1-1–1,

Sovereignty Commission Online; "New Location Acquired by Holy Trinity," *Jackson Daily News*, July 10, 1964, 22. A newspaper advertisement was next to the latter article. Holy Trinity clearly sought to steer disaffected Methodist church people to their congregation. See "An Open Letter to Methodist Laymen in the Jackson Area," newspaper advertisement, unattributed, undated, Box 2, Folder 5, Robert E. Bergmark Papers, Millsaps College Archives.

11. "Open Door Worship Policy Proposed by Presbyteries," *Jackson Daily News*, April 27, 1964, 1; "Church to Drop All-Negro Units," *New York Times*, April 28, 1964, 29; "Presbyterian Mixing Stand Draws Protest," *Jackson Daily News*, April 28, 1964, 15 (quotes from Dr. Miller). The Central Mississippi Presbytery had voted earlier to oppose the NCC's Delta Project, saying the project would "promote lawlessness and the flagrant violation of the inherent rights of all the citizens of the state of Mississippi." See "Presbytery Opposing NCC 'Operation Delta,'" *Clarion-Ledger*, April 17, 1964, 8.

12. "Presbyterians Eye Implementation of Strong Civil Rights Policy," *Jackson Daily News*, April 27, 1964, 8. The story of church desegregation efforts in Memphis is covered thoroughly in Stephen R. Haynes's *The Last Segregated Hour: The Memphis Kneel-Ins and the Campaign for Southern Church Desegregation* (New York: Oxford University Press, 2012).

13. Philip Wogaman, "Focus on the Central Jurisdiction," *Christian Century*, October 23, 1963, 1296.

14. For an excellent comparison of the competing visions of the Committee of Thirty-Six and the Committee of Five ahead of the 1964 general conference, see the following article for essays written by the groups' respective chairmen, Charles C. Parlin and Dr. W. Astor Kirk. "Methodism's Symbol of Racial Segregation," *Concern*, April 15, 1964, 7–9.

15. John F. Baggett and Philip M. Dripps, "Christian Unity, the Methodist Church, and Jackson," *Behold*, December 1963, 5–8; H. Eugene Peacock, "How Shall We Work Together to Achieve the Goals?," *Behold*, December 1963, 9–12. Dr. H. Eugene Peacock was pastor of Dexter Avenue Methodist Church in Montgomery, and the essay was taken from a sermon he delivered at the Chicago Temple in November 1963 during a special service for those interested in the Jackson witness.

16. Gerald Forshey to "Dear Joanie, et al," March 6, 1964, 1–2, Box 9, Folder 444, Ed King Collection, MDAH; New York Area Methodists for Church Renewal to "Dear Fellow Methodists," 23 April 1964, Box 2135-5-4, Folder 6, Methodists for Church Renewal 1964, Methodist Federation for Social Action, GCAH; "Methodists Plan 'Rally For Freedom,'" *Jackson Daily News*, April 28, 1964, 19. The pilgrimage was coordinated by Rev. Gerald Forshey, a member of the Chicago team whom Jackson police arrested at Capitol Street Methodist on October 20, while Rev. Michael L. Kundrat, who was part of the delegation from the Pittsburgh area who came to Jackson in early February, organized the local accommodations and other arrangements.

17. *His Name in Vain* (Jackson, MS: sponsored by a voluntary committee of Jackson, MS, Methodists, 1964). Copies of *His Name in Vain* can be found at the Mississippi Department of Archives and History and the John C. Satterfield Collection, Box 36, Folder 300.52, Archives and Special Collections, J. D. Williams Library, University of Mississippi. Those who contributed essays for *His Name in Vain* included John Satterfield, Rev. Seth Granberry, Thomas H. Watkins, and Nat Rogers.

18. Gerald Forshey to "Dear Joanie, et al," March 6, 1964, 1, Box 9, Folder 444, Ed King Collection, MDAH; "Methodists Plan 'Rally For Freedom,'" *Jackson Daily News*, April 28, 1964, 19; Ida Hannah Sanders, interview with the author; Austin Moore, interview with the author; Joan Trumpauer Mulholland, interview with the author; John Garner to Leon Moore (secretary, general conference), 16 April 1964, Box 1433-6-7, Folder 3, John B. Garner Case, 1964–65 (1981–001), Administrative Records of the Division of Human Relations and Economic Affairs of the General Board of Church and Society, GCAH; King, "White Church, Part IV," 175; Lee H. Reiff to "Dear Fathers and Brethren," undated, Box 9, Folder 441, Ed King Collection, MDAH.

19. Ralph Lord Roy, "MCR, Pittsburgh, and the Future," May 15, 1964, 1, Box 2135-5-4, Folder 6, Methodists for Church Renewal, Methodist Federation of Social Action, GCAH; *Where We Begin* (Pittsburgh: Methodists for Church Renewal, 1964), 1–4, Box 2135-5-4, Folder 6, Methodists for Church Renewal 1964, Methodist Federation for Social Action, GCAH; *Why We Witness* (Pittsburgh: Methodists for Church Renewal, 1964), 1–4, Box 9, Folder 449, Ed King Collection, MDAH.

20. "Real Issues," *Social Questions Bulletin*, May-June 1964, 37.

21. "Methodists Adopt Voluntary Mixing, Southern-Supported Plan Survives Lengthy Hassle," *Jackson Daily News*, May 1, 1964, 1; Margaret Frakes, "Methodists at Pittsburgh: I," *Christian Century*, May 20, 1964, 663.

22. "Kneel-In Scores Methodist Stand," *New York Times*, May 3, 1964, 78; John A. Collins, interview with the author; Paul Minus, interview with the author; Fitts Herbert Skeete, interview with the author; Richard Teller, interview with the author; Al Tomer, interview with the author. Rev. Minus recalled a particularly ironic moment during the general conference. He and his wife went to lunch at a crowded restaurant and were seated at a table with Dr. J. W. Leggett, the district superintendent of the Mississippi Methodist Conference. Dr. Leggett recognized Rev. Minus from their meeting in Jackson, but the two did not speak during this lunch.

23. King, "White Church, Part IV," 176–77. Marti Turnipseed married Millsaps graduate Charles Moore and died in a car accident in 1972. For her civil rights efforts, members of Dexter Avenue Baptist Church in Montgomery, Alabama, honored her with a memorial window.

24. Ibid., 177–79; "Mississippi Lambasted by Tougaloo Chaplain," *Jackson Daily News*, May 2, 1964, 1; King, "White Church, Part IV," 178.

25. *Tonight We Offer Ourselves in a "Living Memorial" for Church Renewal* (Pittsburgh: Methodists for Church Renewal, 1964), 1–4, Box 9, Folder 449, Ed King Collection, MDAH.

26. "Methodist Church General Conference, Pittsburgh, PA, May, 1964," undated photographs, Edwin King private papers.

27. "Kneel-In Scores Methodist Stand," *New York Times*, May 3, 1964, 78; "1,000 Demonstrate against Methodist Integration Delay," *Chicago Sun-Times*, May 3, 1964, 2, 24; Accompanying the *Chicago Sun-Times* and *New York Times* stories was a photograph of Austin Moore carrying the burned cross as he ascended the arena ramp. The local Northeast edition of the Sunday, May 3, *New York Times* carried the picture and the article on the front page.

28. William Astor Kirk, "Committee of Five" (Church Desegregation and the Jackson, MS, Witness, First Methodist Church, Chicago, Illinois, October 4, 2008); "Real Issues," *Social*

Questions Bulletin, May–June 1964, 37; "Merger Gains Tentative OK," *Jackson Daily News,* May 5, 1964, 1.

    29. "Methodist Racial Resolution Argued," *Jackson Daily News,* May 7, 1964, F2.

    30. Gerald Forshey to "Joanie," May 15, 1964, Box 9, Folder 444, Ed King Collection, MDAH; King, "White Church, Part IV," 173.

    31. "Methodist Racial Resolution Argued," *Jackson Daily News,* May 7, 1964, F2.

    32. "Methodists Hear Talk on Conference," *Jackson Daily News,* May 23, 1964, 5.

    33. "Satterfield Urges Stay in Church," *Clarion Ledger,* May 27, 1964, 1, 9; John Satterfield, "Bishop Franklin, Brothers and Sisters ...," undated, 1, 6–7. Box 36, Folder 300.52, John C. Satterfield Collection; John Satterfield, "Extracts From Report to the Mississippi Conference ...," May 26, 1964, 1–2, Box 36, Folder 300.52, John C. Satterfield Collection.

    34. "Satterfield Urges Stay in Church," *Clarion-Ledger,* May 27, 1964, 1, 9; John Satterfield, "Bishop Franklin, Brothers and Sisters ...," undated, 4–6, Box 36, Folder 300.52, John C. Satterfield Collection. The body of this document—especially compared to the newspaper report—makes it clear that the speech consisted of the prepared remarks of John Satterfield at the May 26 session of the Mississippi annual conference. The latter quote is from the *Clarion-Ledger* and is slightly different from what was in his prepared speech.

    35. "Methodists Hear Report of General Conference," *Jackson Daily News,* June 5, 1964, 3. A month later, and just days after President Johnson signed the Civil Rights Act, Bishop Franklin gave the Episcopal address at the Southeastern Jurisdictional Conference of the Methodist Church. He stressed that human relations—and "Negro" relations in particular—were the most pressing concerns in the country. He urged Christians to ask themselves, "What is human, what is Christian?" He proclaimed that all races should be accorded equal rights, whether it was in education, housing, job opportunities, or in the courts. Yet he then said, "Forced segregation cannot be defended nor will forced integration usher in an era of brotherhood and good will." In the effort to shore up resistance to the new civil rights legislation, the *Jackson Daily News* emphasized the last point to its readers. See "Deplores 'Forcing,' Bishop Franklin Urges Human Relations Effort," *Jackson Daily News,* July 8, 1964, 1.

    36. King, "White Church, Part IV," 172.

    37. Gerald Forshey, "Report on the Pilgrimage to Pittsburgh," undated, 1, Gerald Forshey Project.

    38. King, "White Church, Part IV," 181.

    39. Forshey to "Joanie," 15 May 1964, Box 9, Folder 444, Ed King Collection, MDAH; Forshey, "Report on the Pilgrimage to Pittsburgh," undated, 1–2, Gerald Forshey Project. The charred cross remained an important reminder and symbol for Rev. Gerald Forshey. He later commissioned an artist, John Kearney, to add a sculpted crucifix, and he displayed the cross in his living room. After Rev. Forshey died in 2009, his wife, Florence Forshey, presented the cross, called "Crucifixion," to the First United Methodist Church of Chicago at the Chicago Temple, where it can now be viewed publicly.

    40. Joan Trumpauer to Martin Deppe, 29 May 1964, Box 9, Folder 444, Ed King Collection, MDAH; Joan Trumpauer to Gerald Forshey, 29 May 1964, Box 9, Folder 444, Ed King Collection, MDAH; Joan Trumpauer to Michael Kundrat, 29 May 1964, Box 9, Folder 444, Ed King Collection, MDAH; Joan Trumpauer to Darrell Reeck, 29 May 1964, Box 9, Folder 444,

Ed King Collection, MDAH; Joan Trumpauer to Sally Smith, 29 May 1964, Box 9, Folder 444, Ed King Collection, MDAH; Joan Trumpauer to Dick Tholin, 29 May 1964, Box 9, Folder 444, Ed King Collection, MDAH; Joan Trumpauer to Dave Twigg, 29 May 1964, Box 9, Folder 444, Ed King Collection, MDAH.

41. King, "White Church, Part IV," 192–94.

CHAPTER 14
"The Church Needs a Scapegoat"
1964–73

1. Rita Schwerner Bender, interview with the author; Seth Cagin and Philip Dray, *We Are Not Afraid: The Story of Goodman, Schwerner, and Chaney and the Civil Rights Campaign for Mississippi* (New York: MacMillan, 1988), 11, 262–68; William Bradford Huie, *Three Lives for Mississippi* (New York: WCC Books, 1965), 89–90; King, "White Church, Part IV," 201–7. Police officers originally detained the three for speeding (though they had a flat tire) near First Methodist Church in Philadelphia. The church had just called a new senior pastor, Rev. Clay Lee, the assistant pastor of Galloway Memorial Methodist Church in Jackson.

2. The Civil Rights Act of 1964 took effect with the stroke of the president's pen on July 2, 1964. The Jackson Chamber of Commerce and Mayor Allen Thompson—both vocal opponents of the bill—called on city businesses and residents to comply. Of the white religious leaders and moderate or liberal clergy left in the city, only Bishop Richard O. Gerow of the Natchez-Jackson Diocese of the Catholic Church in Mississippi spoke out in the local press to urge compliance with the new legislation. Dr. W. J. Cunningham wrote that he gave a sermon specifically aimed at the young people of the church the Sunday after the bill's passage. He pleaded with the congregation to accept that it was the law of the land, and declared that as good citizens, drawing on the teachings of Paul, Christians must obey the law. In contrast, Governor Paul Johnson instructed citizens to resist compliance until courts considered a challenge to the law. The Jackson Citizens' Council urged defiance and called for a boycott of any white business owner who submitted to the law. On July 7, 1964, a federal judge delivered his final order to Jackson to begin desegregating its public schools in the fall. See "Bishop Urges Catholics to Accept Law," *Jackson Daily News*, July 3, 1964, 1; "Boycott of Integrated Firms Is Asked by Citizens' Council," *Jackson Daily News*, July 7, 1964, 7; Cunningham, *Agony at Galloway*, 71; Charles Sallis and John Quincy Adams, "Desegregation in Jackson, Mississippi," in *Southern Businessmen and Desegregation* (Baton Rouge: Louisiana State University Press, 1982), 243–50.

3. Cases for the thirty-seven defendants were grouped into three separate actions. Those arrested on October 6 and October 20 became *Poole v. City of Jackson*. Those arrested in November 1963 fell under *City of Jackson v. Hougland*. Those arrested in December 1963 and March 1964 comprised *City of Jackson v. John Collins*. The federal suit seeking an injunction to prevent further arrests was *Poole v. Barnett*.

4. R. Jess Brown, "Cases Set in City Court, Jackson, Miss.," memo, undated, Box 9, Folder 438, Ed King Collection, MDAH; John M. Pratt to Grover Bagby, 9 December 1964, 2, Everett Tilson Papers; John M. Pratt, Report on Legal Proceedings and Bail, 1, February 20, 1964, Box

47, Folder 31, National Council of Churches in Christ in the United States, Division of Christian Life and Mission Records, 1945–73, PHS; Fitts Herbert Skeete, interview with the author.

5. Brief for Appellants, US Court of Appeals for the Fifth Circuit, No. 21196, Bette Poole, et al., Appellants, Against Ross R. Barnett, et al., January 27, 1964, 7, Box 50, Folder 15, National Council of Churches of Christ in the United States of America, Division of Christian Life and Mission Records, 1945–73, PHS.

6. Ibid., 8–58; John Pratt to Edward Wright, May 20, 1965, 2, Box 1422-6-7, Folder 2, Jackson Arrest Cases Folder 2, 1963–67, Administrative Records of the Division of Human Relations and Economic Affairs of the General Board of Church and Society, GCAH; Motion by Appellants, US Court of Appeals for the Fifth Circuit, No. 21196, Bette Poole, et al., Appellants, Against Ross R. Barnett, et al., March 13, 1964, Reel 3, Frames 627–631, Randolph Boehm and Blair Hydrick, *Records of the Southern Christian Leadership Conference, 1954–1970, Part 2: Records of the Executive Director and Treasurer.* The motion cited "Judge Due to Rule on Suit to Speed Up Negro Registration," *New York Times*, March 9, 1964, 42.

7. Brief of the Commission on Religion and Race of the National Council of Churches of Christ in the United States of America, John McKee Pratt, US Court of Appeals for the Fifth Circuit, No. 21196, Bette Poole, et al., Appellants, Against Ross R. Barnett, et al., undated, 1–6, Box 50, Folder 15, National Council of Churches of Christ in the United States of America, Division of Christian Life and Mission Records, 1945–73, PHS; Office of Information of the National Council of Churches, "The Commission on Religion and Race has filed a brief in a federal court in a case involving segregation," news release, April 2, 1964, Box 48, Folder, 10, National Council of Churches of Christ in the United States of America, Division of Christian Life and Mission Records, 1945–73, PHS; John M. Pratt, "Report on Legal Proceedings and Bail," 1–2, February 20, 1964, Box 47, Folder 31, National Council of Churches in Christ in the United States, Division of Christian Life and Mission Records, 1945–73, PHS.

8. Brief of Respondents in Opposition to Petition for Writ of Mandamus and Stay, Thomas Watkins and E. W. Stennett, US Court of Appeals for the Fifth Circuit, No. 21141, Poole, et al., Appellants, Against Ross R. Barnett, et al., undated, 1–32, Box 50, Folder 15, National Council of Churches of Christ in the United States of America, Division of Christian Life and Mission Records, 1945–73, PHS.

9. *Poole v. Barnett*, 336 F.2d 267 (Fifth Cir. 1964).

10. John Pratt to Edward Wright, 20 May 1965, Box 1433-6-7, Folder 2, Jackson Arrest Cases Folder 2, 1963–67, Administrative Records of the Division of Human Relations and Economic Affairs of the General Board of Church and Society, GCAH.

11. Brief of Plaintiff in Civil Action 3641 in US District Court for the Southern District of Mississippi, *Garner v. Griffith*, October 20, 1964, 1–7, Box 1433-6-7, Folder 3, John B. Garner Case, 1964–65, Administrative Records of the Division of Human Relations and Economic Affairs of the General Board of Church and Society, GCAH; Edward Wright to Asa Sokolow, 8 December 1965, Box 1433-6-7, Folder 3, John B. Garner Case, 1964–1965, Administrative Records of the Division of Human Relations and Economic Affairs of the General Board of Church and Society, CGAH.

12. Defendants' Answer in Civil Action 3641 in the District Court of the US for the Southern District of Mississippi, *Garner v. Griffith*, November 10, 1964, 1–3, Box 1433-6-7, Folder 3,

John B. Garner Case, 1964–65, Administrative Records of the Division of Human Relations and Economic Affairs of the General Board of Church and Society, GCAH. Garner never did receive a full hearing in his suit; neither did he recover the bail money from the city. In 1967, his lawyer, R. Jess Brown, inexplicably agreed to a dismissal when the case came up for trial. See John Garner to "Dear Friends," 11 December 1967, Box 1433-6-7, Folder 3, John B. Garner Case, 1964–65, Administrative Records of the Division of Human Relations and Economic Affairs of the General Board of Church and Society, GCAH; John Garner, interview with John Dittmer and John Jones, February 13, 1981, transcript, 14, Mississippi Department of Archives and History.

13. Grover Bagby and John Pratt to Henry Clark et al., 11 November 1965, Box 50, Folder 8, National Council of Churches of Christ in the United States of America, Division of Christian Life and Mission Records, 1945–73, PHS; John Pratt to James Nixon, 2 December 1965, Box 50, Folder 8, National Council of Churches of Christ in the United States of America, Division of Christian Life and Mission Records, 1945–73, PHS; Grover Bagby to Thomas Pryor, 19 April 1966, Box 1433-6-7, Folder 1, Jackson Arrest Cases Folder 1 1963–67, Administrative Records of the Division of Human Relations and Economic Affairs of the General Board of Church and Society, GCAH; John Pratt to "All Those Arrested in the Jackson Ministers' Cases," 3 December 1965, Everett Tilson Papers; Francis Stevens to Bruce Hanson, September 12, 1966, Box 1433-6-7, Folder 3, John B. Garner Case, 1964–65, Administrative Records of the Division of Human Relations and Economic Affairs of the General Board of Church and Society, GCAH; Alvin J. Bronstein to "Gentlemen," 25 November 1966, Everett Tilson Papers.

14. Grover C. Bagby and Leon M. Adkins, "All Persons Are Proper Candidates, Petition and Brief Before the Judicial Council of the Methodist Church, Presented on Behalf of the Secretarial Council of the Interboard Commission on the Local Church," April 1, 1965, 1–79, Susan K. Dunn personal collection; "Digest of Decision on Petition of the Secretarial Council of the Interboard Commission on the Local Church for a Declaratory Decision with Reference to the Right of Local Churches to Determine Who May Attends Its Services of Worship," April 28, 1965, 1–4, Gerald Forshey Project; Grover Bagby, "Memo to Jackson Arrest Cases," May 4, 1965, Gerald Forshey Project; Edward Wright to Asa Sokolow, December 8, 1965, Box 1433-6-7, Folder 3, John B. Garner Case, 1964–65, Administrative Records of the Division of Human Relations and Economic Affairs of the General Board of Church and Society, GCAH; "Methodists Told to Let Negroes In," *Jackson Daily News*, April 24, 1965, 1.

15. "Information Bulletin, Volume 1, Number 9, Published Monthly by a Mississippi Association of Methodist Ministers and Laymen," September 1964, 2, Box 36, Folder 300.52, John C. Satterfield Collection. Bishop Pendergrass, a native of Florida, was elected bishop at the Southeastern jurisdiction conference in July 1964. Dr. Ellis Finger, president of Millsaps College, finished second in the voting. See "Florida Minister Methodist Bishop," *Jackson Daily News*, July 12, 1964, 1.

16. "Methodist Bishop Declares Churches Can't Bar Negroes," *Jackson Daily News*, June 3, 1965, 1, 18; "Methodist Bishop Calls for Open Door to All Services," *Clarion-Ledger*, June 4, 1965, 1, 16. For more on Bishop Pendergrass, see Reiff, *Born of Conviction*, 203–4. In another significant move, conference delegates affirmed the recent decision by the trustees of Millsaps College to desegregate. The trustees made the move to end discrimination against student

applicants on the grounds of race after the federal government announced that faculty members and students would no longer be eligible for federal grants if the school continued its segregation policies.

17. "Information Bulletin, Volume 1, Number 5, Published Monthly by a Mississippi Association of Methodist Ministers and Laymen," May 1964, 2–3, Box 36, Folder 300.52, John C. Satterfield Collection.

18. "Southern Methodists Take Initial Integration Steps," *Jackson Daily News*, July 13, 1964, 6; "Information Bulletin, Volume 2, Number 3, Published Monthly by a Mississippi Association of Methodist Ministers and Laymen," June 1965, 1–4 Box 36, Folder 300.52, John C. Satterfield Collection.

19. "Withdrawal Groundwork Mapped Out," *Clarion-Ledger*, June 21, 1965, 6; Cunningham, *Agony at Galloway*, 63–64; "Methodists of Four Local Churches Join New Group," *Clarion Ledger*, June 25, 1965, 11; "Methodist Group Gains Charter and Organizes," *Clarion-Ledger*, July 25, 1965, A7. See *Agony at Galloway*, 64–67, for more on the efforts to solicit members of Galloway to defect to the Association of Independent Methodists.

20. Cunningham, *Agony at Galloway*, 89; John, Margrit, and Stephen Garner to "Dear Friends," 16 June 1964, 1, Box 1, Folder 3, Garner (John and Margrit) Letters, MDAH.

21. Clarice Campbell, *Civil Rights Chronicle*, 241; Cunningham, *Agony at Galloway*, 88–94.

22. Cunningham, *Agony at Galloway*, 77. Dr. Cunningham does not specify when exactly he proposed to the official board that Bishop Kennedy lead the preaching revival.

23. Bruce L. Williams, "It Happened in Jackson," *Christian Century*, November 3, 1965, 1366. This article states that Dr. Cunningham invited Bishop Kennedy "not long thereafter," that is, not long after the Easter 1964 visits.

24. Ray E. Stevens, *Galloway Church History: Book I*, 194–204; "Negro Attendance at Church Noted," *Clarion-Ledger*, October 15, 1965, 3.

25. Cunningham, *Agony at Galloway*, 62.

26. "Negro Attendance at Church Noted," *Clarion-Ledger*, October 15, 1965, 3. It remained unclear whether or not ushers admitted this group, or if they went into the church unnoticed.

27. Ibid.; Claire Collins Harvey, "From the One Concerned," *Christian Century*, December 22, 1965, 1582. For more on Claire Collins Harvey and Womanpower Unlimited, see Claire Collins Harvey, *Womanpower and the Jackson Movement* (Jackson, MS: Pyramid, 1964) and Tiyi Makeda Morris, "Black Women's Civil Rights Activism in Mississippi: The Story of Womanpower Unlimited," Thesis (PhD), Purdue University (2002).

28. Cunningham, *Agony at Galloway*, 85–86.

29. Bruce L. Williams, "It Happened in Jackson," *Christian Century*, November 3, 1965, 1965; John Pratt and Grover Bagby, 11 November 1965, Box 50, Folder 8, National Council of Churches of Christ in the United States of America, Division of Christian Life and Mission Records, 1945–73, PHS; "Integrated Group Is Turned Away at Church Here," *Clarion-Ledger*, October 18, 1965.

30. John Garner to Grover Bagby, 8 November 1965, Box 1433-6-7, Folder 3, John B. Garner Case, 1964–65, Administrative Records of the Division of Human Relations and Economic Affairs of the General Board of Church and Society, GCAH; John, Margrit and Children to "Dear Friends," 15 December 1965, 1–2, Box 1, Folder 4, Garner (John and Margrit) Letters,

MDAH; Howard Spencer, "The Church in Mississippi—The Last Stronghold of White Supremacy," December 24, 1965, 1–2, Box 9, Folder 451, Ed King Collection, MDAH.

31. Cunningham, *Agony at Galloway*, 109–16; Ray Stevens, *Galloway Church History: Book I*, 210. *Agony at Galloway* reprints a full copy of his letter of resignation (115–16).

32. Ray Stevens, *Galloway Church History: Book I*, 210–11.

33. John, Margrit, and children to "Dear Friends," 15 December 1965, Box 1, Folder 4, Garner (John and Margrit) Letters, MDAH.

34. "Galloway Votes Open Door Policy," *Jackson Daily News*, January 17, 1966, 8; Ray Stevens, *Galloway Church History: Book I*, 217; Cunningham, *Agony at Galloway*, 107, 120–24, 145–46.

35. John, Margrit, and children to "Dear Friends," 19 December 1966, 1, Box 1, Folder 4, Garner (John and Margrit) Letters, MDAH; Cunningham, *Agony at Galloway*, 128–35; Ray Stevens, *Galloway Church History: Book I*, 223–30, 237. *Agony at Galloway* includes a letter from Tatum, which Cunningham indicated was the first letter he received in response to the new open-door policy.

36. Howard H. Spencer and John B. Garner to "All Methodist Bishops Service in the United States," 10 March 1966, 1–2, Box 9, Folder 451, Ed King Collection, MDAH.

37. Howard H. Spencer and John B. Garner to "All Methodist Bishops Serving in the United States," 16 March 1966, Box 1, Folder 4, Garner (John and Margrit) Letters, MDAH; John, Margrit, and children to "Dear Friends," 19 December 1966, 1, Box 1, Folder 4, Garner (John and Margrit) Letters, MDAH. Rev. E. E. Samples presided over the church's desegregation. Rev. Seth Granberry left the church in 1964. According to an internal history, beginning in 1963 Capital Street Methodist experienced a decline in membership, which coincided with Dr. Roy Clark's departure, the initiation of the church's closed-door policy, and the first phases of the church visit campaign. The church lost more members to the Independent Methodist Church and, as a church in a transitional area of downtown Jackson, Capitol Street never recovered. A church that boasted 2,585 members in 1949 had 485 in 1994. The church shut down in 1996. See Robert C. Kelley and Effie P. Johnson, *Capitol Street United Methodist Church History: Volume II, 1950–1996* (Jackson, MS: History Committee of Capitol Street United Methodist Church, 1996).

38. Rev. Thompson was wounded by a shotgun blast as he entered his apartment house in Jackson on August 22, 1965. Threats against his life continued, and he left the state in November 1965 to work at Unitarian headquarters in Boston. See "Reward Offered in Local Shooting," *Jackson Daily News*, August 24, 1965, 1, 10; "Cleric Describes Terror in South," *New York Times*, November 21, 1965, 57.

39. J. Moody McDill, Oral History, transcribed, undated, Margaret McDill Pitts private collection; Margaret McDill Pitts, interview with the author; "Dr. McDill Resigning as Fondren Pastor," *Jackson Daily News*, January 24, 1966, 18.

40. "State and Church to Fete Pastor, One of Ten Outstanding Young Men," *Clarion-Ledger*, January 21, 1973, 1, 3; "Rohrman Says His Honor Was Tribute for State," *Clarion-Ledger*, January 24, 1973, C1; "Rohrman Requests Better State Image," *Jackson Daily News*, January 24, 1973, 10; McLemore, *History of the First Baptist Church*, 309–10.

41. "Integration Try Sunday at First Baptist Told," *Jackson Daily News*, January 29, 1973, 7; "Three Claim Church Bars," *Clarion-Ledger*, January 29, 1973, 6; "Opening the Airways," *Washington Post*, February 12, 1973, B1, B3. The Jackson newspapers reported that the group ushers turned away at the morning services included Frank R. Parker of the Lawyers Committee for Civil Rights Under Law, his wife Carolyn, and Linda Glass.

42. McLemore, *History of the First Baptist Church*, 310; Joe McKeever, interview with the author; Clint (no surname), letters to the editor, *Mississippi Collegian*, February 9, 1973, 2. According to another letter to the editor in this edition, about two busloads of students from Mississippi College travelled down the road to Jackson to attend First Baptist each Sunday.

43. "Church Tells Race Policy," *Delta Democrat-Times*, February 5, 1973; "First Baptist Brings Forward Policy," *Clarion-Ledger*, February 5, 1973, 16; "First, Jackson Clarifies Policy," *Baptist Record*, February 8, 1973, 2; McLemore, *History of the First Baptist Church*, 262, 310–11.

44. "Blacks Admitted to Church," *Delta Democrat-Times*, February 19, 1973, 3; "Burns Tells of Church Visitation," *Clarion-Ledger*, February 19, 1973, 14; Si Brantley, interview with the author.

CHAPTER 15
Afterword
"Doing a Little Something to Pave the Way for Others"

1. Thomas Armstrong, interview with the author; Thomas Armstrong, "Panel: How Did These Events Change You?" (Church Desegregation and the Jackson, MS, Witness, First Methodist Church, Chicago, Illinois, October 4, 2008).

2. Bette Anne Poole Marsh, interview with the author; Bette Anne Poole Marsh, "Panel: How Did These Events Change You?" (Church Desegregation and the Jackson, MS, Witness, First Methodist Church, Chicago, Illinois, October 4, 2008).

3. Ida Hannah Sanders, interview with the author.

4. Joan Trumpauer Mulholland, interview with the author; Doris Browne, interview with the author; Camille Wilburn McKey, interview with the author.

5. Austin Moore, interview with the author.

6. Al Bamsey, interview with the author; David James Randolph, interview with the author; Ed Hiestand, interview with the author; Paul Minus, interview with the author; Paul Lowley, interview with the author.

7. Al Bamsey to Joan Trumpauer, 13 February 1964, Box 9, Folder 446, Ed King Collection, MDAH; Bill Martin, interview with the author; Richard Teller, interview with the author; Ed Hiestand, interview with the author; Randy Lunsford to Joan Trumpauer, 6 March 1964, Box 9, Folder 444, Ed King Collection, MDAH; Sally Smith to Ed King, undated, Box 9, Folder 446, Ed King Collection, MDAH.

8. Al Tomer, interview with the author; John Wagner, interview with the author; Robert L. Meeks to "Mr. and Mrs. King," 27 January 1964, 2, Box 9 Folder 446, Ed King Collection, MDAH; Robert Meeks to Grover Bagby, undated, Box 1433-6-7, Folder 2, Jackson Arrest Cases, 1963–67, Administrative Records of the Division of Human Relations and Economic Affairs of the General Board of Church and Society, GCAH; Ed Craun to Joan Trumpauer,

31 December 1963, Box 9, Folder 446, Ed King Collection, MDAH; Arthur Jeffrey Hopper, interview with the author. For Rev. Tomer's articles, see "Two Worlds Behind a Magnolia Curtain, Part I, The Curtain Makers," *Kenton Times*, December 4, 1963, 1, 5; "Two Worlds Behind a Magnolia Curtain, Part II, The Plight of the Moderate," *Kenton Times*, December 5, 1963, 1; "Two Worlds Behind a Magnolia Curtain, Part III: The Events of Sunday and Conclusions," *Kenton Times*, December 7, 1963, 1

9. Elmer. A. Dickson, Civil Rights Memories, January 21, 2008, 4, Gerald Forshey Project.

10. Rev. Richard Raines, interview with the author.

11. Ed Crouch, interview by Paul Grass, Winter 1994, Rev. William H. Casto Jr., personal collection; Van Bogard Dunn, interview by Paul Grass, Winter 1994, Rev. William H. Casto Jr., personal collection; Arthur Jeffrey Hopper, interview by Paul Grass, Winter 1994, Rev. William H. Casto Jr., personal collection; Van Bogard Dunn, Jeffrey Hopper, Paul M. Minus, and Everett Tilson, "Report on Trip to Jackson, Mississippi, Easter 1964," transcript, 1964, Methodist Theological School in Ohio Library.

12. Walter Dickhaut, interview with the author.

13. Joseph Sprague, interview with the author.

14. Al Tomer, interview with the author; John Wagner, interview with the author; Bill Wells, interview with the author.

15. John A. Collins, interview with the author; Ed Hiestand, interview with the author; Richard Raines, interview with the author; Woodie White, interview with the author.

16. "Aspect, A Project of the Information and Education Committee, Jackson Citizens' Council," July–August Bulletin, 1966, Vol. 3, No. 6, 1–2, Archives and Special Collections, J. D. Williams Library, University of Mississippi.

17. William Winter, interview with the author.

Bibliography

MANUSCRIPTS

Adrian College Archives, Adrian, Michigan
  Collection of the Detroit Conference

American Jewish Archives, Cincinnati, Ohio
  Perry E. Nussbaum Papers, 1947–72

Archives and Special Collections, J. D. Williams Library, University of Mississippi, Oxford, Mississippi
  Thomas Abernathy Collection
  W. J. Cunningham / Galloway Church Collection
  Ed King Collection
  John C. Satterfield Collection
  James Silver Collection
  Student Nonviolent Coordinating Committee Papers, 1959–72

Archives of the Evangelical Lutheran Church in America, Elk Grove, Illinois
  Fry Correspondence
  Subject File: Fry—Negro Question, 1963–64
  Subject File: Fry—Responses to Pastoral Letter, 1963
  Subject File: Fry—Southeastern Synod, 1963–64

ASPECT, A Project of the Information and Education Committee, Jackson Citizens' Council, 1963–68
  Bill Minor Papers
  Citizens' Council Collection
  Holloman (Garland) Papers
  John David Humphrey Sr., Papers, 1952–69
  Segregation Integration Collection

C. Benton Kline Jr. Special Collections and Archives, Columbia Theological Seminary
Session Minutes, 1963–67, Central Presbyterian Church(Jackson, Mississippi)

Disciples of Christ Historical Society, Nashville, Tennessee
	Roy S. Hulan Papers
	General Commission on Archives and History (GCAH), Drew University, Madison, New
		Jersey
	Administrative Records of the Division of General Welfare of the General Board of
		Church and Society
	Administrative Records of the Division of Human Relations and Economic Affairs of the
		General Board of Church and Society
	Administrative Records of the Division of World Peace of the General Board of Church
		and Society
	Church Women United Records
	Council of Bishops Records
	E. Smith Collection
	Methodist Federation for Social Action Records
	Peter Murray Collection
	Seattle Episcopal Area Records
	Woman's Division of Christian Service Records

J. B. Cain Archives in Mississippi Methodism, Millsaps College, Jackson, Mississippi
	Bishops' Papers
	Capitol Street United Methodist Church Papers

Journal, 1963 Session, Mississippi Conference, the Methodist Church, Southeast Jurisdiction

Journal, 1964 Session, Mississippi Conference, the Methodist Church, Southeast Jurisdiction
	Selah Papers

Millsaps College Archives, Jackson, Mississippi
	Robert Bergmark Papers
	Oral History of Contemporary Life and Viewpoint

Mississippi Baptist Historical Commission, Mississippi College, Clinton, Mississippi
	Chester A. Quarles File
	Minutes of the Hinds County Baptist Association, 1960–67
	Oral History Program

Mississippi Department of Archives and History (MDAH), Jackson, Mississippi
	Civil Rights and Methodism (Jackson, Mississippi) Collection
	Ed King Collection
	First Baptist Church, Minutes of Deacon's Meetings

Garner Letters
Selah (William Bryan) Scrapbooks, 1935–86
Sovereignty Commission Online
Tougaloo Nine Library Sit-In Collection

Pitts Theology Library Archives, Emory University, Atlanta, Georgia
    Theodore R. Weber Papers

Presbyterian Historical Society, Philadelphia, Pennsylvania
National Council of Churches in Christ in the United States,
Division of Christian Life and Mission Records, 1945–73

Reu Memorial Library, Wartburg Theological Seminary, Dubuque, Iowa
    Wade J. Koons Pastor File

Special Collections, Mississippi State University, Starkville, Mississippi

Wilson Library, the University of North Carolina at Chapel Hill, Chapel Hill, North Carolina
    North Carolina Collection

Wisconsin Historical Society Archives
    Joan Trumpauer Mulholland Papers

CHURCH RECORDS

Archives of the Diocese of Jackson
Ascension Lutheran Church, Jackson, Mississippi
First Methodist Church, Chicago, Illinois
Fondren Presbyterian Church, Jackson, Mississippi

PERSONAL COLLECTIONS

A. W. Martin
Arthur North
C. Everett Tilson
Edwin King
Margaret McDill Pitts
Martin Deppe
Pat and Phinius Stevens
Richard H. Hulan
Roy C. Clark
Susan K. Dunn
William H. Casto Jr.

BIBLIOGRAPHY

INTERVIEWS (CONDUCTED BY THE AUTHOR)

A. W. Martin, Lubbock, Texas (telephone), June 22, 2009
Albert E. Tomer, Cincinnati, Ohio (telephone), June 16, 2009
Alfred Bamsey, Ann Arbor, Michigan (telephone), June 2, 2009
Arthur Jeffrey Hopper, Westerville, Ohio (telephone), September 10, 2008
Arthur North, Miami, Florida (telephone), May 18, 2009
Austin Moore, Pomona, California (telephone), January 29, 2009
Barry Shaw, Waupaca, Wisconsin (telephone), May 18, 2009
Beatrice Gotthelf, Jackson, Mississippi (telephone), August 14, 2008
Becky Moreton, Oxford, Mississippi, August 4, 2008
Bette Anne Poole Marsh, Chicago, Illinois (telephone), September 17, 2008
Camille Wilburn McKey, Jackson, Mississippi (telephone), June 19, 2009
Carl and Martha Brannan, Tampa, Florida (telephone), November 13, 2008
Caroline Keller-Winter, Cashiers, North Carolina (telephone), June 3, 2009
Charles W. Koons, Johnston, South Carolina (telephone), July 21, 2009
Charles E. Morton, Detroit, Michigan (telephone), June 16, 2009
Cora Jordan, Oxford, Mississippi, July 23, 2008
David James Randolph, Albany, California (telephone), February 13, 2009
David P. Ver Nooy, Beacon, New York (telephone), June 24, 2009
Dick Barnes, Jackson, Mississippi (telephone), February 10, 2006
Doris Browne, Washington, DC (telephone), June 4, 2009
Doug Fancher, Oxford, Mississippi, July 30, 2008
Ed King, Jackson, Mississippi, January 27, 2006
Edgar Hiestand Jr., Oak Park, Illinois (telephone), June 5, 2009
Fitts Herbert Skeete, Bronx, New York (telephone), June 15, 2009
George and Jan Purvis, Jackson, Mississippi (telephone), February 10, 2006
Gerry H. Dunn, Delaware, Ohio (telephone), November 6, 2009
Hazel LeBlanc Whitney, Detroit, Michigan (telephone), May 7, 2009
Henry M. McKay, Asheville, North Carolina (telephone), July 23, 2009
Ida Catherine Hannah Sanders, Jackson, Mississippi (telephone), July 20, 2009
Ivory Philips, Jackson, Mississippi (telephone), September 8, 2008
Jack Moskowitz, Jackson, Mississippi, September 15, 2008
Jack Woodward, Jackson, Mississippi (telephone), February 27, 2009
Jack Zipperer, Murfreesboro, Tennessee (telephone), August 10, 2009
James R. Bullock, Ocala, Florida (telephone), August 5, 2008
Jean Kidd, Jackson, Mississippi, September 15, 2008
Joan Trumpauer Mulholland, Jackson, Mississippi, June 12, 2009
Joe McKeever, New Orleans, Louisiana (telephone), August 15, 2008
John A. Collins, New Rochelle, New York (telephone), September 26, 2009
John Anderson, Jackson, Mississippi, August 27, 2008
John Fontaine, Jackson, Mississippi, June 12, 2009
John Wagner, Westerville, Ohio (telephone), June 3, 2009

Joseph Sprague, London, Ohio (telephone), September 26, 2008
Lenora Marquis, Arlington, Virginia (telephone), March 9, 2006
Lisa Anderson Todd, Washington, DC (telephone), September 22, 2008
Margaret McDill Pitts, Arlington, Virginia, (telephone) February 7, 10, 2006
Margrit Garner, Jackson, Mississippi, June 12, 2009
Mary Hendrick, Jackson, Mississippi, February 1, 2006
Nat S. Rogers, Jackson, Mississippi (telephone), February 29, 2009
Pat and Phinius Stevens, Oxford, Mississippi, May 28, 2009
Paul Lowley, Petoskey, Michigan (telephone), May 21, 2009
Paul Minus, Claremont, California (telephone), September 19, 2008
Pharis Harvey, Watsonville, California (telephone), September 23, 2008
Richard C. Raines Jr., Redwood City, California (telephone), May 26, 2009
Richard H. Hulan, Springfield, Virginia (telephone), September 12, 2008
Richard Teller, Delaware, Ohio (telephone), June 11, 2009
Rita Schwerner Bender, Oxford, Mississippi. March 12, 2010
Robert Kochtitsky, Jackson, Mississippi (telephone), September 17, 2008
Ron Payne, Columbus, Ohio (telephone), September 18, 2008
Roy Clark, Nashville, Tennessee (telephone), January 28, 2009
Seth Granberry Jr., Auburn, Alabama (telephone), September 16, 2008
Si Brantley, Alpharetta, Georgia (telephone), August 18, 2008
Susan Dunn, Charleston, South Carolina (telephone), November 6, 2009
Thomas Armstrong, Chicago, Illinois (telephone), August 21, 2008
Tom Boone, Ocean Springs, Mississippi (telephone), July 23, 2009
Walter Dickhaut, Bangor, Maine (telephone), September 13, 2008
William Hutchinson, Smithfield, Rhode Island (telephone), August 28, 2009
William J. Simmons, Jackson, Mississippi, February 8, 2006
William Wells Jr., Laurinburg, North Carolina (telephone), June 15, 2009
William Winter, Jackson, Mississippi, March 8, 2006
Woodie White, Atlanta, Georgia (telephone), September 22, 2008

NEWSPAPERS AND MAGAZINES

Atlanta Constitution
Atlanta Journal
Baptist Record
Chicago Daily News
Chicago Tribune
The Christian
Christian Advocate
The Christian Century
Christian Science Monitor
Christianity Today
Cincinnati Post & Times

The Citizen
Clarion-Ledger
Commercial Appeal
Commonweal
Concern
Delta Democrat-Times
Ebony
The Episcopalian
Hartford Courant
Jackson Advocate
Jackson Daily News
Kansas City Star
Kenton Times
The Living Church
Look
Los Angeles Times
McComb Enterprise-Journal
Michigan Christian Advocate
Mississippi Collegian
Mississippi Free Press
Mississippi Folklife
Mississippi Methodist Advocate
Mississippi Register
The Nation
New Republic
New South
Newsweek
New York Herald Tribune
New York Times
New York Times Magazine
Northside Reporter
Omaha World-Herald
Pulpit Digest
Social Questions Bulletin
The Southern Patriot
Southern School News
State Times
The Student Voice
Telescope-Messenger
Time
Times-Picayune
Washington Post
Your Smithfield Magazine

UNPUBLISHED WORKS

Branch, Ellis Ray. "Born of Conviction: Racial Conflict and Change in Mississippi Methodism, 1945–1983." Thesis (PhD). Mississippi State University, 1984.
Chamberlain, Daphne Rochelle. "'And a Child Shall Lead the Way: Children's Participation in the Jackson, Mississippi, Black Freedom Struggle, 1946–1970." Thesis (PhD). University of Mississippi, 2009.
Favors, Jelani Manu-Gowen. "Shelter in a Time of Storm: Black Colleges and the Rise of Student Activism in Jackson, Mississippi." Thesis (PhD). Ohio State University, 2006.
Garner, John. 1981. Interview by John Dittmer and John Jones. Transcript. February 13. Mississippi Department of Archives and History, Jackson.
Lawson, James M. 1983. Interview by Dallas A. Blanchard. Transcript. October 24. University Library, University of North Carolina at Chapel Hill.
Morris, Tiyi Makeda. "Black Women's Civil Rights Activism in Mississippi: The Story of Womanpower Unlimited." Thesis (PhD). Purdue University, 2002.

PUBLISHED WORKS

Bailey, Kenneth K. *Southern White Protestantism in the Twentieth Century.* New York: Harper and Row, Publishers, 1964.
Bartley, Numan V. *The Rise of Massive Resistance: Race and Politics in the South During the 1950s.* Baton Rouge: Louisiana State University Press, 1969.
Bass, S. Jonathan. *Blessed Are the Peacemakers: Martin Luther King Jr., Eight White Religious Leaders, and the "Letter from a Birmingham Jail".* Baton Rouge: Louisiana State University Press, 2001.
Boehm, Randolph, and Blair Hydrick. *Records of the Southern Christian Leadership Conference, 1954–1970.* Bethesda, MD: University Publications of America, 1995.
Cagin, Seth, and Philip Dray. *We Are Not Afraid: The Story of Goodman, Schwerner, and Chaney and the Civil Rights Campaign for Mississippi.* New York: MacMillan, 1988.
Campbell, Clarice T. *Civil Rights Chronicle: Letters from the South.* Jackson: University Press of Mississippi, 1997.
Campbell, Clarice T., and Oscar Allan Rogers Jr. *Mississippi: The View from Tougaloo.* Jackson: University Press of Mississippi, 1980.
Campbell, Ernest Q., and Thomas F. Pettigrew. *Christians in Racial Crisis: A Study of Little Rock's Ministry.* Washington, DC: Public Affairs Press, 1959.
Campbell, Will D. *Race and the Renewal of the Church.* Philadelphia: Westminster Press, 1962.
Carson, Clayborne, ed. *The Student Voice, 1960–1965: Periodical of the Student Nonviolent Coordinating Committee.* Westport, CT: Meckler, 1990.
Chappell, David L. *A Stone of Hope: Prophetic Religion and the Death of Jim Crow.* Chapel Hill: University of North Carolina Press, 2004.
Cobb, Craig J. *History of the First Christian Church of Jackson, Mississippi.* Jackson, MS: Public Relations Committee, 1987.

Collins, Donald E. *When the Church Bell Rang Racist: The Methodist Church and the Civil Rights Movement in Alabama*. Macon, GA: Mercer University Press, 1998.

Crespino, Joseph. *In Search of Another Country: Mississippi and the Conservative Counterrevolution*. Princeton: Princeton University Press, 2007.

Cunningham W. J. *Agony at Galloway: One Church's Struggle with Social Change*. Jackson: University Press of Mississippi, 1980.

Daniel, Pete. *Lost Revolutions: The South in the 1950s*. Chapel Hill: University of North Carolina Press, 2000.

Dittmer, John. *Local People: The Struggle for Civil Rights in Mississippi*. Urbana: University of Illinois Press, 1994.

Doyle, William. *An American Insurrection: James Meredith and the Battle of Oxford, Mississippi, 1962*. New York: Anchor Books, 2001.

Dupont, Carolyn. *Mississippi Praying: Southern White Evangelicals and the Civil Rights Movement*. New York: NYU Press, 2013.

The Episcopal Church in Mississippi. Jackson: Episcopal Diocese of Mississippi, 1992.

Evers, Myrlie B., and William Peters. *For Us, the Living*. Garden City, NY: Doubleday, 1967.

Evers-Williams, Myrlie, and Manning Marable. *The Autobiography of Medgar Evers: A Hero's Life and Legacy Revealed through His Writings, Letters, and Speeches*. New York: Basis Civitas Books, 2005.

Findlay, James F., Jr. *Church People in the Struggle: The National Council of Churches and the Black Freedom Movement, 1950–1970*. New York: Oxford University Press, 1993.

Fleming, Cynthia Griggs. *Soon We Will Not Cry: The Liberation of Ruby Doris Smith Robinson*. Lanham, MD: Rowman & Littlefield, 1998.

Grant, David Ruff. *To God Be the Glory: An Autobiography*. Jackson, MS: Dallas Printing Company, 1993.

Harvey, Paul. *Freedom's Coming: Religious Culture and the Shaping of the South from the Civil War through the Civil Rights Era*. Chapel Hill: University of North Carolina Press, 2005.

Haynes, Stephen R. *The Last Segregated Hour: The Memphis Kneel-Ins and the Campaign for Southern Church Desegregation*. New York: Oxford University Press, 2012.

Hensley, J. Clark. *By the Grace of God: A Delightful Journey*. Jackson, MS: Dallas Printing Company, 1992.

Hill, Samuel S., Jr. *Southern Churches in Crisis*. New York: Holt, Rinehart and Winston, 1966.

His Name in Vain. Jackson, MS: sponsored by a voluntary committee of Jackson, Mississippi, Methodists, 1964.

Huie, William Bradford. *Three Lives for Mississippi*. New York: WCC Books, 1965.

Jacoway, Elizabeth, and David R. Colburn, eds. *Southern Businessmen and Desegregation*. Baton Rouge: Louisiana State University Press, 1982.

Johnston, Erle. *Mississippi's Defiant Years, 1953–1973: An Interpretive Documentary with Personal Experiences*. Forest, MS: Lake Harbor Publishers, 1990.

Kelley, Robert C., and Effie P. Johnson. *Capitol Street United Methodist Church History: Volume II, 1950–1996*. Jackson, MS: History Committee of Capitol Street United Methodist Church, 1996.

Kennedy, John F. *Papers of John F. Kennedy, Presidential Papers*, President's Office Files: Presidential Recordings, Logs and *Transcripts: Civil Rights, 1963*. Boston: John F. Kennedy Library, 1984.

King, Ed. "Bacchanal at Woolworth's," in *Freedom Is a Constant Struggle: An Anthology of the Mississippi Civil Rights Movement*. Ed. Susan Erenrich. Montgomery, AL: Black Belt Press, 1999, 27–35.

Kunstler, William. *Deep in My Heart*. New York: Morrow, 1966.

Loevy, Robert D. *To End All Segregation: The Politics of the Passage of the Civil Rights Act of 1964*. Lanham, MD: University Press of America, 1990.

Marsh, Charles. *God's Long Summer: Stories of Faith and Civil Rights*. Princeton: Princeton University Press, 1997.

McLemore, Richard and Nannie. *The History of the First Baptist Church*. Jackson, MS: Hederman Brothers, 1976.

McMillen, Neil R. *The Citizens' Council: Organized Resistance to the Second Reconstruction, 1954–1964*. Urbana: University of Illinois Press, 1971.

Moody, Anne. *Coming of Age in Mississippi*. New York: Delta Trade Paperbacks, 2004.

Moore, Leon T., and J. Wesley Hole. *Journal of the 1964 General Conference of the Methodist Church, Volume II*. Nashville, TN: Methodist Publishing House, 1964.

Nelson, Jack. *Terror in the Night: The Klan's Campaign against the Jews*. Jackson, MS: University Press of Mississippi, 1993.

Newman, Mark. *Getting Right With God: Southern Baptists and Desegregation, 1945–1995*. Tuscaloosa: University of Alabama Press, 2001.

Newman, Mark. "Journalist Under Siege," in *Mississippi Women: Their Histories, Their Lives*. Ed. Susan Ditto, Elizabeth Anne Payne, Marjorie Julian Spruill, and Martha W. Swain. Athens: University of Georgia Press, 2003.

O'Brien, Michael. *We Shall Not Be Moved: The Jackson Woolworth's Sit-In and the Movement It Inspired*. Jackson: University Press of Mississippi, 2013.

Reiff, Joseph T. *Born of Conviction: White Methodists and Mississippi's Closed Society*. New York: Oxford University Press, 2016.

Reiff, Joseph T. "Conflicting Convictions in White Mississippi Methodism: The 1963 'Born of Conviction' Controversy." *Methodist History* 49:3 (2011) 162–75.

Salter, John R., Jr. *Jackson, Mississippi: An American Chronicle of Struggle and Schism*. Hicksville, NY: Exposition Press, 1979.

Silver, James. *Mississippi: The Closed Society*. New York: Harcourt, Brace and World, 1963.

Shattuck, Gardiner H., Jr. *Episcopalians and Race: Civil War to Civil Rights*. Lexington: University Press of Kentucky, 2000.

Sparks, Randy J. *Religion in Mississippi*. Jackson: University Press of Mississippi for the Mississippi Historical Society, 2001.

Stevens, Ray E. *Galloway Church History, Book I*. Jackson, MS: Ray E. Stevens, 1996.

Stevens, Thelma, and A. Dudley Ward. *The Methodist Church and Race: A Guide to Understanding the Jurisdictional System and Race Relations*. Washington, DC: General Board of Christian Social Concerns, September, 1962.

Thomas, James S. *Methodism's Racial Dilemma: The Story of the Central Jurisdiction*. Nashville, TN: Abingdon Press, 1992.

US Senate. Committee on the Judiciary. Literacy Tests and Voter Requirements in Federal and State Elections. 87th Cong., 2nd Session, April 6, 1962.

Webb, Clive. *Fight Against Fear: Southern Jews and Black Civil Rights*. Athens: University of Georgia Press, 2001.

Williams, Michael Vinson. *Medgar Evers: Mississippi Martyr*. Fayetteville: University of Arkansas Press, 2011.

Wise, Sherwood Willing. *The Cathedral Church of St. Andrew: A Sesquicentennial History, 1839–1989*. Jackson, MS: Cathedral Church of St. Andrew, 1989.

Wise, Sherwood Willing. *The Way I See It: Then and Now*. Jackson, MS: n.p, 1996.

Zola, Gary Phillip. "What Price Amos? Perry Nussbaum's Career in Jackson, Mississippi," in *The Quiet Voices: Southern Rabbis and Black Civil Rights, 1880s to 1990s*. Ed. Mark K. Bauman and Berkley Kalin. Tuscaloosa: University of Alabama Press, 1997.

Index

CPSIA information can be obtained
at www.ICGtesting.com
Printed in the USA
BVOW08*0812270217
476734BV00002B/3/P

9 781496 810748